SPANISH GRAMMAR

FOR

INDEPENDENT

LEARNERS

by

Avigail Azoulay

Arie Vicente
Texas A&M University-Commerce

VIC Languages
Texas

la escuela Cemanahuac

S. Randle

Comprado en Cuernavaca Morelos, Mexico 1999 June-July

SPANISH GRAMMAR
FOR
INDEPENDENT LEARNERS

We thank for the use of clip art images:

Click Art. T/Maker Company
Corel Gallery. Corel Corporation
One Mile Up, Inc.
TechPool Studios
Totem Graphics Inc.

For information or order:

VIC Languages, 1400 Ash Street, Commerce, TX 75428
Phone: 903-886-1855 or Toll Free: 1-800-990-7981

Printed in the United States of America

THE SENTENCE

El nuevo estudiante de Perú llegó temprano.
The new student from Peru came early

_____/ _____/

THE NOUN PHRASE   THE VERB PHRASE

TYPES OF SENTENCES

- *DECLARATIVE SENTENCES AND WORD ORDER*
  Pablo juega a las cartas [212 - 213].

- *QUESTIONS*
  ¿Qué come Pablo? [214 - 215]

- *NEGATIVE SENTENCES*
  Pablo no quiere hacer un deporte [216].

- *EXCLAMATORY SENTENCES*
  ¡Qué bonito es el cuadro! [217]

- *IMPERATIVE SENTENCES*
  ¡Abre la puerta por favor! [218]

- *PASSIVE SENTENCES*
  El banquete será preparado por Felipe [219 - 220].

EXPANDED SENTENCES

- *EXPRESSING TIME*
  Pablo estudia por las tardes [223 -229].

- *EXPRESSING CAUSE*
  Pablo estudia francés porque quiere viajar a Francia [230].

- *EXPRESSING GOAL*
  Te compré este libro para que estudies inglés [231].

- *EXPRESSING CONSEQUENCE*
  Está demasiado cansado para manejar bien [232 - 233].

- *EXPRESSING CONDITION*
  Si llueve hoy, saldrán las flores [234].

- *EXPRESSING HYPOTHESIS*
  Si hiciera calor, saldríamos [235].

- *EXPRESSING OPPOSITION*
  Los mayores trabajan mientras que los chicos juegan [236].

- *EXPRESSING CONCESSION*
  Vayas donde vayas, te encontrarán [237].

- *COORDINATION*
  Como pan y mantequilla [238 -239].

THE NOUN PHRASE

El	nuevo	estudiante	de	Perú
DET.	*ADJ.*	*NOUN*	*PREP.*	*NOUN*

DETERMINER

- *INDEFINITE ARTICLE*
  un, una...
  [28 - 30]

- *NUMBERS*
  uno, dos, primero...
  [31 - 32]

- *INDEFINITE ADJECTIVE*
  cada, otro... [33]

- *QUANTITY*
  mucho ... [33]

- *FRACTIONS AND TOTALITY*
  todo... [35]

- *DEFINITE ARTICLE*
  el, la... [36 - 39]

- *POSSESIVE*
  mi,tu, su... [40]

- *DEMONS- TRATIVE*
  este, esta... [41]

ADJECTIVE

- *GENDER*
  Masculine/ Feminine
  alto/alta [45]

- *NOUNS & ADJ. OF NATIONALITY*
  [46]

- *PLURAL*
  alta/altas
  [47]

- *PLACE*
  Before/After the noun
  buen libro
  libro caro
  [48 - 49]

- *COMPARISON*
  más lindo
  [50 - 56]

- *SUPER- LATIVE*
  el más lindo
  [57 - 58]

NOUN

- *GENDER*
  Masculine/ Feminine
  niño/niña
  [16 - 21]

- *PLURAL*
  niño /niños
  [22 -23]

PREPOSITION

- *USES OF PREPOSITIONS*
  a [61]
  ante [62]
  antes de [62]
  bajo [62]
  con/sin [62]
  contra [63]
  de [63]
  de... a [64]
  delante de [64]
  dentro de [64]
  desde [64]
  después de [65]
  detrás de [65]
  durante [65]
  en [65]
  encima de [66]
  enfrente de [66]
  entre [66]
  frente a [66]
  hacia [67]
  hasta [67]
  por/para [67]
  sin [67]
  sobre [67]
  tras [67]

- *OPPOSITION*
  por/para
  [68 - 71]

THE NOUN PHRASE

El nuevo estudiante de Perú

The noun phrase can be replaced by pronouns.

THE PRONOUNS

- *PERSONAL PRONOUNS*

  SUBJECT PRONOUNS [77 -79]
  OBJECT PRONOUNS [80 -87]
  PLACE OF OBJECT PRONOUNS [88 - 89]
  ORDER OF PRONOUNS [90]
  SUMMARY [91]

- *DEMONSTRATIVE PRONOUNS*
  ésta... [92]

- *POSSESSIVE PRONOUNS*
  el mío, la mía... [93]

- *INDEFINITE PRONOUNS*
  alguien, algo... [94 - 95]

- *RELATIVE PRONOUNS*
  que, el cual ... [96 - 99]

- *INTERROGATIVE PRONOUNS*
  quién, qué... [100]

THE VERB PHRASE

llegó   temprano

VERB   ADVERB

VERBS

- *VERB USES*
  ser [104]
  estar [105]
  ser vs. estar [106]
  haber [107]
  saber [108]
  conocer [109]
  hacer [110 - 111]
  gustar [112]

  Pronominal verbs [113 - 116]
  Verbs in the 3rd person [117]

- *VERB FORMS*

  VERB CONJUGATIONS, MODES AND TENSES
  [118 -124]

  THE INDICATIVO
  [125 - 163]

  THE SUBJUNTIVO
  [165 - 185]

  SUBJUNTIVO VS. INDICATIVO
  [186 - 187]

  SUBJUNTIVO: SUMMARY [188]

  THE IMPERATIVO [190 - 192]

  THE NON CONJUGATED MODES
  [193 - 202]

- *CONJUGATIONS* [Appendix]

- *VERB COMPLEMENTS*
  [Appendix]

ADVERBS

- *THE ADVERB*
  [204]

- *CLASSIFICATION*
  [205 - 208]

- *THE PLACE OF THE ADVERB*
  [209]

PREFACE TO THE SECOND EDITION √

Numerous teachers and students who have used the *Spanish Grammar for Independent Learners (SGIL)* have pointed out that the section on *Verb Complements* was extremely useful for them. We have therefore decided to revise and extend this section, which now contains more than one thousand verbs. We have also added an English-Spanish alphabetical verb list.

Acknowledgements √

This new edition has greatly benefitted from extremely pertinent comments by colleagues and students. We especially thank John Tyres and Steve Hards for the invaluable questions and comments which have led us to important improvements. We are grateful to the *Center for Bilingual Multicultural Studies* in Cuernavaca, Mexico, for having invited us to conduct grammar workshops during Summer 98. These workshops confirmed the immense value of the book (known there as "el rojito"), which has become part of the American students' learning experience in Mexico. Our thanks also go to the great number of readers who have manifested enthusiastic reactions to *SGIL*.

We also wish to thank our colleagues and students who offered their kind and patient support in the development of the *Spanish Grammar for Independent Learners.*:
To Edda María Carloz Businaro, who read large portions of the manuscript and provided insights on the Spanish spoken in Mexico;
To Elsa I. Miglierini, who read, edited, discussed, challenged us at every step of the way, and helped shape the final presentation;
To Steve Hards, who made us realize that the computer is not a typewriter, and gave shape to our opening pages;
To Shalom Azoulay, who never doubted during the execution of this project, and provided valuable advice and support.

Many colleagues have been particularly supportive of our efforts and we wish to express our gratitude:
Antonio Barbagallo, Stonehill College; Eladio Cortés, Rutgers University; Juan Fernández-Jiménez, Penn State University; Martha T. Halsey, Penn State University; Mario Martín Flores, Texas A&M University-Commerce; Peter Podol, Lock Haven University; Nicolas Toscano, St. John's University; Teresa Valdivieso, Arizona State University;

and to Amy Grace Vicente, who showed boundless patience, and illuminated our work with her multiple talents.

To all, our warmest thanks.

Avigail Azoulay

has a Ph. D. in Linguistics from University of Paris VIII
(France). Author of the book *Les Tours comportant
l'expression de + adjectif* (Genève: Droz, 1985) and many
articles in linguistics and grammar, she participated in
the translation into French of Noam Chomsky's *Lectures
on Government and Binding.* Dr. Azoulay taught language
and linguistics at The Pennsylvania State University and
Tufts University. In 1992, she was a research fellow at
Harvard University. She also taught at the Massachusetts
Institute of Technology (MIT), where she developed a
French grammar, *La Grammaire en fiches du français,*
which aimed at developing students' autonomy. This
concept constitutes the core of *SGIL.*

Arie Vicente

received a Ph. D. at The Pennsylvania State University in
1988. Dr. Vicente taught at Susquehana University and at
Bentley College , where he was the Director of the Spanish
Program until 1992. He is presently an Associate Professor
at Texas A & M University-Commerce. Several times
President of the North East Texas Association of Language
Educators, he has worked in close collaboration with
Spanish instructors. He is now the President of the Lone Star
Chapter of the AATSP. He has published several books and
articles in Spanish literature (*Lo judío en el teatro español
contemporáneo.* Madrid: Pliegos, 1991) and language,
participated in Long Distance Learning, and authored the
materials for *Cara a Cara,* a Spanish Grammar software
published by Heinle and Heinle.

Avigail Azoulay and Arie Vicente are the authors of several
books in the *Series Grammar in the Classroom* and of the
TOPT. Study Book for the Texas Oral Proficiency Test.

SPANISH GRAMMAR
FOR
INDEPENDENT LEARNERS

SGIL

The purpose of this book is to provide a grammatical system which will accompany every learner throughout the Spanish curriculum and beyond.

The <u>Spanish Grammar for Independent Learners</u> (SGIL) presents grammar in a simple way, with easy to follow explanations and quick access to information. When writing a composition or preparing an oral presentation, you will find answers and guidance; and through working with SGIL in a self-correction mode, you will quickly develop the self-discipline, knowledge and confidence needed to interact effectively in the Spanish language.

BENEFITS OF THE
SPANISH GRAMMAR FOR INDEPENDENT LEARNERS

Saves time and frustration
Each page has specific information and contains simple explanation of grammatical points. Explanations are provided in English, examples translated, and English counterparts presented, for easy understanding. The grammar is completely cross-referenced for quick access to further information if needed.

Encourages independent learning
This grammar presents a strategy for oral and written self-correction, a unique feature that enables students to work actively and independently when searching for grammatical information.

Builds confidence
The self-correction technique also provides an effective tool to achieve language accuracy. Independence and good performance build confidence.

SPECIAL FEATURES OF THE
SPANISH GRAMMAR FOR INDEPENDENT LEARNERS

Summary charts   Summaries organizing the information in visual charts, enable you to check information at a glance, and, at the same, give you an overview of the topic.

Conjugation tables   Complete conjugation tables, in the appendix, give you immediate access to verb forms.

Lexicon   A list of verbs and their complements tells you which preposition to use and whether the verb governs the subjunctive or the indicative.

Self-correction   A technique for preparing for oral communication and for written assignments is presented, and self-correction strategies are provided to help you diagnose and correct your own errors, as you learn the language and use it to communicate your thoughts orally, and in writing.

Detailed index   A detailed index directly refers you to the appropriate pages when you need to look up a rule or the use of a specific grammatical word.

Workbooks   The authors are developing a series of workbooks, addressing different levels of language proficiency, which guide you through a series of diagnostic activities, followed by learning and reinforcement exercises. These workbooks can be used as the main text, with each activity directing you to the specific pages where the relevant explanations enable you to complete each given task. The end of the workbook provides an answer key and advise you on what to do next.

HOW DO I USE THE
SPANISH GRAMMAR FOR INDEPENDENT LEARNERS?

The <u>SGIL</u> can be used in different ways, depending on your specific needs. This section describes a number of possible scenarios (by no means all the possible scenarios), and shows you how the grammar can be consulted in each case.

 *You have **a test** on 3 or 4 chapters in your textbook; but you are not sure that you know a rule, for instance, the place of the adjective (before or after the noun).*

In the index, look up the entry "adjective," and, in this entry, the topic "place of the adjective." The index will refer to page 48 for the general principle, and to page 49 for specific adjectives which undergo a change in meaning when used before or after the noun.

 *You are preparing **an oral presentation,** and you want to say that all of your friends came to the party. You know that **all** is **todo,** but wonder how to use it in a sentence.*

Look up the word "todo" in the index. It will lead you to page 35, where you find the answer together with a note on the differences between English and Spanish in the use of "todo."

 *You are **writing a story** and you need to know how to use expressions such as **for, since, two days ago,** etc., to make your story more coherent.*

Look up "time" in the index. You will find the topic "expressing time" on pages 223 - 229. You can also look up the word "hoy" (today), which will refer you to the same pages.

 *You want to **use a specific verb,** for instance **querer,** in order to say that you want Peter to give you something. You don't remember how to use this verb in Spanish.*

Look up the verb "querer" in the lexicon; it will tell you that "querer" is followed by "que + clause in the *subjuntivo*," and give you an example.

Now you know how to use the verb **querer.** *You know that the verb in the "que clause" is in the subjuntivo; but you don't remember* **the form of the verb dar** *in the subjuntivo.*

Look up the verb "dar" in the verb conjugation tables and you will immediately find the form you need.

 You finished writing an essay; you read it and it looks good. However, you want to make sure that it is well written and that **the language is accurate.**

Turn to the self-correction section in the appendix and follow the guidelines. After only a few self-corrected essays, you will see a dramatic improvement of the language accuracy in your written assignments.

 You want **to review** *the Spanish language, either because you have a comprehensive exam, or because you have studied Spanish long ago and wish to refresh your memory before using the language in your job or registering in a Spanish class. You don't know where to start.*

Since the grammar was specifically designed for independent learning, you will find it easy to handle the review. Take the workbook for intermediate level and begin with the first exercise in the "diagnostic section." After you finish the exercise, compare your answer with the answer key given at the end of the workbook. There, you will find:
(i)   the correct answer
(ii) the page in the grammar book where the specific point is explained
(iii) the exercises in the workbook that you can complete if you had a wrong answer and you want to work more on that specific grammar point.

Have a pleasant journey!

Table of contents

Table of contents √

Table of contents √

Table of contents √

INTRODUCTION

Speaking a language is like going on a bicycle ride. You know where you want to go; but if you cannot ride the bike, you may not be able to get there. If you want to reach your goal, to get to your destination, you have to be in control of the cycling mechanism and to be active in pedaling.

I speak English.
Yo hablo español.
I am bilingual.
Yo soy bilingüe.

The language student, just like the bicycle rider, has a specific purpose: he or she wants to communicate thoughts, feelings, information.

In order to be successful, one has to control the mechanism that we call language.

All the languages of the world have many common properties; for example they all use nouns and verbs, questions, exclamations, negations, and other forms of sentences. There are of course many differences as well. The study of these properties is called **grammar**.

The grammar of the Spanish language is the subject of this book. The explanations in English and the comparisons between Spanish and English will help you understand and, therefore, perform with a higher level of accuracy. For every situation of communication, grammar provides you with the tools to convey meaning in speaking or writing.

2

A basic sentence contains a verb and one or serveral nouns.

Pablo come pizza.
Pablo eats pizza.

This is a **basic sentence**.
The sentence gives a complete message: it describes the situation shown in the picture.

Here, an action is being performed and an individual is involved in that specific action. The action is expressed by the **verb** *comer* and the individual or person doing this action is *Pablo*. Individuals involved in the action are expressed by **nouns**.

Here are other examples of basic sentences:

El bebé está durmiendo.	*The baby is sleeping.*
Yo como un pastelillo.	*I eat a pastry.*
David telefonea a la doctora.	*David phones the doctor.*
Luis da dinero a su hijo.	*Luis gives money to his son.*
La película es buena.	*The film is good.*

In each one of these sentences, the noun which comes before the verb names the main participant in the action. This noun is called the **subject**.

SPANISH

In Spanish the subject can be omitted when it is clearly understood.

Como un pastelillo.

ENGLISH

In English the subject must be present in every sentence.

I eat a pastry.

3

There are several **types of sentences**, which are used to convey the speaker's intention and the situation being described. For instance, you use sentences to make statements, ask questions, express emotions, negate statements, or give orders. The form of the sentences you use reflects the kind of message you want to convey.

Declarative sentences

We use a declarative sentence to make a statement [212 - 213].

Pablo juega a las cartas.
Pablo plays cards.
Me gusta el tango.
I like the tango.

Interrogative sentences

We use an interrogative sentence to ask a question [214 - 215].

¿Qué come Pablo?
What does Pablo eat?
¿Dónde vive Pablo?
Where does Pablo live?

Negative sentences

We use a negative sentence to negate a statement [216].

No tengo dinero.
I don't have any money.
Pablo no quiere hacer un deporte.
Pablo does not want to be involved in a sport.

Exclamatory sentences

We use exclamatory sentences to show surprise, admiration, anger, and other emotions [217].

¡Qué bonito cuadro!
What a nice painting!
¡Cuánto trabajo!
What a lot of work!

Imperative sentences

We use an imperative sentence to give orders or suggestions [218].

¡Abre la puerta por favor!
Open the door, please!
¡No olvides tu libro!
Don't forget your book!

Passive sentences

We use passive sentences to focus on the receiver of the action [219 - 220].

El banquete fue preparado por Luis.
The banquet was prepared by Luis.

We can expand sentences by adding circumstances.

We can expand the basic sentence by giving additional information on the **circumstances** in which this action is performed. Circumstances tell us when, where, why, with whom, or how the action takes place.

When	
We can say when the action takes place [223 -229].	Por las tardes, Luis estudia francés. *In the afternoons, Luis studies French.*
Where	
We can say where the action takes place.	Luis estudia francés en su casa. *Luis studies French at home.*
Why	
We can say why the action takes place [230].	Luis estudia francés porque quiere viajar a Francia. *Luis studies French because he wants to travel to France.*
With whom	
We can say with whom the action is performed.	Luis estudia francés con un profesor particular. *Luis studies French with a private teacher.*
How	
We can say how the action is performed.	Luis estudia francés intensivamente. *Luis studies French intensively.*

We can combine several circumstances in one sentence.

Por las tardes, Luis estudia francés intensivamente en su casa con un profesor particular porque quiere viajar a Francia.

In the afternoons, Luis studies French intensively at home with a privatee teacher because he wants to go to France.

For other circumstances, see [221 -237].

The verb is the main building block of the sentence. It expresses the process.

The verb is the most important word in the sentence because it indicates what is going on in any given situation. The verb can express several types of happenings: actions *(telefonea, está durmiendo)*, states of being *(estoy)*. We will call actions and states by the general name of **processes**.

Pablo telefonea a su hermano.	*Pablo phones his brother.*
El bebé está durmiendo.	*The baby is sleeping.*
Estoy enfermo.	*I am sick.*

Verb tenses communicate when processes take place.

We can find out when the process took place by looking at the form of the verb. The form *como* indicates that the action is occurring at the moment when the speaker says the sentence *Como un pastel*. But if the speaker says *Comí un pastel (I ate a cake)*, the form *comí* tells us that the action is located in the past.

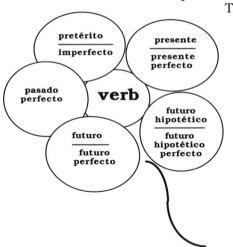

The forms related to the time when the process takes place are called **verb tenses**. We will refer to verb tenses by their names in Spanish: *presente, pretérito, imperfecto, presente perfecto, pasado perfecto, futuro, futuro perfecto, futuro hipotético, futuro hipotético perfecto,* etc.

In Spanish the verb is conjugated.

The verb agrees with its subject. The form of the verb also changes in accordance with its subject. For example, for the verb *comer (to eat),* the forms of the presente are:

yo	como	*I eat*	nosotros/as	comemos	*we eat*
tú	comes	*you eat*	vosotros/as	coméis	*you eat*
él/ella/Ud.	come	*he/she eats*	ellos/ellas/Uds.	comen	*they eat*
		you eat			*you e~*

The agreement of the verb with its subject in each tense is **conjugation** [118].

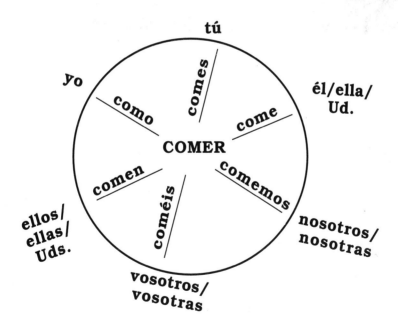

Verb complements are crucial to the complete meaning.

A sentence conveys a complete message when it gives information about the process and the individuals (persons or things) that participate in it. For example, if we want to speak about the process of throwing a ball *(lanzar),* we need to know who throws something and what this person throws.

Remember that the person doing the action is called the subject. The thing being thrown is called the **complement** because it completes the meaning of the verb.

> Luis lanza el balón.   *Luis throws the ball.*

El balón is the complement of the verb *lanzar.* Without it the sentence would not convey a complete message. The sentence *Luis lanza...* is not complete unless we know **what** is being thrown.

Verbs have different requirements for complements.

Some verbs do not require a complement *(está durmiendo)*; others require a noun *(come)*; others are followed by a preposition and a noun *(habla)*; others have several complements *(da).* In the appendix, you will find a complete list of the required complements for some selected verbs.

> Luisa está durmiendo   *Luisa is sleeping.*
> Pablo come pizza.   *Pablo eats pizza.*
> María habla a Juan.   *Maria speaks to Juan.*
> Daré dinero a Juan.   *I will give money to Juan.*

Verb requirements differ from language to language.

When you learn a verb, you have to learn what complement is required in order for the meaning to be complete.

SPANISH	ENGLISH
Aprendo **a** nadar.	*I learn **how** to swim.*
Quiero **que tú nades.**	*I want **you to swim.***
Juego **a** las cartas.	*I play cards.*

8

Nouns name the participants in the process.

We learned that, in order to express or understand a complete message, we need to identify the process and the people or things which participate in it. **Nouns** are used to name the participants in the process.

María habla español.   *María speaks Spanish.*

María and *Spanish* are nouns. They tell us who is speaking, and what language she speaks, i.e., they give us information about the participants involved in the action of speaking.

In Spanish all nouns have gender.

In Spanish, contrary to English, nouns are either feminine or masculine, whether they refer to humans, animals or inanimate things. When you learn nouns, you have to learn their gender.

Like in English, for humans and animals the gender is determined by the natural gender (male/female); for example, *el niño (the boy)* is masculine, and *la niña (the girl)* is feminine. However, unlike English, nouns naming inanimate things also have gender; for example, *el sombrero (the hat)* is masculine, and *la corbata (the tie)* is feminine [16 - 21].

la niña, la gata, la goma, la corbata   are **feminine**.
the girl, the cat, the eraser, the tie

el niño, el gato, el lápiz, el sombrero   are **masculine**.
the boy, the cat, the pencil, the hat

Gender is very important to learn because all the elements related to the noun (determiner and adjectives) have the same gender.

una nuev**a** corbat**a**   *a new tie*
un nuev**o** sombrer**o**   *a new hat*

9

Nouns vary in number.

Nouns can be marked for **number**. They can be used in the singular and the plural forms, just like in English; for example, *la niña (the girl)* is singular, and *las niñas (the girls)* is plural [22 - 23].

la mujer, la falda, la camisa
the woman, the skirt, the shirt

are **singular**.

las mujeres, las faldas, las camisas
the women, the skirts, the shirts

are **plural**.

el hombre, el chaleco, el cinturón
the man, the vest, the belt

are **singular**.

los hombres, los chalecos, los cinturones
the men, the vests, the belts

are **plural.**

Number is very important to learn because all the elements related to the noun (determiner and adjectives) have the same number.

las nuev**as** corbat**as**   *the new ties*
un nuev**o** sombrer**o**   *the new hats*

Common nouns need a determiner.

Consider the following situation:

 A student came late to class.

We can express this situation in several ways:

Carmen llegó tarde a clase.   *Carmen came late to class.*
La estudiante llegó tarde a clase.   *The student came late to class.*

In the first sentence, the subject is expressed by the noun *Carmen* and in the second, by *estudiante*. But, whereas the noun *Carmen* can stand by itself, *estudiante* needs to be accompanied by the word *la*, which is called a **determiner**. The reason is that *Carmen* and *estudiante* belong to two different categories of nouns: **proper** and **common nouns**.

√ **Proper nouns** name a particular person or thing *(Carmen)*. They do not come with a determiner.

√ **Common nouns** name a general class of people or things *(estudiante)*. They need a determiner.

It is possible to use other determiners before the noun *estudiante* [26 - 41]:

una *(a)* estudiante; **esta** *(this)* estudiante; **su** *(her)* estudiante

Determiners agree with the noun.

The determiner always **agrees** in gender and number with the noun. The determiner will be feminine or masculine, and singular or plural in accordance with the noun.

El estudiante compró **una corbata.**   *The student bought a tie.*
La profesora explicó **la lección.**   *The teacher explained the lesson.*
Los niños juegan a **la pelota.**   *The children play ball.*
Las bolsas son de cuero.   *The purses are made of leather.*

11

The adjective describes the person or thing named by the noun.

In the same situation as the one described in the previous page, we can also say:

La nueva estudiante chilena llegó tarde a clase.	*The new Chilean student came late to class.*

In this sentence, we have added information about the student. We know that she is a new student *(nueva),* and that she comes from Chile *(chilena).* These two pieces of information are given by **adjectives**, words which describe the person named by the noun.

Adjectives agree with the noun.

Adjectives **agree** in gender and number with the noun. The adjectives will be feminine or masculine, and singular or plural in accordance with the noun [44 - 47].

Yo compré **una camisa blanca.**	*I bought a white shirt.*
No me gustan **las tartas heladas.**	*I don't like frozen cakes.*
Yo compré **un carro blanco.**	*I bought a white car.*
Me gustan **los platos picantes.**	*I like hot dishes.*

Adjectives come before or after the noun.

Some adjectives come **before** the noun *(magnífico),* others come **after** the noun *(mexicana, delicioso, tinto).* In English adjectives come before the noun [48 - 49].

SPANISH	ENGLISH
el **magnífico** monumento	*the **superb** monument*
la estudiante **mexicana**	*the **Mexican** student*
un plato **delicioso**	*a **delicious** dish*
un vino **tinto**	*a **red** wine*

12

THE NOUN
AND
THE NOUN PHRASE

13

THE NOUN

In Spanish all nouns have gender.

Contrary to English, nouns are either feminine or masculine, whether they refer to humans, animals, or inanimate things.

 For humans and animals the gender is determined by the natural gender (masculine for males, feminine for females). However, in Spanish the gender is also represented in the ending of the nouns.

The ending indicates whether a noun is masculine or feminine.

Nouns ending in O in the masculine take the ending A in the feminine.

el esposo	la esposa	*husband/wife*
el hermano	la hermana	*brother/sister*
el niño	la niña	*boy/girl*
el gato	la gata	*cat/she-cat*

Nouns ending in consonants D, L, N, R, S, Z, in the masculine take the ending A in the feminine.

el doctor	la doctora	*doctor*
el león	la leona	*lion*
el japonés	la japonesa	*Japanese man/woman*

In some cases the masculine and the feminine are expressed by two different words.

el hombre	la mujer	*man/woman*	el buey	la vaca	*ox/cow*
el marido	la esposa	*husband/wife*	el toro	la vaca	*bull/cow*
el padre	la madre	*father/mother*	el caballo	la yegua	*horse/mare*
el rey	la reina	*king/queen*	el carnero	la oveja	*sheep*
el yerno	la nuera	*son-in-law/ daughter-in-law*	el gallo	la gallina	*rooster/hen*
			el macho	la hembra	*male/female*
			el potro	la jaca	*colt/poney*

16

In some cases the masculine and the feminine are identical.

√ **For human beings,** when the masculine and the feminine are the same, the difference is indicated by the article.

el / la anestesista	*anaesthetist*	el / la pediatra	*pediatrician*
el / la dentista	*dentist*	el / la periodista	*journalist*
el / la estudiante	*student*	el / la pianista	*pianist*
el / la joven	*young man/ woman*	el / la policía	*policeman/ woman*
el / la lingüista	*linguist*	el / la taxista	*taxi driver*
el / la médico	*doctor*	el / la turista	*turist*
el / la oficinista	*office clerk*		

 Note that *una persona (a person)* and *una víctima (a victim)* are always feminine even when they are used to refer to men.

√ **When speaking about animals,** we use a generic form which is either masculine or feminine, independently of the natural gender of the animal.

el águila	*eagle*	la ballena	*whale*
el elefante	*elephant*	la rata	*rat*
el armadillo	*armadillo*	la serpiente	*snake*

When the situation requires to be specific about the natural gender, then we use the words *macho (male)* and *hembra (female)*.

el águila macho   el águila hembra   or   la hembra del águila
la ballena macho la ballena hembra or   la hembra de la ballena

la abeja   *la rana*   *el ciervo*   *la mosca*

Nouns which refer to inanimate things are either masculine or feminine. As a general rule, we know the gender of a noun by looking at the ending.

The ending indicates whether a noun is masculine or feminine.

el baño		*la casa*
el carro	**- O**	*la mesa*
el cuchillo		*la cuchara*
el cuaderno	**- A**	*la mochila*

Nouns ending in O are masculine.

el baño *(bath)*, el carro *(car)*, el cuaderno *(notebook)*, el cuchillo *(knife)*

 Exceptions: la foto *(picture)*, la mano *(hand)*, la moto *(motorcycle)*, la radio (*radio* is feminine in Spain)

Nouns ending in A are feminine.

la casa *(house)*, la cuchara *(spoon)*, la mochila *(backpack)*, la roca *(stone)*, la rosa *(rose)*, la toalla *(towel)*

 Exceptions: el clima *(weather)*, el día *(day)*, el drama *(drama)*, el idioma *(language)*, el mapa *(map)*, el planeta *(planet)*, el problema *(problem)*, el programa *(program)*, el sistema *(system)*, el tema *(theme)*, el telegrama *(telegram)*

Nouns beginning with A or HA and ending in A are feminine.

However, we use the masculine form of the articles *el/un* in order to avoid repeating the sound **A** (**la a**lma, etc.):

el agua *(water)*, el alma *(soul)*, el arma *(weapon)*, el habla *(speech)*, el hacha *(axe)*, el hada *(fairy)*
el hambre *(hunger)* follows the same rule.

Although these nouns are preceded by *el*, they are still feminine and the adjectives that modify them come in the feminine form:

el agua fresca *(fresh water)*, el arma biológica *(biological weapon)*

el chiste
el café

- E

la fuente
la leche

Nouns ending in E can be either masculine or feminine.

masc.: el café *(coffee)*, el chiste *(joke)*, el peine *(comb)*, el paquete *(package)*
fem.:   la fuente *(fountain)*, la leche *(milk)*, la llave *(key)*, la noche *(night)*

Nouns ending in a consonant are masculine.

el bar *(bar)*, el césped *(lawn)*, el cristal *(crystal)*, el énfasis *(emphasis)*, el jabón *(soap)*, el lápiz *(pencil)*

 Exceptions: some nouns ending in a consonant are feminine; they usually end in D, Z, and L: la sed *(thirst)*, la luz *(light)*, la piel *(skin)*.

The suffix indicates whether a noun is masculine or feminine.

Nouns can be formed by adding an ending to a verb, an adjective, or another noun. These endings are called **suffixes.** We know the gender of a noun by looking at the suffix.

Masculine

- aje
el equipaje *(luggage)*
- ete
el banquete *(banquet)*
- ón
el jarrón *(vase)*, el salón *(lobby)*
- dor / tor / sor
el calentador *(heater)*
el tractor *(tractor)*
el ascensor *(elevator)*
- il
el redil *(sheepfold)*

Feminine

- dad
la soledad *(solitude)*
- tad
la amistad *(friendship)*
- ez
la escasez *(shortage)*
- ie
la calvicie *(baldness)*
- ión
la canción *(song)*
la opinión *(opinion)*

Some nouns come in the feminine or the masculine with different meanings

Certain nouns are identical in form, but can be either masculine or feminine, as shown by the article that precedes it. Their meaning is then different.

el batería	*drummer*	la batería	*battery*
el capital	*capital (money)*	la capital	*capital (city)*
el cólera	*cholera*	la cólera	*anger*
el corte	*cut*	la corte	*law court*
el cura	*priest*	la cura	*cure*
el frente	*front (in front)*	la frente	*forehead*
el guía	*guide*	la guía	*guidebook*
el margen	*border*	la margen	*riverbank*
el parte	*message*	la parte	*portion*
el pendiente	*earring*	la pendiente	*slope*
el policía	*policeman*	la policía	*police*

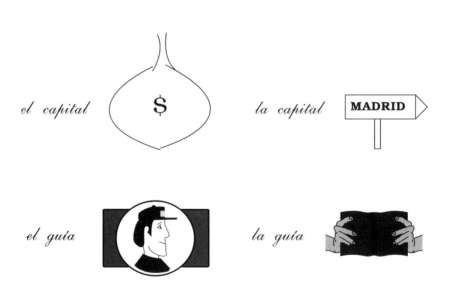

el capital   la capital   el guía   la guía

Here are some generalizations.

Geographical names are masculine.

Seas	Rivers	Mountains	Lakes
el Atlántico	el Nilo	los Pirineos	el Titicaca
el Mediterráneo	el Río Grande	el Everest	el Victoria
el Pacífico	el Amazonas	los Andes	el Ontario

Names of trees take the ending O and are therefore masculine. Names of fruits take the ending A and are therefore feminine.

Trees		Fruit	
el almendro	*almond tree*	la almendra	*almond*
el banano	*banana tree*	la banana	*banana*
el cerezo	*cherry tree*	la cereza	*cherry*
el manzano	*apple tree*	la manzana	*apple*
el naranjo	*orange tree*	la naranja	*orange*

Exceptions:

el cocotero (regular)	*coconut palm*	el coco	*coconut*
la higuera	*fig tree*	el higo	*fig*
el nogal	*walnut tree*	la nuez	*walnut*
la palmera	*palm tree*	el datil	*date*
la viña	*vineyard*	la uva	*grape*
el limonero (regular)	*lemon tree*	el limón	*lemon*

Names of languages are masculine.

el árabe *(Arabic)*, el español *(Spanish)*, el inglés *(English)*, el francés *(French)*, el portugués *(Portuguese)*, el quechua *(Quichua)*

Names of sciences end in A and are therefore feminine.

la biología *(biology)*, la física *(physics)*, las matemáticas *(mathematics)*, la medicina *(medicine)*, la oceanografía *(oceanography)*, la química *(chemistry)*

Names of days are masculine.

el domingo, el lunes, el martes, el miércoles, el jueves, el viernes, el sábado

> **To turn a noun into the plural, we add an ending to the singular form.**

1. We add S to nouns ending in an unstressed vowel (A, O, E) or É.

el libro	los libros	*book*	la llave	las llaves	*key*
el café	los cafés	*café*	la mesa	las mesas	*table*

2. We add ES:

√ to nouns ending with a consonant (except S).

el pan	los panes	*bread*	el reloj	los relojes	*watch*
el color	los colores	*color*	el balón	los balones	*ball*

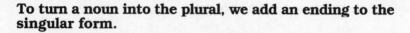 **Note** that for the nouns ending in **Z,** the final **Z** changes to **C** when we add **ES.** This is a consequence of the spelling of the sound [s]/[th]; see [251].

el pez	los peces	*fish*	una vez	dos veces	*times*
el juez	los jueces	*judge*	la voz	las voces	*voice*

√ to nouns ending with EY.

el buey	los bueyes	*ox*
la ley	las leyes	*law*
el rey	los reyes	*king*

√ to nouns ending with Á,Ó,Í,Ú.

el rubí	los rubies	*ruby*
el marroquí	los marroquies	*Morrocan*
el hindú	los hindues	*Hindu*

Exceptions: papá, papás *(father);* mamá, mamás *(mother);* dominó, dominós *(domino);* sofá, sofás *(sofa)*

√ to noun ending in a stressed vowel followed by S.

el francés	los franceses	*French people*
el país	los paises	*country*
el revés	los reveses	*the underside*
el mes	los meses	*month*

22

Some nouns do not change in the plural.

Nouns ending with an unstressed vowel followed by S in the singular do not change in the plural.

la / las crisis	*crisis*	la / las dosis	*dose*
el / los cumpleaños	*birthday*	el / los lunes	*Monday*
		el / los virus	*virus*

Some nouns are always plural.

los alicates	*pliers*	las tinieblas	*darkness*
los anteojos	*glasses*	las vacaciones	*holidays*
las bragas	*panties (Spain)*	los víveres	*provisions*
los celos	*jealousy*	las Letras	*Literature*
las esposas	*handcuffs*	las partes	*private parts (Spain)*
las gafas	*glasses*	los adentros	*innermost thoughts*
los pantalones	*trousers*	los bienes	*goods*
las tijeras	*scissors*		

los anteojos

Some nouns have a different meaning in the singular and the plural.

celo	*zeal*	celos	*jealousy*
corte	*cut/court*	Cortes	*parliament*
honra	*honor*	honras fúnebres	*funeral rites*

Some nouns have a singular form with a collective meaning.

These nouns are followed by a verb in the singular.

Toda mi familia va a venir.	*My whole family will come.*
El pueblo de Madrid se rebela.	*The people of Madrid are rebelling.*
La gente sale a pasear.	*People go out for a walk.*

23

THE DETERMINER

There are two kinds of nouns: the proper nouns and the common nouns. **Proper nouns** name a particular person or thing (Pablo, Madrid). **Common nouns** name a general class of people or things (niño, ciudad) [11].

Common nouns need a determiner.

It is easy to identify the person named "Pablo" or the city called "Madrid". However, when we use the noun "niño", we need more information in order to identify the specific person or thing about whom (which) we are talking. For example, we can point to a specific boy and say "este niño" *(this boy)*. The word we have added to the noun is called a **determiner** [11]. There are several kinds of determiners:

Indefinite determiners Indefinite determiners do not specify the identity of the person or thing named by the noun.	Examples
The indefinite article 	Tengo **unos** amigos en Chile. *I have some friends in Chile.*
The cardinal numbers	**Ocho** caballos compitieron. *Eight horses competed.*
The indefinite adjective	Voy a España **cada** verano. *I go to Spain every summer.*
The expressions of quantity	**Ningún** estudiante vino a la reunión. *No student came to the meeting.*

The second class of determiners is called the class of **definite determiners.**

Definite determiners Definite determiners help identify the person or thing named by the noun.	Examples
The definite article 	**La** moto de Ana es nueva. *Ana's motorcycle is new.*
The possessive determiner	**Mi** hermana se llama Ana. *My sister's name is Ana.*
The demonstrative determiner	**Esta** casa es bonita. *This house is nice.*

The **indefinite article** is an indefinite determiner. It does not specify the identity of the person or thing named by the noun. It corresponds to the English *a* and *some.*

FORM

	Singular	Plural
masculine	un	unos
feminine	una	unas

Un estudiante entró en la clase.	*A student went into the classroom.*
Tengo **unos** lápices y **unas** gomas.	*I have some pencils and some erasers.*

USES

The indefinite article introduces something that has not been mentioned before.

Yo leo **una** novela policíaca.	*I read a detective novel.*
Hay **una** biblioteca en la plaza.	*There is a library in the square.*

The indefinite article is used in a generic statement.

A noun with the indefinite article has a generic meaning. This means that the statement in the sentence is true of any person or thing named by the noun.

Un buen estudiante no falta nunca a la escuela.	*A good student never misses school.*
Una niña scout ayuda a sus camaradas.	*A girl scout helps her friends.*

The plural indefinite article followed by an expression of quantity means *approximately.*

Me quedan **unas cuarenta** páginas por leer.	*I have about 40 pages to read.*
¡Dáme **unos** dólares!	*Give me a few dollars!*

OMISSION OF THE INDEFINITE ARTICLE

We omit the plural definite article to express generality.

The indefinite articles *unos/unas* are used to refer to individual people or things; when the indefinite article is omitted, the noun refers to things or people in general.

WITHOUT THE ARTICLE	WITH THE ARTICLE
Compré libros. *I bought books.*	Compré **unos** libros. *I bought some books.*
En este pueblo tengo amigos. *I have friends in this town.*	En este pueblo tengo **unos** amigos. *I have some friends in this town.*
Comí pasteles deliciosos. *I ate delicious cakes.*	Comí **unos** pasteles deliciosos. *I ate some good cakes.*
Books, friends, cakes give general information; identifying them would not be relevant.	*Books, friends, cakes* are individual entities which can be easily identified.

We omit the indefinite article *un/una* before mass nouns.

A mass noun names things which cannot be counted, like substances (sugar, coffee) or abstract qualities (courage, beauty). Like in English, when we do not specify what kind of thing or how much exactly, we omit the indefinite article.

He bebido té para el desayuno. *I drank tea at breakfast.*	He bebido **un** té estupendo. *I drank a wonderful tea.*

 Note that **when we add an adjective** *(estupendo)*, describing a kind of tea, we use the indefinite article.

We omit the indefinite article before *ciento, medio, mil,* and *otro.*

¡Déme medio kilo de sardinas y otro pollo!	*Give me half a kilo of sardines and another chicken.*

29

OMISSION OF THE INDEFINITE ARTICLE

After the verb *ser*, the use or the omission of the indefinite article have different meanings.

WITH THE INDEFINITE ARTICLE

We use the indefinite article after the verb *ser* when the noun serves **to identify an unknown person.** This can be done by mentioning the profession, nationality, political affiliation, religion, marital status, or any other identifying information.

¿Quién es Julia Rodríguez?	*Who is Julia Rodriguez?*
__ Es **una** abogada.	*__ She is a lawyer.*
__ Es **una** cubana	*__ She is a Cuban.*
__ Es **una** ecologista.	*__ She is an ecologist.*

When the noun is accompanied by an adjective, then we always use the indefinite article.

__ Es **una** buena abogada.	*__ She is a good lawyer.*
__ Es **una** cubana exiliada.	*__ She is a Cuban in exile.*
__ Es **una** ecologista famosa.	*__ She is a famous ecologist.*

WITHOUT THE ARTICLE

We do not use the indefinite article after the verb *ser* when we speak about the **properties of a specific person** who is the focus of attention.

¡Háblame de Julia Rodríguez!	*Tell me about Julia Rodriguez!*
__ Es abogada.	*__ She is a lawyer*
__ Es cubana	*__ She is a Cuban.*
__ Es ecologista.	*__ She is an ecologist.*
__ Es soltera.	*__ She is an unmarried woman.*

 Note that if you speak about yourself or about anybody who is part of the conversation and has already been identified, you cannot use the indefinite article, except when there is an adjective.

Yo soy abogada.	*I am a lawyer.*
Yo soy una buena abogada.	*I am a good lawyer.*

Cardinal numbers are indefinite determiners. They do not specify the identity of the persons or things named by the noun, but only tell how many. They correspond to the English cardinal numbers.

0	cero	10	diez	20	veinte	30	treinta
1	uno/un/una	11	once	21	veintiuno	31	treinta y uno
2	dos	12	doce	22	veintidós	40	cuarenta
3	tres	13	trece	23	veintitrés	41	cuarenta y uno
4	cuatro	14	catorce	24	veinticuatro	50	cincuenta
5	cinco	15	quince	25	veinticinco	51	cincuenta y uno
6	seis	16	diez y seis	26	veintiséis	60	sesenta
7	siete	17	diez y siete	27	veintisiete	70	setenta
8	ocho	18	diez y ocho	28	veintiocho	80	ochenta
9	nueve	19	diez y nueve	29	veintinueve	90	noventa

100	cien* / ciento	1.000	mil
101	ciento uno	1.000.000	un millón
200	doscientos / as	1.000.000.000.000	un billón
500	quinientos / as		

* We use **cien** when it is followed by the noun *(cien páginas)*, or by *mil (cien mil dólares)*, or when the noun is understood: *¿Cuántos libros tienes? — Tengo cien.* [*Libros* is understood.]
* We use **ciento** in combination with other numbers: dos cientos, ciento veinte.

Pay attention to the following differences.

1. **When a comma is used in Spanish,** English uses a dot and vice-versa. In Mexico the dot is used for decimals, like in English.

	Spanish	English
seven	7,00	7.00
seven thousand	7.000	7,000
seven hundred thousand	700.000	700,000

2. **The US English *billion*** is not the equivalent of the Spanish *billón*.

	Spanish	US English
1 000 000 000	mil millones	a billion
1 000 000 000 000	un billón	a trillion

3. **We use cardinal numbers** to indicate the date: day, month, year:

el dos de mayo de 1996 (2-5-96)   *May 2nd, 1996 (5-2-96)*

 Note that for the 1st day of the month, we can use either the cardinal or the ordinal number: el primero/el uno de mayo *May 1st.*

Ordinal numbers are used with a noun to indicate **the order** in which a person or a thing comes in a series.

FORM

The first 12 ordinal numbers have a specific form. From number 13 on, the cardinal number is used to convey ordinal meaning.

primero*	*first*	quinto	*fifth*	noveno	*ninth*
segundo	*second*	sexto	*sixth*	décimo	*tenth*
tercero*	*third*	séptimo	*seventh*	undécimo	*eleventh*
cuarto	*fourth*	octavo	*eighth*	duodécimo	*twelfth*

> * The forms **primero** and **tercero** are used when the noun is understood:
> Llegó (el) primero.   *He arrived first.*
> * The forms **primer** and **tercer** are used before masculine nouns:
> el primer lunes   *the first Monday*

> ***Ordinal numbers agree in gender and number with the noun.***

el segundo piso/la segunda fila	*the second floor/the second row*
los segundos anteojos/las segundas tijeras	*the second glasses/the second pair of scissors*

USE

1. Ordinal numbers must come with a determiner.

Luis vive en el quinto piso.	*Luis lives on the fifth floor.*
Es la sexta vez que viajo a Jaén.	*It is the sixth time I go to Jaen.*

2. With proper names, we use the ordinal number after the name to refer to a specific person. It becomes part of the proper name. We do the same when referring to a specific century.

Carlos V/Francisco I	*Charles V/François I*
[Read: Carlos quinto/ Francisco primero]	
el siglo II/el siglo XX	*the 2nd century/the 20th century*
[Read: el siglo segundo/ el siglo veinte]	

Indefinite Adjectives √

The **indefinite adjectives** are indefinite determiners. They do not specify the identity of the persons or things named by the noun. They correspond to the English indefinite *certain, each, any, different, other...*

Masculine sing./pl.		Feminine sing./pl.		English
algún	algunos	alguna	algunas	*any, a certain, some*
cada	[no plural]	cada	[no plural]	*every, each*
cierto	ciertos	cierta	ciertas	*certain* [no information on quantity or identity]
cualquier	[no plural]	cualquier	[no plural]	*any*
diferente	diferentes	diferente	diferentes	*different*
otro	otros	otra	otras	*another* (sing.), *other* (pl.)
todo	[no plural]*	toda	[no plural]*	*each and every*
[no sing.]	varios	[no sing.]	varias	*various* [small quantity + idea of variety]

* This use of **todo** is different from the one given in [35]

¿Conoces **algún** o **alguna** estudiante que sepa portugués?

Do you know any student who would speak Portuguese?

Cada estudiante en esta clase habla dos lenguas.

Each student in this class speaks two languages.

Ciertas alumnas visitaron Quebec.

Certain students visited Quebec.

Cualquier estudiante conoce la historia de Colón.

Any student (whatsoever) knows the story of Columbus.

Conozco **diferentes** estudiantes que pueden hacer este trabajo.

I know different students who can do this job.

Otras estudiantes harán el viaje a México.

Other students will go on the trip to Mexico.

Todo estudiante de primer año debe presentarse en la secretaría.

Each and every first year student must report to the secretary's office.

Hay **varias** soluciones para cada problema.

There are various solutions for each problem.

Expressions of quantity are indefinite determiners. They do not specify the identity of the persons or things named by the noun, but only **tell how many.** They correspond to the English expressions of quantity: *many, few, a pound of...*

Masculine sing./pl.		Feminine sing./pl.		English
bastante	bastantes	bastante	bastantes	*enough*
demasiado	demasiados	demasiada	demasiadas	*too many/much*
más	más	más	más	*more*
menos	menos	menos	menos	*less, fewer*
mucho	muchos	mucha	muchas	*many, much*
ningún	ningunos	ninguna	ningunas	*no*
poco	pocos	poca	pocas	*few, little*
suficiente	suficientes	suficiente	suficientes	*enough*
tanto*	tantos	tanta	tantas	*as/so much, as/so many*

* **tanto/os** and **tanta/as** can be used after a number, or to indicate time:
30 y tantos/as	*30 something*
30 y tantos años	*over 30 years of age*
a las tantas de la noche	*at some time in the small hours*

⮕ **Note** that many nouns can be used as expressions of quantity: un kilo de (*a kilo of*), una taza de (*a cup of*), una caja de (*a box of*), una cuchara de (*a spoonful of*), un par de (*a couple of*)...

Ninguna biblioteca tiene **más** libros que la nuestra.	*No library has more books than ours.*
Hay **demasiada** gente que come **mucha** carne y **pocas** legumbres.	*There are too many people who eat too much meat and few vegetables.*
No tenemos **suficiente** dinero para comprar una casa más grande.	*We do not have enough money to buy a bigger house.*
Nunca he visto **tantos** pájaros en el jardín.	*I have never seen so many birds in the garden.*
Para hacer flan se necesita **una cucharada de** azúcar, **un vaso de** leche, y huevos.	*To make a flan, one needs one spoon of sugar, a cup of milk, and eggs.*

FRACTIONS

Fractions are expressions which specify a part or **portion** of a whole
(half, a quarter...).

la mayoría	*most*	la mitad	*half (1/2)*
una parte	*part*	la tercera parte	*a third (1/3)*
diez por ciento	*ten per cent (10%)*	la cuarta parte	*a quarter (1/4)*

 Note that fractions are always followed by the preposition **de** and a
full noun phrase (a noun and its determiner). If the noun phrase is
omitted, then *de* is also omitted.

Yo quiero la mitad **del** pastel.	*I would like half the cake.*
¿Cuánto tomas? — La mitad.	*How much would you like? — A half.*

TOTALITY

To express the **totality** of something, we use the expressions *todo/s* and
toda/s, which are equivalent to the English *all.*

Masculine sing./pl.	Feminine sing./pl.	*English*
todo todos	toda todas	*all, whole, entire*

 Note that **todo** comes before the complete noun phrase (the noun and
its determiner). Contrary to English, *todo* is never followed by a
preposition (todos mis amigos, *all **of** my friends*).

todo el mundo; **toda** la familia	*the whole world; the whole family*
todos los árboles; **todas** las casas	*all the trees, all the houses*
todo el día; **todos** los días	*the whole day; every day*

 Also note that it is different from the indefinite adjective **todo** [33],
which comes only in the singular and means *each and every.*

Expressions with *todo/os/a/as*

a toda velocidad	*at full speed*
con toda prisa	*in all haste*
en toda California	*all over California*
todo lo demás	*all the rest*

The **definite article** is a definite determiner. It helps identify the person or thing named by the noun. The English definite article is *the*.

FORM

Gender	Singular	Plural
masculine	el	los
feminine	la	las
neutral	lo	

The neutral article **lo** comes before adjectives and participles which are used as abstract nouns, and before relative clauses.

Lo importante es tener salud.	*What is important is to be healthy.*
Lo mejor que puedes hacer es esperar.	*The best thing you can do is wait.*
Juan no llegó; me imagino **lo** peor.	*Juan did not arrive; I imagine the worst.*

CONTRACTED FORMS OF THE DEFINITE ARTICLE

When the article **el** comes after prepositions **a** or **de,** the two words are **contracted** into a single word in the following way:

a	**+**	**el**	**=**	**al**
de	**+**	**el**	**=**	**del**

Luis va **al** estadio para jugar al fútbol.	*Luis goes to the stadium to play soccer.*
El entrenador **del** equipo es de Cuba.	*The coach of the team is from Cuba.*
Hablaré **al** director **del** viaje.	*I will talk to the principal about the trip.*

 Note that the contraction does not occur with the other definite articles. Compare the sentences above with the following.

Luis va **a la** escuela para jugar **a la** pelota.
El entrenador **de la** clase es de Cuba.
Hablaré **a la** directora **de los** viajes de estudios.

USES

The definite article is used with a noun which has been mentioned previously or which is known to both speaker and listener.

Un estudiante llegó. . . **El** estudiante llevaba una camisa azul.	*A student arrived... The student wore a blue shirt.*
¡Dáme **el** libro!	*Give me the book!* (The listener knows which book.)

The definite article is used with a noun to refer to a specific person or thing.

The noun can be specified by an adjective, a preposition and a noun phrase (*de...*), or a relative clause (*que/donde...*).

La hermana de Juan vive en Miami.	*Juan's sister lives in Miami.*
El señor que te presenté el mes pasado obtuvo **el** puesto.	*The man I introduced to you last month got the position.*
El pueblo donde vivo está a 50 km de **la** capital.	*The town where I live is 50 km from the capital.*

The definite article is used in the same way with proper nouns.

El San Antonio colonial era un pueblo. [vs.: San Antonio es una gran ciudad.]	*Colonial San Antonio was a village.* [vs.: *San Antonio is a big city.*]
El San Antonio del siglo XVIII era un pueblo.	*San Antonio in the 18th century was a village.*
El San Antonio en el que vivió mi bisabuela era un pueblo.	*The San Antonio where my great grandmother lived was a village.*
El Goya de los últimos años vivió triste y solitario.	*The later Goya lived sad and lonely.*

37

USES

The definite article has a generic sense.

The definite article, used in the singular, has a generic meaning: speaking about one individual, it gives a statement which is characteristic of a class of individuals.

El gato es un animal cariñoso.	*The cat is an affectionate animal.*
El agricultor se levanta temprano.	*The farmer gets up early.*
El machete sirve para cortar caña.	*The machete is used to cut cane.*

The definite article presents a generalization.

1. **The definite article, used in the plural,** has a general or collective meaning. It tells a statement which is believed to be true of all the members of a group.

Los españoles usan aceite de oliva.	*The Spaniards use olive oil.*
Las enfermeras trabajan mucho.	*The nurses work hard.*

 Note that this use of plural generalization is the form used in expressing stereotypes.

2. **The definite article is also used with specific verbs** whose meaning implies a generalization.

Me gustan las frutas.

Me encantan las frutas.

The use of the definite article with the verb *gustar* implies not a specific pear, but the whole class of fruit called *pears*. The definite article is used with other verbs like *gustar*, such as *encantar, adorar, odiar, preferir,* etc.

Prefiero el helado.

USES

3. **Abstract and general concepts** take a definite article in Spanish, but do not take any article in English.

SPANISH	ENGLISH
No me interesa **la** política.	*I am not interested in politics.*
La televisión fomenta **la** pasividad.	*Television encourages passivity.*
La arquitectura colonial es bella.	*Colonial architecture is beautiful.*
Estudiamos **la** religión azteca.	*We study Aztec religion.*
Se ha desarrollado **el** turismo.	*Turism has been developed.*
La cultura rural es diferente de **la** cultura urbana.	*Rural culture is different from urban culture.*
Se especializa en **la** cultura maya.	*He specializes in Mayan culture.*
El Presidente dio un discurso sobre el futuro de **la** investigación científica.	*The President gave a speech on the future of scientific research.*
La contaminación del agua causó el pánico en la ciudad.	*Water pollution caused panic in the city.*

The definite article is used before a title or a name.

La Universidad de Yale es famosa.	*Yale University is famous.*
El Presidente Lincoln fue asesinado en 1865.	*President Lincoln was assassinated in 1865.*
Te presento a **la** Señora Suárez.	*Let me introduce you to Mrs. Suarez.*
La Callas fue una cantante famosa.	*Callas was a famous opera singer.*

 Note that the singular article is used only for famous women. The plural is used for both famous men and women. **Los** is also used for families *(Los Fuente, The Fuentes)*.

 Note also that when we speak directly to a person, we do not use the article before the name or title.

Buenos días Señora Suárez.	*Good morning Mrs. Suarez.*

The **possessive determiner** is a definite determiner. It specifies which person or thing is named by the noun, by indicating possession. Like all determiners, the possessive determiner agrees in gender and number with the noun which follows.

FORM

Following noun belongs to	Following noun is masculine sing. / pl.		Following noun is feminine sing. / pl.		English
me you (sing.) her/him/ you (formal)	mi tu su	mis tus sus	mi tu su	mis tus sus	*my* *your* *his/her/* *its/your*
us you (pl.) them/you (pl. formal)	nuestro vuestro su	nuestros vuestros sus	nuestra vuestra su	nuestras vuestras sus	*our* *your* *their/* *your*

USES

The possessive determiner expresses possession.

Invité a todos **mis** amigos.	*I invited all of my friends.*
Esta es **mi** moto.	*This is my motorcycle.*
Olvidé **mis** cuadernos en casa.	*I forgot my notebooks at home.*

 Note that when the possession is obvious (body parts, clothing, car, etc.), we do not need the possessive determiner.

Sacó **la** cabeza por la ventana.	*He stuck his head out of the window.*
Me puse **la** corbata y **el** sombrero.	*I put on my tie and my hat.*
Tomé **la** cartera.	*I took my wallet.*
Camina con **las** manos en los bolsillos.	*He walks with his hands in his pockets.*

When the noun has a modifier (adjective or preposition + noun phrase), we do use the possessive determiner.

Estiré mis piernas cansadas.	*I stretched my tired legs.*

Demonstrative Determiners

The **demonstrative determiner** is a definite determiner. It specifies which person or thing is named by the noun, by pointing to it.

FORM

Proximity	Masculine sing./ pl.		Feminine sing. / pl.		English
near the speaker	este	estos	esta	estas	*this / these*
near the listener	ese	esos	esa	esas	*that / those*
far from both	aquel	aquellos	aquella	aquellas	*that / those*

USES

The demonstrative determiner is used to refer to an individual or thing by pointing to it, physically or mentally.

Voy a comprar **esta** falda azul
y **este** jersey blanco.

I will buy this blue dress and this white sweater.

¡Dáme **aquella** foto que tomamos
en la cima del Popocatépetl!

Give me that picture we took on the top of the Popocatepetl.

Recuerdo **aquel** día que fuimos a
Veracruz.

I remember that day when we went to Veracruz.

The demonstrative determiner is used to refer to something which has been mentioned before.

Compré muebles y ropa. **Estas**
compras me han dejado sin ahorros.

I bought furniture and clothes. This shopping used up my savings.

 esta ... aquellos ... ese ...

41

THE ADJECTIVE

The **adjective** describes the person or thing named by the noun. It gives properties of the noun: shape, color, value, physical characteristics, character, origin, etc.

el libro **azul**	*the blue book*
el **nuevo** estudiante **español**	*the new Spanish student*
el niño con pelo **corto rizado**	*the boy with short curled hair*

Adjectives in Spanish differ from adjectives in English by two important properties:

(i)   they agree with the noun that they describe
(ii) they come either before or after the noun

Adjectives agree with the noun.

Adjectives **agree** in gender and number with the noun. The adjectives will be feminine or masculine, and singular or plural in accordance with the noun.

u**na** camis**a blanca** (fem. sing.)	*a white shirt*
la**s** tart**as heladas** (fem. pl.)	*the frozen cakes*
un carr**o blanco** (masc. sing.)	*a white car*
l**os** plat**os picantes** (masc. pl.)	*the hot dishes*

Adjectives come before or after the noun.

Some adjectives come **before** the noun *(buena)*, others come **after** the noun *(mexicanas)*. In English adjectives always come before the noun.

la **buena** maestra	*the **good** teacher*
las estudiantes **mexicanas**	*the **Mexican** students*

las estudiantes mexicanas

la buena maestra

Adjectives vary in gender and number in agreement with the noun which they modify.

Adjectives ending in O in the masculine change their O ending to A in the feminine.

corto	corta	*short*
cubano	cubana	*Cuban*
pequeño	pequeña	*small*

Adjectives ending in ÁN, ÓN, OR, ÉS in the masculine take A in the feminine.

charlatán	charlatana	*talkative*
llorón	llorona	*crybaby*
trabajador	trabajadora	*hard-working*
burgués	burguesa	*bourgeois*

Adjectives ending in A, E do not change in the feminine.

hipócrita	hipócrita	*hypocrit*
homicida	homicida	*homicide*
bilingüe	bilingüe	*bilingual*
torpe	torpe	*clumsy*

Adjectives ending in AL, AR, IZ, OZ do not change in the feminine.

crucial	crucial	*crucial*
polar	polar	*polar*
feliz	feliz	*happy*
veloz	veloz	*fast*

Adjectives in the comparative form do not change in the feminine.

inferior	inferior	*inferior*	superior	superior	*superior*
mayor	mayor	*bigger*	menor	menor	*smaller*
mejor	mejor	*better*	peor	peor	*worse*

The formation of nouns and adjectives of **nationality** does not follow specific rules. It is often hard to know, given the name of a country, what would be the name of the citizens of that country. Below is the list of all the Spanish speaking countries and states followed by the corresponding nationality, as well as the most important cities followed by the names of their inhabitants.

• **Argentina** (la)	argentino
Buenos Aires	porteño /
	bonaerense
• **Bolivia**	boliviano
La Paz	paceño
• **Colombia**	colombiano
Bogotá	bogotano
Medellín	medellinense
• **Costa Rica**	costarriqueño
	costarricense
San José	josefino
• **Cuba**	cubano
La Habana	habanero
Santiago	santiaguero
• **Chile**	chileno
Santiago	santiaguino
Valparaíso	porteño
• **Ecuador** (el)	ecuatoriano
Quito	quiteño
• **El Salvador**	salvadoreño
• **España**	español
Madrid	madrileño

Regions of Spain

Andalucía	andaluz
Aragón	aragonés
Asturias	asturiano
Cantabria	cántabro
Castilla	castellano
Cataluña	catalán
Extremadura	extremeño
Galicia	gallego
Navarra	navarro
País Vasco	vasco
Valencia	valenciano

• **Guatemala**	guatemalteco
• **Honduras**	hondureño
• **México**	mexicano
México D.F.	capitalino
Puebla	poblano
Guadalajara	tapatío
• **Nicaragua**	nicaragüense
Managua	managüense
• **Panamá**	panameño
• **Paraguay**	paraguayo
• **Perú** (el)	peruano
Lima	limeño
Cuzco	cuzqueño
• **Puerto Rico**	puertorriqueño
• **Santo Domingo**	dominicano
• **Uruguay** (el)	uruguayo
• **Venezuela**	venezolano
Caracas	caraqueño
Tegucigalpa	tegucigalpense

Estados Unidos

estadounidense
norteamericano

• In the US there are about 30 million Hispanics. The words **hispano/ latino** refer to the people with Hispanic background from Latin America, Spain, and US territories that were once settled by Spain.

The Plural of Adjectives √

The plural of adjectives follows the same basic rule as the plural of nouns [22 - 23].

> **To form the plural, we add S to adjectives ending in an unstressed vowel.**

rosa	rosas	*pink*
grande	grandes	*big*
corto	cortos	*short*

> **We add ES to adjectives ending with a consonant or a stressed vowel.**

fácil	fáciles	*easy*
mejor	mejores	*better*
portugués	portugueses	*Portuguese*
israelí	israelíes	*Israeli*
hindú	hindúes	*Hindu*

 Note that for the nouns ending in **Z**, the final **Z** changes to **C** when we add **ES**. This is a consequence of the spelling of the sound [s]/[th]; see [251].

veloz	veloces	*fast*
capaz	capaces	*able*
sagaz	sagaces	*clever*

los carros rápidos

los carros lentos

47

In Spanish, adjectives can come either before or after the noun depending on their meaning and their connection to the noun.

Most adjectives come after the noun.

These are adjectives which modify the noun by way of **classification.** They define a subset in the set indicated by the noun (in the set of shoes, there is a pair which is new).

los zapatos **nuevos** de Luis	*Luis' new shoes*
una revista **interesante**	*an interesting magazine*
una cuerda **larga**	*a long rope*

Adjectives indicating color, nationality, membership to a political or religious group, come essentially after the noun:

un lápiz **rojo**	*a red pencil*
un ciudadano **guatemalteco**	*a Guatemalan citizen*
la alcaldesa **republicana**	*the republican mayor*

Long adjectives or **adjectives followed by a modifier** are placed after the noun.

una historia **impresionante**	*an impressive story*
un padre **orgulloso de su hija**	*a father proud of his daughter*
un concierto **bastante bueno**	*quite a good concert*

Some adjectives come before the noun, with a special meaning.

Adjectives that come before the noun combine closely with the noun to **reinforce its meaning.**

una **alegre** primavera	*a joyful spring*
una **oscura** noche	*a dark night*
un **verde** prado	*a green field*

The Place of the Adjective √

Adjectives can be placed before the noun for **emphasis and emotional effect.**

una **extraordinaria** aventura	*an extraordinary adventure*
un **maravilloso** paisaje	*a marvelous landscape*

Some adjectives usually come before the noun and add **a nuance of moral or esthetic appreciation:** *bello, buen, gran, horrible, mal, mejor, nuevo, peor, pequeño, verdadero,* etc...

la **peor** pesadilla	*the worst nightmare*
la **verdadera** razón	*the real reason*

➤ **Note** that the adjectives *bueno* (masc. sing.), *grande* (masc. and fem. sing.), malo (masc. sing.), have a shortened form before the noun: *buen, gran, mal.*

un **buen** amigo	*a good friend*
una **gran** ciudad	*a big city*
un **mal** tiempo	*bad weather*

Some adjectives come before or after the noun, with meaning changes.

la **antigua** mesa	*the old table*	la mesa **antigua**	*the antique table*
un **buen** profesor	*a good teacher*	un profesor **bueno**	*a kind teacher*
un **gran** hombre	*an important man*	un hombre **grande**	*a big man*
el **mismo** presidente	*the same president*	el presidente **mismo**	*the president himself*
un **nuevo** libro [newly acquired]	*a new book*	un libro **nuevo** [recent]	*a new book*
un **pobre** hombre	*a poor guy*	un hombre **pobre**	*a man who is poor*
un **sencillo** soldado	*a private soldier*	un soldado **sencillo**	*a simple-minded soldier*
un **solo** estudiante	*only one student*	un estudiante **solo**	*a lonely student*
una **triste** aventura	*a dreadful adventure*	una aventura **triste**	*a sad adventure*
el **único** médico	*the only doctor*	un médico **único**	*a unique doctor*
un **viejo** amigo	*a long-standing friend*	un amigo **viejo**	*a friend who is old*

In our daily experience, we come in contact with people, objects and concepts. When we make a choice between things we want to buy, or evaluate different solutions to a problem, or decide which movie we want to see, we **make comparisons.** In every new situation, we evaluate, make judgments and choices based on comparisons. More specifically, comparison is a strategy that we constantly use when we learn other languages and cultures.

When we compare things, we use three degrees of comparison:
a higher degree; a lower degree; and an equal degree of comparison.

The **higher and lower degrees of comparison** contrast two things which show differences with respect to the same property.

For example, we can compare the following two sail boats, saying which one is bigger or smaller.

We can also express the fact that two things have an **equal degree** of the same property.

These two sail boats are equal in size.

We can express the similarities and the differences between things by using **comparative forms.** When we compare two things, we view one thing as having a property of a higher, lower or equal degree than the other.

EXPRESSING A HIGHER (LOWER) DEGREE

To indicate a higher (or lower) degree of comparison, we use the adverb *más (menos)* before the adjective, the adverb, or the noun and *que* or *de lo que* [52] after. This form corresponds to the English *more (less). . . than.* In all the following rules and examples, we will write the comparison of lower degree in parenthesis.

más (menos) +	**adjective** **adverb** **noun**	**+ que...**

Juan es **más (menos) alto que** Luis.	*Juan is taller (less tall) than Luis.*
Yo camino **más (menos) rápido que** Luis.	*I walk faster (less fast) than Luis.*
María tiene **más (menos) libros que** yo.	*María has more (less) books than I.*
Compro **más (menos) libros que** antes.	*I buy more (less) books than before.*

La policía es más alta que el obrero.

El obrero es menos alto y más gordo que ella.

When the second part of the comparison is a clause which begins with *que*, we use the form *de lo que*.

más (menos) +	**adjective** **adverb** **noun**	+ **de lo que** +	**clause**

The expression *de lo que* is used before a clause which is not introduced by a conjunction, such as *cuando, antes de, para*, etc.

El carro es **más (menos) rápido de lo que** crees.

The car is faster (less fast) than you think.

Tiene **más (menos) dinero de lo que** dice.

He has more (less) money than he says he has.

Some adjectives and adverbs have a special form to indicate the higher degree of comparison.

bueno/a/os/as; bien	*good; well*	mejor/mejores	*better*
malo/a/os/as; mal	*bad; badly*	peor/es	*worse*
grande/es	*big*	mayor	*bigger*
pequeño/a/os/as	*small*	menor/es	*smaller*

El chocolate es **mejor que** el café.

Chocolate is better than coffee.

El viaje fue **peor de lo que** había imaginado.

The trip was worse than I had imagined.

Expressions:

el hermano menor/mayor

the younger/older brother

la hermana menor/mayor

the younger/older sister

ser mayor de edad

to be of age

Other words are used to compare people or things: *superior, inferior, anterior, posterior.* They are followed by the preposition **a.**

>   Tuve una nota inferior/superior **a** la tuya.

>   *I had a grade lower/higher than yours.*

We can compare numbers of things.

The comparison has the following form:

number + **noun** +	**más (menos) que**		
number + **noun** +	**más (menos) de lo que**	+	**clause**

>   Tengo 10 dólares **más (menos) que** tú.

>   *I have $10 more (less) than you.*

>   Me envió dos libros **más (menos) de los que** había encargado.

>   *He sent me two books more (less) than what I had ordered.*

We also say:

>   Tengo **más (menos) de** 10 dólares en mi bolsillo.

>   *I have more (less) than $10 in my pocket.*

>   He visitado **más (menos) de** doce paises.

>   *I have visited more (less) than 12 countries.*

En la ciudad hay más de diez rascacielos.

We can compare verbs.

To indicate a higher degree when comparing verbs, we use *más que* and *más de lo que* after the verb.

verb	+	**más (menos) que**
verb	+	**más (menos) de lo que** + **clause**

The expression *de lo que* is used before a clause which is not introduced by a conjunction, such as *cuando, antes de, para,* etc.

Juan trabaja **más (menos) que** Luis.	*Juan works more (less) than Luis.*
Yo trabajo **más (menos) que** cuando no tenía computadora.	*I work more (less) than when I did not have a computer.*
María lee **más (menos) de lo que** crees.	*Maria reads more (less) than you think.*

 Note that we can omit the second part of the comparison:

Estas pilas duran **más (menos)**.	*These batteries last longer (less).*
En esta clase leemos **más (menos)**.	*In this class we read more (less).*

Expressions with *más*

más y más	*more and more*
más o menos	*more or less*
2 libros de más	*2 extra books*
5 pesos nada más	*only 5 pesos*
¿Qué más da?	*What difference does it make?*
¿Qué más?	*What else?*
¿Quieres más?	*Would you like more?*
¡Nada más!	*That's all!*

EXPRESSING AN EQUAL DEGREE

To indicate an equal degree of comparison, we use the word *tan* before the adjective, adverb or noun and *como* after. This form corresponds to the English *as. . . as.*

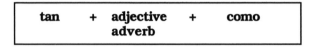

tan	+	adjective adverb	+	como

Juan es **tan alto como** Luis.   *Juan is as tall as Luis.*

Juan trabaja **tan rapidamente como** Luz.   *Juan works as fast as Luz.*

Luis es **tan conocido como** lo fue su padre.   *Luis is as famous as his father was.*

When we use nouns in the comparison, *tan* agrees in gender and number with the noun.

tanto / tanta tantos / tantas	+	noun	+	como

Tengo **tanto interés** en las matemáticas **como** en la física.   *I am interested in math as much as in physics.*

Nuestra universidad tiene **tantos estudiantes como** la de Dallas.   *Our university has as many students as the one in Dallas.*

To indicate an equal degree when comparing verbs, we use *tanto como* after the verb.

verb	+	tanto	+	como

No puedo madrugar **tanto como** tú.   *I can't wake up as early as you.*

Luisa trabaja **tanto como** cuando tenía su propia compañía.   *Luisa works as much as when she had her own company.*

Expressions of similarity are related to comparison of equal degree.

como	Es delgada como su madre.	*She is thin like her mother.*
mismo	Tienen la misma edad.	*They have the same age.*
igual	Los dos modelos son iguales.	*The two models are alike.*
idéntico	Estos gemelos son idénticos.	*These twins are identical.*

  Note that *como* is an adverb, and therefore does not vary in gender and number. *Mismo, igual,* and *idéntico* are adjectives, and agree with the noun.

Expressions with *más. . . que*

más astuto que un zorro	*as cunning as a fox*
más blanco que la nieve	*as white as snow*
más bueno que el pan	*as good as gold*
más contento que unas pascuas	*as happy as a lark*
más duro que una piedra	*as tough as nails*
más feo que Picio	*as ugly as sin*

Expressions with *como*

aburrirse como una almeja/ostra	*to be bored stiff*
beber como una cuba	*to drink like a fish*
cantar como un jilguero	*to sing like a canary*
comer como una fiera/vaca	*to eat like a horse*
correr como un galgo	*to run like a greyhound*
dormir como un tronco	*to sleep like a log*
estar como agua para chocolate	*to be very angry*
fumar como un carretero	*to smoke like a chimney*
gritar como un descosido	*to shout at the top of one's lungs.*
llevarse como perro y gato	*to fight like cats and dogs*
nadar como un pez	*to swim like a fish*
ser fuerte como un roble	*to be as strong as an ox*
ser más tonto que Abundio	*to be very dumb*
ser tan claro como el agua	*to be as clear as crystal*
trabajar como un buey	*to work like a horse*
venderse como pan caliente/churros	*to sell like hot cakes*

Some proverbs

Más moscas se cazan con miel que con vinagre.	*You can catch more flies with honey than with vinegar.*
Más vale pájaro en mano que cien volando.	*A bird in the hand is worth two in the bush.*
Más vale tarde que nunca.	*Better late than never.*

56

EXPRESSING THE HIGHEST (LOWEST) DEGREE

The **superlative** expresses the highest (lowest) degree of comparison. To form the superlative, we use the definite article and the noun before the comparative expression and *de/que. . .* after the adjective.

> definite article + noun + **más (menos)** + adjective + **de...**
> **que...**

Esta es **la casa más bonita del** pueblo y **la más grande que** he visto.	*This is the most beautiful house in the town and the biggest I have seen.*
He visto **la película más interesante de** mi vida.	*I saw the most interesting movie in my life.*
Este programa de verano es **el mejor de** todos.	*This Summer Program is the best of all.*
Luisa es **la mejor estudiante de** su clase pero la menos trabajadora.	*Luisa is the best student in her class but she least working.*
Vimos **la película más aburrida que** puedes imaginarte.	*We saw the most boring movie that you can imagine.*
Es **la mejor escritora** de lengua española.	*She is the best writer in Spanish.*

Special cases:

• **Adjectives can be used as abstract nouns.** Then, the article **lo** comes before the comparative form.	**Lo** mejor sería que vengas con nosotros. *It will be best that you come with us.* El zoo es **lo** más interesante de todo. *The zoo is the most interesting of all.*
• **With adverbs,** we use the neutral definite article **lo.**	¡Haz tu trabajo **lo** más rapidamente que puedas! *Do your work as fast as you can!*
• **With adjectives,** we can also express the highest degree with **altamente, muy, sumamente:**	Estás **muy** contenta de la visita. *She is very happy with the visit.* Es un viaje **sumamente** caro. *It is a very expensive trip.*

57

The Superlative √

OTHER WAYS OF EXPRESSING THE HIGHEST DEGREE

We can also express the superlative by adding the suffix **-ísimo** to the stem of the adjective and of the adverb.

adjective	+	**ending -ísimo/a/os/as**
adverb	+	**ending -ísimo/-ísimamente**

bueno	buenísimo	fuerte	fuertísima
cerca	cerquísima	mala	malísima
entretenida	entretenidísima	padre	padrísimo (Mexico)

La tienda está **cerquísima.**	*The store is very close.*
Es un actor **guapísimo.**	*He is a very handsome actor.*
Tuve un dolor **fuertísimo.**	*I had a very strong pain.*
Lo hicieron **malísimamente.**	*They did it very badly.*

In colloquial language, between friends, sometimes a highest degree can be indicated with the prefixes **archi-, super-, requete-** attached to the adjective:

archi-/super-/requete-	+	**adjective**

Este helado está **requetebueno.**	*This ice cream is very good.*
Llevaba un vestido **superelegante.**	*She was wearing a very elegant dress.*

guapo	*muy guapo*	*guapísimo*	*superguapo*
feo	*muy feo*	*feísimo*	*superfeo*
caro	*muy caro*	*carísimo*	*supercaro*
barato	*muy barato*	*baratísimo*	*superbarato*
bueno	*muy bueno*	*buenísimo*	*superbueno*
malo	*muy malo*	*malísimo*	*supermalo*

58

THE PREPOSITION

Prepositions are words or expressions which link elements in the sentence.

Prepositions connect verbs, nouns, and adjectives with their complements. English, like Spanish, uses prepositions as linking words. However, they do not always use the same preposition to convey the same meaning.

When you learn Spanish, you have to check the use of each preposition. It is also helpful to have a clear understanding of the most important differences between English and Spanish uses of prepositions. Finally, you can pay special attention to specific prepositions such as *por* and *para* [68 - 71].

Luis corrió...
 en la ciudad,
  delante del Ayuntamiento,
  detrás de la farmacia,
  en medio de la plaza,
  alrededor de la fuente,
  en la acera,
  debajo del puente,
  sobre el césped,
  entre las flores,
  fuera de la ciudad,
  hacia el molino,
 por el campo,

 contra (el) reloj,
 durante la mañana,
 en zapatillas de tenis,
 para estar en forma,
 sin parar,
 hasta el agotamiento,
 con su amiga,
 antes de la carrera.

Luis ran...
 in the city,
  in front of the City Hall,
  behind the pharmacy,
  in the middle of the square,
  around the fountain,
  on the sidewalk,
  under the bridge,
  on the lawn,
  among the flowers,
  outside the city,
  toward the mill,
 in the countryside,

 against the clock,
 in the morning,
 in sneakers,
 to be in shape,
 without stopping,
 until exhaustion,
 with her friend,
 before the race.

List of Prepositions √

a

destination	Iré a Paris/a Italia. Iré al oeste/al sur.	*I will go to Paris/to Italy.* *I will go to the west/south.*
place	Me siento a la mesa. Le gusta estar al sol.	*I sit at the table.* *She likes to be in the sun.*
distance	La casa está a 20 km. A los 20 km me paré.	*The house is 20 km away.* *After 20 km I stopped.*
time	Vendré a las tres. Estamos a 30 de mayo.	*I will come at 3 o'clock.* *Today is May 30th.*
expressions	a deshora a finales del año al día siguiente a principios de a tiempo	*at the wrong time* *at the end of the year* *on the next day* *at the beginning of* *on time*
price	¿A cuánto están las uvas? Lo compré a veinte dólares. Las uvas están a 3 dólares la libra.	*How much do the grapes cost?* *I bought it for 20 dollars.* *Grapes are $ 3 a pound.*
manner or **means**	Lo haré a mi manera. Fue a la playa a pie. Hay que coser a máquina o a mano.	*I will do it in my own way.* *I walked to the beach.* *You have to sew on a machine or by hand.*
command	¡A correr! ¡A la cama!	*Run!* *Go to bed!*
purpose	Vengo a estudiar.	*I come to study.*
indirect object	Ofrecí un regalo a Pablo. A ella le gusta Guanajuato.	*I offered a present to Pablo.* *She likes Guanajuato.*
direct object (human)	Ví a mi amigo. Llevó a su hermano a casa.	*I saw my friend.* *He took his brother home.*
expressions	estar al corriente a escondidas tomar a pecho No sé a punto fijo. Lo hizo a regañadientes.	*to be informed* *covertly* *to take to heart* *I do not know for certain.* *He did it unwillingly.*

61

ante

in the presence of	Se presentó ante el juez.	*He appeared before the judge.*
expressions	ante todo ante la posibilidad de ante las circunstancias	*first of all* *faced with the possibility of* *under the circumstances*

antes de

time	Ven antes del mediodía. Leo antes de acostarme.	*Come before midday.* *I read before going to sleep.*

bajo

place	¡Desliza la llave bajo la puerta!	*Slide the key under the door!*
expressions	bajo control bajo fianza 10 grados bajo cero	*under control* *on bail* *ten degrees below zero*

con / sin

association	¡Un café con leche por favor!	*I would like coffee with milk, please.*
	Voy con/sin Luis.	*I'm going with/without Luis.*
	Me encontré con ella la semana pasada.	*I met her last week.*
manner	Habló con/sin tacto. Camina con/sin muletas.	*He spoke with/without tact.* *He walks with/without crutches.*
cause	Te vas a cansar con tanto trabajo.	*You're going to be tired, working so much.*
	No ganarás dinero sin trabajar.	*You won't earn money without working.*
opposition	Con todo lo que gana, no le alcanza para vivir.	*In spite of all the money he earns, he can't make ends meet.*

62

contra

place	La mesa está contra la pared.	*The table is against the wall.*
opposition	La policía está contra la huelga.	*The police is against the strike.*

de

linking a noun with its complement (equivalent to English "of")

time	Es una película de 2 horas.	*It is a two hour movie.*
material	Llevo un anillo de oro.	*I wear a gold ring.*
	Compré un vestido de seda.	*I bought a silk dress.*
rate, price	Tuvo un aumento del 2%.	*He got a 2% raise.*
	Tengo un carro de 15.000 dólares.	*I have a 15,000 dollar car.*
age	Tengo una hija de 12 años.	*I have a 12 year old daughter.*
belonging	Esta es la mochila de Pedro.	*This is Pedro's backpack.*
	Las casas del pueblo son bonitas.	*The houses in the village are nice.*

following verbs or adjectives

origin	La directora es de Bolivia.	*The principal is from Bolivia.*
professional activity	Estoy de camarero.	*I work as a waiter.*
cause	Está lívido de miedo.	*He is pale with fear.*
	Estoy cansado de trabajar.	*I am tired of working.*
expressions	de improviso	*unexpectedly*
	de memoria	*by heart*
	de nuevo	*again*
	de repente	*suddenly*
	de todas formas	*in any case*
	de veras	*truly*

de. . . a

distance	De aquí a allí hay 2 millas.	*From here to there, there are 2 miles.*
time	La conferencia será de 5 a 7.	*The lecture will be from 5 to 7.*
quantity	Llegaron de 10 a 15 autobuses.	*10 to 15 buses came.*

delante de

space	El auto está delante de la casa.	*The car is in front of the house.*
	Juan está sentado delante de mí.	*Juan is sitting in front of me.*
	Prohibido estacionar delante del banco.	*It is forbidden to park in front of the bank.*

dentro de

space	Dentro de la casa hay un patio.	*There is a patio inside the house.*
time	Regreso dentro de unos días.	*I will be back in a few days.*

expressions

	dentro de lo posible	*within one's possibilities*
	dentro de poco	*shortly*

desde

space	Se ve el volcán desde la puerta.	*The volcano can be seen from the door.*
time	No la he visto desde ayer.	*I haven't seen her since yesterday.*
	Estoy enfermo desde hace 5 días.	*I have been sick for 5 days.*

64

después de

time Llegaré depués de la cena. *I will arrive after dinner.*

detrás de

space Se escondió detrás de la columna. *He hid behind the pilar.*
El parque está detrás de la casa. *The park is behind the house.*

durante

time Viajó durante el verano. *He traveled during the summer.*
No voy al cine durante la semana. *I don't go to the movies on week days.*
Hablamos durante dos horas. *We spoke for two hours.*

en

space Mis primos están en Sevilla. *My cousins are in Sevilla.*
Llegaremos a Quito en 9 km. *We have 9 more km to Quito.*
El libro está en el suelo. *The book is on the floor.*

time Estaré en 5 minutos. *I will be there in 5 minutes.*
Vendré en el verano. *I will come in the summer.*

transportation
Voy a la universidad en autobús. *I go to the university by bus.*

quantity Vendí mi carro en 3.000 dólares. *I sold my car for 3,000 dollars.*
La gasolina aumentó en un tres por ciento. *Gas increased by 3%.*

expressions

en broma/serio	*as a joke/seriously*	en lugar de	*instead of*
en busca de	*in search of*	en resumen	*in short*
en cambio	*on the other hand*	en seguida	*immediately*
en estado	*pregnant*	en vivo	*live (television broadcast)*
en la actualidad	*at present*		
en la televisión	*on TV*		
en la radio	*on the radio*	en voz alta	*aloud*
		en voz baja	*speaking softly*

List of Prepositions √

---

encima de

place La paloma está encima del tejado. *The dove is on top of the roof.*
¡No saltes encima de la cama! *Don't jump on the bed!*

enfrente de

place La escuela está enfrente de mi *The school is in front of my house.*
casa.

entre

space La librería está entre el cine y *The bookstore is between the*
el restaurante. *cinema and the restaurant.*

Entre los candidatos que se *Among the candidates who*
presentaron, el último fue el *applied, the last one was the best.*
mejor.

quantity Había entre 20 y 30 personas. *There were 20 to 30 people.*
Entre todos, había unos 20. *There were 20 people in all.*
Entre esto y lo otro, no me di *With this and that, I did not realize*
cuenta de la hora. *what time it was.*

frente a

implies the idea of facing something (in space or figuratively)

¡Pónte frente a la cámara y sonríe! *Face the camera and smile!*
Frente a una situación como esta, *When facing a situation such as*
hay que permanecer tranquilos. *this, we have to stay calm.*

expression
chocar de frente *to crash head on*
estar al frente de *to be at the head of*

66

List of Prepositions   √

---

hacia

direction	Caminamos hacia el sur.	*We are walking southward.*
	Pasaron hacia el otro lado del río.	*They crossed the river.*
time	Salgo hacia el día 9.	*I'm leaving around the 9th.*

hasta

place Paso.	No hay gasolinera hasta Paso.	*There's no gas station until El El*
time	Estaremos aquí hasta las diez. Hasta la vista.	*We'll be here until 10 o'clock. See you later.*

por/para   *see opposition para/por* [68 - 71]

sin   *see con* [62]

sobre

place	¡Pon el libro sobre la mesa!	*Put the book on the table!*
time	Llegaré sobre las dos.	*I'll arrive around 2 o'clock.*
about	Es un libro sobre el bilingüismo.	*It is a book about bilingualism.*

tras

tras	Tras la montaña, hay una casita.	*Beyond the mountain, there is a small house.*
time	Los autobuses salieron uno tras otro.	*The buses left after one another.*

Opposition por/para √

The prepositions *por* and *para* require special attention because the words are somehow similar, and in most situations where *para* is used, we can also use *por* with a different meaning. It is therefore important to understand the meanings conveyed by the use of these prepositions in order to distinguish between them. The crucial difference between *por* and *para* is the following:

> **PARA** is related to **direction, intention, expectation, purpose** (subjective concepts rather than actual facts).
>
> **POR** is related to **specific place/time, cause, source** (actual or timeless facts rather than subjective purpose or intention).

 Note that this difference reminds us of the difference between the *subjuntivo,* which is the mode of intentionality rather than reality, and the *indicativo,* which is the mode of real factual processes.

por	para
indicating space	*indicating space*
• **Conveys the meaning of being within a specific place.**	• **Conveys the meaning of goal, destination.**
Pasamos por Houston cuando viajamos al sur.	Ibamos para Houston, pero el mal tiempo nos desvió y llegamos a San Antonio.
We went through Houston on our way to the South.	*We were heading to Houston, but the weather conditions made us change direction, and we ended up in San Antonio.*
¿Por dónde va el autobús?	¿Para dónde va el autobús?
What route does the bus take? (What is its usual itinerary?)	*Where does this bus go?* (What is its destination?)
La oficina está por la Ópera.	Luis salió para su oficina.
The office is near the Opera house.	*Luis left to his office.*
Envié el paquete por avión.	Envié el paquete para el avión.
I sent the package by air mail. (The package is in the plane as a means of transportation.)	*I sent the package for it to reach the plane.* (The destination of the package is the plane.)

68

Opposition por / para √

---

por

para

expressing time

expressing time

• **Conveys the meaning of happening at a specific moment in time.**

• **Conveys the meaning of having the intention to do something at a moment in time.**

¿Cúando trabajas?
Yo trabajo por la noche.

When do you work?
I work at night.
(At a specific moment.)

¿Para cúando lo tendrán?
Estará listo para mañana.

When will you have it ready?
It will be ready tomorrow.
(The intention is to get it tomorrow.)

Fuimos a América por 5 años.

We were in America for 5 years.
(We stayed there 5 years.)

Fuimos a América para 5 años, pero nos quedamos 10.

We went to America to spend 5 years, but we stayed there for 10 years.

Recibí una paga extra por Navidad.

I received an extra paycheck for Christmas.
(The check was given because it was Christmas.)

Compré los regalos para la Navidad.

I bought presents for Christmas.
(The presents were bought with the intention of offering them at Christmas.)

expressing cause, source

expressing purpose

• **Conveys the meaning of a cause as an objective fact.**

• **Conveys the meaning of subjective purpose.**

¿Por qué vas a México?
Voy a México por sus playas.

Why do you go to Mexico?
I go to Mexico because of its beaches.
(The beaches represent the reason why I go there.)

¿Para qué vas a México?
Voy a México para estudiar.

Why are you going to Mexico?
I go to Mexico to study.
(It is my intention to study there.)

México es famoso por sus playas.

Mexico is famous for its beaches.

Para buenas playas, las de México.

If you want good beaches, there is Mexico.

Le dieron la beca por haber escrito el mejor ensayo.

She was awarded a grant for having written the best essay.
(She wrote the best essay.)

Le dieron la beca para que escribiera un ensayo.

She was given a grant to write an essay.
(The intention is to write an essay.)

por

para

expressing cause, source
(continued)

Esta canción fue escrita por Juan.

This song was written by Juan.
(The agent in a passive sentence is understood as the cause or the source of the process.)

Hubo una exposición de dibujos hechos por niños.

There was an exhibition of drawings made by children.

No puede ver esta película por su edad.

He cannot see this movie because of his age.
(His age is the cause for not being allowed to see the movie.)

Tengo dos capítulos por leer.

I have two chapters left to read.
(Of several chapters which I had to read, I read all but two.)

expressing purpose
(continued)

Esta canción fue escrita para Juan.

This song was written for Juan.
(Juan is the intended recipient of the song.)

Hubo una exposición de dibujos de pintores famosos para niños.

There was an exhibition of drawings by famous children painters.

Ve películas apropiadas para su edad.

He sees movies appropriate for his age.

(The movies were made with the intention of addressing people that age.)

Tengo dos capítulos para leer.

I have two chapters which I intend to read.
(I only have two chapters to read.)

---

expressions of quantity and proportion with *por*

Lo compré por 15 dólares.	*I bought it for $15.*
Manejó a 75 millas por hora.	*He drove at 75 miles per hour.*
El interés es del doce por ciento.	*The interest is 12 %.*
Cuatro por cuatro son diez y seis.	*Four times four is sixteen.*

expressions with *por* useful for narration and reasoning

por cierto	*certainly*	por otra parte	*on the other hand*
por consiguiente	*consequently*	por supuesto	*of course*
por lo general	*in general*	por lo visto	*apparently*
por lo menos	*at least*	por fin/último	*at last*
por un lado	*on the one hand*	por esto/lo tanto	*therefore*

Un viaje a la Misión de San José

Era un viaje organizado **para** estudiantes de español de nivel avanzado. Ibamos **para** pasar todo el día en San Antonio y sus alrededores. Salimos de Dallas **por** la noche y nos paramos **para** dormir a la entrada de la ciudad de San Antonio. **Por** la mañana, llegamos a la Misión. La Misión de San José fue fundada en el siglo XVIII **por** Miguel Nuñez. Esta Misión es conocida **por** el nombre de "La Perla de las Misiones" y es famosa **por** su ventana del sur. Todos teníamos un cuaderno **para** tomar notas, y algunos una cámara fotográfica **para** sacar unas fotos de la Misión. Naturalmente, llevábamos un buen sombrero **para** protegernos del ardiente sol.

Estuvimos en la Misión **por** tres horas. **Por** la tarde caminamos **por** el centro de San Antonio y, **por** último, fuimos al Mercado **para** comprar artesanías del sur.

Compré, **por** 30 dólares, un ajedrez de alabastro **para** mi

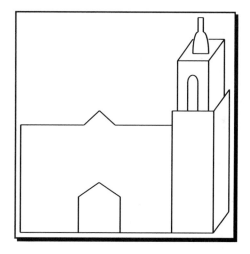

familia. En el autobús, me dormí **por** un rato y, en mi sueño, vi pasar **por** el patio de la Misión a los pastores y vaqueros que se ocupaban del ganado mientras que un grupo de niños iban a los pórticos **para** estudiar. Uno de ellos me tiraba de la manga y fue entonces cuando me desperté al sentir que era mi compañero Luis quien me estaba avisando que habíamos llegado a casa.

THE PRONOUNS

Pronouns are used to replace a noun or a noun phrase which has already been mentioned. There are several types of pronouns.

PRONOUNS	EXAMPLES
• **PERSONAL PRONOUNS** √ Regular personal pronouns replace nouns or noun phrases. 	Juan entró en el tren. **El** estaba herido. Todos los pasajeros **le** ayudaron. *Juan got into the train. He was wounded. All the passengers helped him.*
√ Neutral personal pronouns stand for adjectives or clauses.	¿Estás contenta? — Sí, yo **lo** estoy. *Are you happy? — Yes, I am.* María ha tenido éxito. — Sí, **lo** sé. *Maria succeeded. — Yes. I know.*
• **DEMONSTRATIVE PRON.** √ They replace nouns or noun phrases, and at the same time point to the people or things to which they refer.	He visitado varias casas, pero solo me gusta **ésta.** *I visited many houses, but I only like this one.*
• **POSSESSIVE PRON.** √ They replace noun phrases with a possessive determiner.	He enviado mi carta y **la tuya.** *I sent my letter and yours.*

• **INDEFINITE PRON.** √ They mention people or things, but do not identify specific individuals or things.	¿Me llamó **alguien?** *Did anybody call me?*
• **RELATIVE PRON.** √ They introduce a relative clause, i.e., a clause that describes a noun.	¡Pásame el libro **que** compraste! *Give me the book you bought!*
• **INTERROGATIVE PRON.** √ They ask for specific information.	¿**Qué** hiciste ayer? *What did you do yesterday?* ¿qué?
• **EXCLAMATORY PRON.** √ They are used for emphasis in exclamatory sentences.	¡**Qué** bonito! *How nice!*

Personal pronouns are pronouns that replace nouns or noun phrases which have already been mentioned or which are known to the speaker and the listener.

When you learn pronouns, you have to take into consideration three important questions: (i) what is the form of the pronoun?; (ii) what is the place of the pronoun?; and (iii) in what order do pronouns come?

THE FORM OF PRONOUNS

There are several types of personal pronouns, depending on their relation to the verb.

THE PLACE OF PERSONAL PRONOUNS

The personal pronouns come before or after the verb, depending on the form (mode) of the verb.

THE ORDER OF PERSONAL PRONOUNS

When two or more pronouns are used, they come in a specific order, depending on their relation to the verb, and the form (mode) of the verb.

PERSONAL PRONOUNS: A SUMMARY

The **subject pronouns** refer to the subject of the verb:

YO	**1st person singular; masc. or fem.** √ refers to the speaker.	*I*
TÚ	**2nd person singular; masc. or fem.** √ refers to the person spoken to. √ indicates an informal style, used with friends, people who belong to the same social circle or when the speaker is explicitly allowed to do so. √ in many parts of South and Central America the form **vos** is used [78].	*you*
ÉL **ELLA**	**3rd person singular; masc./ fem.** √ refers to the person spoken about.	*he* *she*
USTED **(Ud.)**	**3rd person singular; masc. or fem.** √ it is the polite, formal pronoun used to address one person with whom the speaker is not close or familiar (abbreviated Ud. or Vd.).	*you*
NOSOTROS **NOSOTRAS**	**1st person plural; masc./ fem.** √ refers to a group including the speaker.	*we*
VOSOTROS **VOSOTRAS**	**2nd person plural; masc./ fem.** √ refers to a group of people addressed by the speaker. √ used in Spain only.	*you*
ELLOS **ELLAS**	**3rd person plural; masc./ fem.** √ refers to the group of people spoken about.	*they*
USTEDES **(Uds.)**	**3rd person plural; masc. or fem.** √ refers to the group of people spoken to. √ is the formal form of address in Spain. √ is used for both formal and informal address in Latin America.	*you*

Spanish and English subject pronouns are different in their uses. While in English the subject pronoun always precedes the verb, in Spanish the subject pronoun can be omitted, or placed before or after the verb in specific situations.

SECOND PERSON INFORMAL PRONOUNS

All the varieties of Spanish spoken in different countries have the same forms for the second person formal pronouns: **Ud.** and **Uds.** However, the second person **informal pronouns** are different.

	2nd. pers. sing.	**2nd. pers. pl.**
Mexico	tú sabes	Uds. saben
Spain	tú sabes	vosotros sabéis
Argentina	vos sabés	Uds. saben

OMISSION OF THE SUBJECT PRONOUN

Whenever the subject has been clearly identified, the subject pronoun is omitted. This omission does not create ambiguity nor cause misunderstandings since the verb endings are a clear indication of the person, tense, and mode.

Pedro me llamó ayer. Me dijo que acababa de llegar de viaje y me preguntó si quería ir al cine.

Pedro called me yesterday. He told me that he had just arrived from a trip and asked me if I wanted to go to the movies.

The two participants in this situation are identified in the first sentence. Therefore, all the subsequent subject pronouns are omitted.

THE SUBJECT PRONOUN PRECEDES THE VERB

1. The subject pronoun is used **before the verb** to put a strong emphasis on the subject.

    Ella respondió pronto.

    SHE responded quickly.

2. The subject pronoun is also used before the verb to avoid ambiguity when the verb ending can refer to different persons.

    Yo quería ir al cine.

    I wanted to go to the movies.

Quería can mean *I wanted* or *she/he wanted*. In the absence of a context which would help identify the subject, we use the pronoun.

78

THE SUBJECT PRONOUN FOLLOWS THE VERB

When a pronoun is used for emphasis or to avoid ambiguity, the
pronoun usually comes before the verb, except in the following cases.

1. For special emphasis:

Te lo prometo **yo.**	*I promise it to you, myself.*
Lo hizo **él.**	*He did it himself.*

    Note that when the subject pronoun follows the verb, as in the
   examples above, the pronoun bears a heavy stress and there is a
   strong emphasis implied. The first sentence implies: "I really
   commit myself to do it;" and the second means: "He, and nobody
   else, did it."

2. In questions:

¿Por qué cortas **tú** el pasto? Esta vez era mi turno.	*Why are you mowing the lawn? This time it was my turn.*

3. To reinforce a command given in the *imperativo:*

¡Hazlo **tú!** / ¡Hazlo **tú** mismo!	*Do it yourself!*

4. After quotations in reported speech:

Después del accidente, la policía pidió a un testigo que describiera los hechos. "Ví que el avión estaba bajando hacia la casa", dijo **ella.**	*After the accident, the police asked a witness to describe what happened. "I saw the plane coming down towards the house," she said.*
— ¿Cuándo llegaste? preguntó **él.**	*— When did you arrive? he asked.*
— Por la noche, respondió **ella.**	*— Last night, she answered.*

5. The subject pronoun usually comes after the verb when certain
   adverbs, such as *quizás, ya, nunca, bastante,* etc., are used in the
   beginning of a sentence:

Ya está **ella** en el aeropuerto.	*She is already at the airport.*

 Note that in formal letters and business correspondence, the use of
yo in particular is avoided because it is considered pretentious.
In oral communication, however, **yo** is used very often to focus the
attention on the speaker, his or her opinions, reactions, or ideas.

The object pronouns replace the object of the verb (the noun or noun phrase which are the complements of the verb [8]). When the verb is followed by a direct object (a noun phrase not preceded by a preposition), we use a **direct object** pronoun:

Compré el libro → **Lo** compré.   *I bought the book; I bought it.*

Persons	Pronouns	English
1st pers. sing. masc. or fem.	**me**	*me*
2nd pers. sing. masc. or fem.	**te**	*you*
3rd pers. sing. masc.	**lo (le*)**	*him, it, you*
3rd pers. sing. fem.	**la**	*her, it, you*
1st pers. pl. masc. or fem.	**nos**	*us*
2nd pers. pl. masc. or fem.	**os**	*you*
3rd pers. pl. masc.	**los**	*them, you*
3rd pers. pl. fem.	**las**	*them, you*
* see the note below.		

¿Viste la nueva película?
— Sí, **la** ví.
— No, pero **la** quiero ver esta noche.
— No, no quiero ver**la.**

Have you seen the new movie?
— Yes, I saw it.
— No, but I want to see it tonight.
— No, I don't want to see it.

¿**Me** llamarás mañana?
— No. Lláma**me** tú.

Will you call me tomorrow?
— No, YOU call me.

 Note that in certain varieties of Spanish (in some regions of Spain):

(i) the pronouns **le/les** are used to refer to human beings instead of the 3rd pers. masculine **lo/los** (meaning *him/them).* This phenomenon is known as "leísmo":

¿Has visto a Juan?
— Sí, **le** he visto.

Have you seen Juan?
— Yes, I saw him.

(ii) the pronouns **le/les** are used to refer to formal *Ud.* and *Uds.*:

Me alegro de conocer**le**/conocer**les.**   *I am pleased to meet you.*

80

The Neutral Pronoun LO √

Spanish has a **neutral pronoun, *lo,*** used as a substitute for a property (usually expressed by an adjective), or for a whole thought (usually expressed by a clause).

Lo replaces an adjective or a preposition + noun phrase, which describe the subject.

¿Es la casa nueva?
— Sí, **lo** es (lo = nueva)

Is the house new?
— Yes, it is.

¿Es la casa de madera?
— Sí, **lo** es (lo = de madera)

Is the house made of wood?
— Yes, it is.

Lo replaces the *infinitivo*.

¿Necesitas ponerte a régimen?
— Sí, **lo** necesito
(lo = ponerme a régimen)

Do you need to go on a diet?
— Yes, I do.

¿Deseas conocer otros países?
— Sí, lo deseo mucho.
(lo = conocer otros paises)

Would you like to know other countries? — Yes, I'd like it very much.

Lo replaces a clause.

¡Luis! Juan ganó la lotería.
— Todo el mundo **lo** sabe.
(lo = que Juan ganó la lotería)

Luis! Juan won the lottery.
— Everybody knows that.

¿Cuándo sale el tren?
— No sé, voy a preguntar**lo.**
(lo = cuando sale el tren)

When is the train leaving?
— I don't know, I'm going to ask.

Lo sé.   Lo digo.   Lo creo.   Lo dudo.

Lo pienso.   **Lo niego.**   **Lo siento.**

We use an **indirect object pronoun** when the verb is followed by an indirect object (a noun phrase which follows the preposition **a** and is the recipient or beneficiary of the action). The indirect object pronouns are used for humans and animals only, and not for inanimate things.

¿Has telefoneado a Juana?   *Have you phoned Juana?*
— Sí, **le** he telefoneado.   *— Yes, I phoned her.*

Persons	Pronouns	*English*
1st pers. sing. masc. or fem.	**me**	*me*
2nd pers. sing. masc. or fem.	**te**	*you*
3rd pers. sing. masc. or fem.	**le / se**	*him, her, it, you*
1st pers. pl. masc. or fem.	**nos**	*us*
2nd pers. pl. masc. or fem.	**os**	*you*
3rd pers. pl. masc. or fem.	**les / se**	*them, you*

¿Tuvo suerte Juan en la entrevista?   *Did Juan have any luck in the*
— Sí, **le** ofrecieron el empleo.   *interview? — Yes, he got the job.*

¡Da**me** tu número de teléfono!   *Give me your phone number.*

The pronouns *le* and *les* change into *se* when they come before the direct object pronouns *lo/los/la/las*

Yo di el mensaje a Teresa.   *I gave the message to Teresa.*
     lo   le

Yo **le** di el mensaje.   *I gave her the message.*
Yo **se lo** di.   *I gave it to her.*

 Note the special use of the indirect object pronouns with reflexive verbs to express that a person is the victim of an unexpected event.

Se me quemó la comida.   *My meal burned.*

82

When the direct or indirect object refers to the same person as the subject, we use **reflexive pronouns** [113 - 116]. The English reflexive pronouns are *myself, yourself,* etc.

Yo **me** peino.   *I comb my hair.*

When the action is directed from the subject to the object and from the object to the subject, we call the construction "reciprocal" [113 - 116]. This construction uses the **reciprocal pronouns,** which are identical to reflexive pronouns in Spanish. The English reciprocal pronouns are *each other* and *one another.*

Pedro y Luis **se** insultaron.   *Pedro and Luis insulted each other.*

Persons	Pronouns	English
1st pers. sing. masc. or fem.	**me**	*myself*
2nd. pers. sing. masc. or fem.	**te**	*yourself*
3rd pers. sing. masc. or fem.	**se**	*himself, herself, itself, yourself*
1st pers. plur. masc. or fem.	**nos**	*ourselves*
2nd pers. plur. masc. or fem.	**os**	*yourselves*
3rd pers. plur. masc. or fem.	**se**	*themselves, yourselves*

Pay attention to the difference between Spanish and English in the use of reflexive pronouns with actions related to personal care:

Me lavo los dientes.   *I brush my teeth.*
Me seco el cabello.   *I dry my hair.*
Me pongo la camisa.   *I put my shirt on.*

 Note that we can reinforce the reciprocal form by adding **uno al otro** after the verb, especially when both reflexive and reciprocal meanings are possible:

Se miraron.   *They looked at themselves / each other.*
Se miraron **una a la otra.**   *They looked at each other.*

Se compran regalos.   *They buy presents for themselves / each other.*

Se compran regalos **uno para el otro.**   *They buy presents for each other.*

The **pronoun *se*** can be used with a passive meaning. In order to understand this use of *se*, examine the following situation:

There is a specific house that we saw on the hill.

Talking about this house we can say:

(1) La Señora Salcedo vendió la casa a un famoso artista.   *Mrs. Salcedo sold the house to a famous artist.*

(2) La casa fue vendida el año pasado.   *The house was sold last year.*

(3) Se vendió la casa el año pasado.   *The house was sold last year.*

Sentence 1 focuses on la Señora Salcedo and tells us what she did with the house.

Sentence 2 focuses on the house and tells us what happened to it. It is however a form which belongs to a written style, and is rarely used in oral speech. The person who sold the house is no longer important and can be omitted.

Sentence 3 is the **most widely used** in spoken Spanish. The person who sold the house is irrelevant in this message, **the focus being on the house itself and the fact that it was sold.** We use this construction especially when we speak about things rather than people.

Other examples:

Este verano **se** quemaron dos montes.   *Two hills burnt this summer.*

Se hablan varias lenguas en este país.   *Several languages are spoken in this country.*

No **se** estudia la música en esta escuela.   *Music is not taught at this school.*

Se limpian las playas todos los días.   *The beaches are cleaned every day.*

Se renovaron los edificios antiguos de la ciudad.   *The old buildings of the city were renovated.*

The Impersonal SE √

En el ayuntamiento
Se vota
Se ayuda
a los pobres.
Se inscribe a los
recién nacidos

The **impersonal pronoun** *se* is used to express the fact that the agent of the action (the person doing the action) is not specific; for instance, *alguien (somebody).* The focus is **on the action** rather than on the people doing it. Then, the verb is always in the 3rd person singular form.

Durante las fiestas, **se** canta y **se** baila por las calles.	*During the "fiestas," people sing and dance in the streets.*
Hay locales donde no **se** puede fumar.	*There are places where one is not allowed to smoke.*
En este restaurante se recibe bien a los clientes.	*In this restaurant, they serve the customers well.*

When the verb is followed by a noun or a noun phrase, the passive **se** [84] is preferred.

En el mercado de las pulgas, **se** venden ropas viejas y utensilios usados.	*At the flea market, old clothes and used utensils are sold.*

Although the impersonal **se** is possible: *se vende ropas viejas,* it is not used in the spoken language.

The preceding pages have shown the several uses of the pronoun **se.** Here is a summary :

Uses of SE	Examples	English
Reflexive Direct Object [83]	Pedro **se** lava.	*Pedro washes himself.*
Reflexive Indirect Object [83]	Luis **se** lava las manos. (Luis lava las manos a Luis.)	*Luis washes his hands.*
Reciprocal Direct Object [83]	León y Gloria **se** admiran mucho. (León admira a Gloria y Gloria admira a León.) a = direct object.	*Leon and Gloria admire each other a lot.*
Reciprocal Indirect Object [83]	León y Gloria **se** ofrecieron unos regalos. (León ofreció regalos a Gloria y Gloria ofreció regalos a León.) a = indirect object, the recipient of the presents.	*Leon and Gloria offered presents to each other.*
Indirect Object Substitute for le, before lo/los/la/las [82]	León **se** lo ha ofrecido. (León ha ofrecido el regalo a Gloria.)	*Leon offered it to her.*
Passive SE [84]	**Se** vendió la casa.	*The house was sold.*
Impersonal SE [85]	Aquí **se** puede fumar.	*Here one is allowed to smoke.*

When the verb is followed by a prepositional object (a noun phrase preceded by a preposition **other than** *a*), we use a pronoun **object of a preposition**.

Este regalo es **para tí.**   *This present is for you.*

Persons	Pronouns	English
1st pers. sing. masc. or fem.	**mí**	*me*
2nd pers. sing. masc. or fem.	**tí**	*you*
3rd pers. sing. masc.	**él/Ud.**	*him, it, you*
3rd pers. sing. fem.	**ella/Ud.**	*her, it, you*
1st pers. pl. masc. and fem.	**nosotros/as**	*us*
2nd pers. pl. masc. and fem.	**vosotros/as**	*you*
3rd pers. pl. masc.	**ellos/Uds.**	*them, you*
3rd pers. pl. fem.	**ellas/Uds.**	*them, you*

¿Puedes ocuparte de mi bebé?   *Would you take care of my baby?*
— Sí, me ocuparé **de él.**   *— Yes, I'll take care of him.*

He preparado un pastel **para tí.**   *I baked a cake for you.*

Puedes confiar **en ellos.**   *You can trust them.*

La visito más que **a tí.**   *I visit her more than (I visit) you.*

When the pronouns **mí** and **tí** follow the preposition **con,** we use the contracted forms **conmigo** and **contigo** (with me/you):

¿Juan estudió **contigo?**   *Did Juan study with you?*
— No, no estudió **conmigo.**   *— No, he did not study with me.*

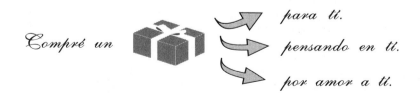

$$Compré\ un\ \fbox{}\ \Rightarrow\ para\ ti.$$
$$\Rightarrow\ pensando\ en\ ti.$$
$$\Rightarrow\ por\ amor\ a\ ti.$$

87

Object personal pronouns come **before or after the verb,** depending on the form (or mode) of the verb.

Object pronouns come before the verb when the verb is in a conjugated form, except in the affirmative *imperativo.*

Te daré la foto.	*I'll give you the picture.*
Luis **me** ha escrito de Brasil.	*Luis wrote to me from Brazil.*
Recibí la carta; pero no **la** leí.	*I received the letter; but I did not read it.*
Llegó tarde porque **no se** despertó a tiempo.	*He came late because he did not wake up on time.*
Abre la carta; pero no **la** leas.	*Open the letter; but don't read it.*
No **me** digas el secreto.	*Don't tell me the secret.*

Object pronouns are attached to the end of the verb in the affirmative *imperativo,* and in non-conjugated modes: the *infinitivo,* and the *gerundio.*

Abre la carta y lée**la.**	*Open the letter and read it.*
Dí**me** el secreto.	*Tell me the secret.*
¡Cánta**me** una canción!	*Sing me a song!*
Compré la novela para leer**la.**	*I bought the novel in order to read it.*
Perdió el tren por no despertar**se** a tiempo.	*He missed the train because he did not wake up on time.*
Los mariachis comenzaron dedicándo**nos** una canción.	*The mariachis began by dedicating a song to us.*

El balón

Juana **lo** tira a Elena. Elena **lo** toma y **lo** entrega a Eva que no consigue recoger**lo.** El balón **le** pega en el hombro y rebota hacia María. María, tomándo**lo** con las dos manos, **lo** coloca a su derecha y corre protegiéndo**lo.** Luisa, que estaba esperándo**lo, lo** recibe, salta y **lo** mete en la canasta.

88

THE *INFINITIVO* FOLLOWS ANOTHER VERB

When the *infinitivo* **follows another verb,** the pronoun can be attached to the *infinitivo* ending; or it can precede the first verb.

No pudieron avisar**le** que su madre estaba enferma.   *They could not inform*
No **le** pudieron avisar que su madre estaba enferma.   *her that her mother*
                                                          was sick.

Quiero despertar**me** a las ocho.   *I want to wake up*
Me quiero despertar a las ocho.   *at 8 o'clock.*

However with verbs like *dejar* (let), *hacer* (do), *ordenar* (order), *mandar* (order), the meaning is not the same when the pronoun is placed before the first verb and when it is after the *infinitivo*.

Hice coser**le** una falda.   *I had a dress sewn*
(le = mi hija)   *for her.*
(The dress is for my daughter.)

Le hice coser una falda.   *I made her sew*
(le = mi hija)   *a dress.*
(My daughter is sewing a dress.)

THE *GERUNDIO* FOLLOWS ANOTHER VERB

When the *gerundio* **follows the verbs** *estar* (be), *seguir* (continue), *andar* (be in the process of), the pronoun can be attached to the *gerundio* ending; or it can precede the first verb.

Yo estaba hablándo**le** cuando llegó el telegrama.   *I was talking to him/*
Yo **le** estaba hablando cuando llegó el telegrama.   *her when the telegram*
                                                         arrived.

La tía Pepa siempre anda regañándo**nos.**   *Aunt Pepa is always*
La tía Pepa siempre **nos** anda regañando.   *nagging us.*

When **several pronouns** are used in the same sentence, they must come in a specific order. We will illustrate the rules for ordering pronouns with dialogues based on the following situation.

   Josefina lends her bike to her brother, Octavio.

Subject pronouns
are omitted as much as possible, and when present, they come before the verb and before all other pronouns.

O. — ¡Josefina, préstame tu bicicleta!
Josefina, lend me your bike!

J. — **Tú** me la pides siempre.
You always ask for it.

When a direct object pronoun and an indirect object pronoun
are used in connection with the same verb, then the indirect object comes before the direct object.

O. — **Te la** devolveré mañana.
I'll give it back to you tomorrow.

J. — **Te la** presto por un día.
I'll lend it to you for one day.

J. — ¡No **me la** rompas y devuélve**mela** limpia!
Don't break it and give it back to me clean!

Le/les change to se.
The indirect object pronouns **le** and **les** change to **se** when they come before **lo/los** and **la/las**.

J. — ¡No **se la** prestes a nadie!
Don't lend it to anyone!

Reflexive pronouns
can be used in conjunction with direct object pronouns. In that case, they are indirect objects and therefore come before the direct object pronouns.

J. — ¡No **te** olvides el casco!
Don't forget the helmet!

O. — Siempre **me lo** pongo.
I always wear it.

Pronouns used as objects of prepositions
always follow the preposition, and therefore do not interfere with the other pronouns.

O. — Olvidé decirle a papá que regresaré a las seis.
I forgot to tell Dad that I'll be back at 6 o'clock.

J. — No te preocupes; yo se lo diré por **ti.**
Don't worry; I'll tell him for you.

90

To decide which pronouns to use, you have to ask the following questions.

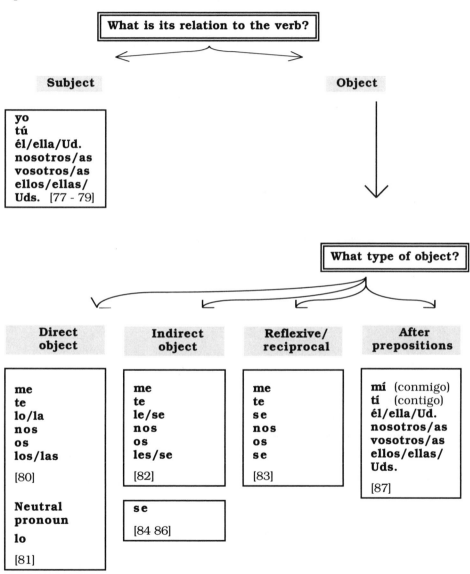

┌─────────────────────────────────┐
│ **What is its relation to the verb?** │
└─────────────────────────────────┘

Subject

┌──────────────────┐
│ **yo** │
│ **tú** │
│ **él/ella/Ud.** │
│ **nosotros/as** │
│ **vosotros/as** │
│ **ellos/ellas/** │
│ **Uds.** [77 - 79] │
└──────────────────┘

Object

┌──────────────────────┐
│ **What type of object?** │
└──────────────────────┘

Direct object	**Indirect object**	**Reflexive/ reciprocal**	**After prepositions**
me	**me**	**me**	**mí** (conmigo)
te	**te**	**te**	**tí** (contigo)
lo/la	**le/se**	**se**	**él/ella/Ud.**
nos	**nos**	**nos**	**nosotros/as**
os	**os**	**os**	**vosotros/as**
los/las	**les/se**	**se**	**ellos/ellas/**
[80]	[82]	[83]	**Uds.**
			[87]

Direct object — Neutral pronoun
lo
[81]

Indirect object
se
[84 86]

Demonstrative pronouns replace nouns or noun phrases, and at the same time point to the people or things to which they refer.

Proximity	Masculine sing. pl.		Feminine sing. pl.		Neutral	*English*
Near speaker	**éste**	**éstos**	**ésta**	**éstas**	**esto**	*this one*
Near listener	**ése**	**ésos**	**ésa**	**ésas**	**eso**	*that one*
Far from both	**aquél**	**aquéllos**	**aquélla**	**aquéllas**	**aquello**	*that one there*

1. **The demonstrative pronoun serves to point to** someone or something, indicating if it is near or far in time or in space.

   Es difícil escoger entre tantos zapatos: **éstos** me gustan mucho, pero **aquéllos** son más baratos.

   It is difficult to choose between so many shoes; I like these, but those are less expensive.

   Éste es un buen equipo.

   This is a good team.

2. **The neutral pronoun *esto*** announces what is going to be said; ***eso*** announces what has just been said:

   Acuérdense de **esto:** está prohibido fumar aquí.

   Remember this: it is forbidden to smoke here.

   Está prohibido fumar aquí: acuérdense de **eso.**

   It is forbidden to smoke here: remember that.

3. **Demonstrative pronouns** are used instead of the noun or noun phrase: this is the usual use of pronouns. However, in Spanish, the demonstrative pronoun **can also be used after a noun.** Then, the noun is preceded by the definite article. This use is emphatic.

   Me gusta **el** libro **éste.**

   I like this book.

Expressions with neutral demonstrative pronouns:

en esto	*at this point*	es por eso	*that's why*
por esto	*for this reason*	¿Qué es eso?	*What's that?*
por eso	*therefore*	Eso digo yo.	*I quite agree*

The **possessive pronouns** replace noun phrases with a possessive determiner.

| Masculine | | Feminine | | *English* |
sing.	pl.	sing.	pl.	
el mío	**los míos**	**la mía**	**las mías**	*mine*
el tuyo	**los tuyos**	**la tuya**	**las tuyas**	*yours*
el suyo	**los suyos**	**la suya**	**las suyas**	*his/hers/ yours*
el nuestro	**los nuestros**	**la nuestra**	**las nuestras**	*ours*
el vuestro	**los vuestros**	**la vuestra**	**las vuestras**	*yours*
el suyo	**los suyos**	**la suya**	**las suyas**	*theirs/yours*
There is also a neutral form of the possessive pronoun: **lo mío / lo tuyo / lo suyo / lo nuestro / lo vuestro / lo suyo.** These pronouns are used when the reference is indeterminate: lo mío = whatever is mine, etc.				*mine, etc.*

¡Llama primero a mi abogado y después **al tuyo!** [a + el = al]	*Call my lawyer first, and then yours.*
Los padres de Gloria y **los míos** vendrán a la boda.	*Gloria's parents and mine will come to the wedding.*
¡No toques **lo mío!**	*Don't touch my things.*

 Note that possessive pronouns are used instead of the noun or noun phrase: this is the usual use of pronouns. However, in Spanish, the possessive pronouns **can also be used after a noun.** Then, the noun is preceded by a determiner.

¿Antonio, es este tu carro? — No, este carro es de mi madre; **el** carro **mío** está en el garage.	*Antonio, is this your car?* *— No, this is my mother's car; mine is in the garage.*
Un abuelo **suyo** murió en la Guerra Civil.	*One of his grandfathers died in the Civil War.*

Expressions with the possessive *suyo*:

Cada cual a lo suyo.	*It's best to mind one's own business.*
salirse con la suya	*to get one's way*
los suyos	*his/her people*

93

Indefinite pronouns mention people or things, but do not identify them. There are two types of indefinite pronouns:

(i) indefinite pronouns which are always pronouns: they never come with a noun

(ii) indefinite pronouns which can also be used as determiners: they come with a noun.

FIRST TYPE : INDEFINITE PRONOUNS WHICH ARE ALWAYS PRONOUNS

These indefinite pronouns are invariable: they do not have feminine and plural forms.

Pronouns	Use	English
alguien	√ refers to male and female	*someone*
algo	√ refers to things	*something*
nadie	√ negative; refers to humans	*nobody*
nada	√ negative; refers to things	*nothing*
cualquiera	√ refers to people or things	*anybody, whoever*

¿Vino **alguien** esta mañana?
— No, no vino **nadie**.

Did anybody come this morning?
— No, nobody came.

¿Compraste **algo** en la tienda?
— No, no compré **nada.**

Did you buy anything at the store?
— No, I didn't buy anything.

Esta pregunta es tan fácil que
cualquiera la puede responder.

This question is so easy that
anybody could answer it.

Aburrimiento

No hay **nada** que hacer.
No hay **nadie** que me hable.
¿Hay **alguien** que me escuche?
¿Hay **algo** que merezca la pena?
Cualquiera que me oiga sabrá que estoy aburrido.

Boredom

I have nothing to do.
Nobody talks to me.
Is there anyone who would listen to me?
Is there anything worth doing?
Anyone who hears me will know that I am bored.

94

SECOND TYPE: PRONOUNS WHICH ARE ALSO USED AS DETERMINERS

Like other determiners, these indefinite pronouns vary in gender and number: they come in masculine and feminine as well as singular and plural forms.

Pronouns	Use	English
alguno	√ refers to people and things	*some*
ninguno	√ refers to people and things √ has no plural	*none*
mucho	√ can come with the neutral **lo** and a relative clause *(lo mucho que sabes).*	*much/many/ a lot*
otro	√ can be used in conjunction with **uno** *(uno. . . otro).*	*other/ another one*
poco	√ can come with the neutral **lo** and a relative clause *(lo poco que hay).*	*few/little*
todo	√ in the singular, it comes only in the neutral **todo.** √ in the plural, both masculine and feminine are possible.	*everything* *all*
uno	√ can also be used in conjunction with **otro** *(el uno. . . el otro).*	*one*

¿Tiene Ud. corbatas de seda?
— Si, me quedan **algunas.**
— No, no me queda **ninguna.**

Do you have silk ties?
— Yes, I have some left.
— No, I have none.

¿Has terminado el trabajo?
— No, me queda **mucho** por hacer.

Have you finished your work?
— No, I still have a lot to do.

Yo vivo en este barrio y mi hermana vive en **el otro.**

I live in this neighborhood, and my sister lives in the other one.

Quien **mucho** abarca **poco** aprieta.

You can bite off more than you can chew.

La nieve lo cubrió **todo.**

The snow covered everything.

¡Dame **uno** y te daré **el otro!**

Give me one, and I'll give you the other one.

The **relative pronoun** is a pronoun used to introduce a clause whose purpose is to add information about the noun. Examine the following dialogue between Julio y Paula:

J. — Compré el diccionario.	*I bought the dictionary.*
P. — ¿Qué diccionario?	*Which dictionary?*
J. — El diccionario que nos recomendó el profesor.	*The dictionary that the teacher recommended.*

Julio could anticipate Paula's question and directly say:

Compré el diccionario **que nos recomendó el profesor.**

In this sentence, *que* is called **relative pronoun,** *que nos recomendó el profesor* is the **relative clause,** and *el diccionario* is the **antecedent.** The relative pronoun replaces the antecedent.

The relative clause always begins with a relative pronoun.

Este es el médico. . .
(i) **que** trabaja para la Cruz Roja.
(ii) **que** invitó el presidente.
(iii) **a quien** le dieron la medalla de oro.

This is the doctor. . .
(i) who works for the Red Cross.
(ii) whom the president invited.
(iii) to whom the Gold Medal was awarded.

The relative clause always comes immediately after the noun it relates to (the antecedent).

Yo compré **la casa que está al otro lado del río.**

I bought the house which is on the other side of the river.

La casa que está al otro lado del río es mía.

The house which is on the other side of the river is mine.

La casa en la cual estuvimos se vendió la semana pasada.

The house in which we stayed was sold last week.

> **The three stages in the formation of a relative clause are the following: find the relation of the relative pronoun to the verb; identify the relative pronoun; and join the relative clause with the main clause to form one sentence.**

 Conchita es la tenista _____ ganó la copa.

Steps	Example
1. Find the relation of the relative pronoun to the verb.	We have to consider how the relative pronoun (or the noun phrase for which it stands) relates to the verb in the relative clause. The meaning of the relative clause is: *La tenista* ganó la copa. In the relative clause, *la tenista* is the subject of the verb *ganó*.
2. Identify the relative pronoun.	*La tenista* ganó la copa. The relative pronoun for subjects is **que**.
3. Write the whole sentence.	*Conchita es la tenista que ganó la copa.* *Conchita is the tennis player who won the cup.*

Here are other examples of relative clauses related to *la tenista:*

 Conchita es la tenista _____ los periódicos hablan bien.

1. Los periódicos hablan bien **de la tenista.**
2.   **(de quien)**
3. *Conchita es la tenista de quien los periódicos hablan bien.*
   Conchita is the tennis player of whom the newspapers say good things.

 Conchita es la tenista _____ entrenador es famoso por su rigor.

1. **El entrenador de Conchita** es famoso por su rigor.
2. **(cuyo entrenador)**
3. *Conchita es la tenista cuyo entrenador es famoso por su rigor.*
   Conchita is the tennis player whose coach is well-known for his severity.

97

> **The form of the relative pronoun depends on its relation to the verb in the relative clause.**

To determine the form of a relative pronoun, you have to know its function in the relative clause. Here are the relative pronouns.

1. **The relative pronoun is the subject of the verb in the relative clause:** the pronoun is **que.**

   The pronoun **que** refers to people and things.

Aquí está la niña **que** habla chino.	*Here is the girl who speaks Chinese.*
Aquí está la carta **que** llegó ayer.	*Here is the letter that arrived yesterday.*

2. **The relative pronoun is the direct object of the verb in the relative clause.** The pronouns are the following:

   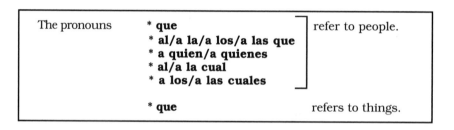

The pronouns	* **que**	refer to people.
	* **al/a la/a los/a las que**	
	* **a quien/a quienes**	
	* **al/a la cual**	
	* **a los/a las cuales**	
	* **que**	refers to things.

   The pronouns *quien* and *cual* agree in number with the antecedent. The definite article before *cual* gives more precision on the gender and number.

   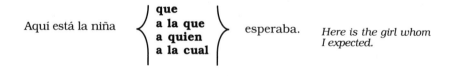

Aquí está la niña	que a la que a quien a la cual	esperaba.	*Here is the girl whom I expected.*

Aquí está la carta **que** esperaba.	*Here is the letter that I expected.*

3. **The relative pronoun follows a preposition in the relative clause.** The pronouns are the following:

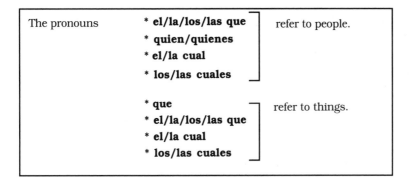

| The pronouns | * el/la/los/las que
* quien/quienes
* el/la cual
* los/las cuales | refer to people. |
| | * que
* el/la/los/las que
* el/la cual
* los/las cuales | refer to things. |

Aquí está la niña
con la que
con quien
con la cual
vas a estudiar.

Here is the girl with whom you are going to study.

Aquí está el libro
con el que
con el cual
vas a estudiar.

Here is the book with which you are going to study.

4. **The relative pronoun expresses possession, belonging.**
The pronouns are **cuyo/cuyos** and **cuya/cuyas.**

These pronouns are used to refer to people and things.

Aquí está la niña **cuya madre** es bibliotecaria.

Here is the girl whose mother is a librarian.

Aquí está el barco **cuyo capitán** se hizo famoso.

Here is the boat whose captain became famous.

In Spanish, like in English, question words come at the beginning
of the sentence. We determine which pronoun to use depending on
the type of information requested.

Information	Question Word	English
a person	**quién/quiénes**	*who/whom*
a thing	**qué**	*what*
a choice among people / things	**cuál/cuáles**	*which one*
place	**dónde**	*where*
time	**cuándo**	*when*
manner	**cómo**	*how*
quantity	**cuánto**	*how much*
	cuánto/a/os/as	*how much/many*
cause	**por qué**	*why*

¿**Quién** es? — *Who is it?*
¿**A quién** has visto? — *Who(m) have you seen?*
¿**De quién** es este paraguas? — *Whose umbrella is this?*
¿**Con quién** has viajado? — *With whom did you travel?*
¿**Para quién** es el regalo? — *For whom is the present?*

¿**Qué** pasó ayer aquí? — *What happened here yesterday?*
¿**Qué** miras? — *What are you looking at?*
¿**Qué** sandalias prefieres? — *Which sandals do you prefer?*
¿**De qué** hablaron? — *What did they talk about?*
¿**Para qué** vas a Chile? — *What are you going to Chile for?*

¿**Cuál** prefieres? — *Which one do you prefer?*
¿**Cuál** de estos te gusta? — *Which one of those do you like?*
¿**De cuál** ventana cayó? — *From which window did it fall?*
¿**Con cuál** pincel pintas el fondo? — *With which brush do you paint the background?*

¿**Dónde** está Luis? — *Where is Luis?*
¿**De dónde** es Luis? — *Where is Luis from?*
¿**A dónde** va Luis? — *Where is Luis going?*

¿**Cuándo** sales? — *When are you leaving?*
¿**Para cuándo** estará listo? — *When is it going to be finished?*
¿**Hasta cuándo** te quedas aquí? — *Until when are you going to stay here?*
¿**Cómo** estás? — *How are you?*
¿**Cómo** se hace la paella? — *How do you make paella?*

¿**Cuánto** cuesta este reloj? — *How much is this watch?*

100

THE VERB
AND
THE VERB PHRASE

101

INTRODUCTION

Ser expresses essential / inherent properties.

The verb *ser (to be)* is used to tell about the properties that identify or characterize something or someone: **the essence**.

Identity
Ser identifies a person or thing.

¿Qué es? — Es una mesa.
What is it? It's a table.
¿Quién es? — Es Juan.
Who is this? This is Juan.

Material
Ser is used to say what a thing is made of.

¿De qué es la mesa? — Es de madera de pino.
What is the table made of? It is made of pine wood.

Origin
Ser is used to say where a person or thing comes from.

¿De dónde es la mesa? — Es de China.
Where does the table come from? It is from China.

Ownership
Ser is used to say to whom a thing belongs.

¿De quién es la mesa? — Es mía.
Whose table is it? It's mine.
¿Para quién es la mesa? — Es para mí.
For whom is the table? It is for me.

Quantity
Ser is used to indicate how many persons or things there are.

¿Cuántas son? — Son cuatro.
How many are they? They are four.

Essential properties
Ser is used to express properties that define the nature of a person or thing.

¿Cómo es la mesa? — Es fuerte y cara.
How is the table? It is strong and expensive.
La mesa es para trabajar en la cocina.
The table is used to work in the kitchen.

Time / Hour
Ser is used to tell time.

¿Qué hora es? — Son las diez.
What time is it? It is 10 o'clock.
¿Qué día es? — Es lunes.
What day is today? It is Monday.

Impersonal expressions

es difícil/necesario/posible...
it is hard/necessary/possible...

Estar expresses incidental properties.

The verb *estar* (also translated as the English *to be*) is used to express incidental properties, properties that are not essential to the identification of a person or a thing. *Estar* indicates **non inherent** or temporary properties.

Non essential properties	¿Cómo está la mesa? — Está rota. *How is the table? It's broken.* ¿A cuánto está el ajo? — Está a 90 pts. el kilo. *How much does garlic cost? It costs 90 pesetas a kilo.*
Location in space	¿Dónde está la mesa? — Está en la esquina. *Where is the table? It's in the corner.*
Location in time	¿A cuántos estamos? — Estamos a 2 de junio. *What is today's date? It's June 2nd.*
Position	Juan está apoyado en la mesa. *Juan is leaning on the table.*
Opinion	¿Por qué candidato estás? — Estoy por el mejor. *Which candidate are you for? I am for the best one.*
On-going action in progressive tenses [159]	¿Qué está haciendo Luis? — Está leyendo. *What is Luis doing? He is reading.*
Expressions	¿Estamos? *Do we agree?* Está bien. *That's enough.* está visto que... *it is clear that...* estar de acuerdo *to agree* estar equivocado *to be wrong* estar de viaje *to be on a trip* estar de regreso *to be back*
	Note that *vivo (alive)* and *muerto (dead)* are used with *estar:* Pedro está vivo / muerto. *Pedro is alive / dead.*

Sometimes it is possible to use either *ser* or *estar* with a specific expression. In these cases the choice of verb conveys a different meaning. Here are some examples:

We can use *ser* or *estar* with names of professions.

José es profesor.

Jose is a teacher.
(It's his profession.)

José está de profesor.

Jose is working as a teacher
(Although he is not in the teaching profession.)

We can use *ser* or *estar* with certain adjectives.

La pera es buena para la salud.
Esta pera está buena.

Pears are good for your health.
This pear is tasty.

Su padre es joven/viejo.
Su padre está joven/viejo.

His father is young/old.
His father is (looks) young/old.

Es listo.
Está listo.

He is smart.
He is ready.

Este niño es malo.
Este niño está malo.

This child is naughty.
This child is sick.

Este gato es vivo.
Este gato está vivo.

This cat is alert.
This cat is alive.

Las manzanas son verdes.
Las manzanas están verdes.

The apples are green.
The apples are unripe.

Ser + Verb in the *participio* = passive form [219]
Estar + Verb in the *gerundio* = progressive form [159]

In construction with verbs, *ser* is followed by the *participio* to form passive sentences, while *estar* is followed by the *gerundio* to form the progressive.

Juan estaba comiendo la pera.
La pera fue comida.

Juan was eating the pear.
The pear was eaten.

106

The verb *haber* means *to have. Haber* is first and foremost an auxiliary, a helping verb used to form compound tenses.

Haber is the auxiliary used to form compound tenses in Spanish.

In this use, it is the equivalent of the English auxiliary *to have.*

He leído este libro.	*I have read this book.*
Luis había estado enfermo.	*Luis had been sick.*
Me alegro de haberte visto.	*I am happy to have seen you.*

Haber + Noun Phrase = *there is / there are*

Haber is also used in the impersonal construction corresponding to the English *there is/are.*

Hay un florero en la mesa.	*There is a vase on the table.*
Hay muchas velas en la mesa.	*There are many candles on the table.*
Había un libro en la mesa.	*There was a book on the table.*
Habrá una cena en esta sala.	*There will be a dinner in this room.*

Haber que + Verb in the *infinitivo* = *it is necessary to*

In this impersonal construction, *haber que* is followed by a verb in the *infinitivo* and means *it is necessary to...*

Hay que leer el libro para entender la película.	*It is necessary to read the book in order to understand the movie.*
Habrá que salir temprano.	*It will be necessary to go out early.*
Había que verlo.	*You should have seen him.*

 Note that there is an important difference between the English *to have* and the Spanish *haber.* In English, *to have* is also a verb meaning *to possess (I have a blue car). Haber* does not have this use.

107

The verbs *saber* and *conocer* are both translated into the English *to know*. There are, however, differences in the way we use them.

Saber + Noun or Noun Phrase = *to possess knowledge*

Saber can be followed by a noun or noun phrase and means *to know, to possess knowledge* or *wisdom.*

Sabe español y francés.	*He knows Spanish and French.*
No sabe nada.	*He does not know anything.*
	(He is ignorant.)

Saber + Verb in the *infinitivo* = *to know how to*

Saber can be followed by a verb in the *infinitivo*. It means *to know how to.*

Sabe jugar al tenis.	*She knows how to play tennis.*
Yo sé nadar pero no sé bucear.	*I can swim but I don't know how to dive.*

Saber + *algo / nada* + *de* + Noun or Noun phrase = *to have news about something or someone*

Saber can be followed by the expressions *algo de, nada de,* and a noun or a noun phrase to mean *to hear about, to have news about.*

No sé nada de Luis.	*I have no news about Luis.*
¿Sabes algo de tu primo?	*Do you have news about your cousin?*

Expressions with the verb *saber*

¿Yo que sé?	*How should I know?*
¡Vete / vaya a saber!	*God knows.*
No se sabe.	*Nobody knows.*

Conocer √

Conocer + Noun or Noun Phrase = *to be familiar with*

Conocer can be followed by a noun or noun phrase and means *to be acquainted/familiar with.*

Conozco el nuevo libro.	*I am familiar with the new book.*
Pablo no conoce París.	*Pablo does not know Paris.*
¿Conoce Usted a Luis?	*Do you know Luis?*

Conocer + *a* + Noun or Noun phrase = *to meet*

Conocer can be followed by a noun or a noun phrase describing a human being and means *to meet.*

Conocí a mi esposa en Boston.	*I met my wife in Boston.*

Conocer + Noun or Noun Phrase = *to recognize*

Conocer can be followed by a noun or noun phrase and means *to recognize.*

No la conocí en esta foto.	*I did not recognize her on this picture.*
Lo conozco por su voz.	*I recognize him from the sound of his voice.*

Expressions with the verb *conocer*

dar a conocer algo	*to release some piece of information*
dar a conocer a alguien	*to introduce somebody*
Me conozco.	*I know myself.*
se conoce que...	*it is clear/well known that...*

109

The verb *hacer* has several uses:

Hacer means *to do, to make.*

Yo siempre hago mi tarea.	*I always do my homework.*
¿Qué vas a hacer?	*What are you going to do?*
Mi madre hace buenas galletas.	*My mother makes good cookies.*
El perro me hizo correr.	*The dog made me run.*

Hacer is used in weather expressions.

¿Qué tiempo hace?	*How is the weather like?*
— Hace frío/calor/fresco...	*— It is cold/hot/fresh...*
— Hace 40 grados.	*— It is 40 degrees.*
(In Mexico: Estamos a 40 grados.)	

Hacer is used with time expressions with the meanings *for* and *ago.*

It is used in the following construction:

> HACER + EXPRESSION OF TIME + *QUE* + SENTENCE

¿Cuánto tiempo hace que...?	*How long ago/ for how long...?*
Hace dos horas que espero el tren.	*I have waited for the train for 2 hours.*

Depending on the tense of *hacer* and the tense of the following verb, the meaning can be *for* or *ago.* Look at the following situation and examples, and find the explanations on the next page.

July 7, 1996 (now): I am now a professional tennis player.
July 1, 1990: I started playing tennis professionally.

Hace 6 años que yo juego al tenis. Juego al tenis desde hace 6 años.	*I have played tennis for 6 years.*
Hace 6 años que yo empecé mi carrera en el tenis.	*I started my career in tennis 6 years ago.*
En 1993, hacía 3 años que yo jugaba al tenis.	*In 1993, I had played tennis for 3 years.*
En 1993, hacía 3 años que yo había empezado mi carrera en el tenis.	*In 1993, it had been 3 years since I had started my career in tennis.*

Hace + expression of time + *que* + . . . Verb in *presente* or *presente progresivo* = *for*

This construction is used to express an action which started some time ago and is still going on at the moment of speech.

Hace un mes que trabajo en Perú.	*I have worked in Peru for one month.*
Hace un mes que estoy trabajando en Perú.	*I have been working in Peru for one month.*

Hacía + expression of time + *que* + . . . Verb in *imperfecto* or *pasado progresivo* = *for.*

This construction is used to express an action which started some time before a specific moment in the past, and was still going on at that moment.

Hacía dos años que tomaba cursos de inglés.	*I had taken English classes for 2 years.*
Hacía dos años que estaba tomando cursos de inglés.	*I had been taking English classes for two years.*

Hace + expression of time + *que* + . . . Verb in the *pretérito* = *ago*

This construction expresses an action that took place and was completed before the moment of speech.

Hace mucho tiempo que compré este carro.	*I bought this car a long time ago.*

Hacía + expression of time + *que* + . . . Verb in the *pasado perfecto* = *ago*

This construction expresses an action that took place and was completed before a specific moment in the past.

Hacía mucho tiempo que había comprado este carro.	*I had bought this car a long time ago.*

> **The subject of *like* in English corresponds to the indirect object of *gustar* in Spanish.**

The verb *gustar* means *to like, to be fond of.* But this verb is used in completely different ways in English and in Spanish.

ENGLISH	SPANISH
√ The subject of the verb *like* is the person who likes something.	√ The subject of the verb *gustar* is the thing being liked.
<u>Eva</u> like**s** <u>comedies.</u> subject direct object	<u>A Eva</u> <u>le</u> gust**an** <u>las comedias.</u> ind. object subject
<u>Eva</u> like**s** <u>to read.</u> subject direct object	<u>A Eva</u> <u>le</u> gusta <u>leer.</u> ind. object subject
The 3rd person singular ending on the verb *like**s*** shows that it agrees with Eva, which is its subject.	The subject comes after the verb. The ending on the verb *gust**an*** shows that it agrees with *las comedias,* which is its subject.
Comedies is the direct object, the thing being liked.	The person who likes them comes before the verb, preceded by the preposition *a.* It is repeated in the form of an indirect object personal pronoun [82]. *Le* and *a Eva* express the indirect object.
	√ The verbs *antojarse (feel like), apasionar (adore),* and *encantar (to be delighted)* are used in the same way.

Here are the **pronouns** which express the person who likes something.

(A mí) **me** gusta/gustan...   (A nosotros/as) **nos** gusta/gustan...
(A tí) **te** gusta/gustan...   (A vosotros/as) **os** gusta/gustan...
(A él/ella/Ud.) **le** gusta/gustan...   (A ellos/ellas/Uds.) **les** gusta/gustan...

Expressions using *gustar*

¿Gustas? / ¿Gusta Ud.?   *Would you like...?*
Como gustes. / Como Ud. guste.   *As you wish.*

1. Pablo lava el carro.
   Pablo washes the car.

2. Pablo se lava.
   Pablo washes himself.

3. Pablo y María se hablan por teléfono.
Pablo and María speak to each other on the phone.

√ **In the first situation,** the subject (the person doing the action) and the object (the receiver, or the thing on which the action is done) are different *(Pablo; the car)*. The verb is used in a regular construction: the verb is *lavar.*

√ **In the second situation,** the subject and the object are the same person. *Pablo* is the one who performs the action of washing and he is also the receiver of this action. The verb is used in a pronominal construction: *lavarse.* We use a pronoun *(se)*, called **reflexive pronoun.**

√ **In the third situation,** *Pablo* and *María* are subjects and indirect objects at the same time and the action is directed from *Pablo* to *María*, and from *María* to *Pablo.* It is a reciprocal action: *hablarse.* We use the pronoun *se*, called **reciprocal pronoun.**

REFLEXIVE VERBS

In reflexive verbs, the action goes from the subject to himself or herself.

The subject is at the same time the agent and the receiver.

acostarse	*to go to bed*	bañarse	*to take a bath*
dormirse	*to fall asleep*	lavarse	*to wash*
despertarse	*to wake up*	vestirse	*to dress*

Luisa **se levanta** a las siete. Toma el café escuchando las noticias. **Se ducha** con agua muy caliente y **se peina.** Después de **vestirse,** sale para la universidad.

Luisa gets up at seven o'clock. She drinks coffee while listening to the news. She takes a shower with very warm water and she combs her hair. After putting her clothes on, she goes to the university.

RECIPROCAL VERBS

In reciprocal verbs, the action goes from the subject to the object and from the object to the subject.

For example Pablo loves Luisa, and Luisa loves Pablo. This corresponds to the English *each other.*

amarse	*to love each other*	telefonearse	*to phone each other*
odiarse	*to hate each other*	verse	*to see each other*

Los dos gallos **se miraron, se incitaron** a luchar, **provocándose** con el pico y **se abalanzaron** uno sobre el otro.

The two fighting cocks looked at each other, incited each other to fight, provoking each other with their beak, and threw themselves at each other.

114

INHERENTLY PRONOMINAL VERBS

Inherently reflexive verbs are verbs which come only in the reflexive form.

acercarse a	*to approach*	enfadarse	*to get angry*
acordarse de	*to remember*	enterarse de	*to find out*
alegrarse de	*to be glad*	esforzarse	*to exert oneself*
atreverse a	*to dare to*	fijarse en	*to notice*
burlarse de	*to make fun of*	quejarse de	*to complain*
callarse	*to be silent*	reirse de	*to make fun of*
convertirse en	*to become*	suicidarse	*to commit suicide*
desmayarse	*to faint*		

Siempre que **se acerca** a la casa de su abuela, **se acuerda** de su niñez.

Whenever he gets close to his grandmother's house, he remembers his childhood.

Se enfadó al **enterarse** que **se habían burlado** de él.

He got angry when he found out that they had made fun of him.

PASSIVE PRONOMINAL VERBS

Passive pronominal verbs express a passive meaning: the receiver is the subject.

This form is used to express the passive meaning when the receiver of the action is not human and the agent is irrelevant. It is always used in the 3rd person singular or plural, and expresses a habitual action or generality:

El vino blanco se toma con el pescado.

One drinks white wine with fish.

115

When the verb is conjugated, we add the reflexive or reciprocal pronoun before the verb.

yo	**me**	lavo	nosotros/as	**nos**	lavamos
tú	**te**	lavas	vosotros/as	**os**	laváis
él/ella/Ud.	**se**	lava	ellos/ellas/Uds.	**se**	lavan

In the non-conjugated modes (*infinitivo* and *gerundio*), we attach the reflexive or reciprocal pronoun as an ending to the verb.

REFLEXIVE

Tú puedes matricular**te** en la universidad.	*You can register at the university.*
Jorge se cortó, afeitándo**se** con una nueva cuchilla.	*Jorge cut himself while shaving with a new razor.*

RECIPROCAL

Les gusta enviar**se** fotos.	*They like to send pictures to each other.*
Pablo y Luisa continúan escribiéndo**se** cartas.	*Pablo and Luisa continue to write letters to each other.*

When the *infinitivo* follows a conjugated verb, we can either place the pronoun before the conjugated verb or attach it to the *infinitivo* ending [89]:

He jugado a la pelota y **me** quiero duchar.
He jugado a la pelota y quiero duchar**me.**
I have played ball, and I want to take a shower.

In the *imperativo*, the pronoun attaches to the verb ending in the affirmative form, and precedes the verb in the negative form:

AFFIRMATIVE

¡Lávate ahora y acuéstate!	*Wash now and go to bed!*

NEGATIVE

¡No te laves ahora y no te acuestes!	*Don't wash now and don't go to bed!*

Verbs Which Come only in the 3rd Person Singular √

Some verbs are used in the 3rd person singular only. This class of verbs contains verbs that describe natural phenomena, weather conditions, and the existential expression *hay (there is/are)*.

Natural phenomena	amanecer:	amanece	*to dawn*
	anochecer:	anochece	*to get dark*
Weather conditions	helar:	hiela	*to freeze*
	granizar:	graniza	*to hail*
	llover:	llueve	*to rain*
	nevar:	nieva	*to snow*
	relampaguear:	relampaguea	*to lighten*
	tronar:	truena	*to thunder*
	Note that *hacer* can also be used in weather expressions such as:		
	hace calor		*it is hot*
	hace fresco		*it is cool*
	hace frío		*it is cold*
	hace sol		*it is sunny*
	hace viento		*it is windy*
Existential expression	hay		*there is/are*

√ In the conjugated modes, these verbs can come in all tenses:

En invierno nevaba mucho.   *In winter it snowed a lot.*
Mañana no hará calor.   *Tomorrow it will not be hot.*

√ These verbs can also be used in the non-conjugated modes *(infinitivo, gerundio, participio)*:

Va a llover.   *It is going to rain.*
Si continúa nevando, no podré salir.   *If it goes on snowing, I won't be able to go out.*

117

The form of the verb gives information on the subject, the speaker's attitude, and the time of the action.

The form of the verb in a sentence depends on several factors:
(i) the subject; (ii) the verb group; (iii) the mode; (iv) the tense.

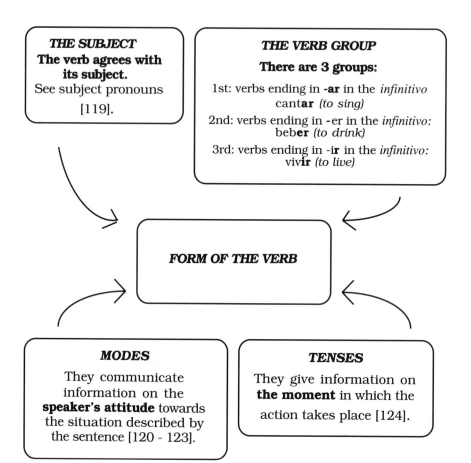

THE SUBJECT
The verb agrees with its subject.
See subject pronouns [119].

THE VERB GROUP

There are 3 groups:

1st: verbs ending in **-ar** in the *infinitivo*
cant**ar** *(to sing)*

2nd: verbs ending in -er in the *infinitivo:*
beb**er** *(to drink)*

3rd: verbs ending in -ir in the *infinitivo:*
viv**ir** *(to live)*

FORM OF THE VERB

MODES
They communicate information on the **speaker's attitude** towards the situation described by the sentence [120 - 123].

TENSES
They give information on **the moment** in which the action takes place [124].

Subject Pronouns √

A verb is preceded by its subject, which comes in the form of a noun, noun phrase, or pronoun. The subject pronouns are [77 - 79]:

YO	**1st person singular; masc. or fem.** √ refers to the speaker.	*I*
TÚ	**2nd person singular; masc. or fem.** √ refers to the person spoken to. √ indicates an informal style, used with friends, people who belong to the same social circle or when the speaker is explicitly allowed to do so. √ in many parts of South and Central America, the form **vos** is used [78].	*you*
ÉL **ELLA**	**3rd person singular; masc./ fem.** √ refers to the person spoken about.	*he* *she*
USTED	**3rd person singular; masc. or fem.** √ it is the polite, formal pronoun used to address one person with whom the speaker is not close or familiar (abbreviated Ud. or Vd.).	*you*
NOSOTROS **NOSOTRAS**	**1st person plural; masc./ fem.** √ refers to a group including the speaker.	*we*
VOSOTROS **VOSOTRAS**	**2nd person plural; masc./ fem.** √ refers to a group of people addressed by the speaker. √ used in Spain only.	*you*
ELLOS **ELLAS**	**3rd person plural; masc./ fem.** √ refers to the group of people spoken about.	*they*
USTEDES	**3rd person plural; masc. or fem.** √ refers to the group of people spoken to. √ is a formal expression in Spain. √ is used for both formal or informal in Latin America.	*you*

Modes express the speaker's attitude.

In order to determine which mode has to be used, we have to consider how the speaker views the situation which he or she is describing. There are several ways to represent a situation or a process.

The speaker can present an action as real or unreal.

When describing a situation, a speaker can view and represent the situation as a fact which **takes place in reality.**

For instance, when Peter says:

I bought a car.

he is making a statement on something that really happened.

Paul can tell us that the action of buying a car is not happening because some conditions have not been met.

If I had money, I would buy a car.

This means that he does not buy a car because he has no money. The action of buying a car is **hypothetical,** not real.

The speaker can present an action indirectly through his reactions to it.

Louis can also speak, not directly about buying a car, but about **his reaction to this action.** When he says:

I wish I could buy a car.
I am glad I bought a car.

he is not making a statement about buying a car, but rather about his feeling or his desire with respect to this specific action.

The speaker can give a command for an action to be performed.

Finally, Louis can request his father to buy a car, saying:

Buy a car, please!

In this situation, we do not know whether a car will be bought or not.

These different perspectives are expressed in Spanish through the different modes.

There are **three modes** which indicate the speaker's attitude towards the process described in the sentence.

We use the *indicativo* to describe a process as real or unreal (hypothetical).

The sentence can state that the process really occurs.

Yo **compré** un carro.	*I bought a car.*
Voy al cine.	*I am going to the movies.*

When the process is not real, we use hypothetical tenses, which are also called *condicional.*

Si tuviera dinero, **compraría** un carro.	*If I had money I would buy a car.*
Si fuera rico, **viajaría.**	*If I were rich, I would travel.*

We use the *subjuntivo* to describe a process viewed through a subjective reaction to it, and not in its reality.

Whether the process is real or not is irrelevant. The main message is the speaker's feeling or subjective reaction to it.

Quiero que tú **compres** un carro.	*I wish you would buy a car.*
Espero que **vengas.**	*I hope you'll come.*

We use the *imperativo* to give suggestions, commands, orders.

¡Cómprame un carro!	*Buy me a car!*
¡Levántate y **corre!**	*Get up and run!*

122

There are three other modes, which are not conjugated: the form of the verb does not change with the subject.

The *infinitivo* is the form we use when we refer to the verb; it is the name of the verb.

The *infinitivo* is the form that is listed in a Spanish dictionary, for example: *saltar (to jump)*.

In the English infinitive, the verb follows the particle *to (to sing)*. Like in English, the Spanish *infinitivo* is used in specific contexts:

√ after another verb:

Yo quiero **salir.**	*I want to go out.*
Me gusta **tomar** fotos.	*I like to take pictures.*

√ after prepositions:

Compré el libro para **estudiar** inglés.	*I bought the book in order to learn English.*

The *gerundio* is used with the auxiliary *estar* to express an on-going action, an action in progress.

It corresponds to the English verb form ending in *-ing: hablando (speaking), leyendo (reading).*

Lucía está **hablando** con Juan.	*Lucía is speaking with Juan.*
Estoy **leyendo** una novela.	*I am reading a novel.*

The *participio* is used after the auxiliary *haber* to form compound tenses.

It corresponds to the English past participle: *terminado (finished), caído (fallen down).*

Hemos **terminado** el proyecto.	*We have finished our project.*
Me he **caído** en la pista.	*I have fallen down on the track.*

123

Tenses communicate when the process takes place.

A process always takes place in time. We perceive events in our lives and in history as being part of chronology. We conceive of our lives as series of successive periods of time: infancy, childhood, youth, adulthood, mature age, and old age. Our world is divided into periods: centuries, decades, years, months, weeks, days, hours, etc.

Our communication is embedded in time. Every act of communication occurs at a specific moment in time. Both speaker and listener, writer and reader understand what is said only if the processes can be located in time: before, after, or during a specific moment in time.

For example, we can describe a process which occurred:

√   before the moment in which we speak or write, which we can call the present moment (NOW):

> Isabel ha ido a Madrid muchas veces.   *Isabel has been to Madrid many times.*
> José fue a la playa la semana pasada.   *Jose went to the beach last week.*
> Los niños han jugado a la pelota.   *The children have played ball.*

√   during the present moment:

> Paco está tocando la guitarra.   *Paco is playing the guitar.*
> Luisa habla muchas lenguas.   *Luisa speaks many languages.*

√   after the present moment:

> Yo telefonearé al doctor.   *I will call the doctor.*
> Carmen será abogada.   *Carmen will be a lawyer.*

We can find out when the process took place by looking at the form of the verb. For instance, the specific form **ha ido** indicates a past process whereas **será** tells us that the process is located in future time.

The forms related to the time of occurrence of the process is what we call **verb tenses**. We will refer to verb tenses by their Spanish names: *presente, pretérito, imperfecto,* etc.

Simple tenses are tenses formed with one word only.
Compound tenses are formed with two words: the auxiliary *haber* and the *participio* of the verb (194-195).

124

THE INDICATIVO

Estoy contenta: he recibido mi billete de avión para ir a Puerto Rico. He decidido ir este año porque mis amigos, que han pasado las vacaciones allí, me hablan siempre de lo bien que lo pasaron. Siempre he querido visitar esta isla y pasearme en las calles del viejo San Juan.

Luisa dijo que **estaba** contenta: **había recibido** su billete de avión para ir a Puerto Rico. **Había decidido** ir ese año porque sus amigos, que **habían pasado** las vacaciones allí, le **hablaban** siempre de lo bien que lo **habían pasado**. Siempre **había querido** visitar esta isla y pasearse en las calles del viejo San Juan.

Uses of the *Presente del Indicativo* √

The *presente del indicativo* is used to describe a habitual process or an action done on a regular basis.

Voy al cine los domingos.	*I go to the movies on Sundays.*
Me levanto a las siete.	*I get up at 7 o'clock.*

The *presente del indicativo* describes a process which takes place at the moment of speech.

It describes an action which takes place as we speak.

Jaime **canta** con sus amigos.	*Jaime sings with his friends.*
Juan **pasa** el balón a Luis.	*Juan throws the ball to Luis.*

The *presente del indicativo* expresses a general timeless truth.

Jaime **canta** bien.	*Jaime sings well.*
En verano **hace** calor.	*Summer is hot.*

The *presente del indicativo* describes a process which is about to take place in the immediate future.

It is then used with a future time adverb, or a time expression.

Jaime **canta** mañana en la Ópera.	*Jaime is singing tomorrow at the Opera.*
Tomo el avión el miércoles.	*I fly on Wednesday.*

The *presente del indicativo* expresses a condition introduced by the word *si*.

Si Jaime **canta** bien el año próximo, recibirá el premio.	*If Jaime sings well next year, he will receive the award.*
Si **vienes** mañana, te daré el libro.	*If you come tomorrow, I will give you the book.*

A conjugated verb has two parts: the stem and the ending. The **stem** indicates the basic part of the verb. The **ending** is added to the stem and indicates the tense and the person. When you conjugate a verb, you must therefore find the stem first and then learn the endings.

REGULAR VERBS

To conjugate a verb in the *presente del indicativo*:

(1) Find the stem.

Take the *infinitivo* and delete the *infinitivo* ending (-**ar** for the 1st group; -**er** for the 2nd group; and -**ir** for the 3rd group):

Infinitivo:	hablar	—— stem:	**habl-**	*(to speak)*
Infinitivo:	beber	—— stem:	**beb-**	*(to drink)*
Infinitivo:	vivir	—— stem:	**viv-**	*(to live)*

(2) Learn the endings.

1st group (-ar):	**o, as, a,**	**amos, áis, an**
2nd group (-er):	**o, es, e,**	**emos, éis, en**
3rd group (-ir):	**o, es, e,**	**imos, ís, en**

	HABLAR	**BEBER**	**VIVIR**
yo	hablo	bebo	vivo
tú	hablas	bebes	vives
él/ella/Ud.	habla	bebe	vive
nosotros/as	hablamos	bebemos	vivimos
vosotros/as	habláis	bebéis	vivís
ellos/ellas/Uds.	hablan	beben	viven

Forms of the *Presente del Indicativo*

IRREGULAR VERBS

Four verbs are presented here, before all other irregular verbs: *ser (to be), estar (to be), ir (to go), haber (to have).* These verbs are very important because of their high frequency in the language.

	SER	**ESTAR**	**IR**	**HABER**
yo	soy	estoy	voy	he
tú	eres	estás	vas	has
él/ella/Ud.	es	está	va	ha
nosotros/as	somos	estamos	vamos	hemos
vosotros/as	sois	estáis	vais	habéis
ellos/ellas/Uds.	son	están	van	han

IRREGULAR PATTERNS

Apart from the previous irregular verbs, there are verbs that follow irregular patterns in the *presente del indicativo*. They undergo changes in their stems.

(1) The last stem vowel E changes to IE.

E becomes IE in all persons except for *nosostros/vosotros.*

pensar ⸺ stem: p**e**ns-   *(to think)*

	PENSAR	VERBS LIKE PENSAR
yo	p**ie**nso	
tú	p**ie**nsas	
él/ella/Ud.	p**ie**nsa	
nosotros/as	pensamos	
vosotros/as	pensáis	
ellos/ellas/Uds.	p**ie**nsan	

VERBS LIKE PENSAR

-ar: acertar; alentar; apretar; arrendar, atravesar; calentar; cerrar; comenzar; confesar; despertar; empezar; encerrar; enterrar; errar*; fregar; gobernar; manifestar; merendar; negar; pensar; recomendar; regar; reventar; segar; sembrar; sentar(se); tropezar

-er: ascender; atender; defender; descender; encender; entender; perder; querer

-ir: adherir; adquirir; advertir; arrepentirse; convertir; digerir; divertir; herir; hervir; invertir; mentir; preferir; referir; sentir

☞ **Note** that *errar* takes a **Y** instead of **I:**
yerro, yerras, yerra, yerran

129

(2) The last stem vowel O changes to UE.

O becomes UE in all persons except for *nosotros/ vosotros*.

dormir ——— stem: dorm-   *(to sleep)*

	DORMIR	VERBS LIKE DORMIR
yo	d**ue**rmo	**-ar:** acordarse; acostarse; almorzar;
tú	d**ue**rmes	apostar; avergonzarse; colgar;
él/ella/Ud.	d**ue**rme	comprobar; contar; consolar; costar;
nosotros/as	dormimos	demostrar; encontrar; mostrar; probar;
vosotros/as	dormís	recordar; renovar; rogar; soltar; sonar;
ellos/ellas/Uds.	d**ue**rmen	soñar; volar; volcar
		-er: cocer; morder; mover; resolver
		soler; torcer; volver
		-ir: dormir(se); morir

The verb **jugar** *(to play)* is the only verb which follows a similar pattern (**U** becomes **UE**):

yo	j**ue**go
tú	j**ue**gas
él/ella/Ud.	j**ue**ga
nosotros/as	jugamos
vosotros/as	jugáis
ellos/ellas/Uds.	j**ue**gan

(3) The last stem vowel E changes to I for some -ir verbs.

E becomes I in all persons except for *nosostros/ vosotros*.

repetir ——— stem: repet-   *(to repeat)*

	REPETIR	VERBS LIKE REPETIR
yo	rep**i**to	competir; conseguir; corregir;
tú	rep**i**tes	despedir; elegir; freír; impedir;
él/ella/Ud.	rep**i**te	medir; pedir; perseguir;
nosotros/as	repetimos	reír; reñir; seguir; servir;
vosotros/as	repetís	sonreír; vestirse
ellos/ellas/Uds.	rep**i**ten	

(4) The last stem vowel U changes to UY for some -ir verbs.

U becomes UY in all persons except for *nosotros/ vosotros*.

construir —— stem: constr-   *(to build)*

	CONSTRUIR
yo	constr**uy**o
tú	constr**uy**es
él/ella/Ud.	constr**uy**e
nosotros/as	construimos
vosotros/as	construís
ellos/ellas/Uds.	constr**uy**en

VERBS LIKE CONSTRUIR
All verbs ending in **-uir** in the *infinitivo*.

(5) Some verbs change only in the 1st person singular *(yo)*.

C becomes G.

hacer —— stem: hac-

	HACER *(to do)*
yo	ha**g**o
tú	haces
él/ella/Ud.	hace
nosotros/as	hacemos
vosotros/as	hacéis
ellos/ellas/Uds.	hacen

VERBS LIKE HACER
deshacer; satisfacer

N becomes NG.

poner —— stem: pon-

	PONER *(to put)*
yo	pon**g**o
tú	pones
él/ella/Ud.	pone
nosotros/as	ponemos
vosotros/as	ponéis
ellos/ellas/Uds.	ponen

VERBS LIKE PONER
All the verbs formed with **poner:** componer; disponer; exponer; imponer; oponer; proponer; reponer; suponer; etc.

Note that *tener* [133] also has a **G** in the 1st pers. sing.

131

L becomes LG.

salir —— stem   sal-   *(to go out)*

	SALIR
yo	sal**g**o
tú	sales
él/ella/Ud.	sale
nosotros/as	salimos
vosotros/as	salís
ellos/ellas/Uds.	salen

VERBS LIKE SALIR
All verbs ending with **-alir**, like sobresalir, and **-aler**, like valer.

Add IG between the stem and the ending O.

traer —— stem: tra-   *(to bring)*

	TRAER
yo	tra**ig**o
tú	traes
él/ella/Ud.	trae
nosotros/as	traemos
vosotros/as	traéis
ellos/ellas/Uds.	traen

VERBS LIKE TRAER
All verbs formed with **traer,** like atraer; contraer; distraer; extraer; sustraer; etc., and the verb caerse.

C becomes ZC.

conocer —— stem: conoc-   *(to know)*

	CONOCER
yo	cono**zc**o
tú	conoces
él/ella/Ud.	conoce
nosotros/as	conocemos
vosotros/as	conocéis
ellos/ellas/Uds.	conocen

VERBS LIKE CONOCER
-er: agradecer; complacer; crecer; desconocer; desobedecer; merecer; nacer; obedecer; ofrecer; parecer; pertenecer; reconocer.
-ir: conducir; introducir; producir; reducir; reproducir; seducir; traducir.

Some verbs are completely irregular in the 1st person only.

	SABER *(to know)*	**DAR** *(to give)*	**VER** *(to see)*
yo	s**é**	d**oy**	v**eo**
tú	sabes	das	ves
él/ella/Ud.	sabe	da	ve
nosotros/as	sabemos	damos	vemos
vosotros/as	sabéis	dais	veis
ellos/ellas/Uds.	saben	dan	ven

(6) Some verbs combine two irregularities.

1. 1st person: N becomes NG.
2. E becomes IE in all other persons except for *nosotros/vosotros.*

tener —— stem: ten-   *(to have)*

	TENER	VERBS LIKE TENER
yo	te**ng**o	All verbs formed with **tener,** like:
tú	ti**e**nes	contener; detener; entretener;
él/ella/Ud.	ti**e**ne	mantener; retener; obtener; etc.
nosotros/as	tenemos	**-ir:** venir; intervenir; prevenir
vosotros/as	tenéis	
ellos/ellas/Uds.	ti**e**nen	

1. 1st person: C becomes G.
2. E becomes I in all persons except for *nosotros / vosotros.*

decir —— stem: dec-   *(to say)*

	DECIR	VERBS LIKE DECIR
yo	di**g**o	All verbs formed with **decir:**
tú	di**c**es	bendecir; maldecir; predecir
él/ella/Ud.	di**c**e	
nosotros/as	decimos	
vosotros/as	decís	
ellos/ellas/Uds.	di**c**en	

133

(7) Some verbs change their spelling in order to maintain the pronunciation of the last stem consonant.

Two rules of pronunciation are relevant for the following verbs:

Pronunciation of the letter C

The letter **c** is pronounced:
[s] or [th] before **e** and **i** (**ce**rca),
[k] before **o** and **a** (cer**ca**).

Pronunciation of the letter G

The letter **g** is pronounced:
[j] before **e** and **i** (**ge**ranio).
[g] before **o** and **a** (**go**l).

C changes to Z before O and A.

The 1st person singular ending is **-o**. In order to avoid a change in pronunciation and to maintain the sound [s] / [th], we write the letter **z** instead of **c**.

G changes to J before O and A.

The 1st person singular ending is **-o**. In order to avoid a change in pronunciation and to maintain the sound [j], we write the letter **j** instead of **g**.

CONVENCER
(to convince)

yo	conven**z**o
tú	convences
él/ella/Ud.	convence
nosotros/as	convencemos
vosotros/as	convencéis
ellos/ellas/Uds.	convencen

VERBS LIKE CONVENCER
cocer (also O > UE [130]); ejercer; torcer (also O > UE [130]); vencer.

CORREGIR
(to correct)

yo	corri**j**o
tú	corriges
él/ella/Ud.	corrige
nosotros/as	corregimos
vosotros/as	corregís
ellos/ellas/Uds.	corrigen

VERBS LIKE CORREGIR
-er: coger; encoger; escoger; proteger; recoger
-ir: dirigir; exigir; surgir

 Note that the verb *corregir* also exhibits the change E > I, described in [130].

134

USE

When we want to describe an action which is going on at the moment of speech, we use the **progressive form,** just like in English.

The process is happening at the very moment we are talking: the action is in progress.

En esta foto, José **está describiendo** su proyecto y ellos **están escuchando** y **están tomando** notas.

In this picture, Jose is describing his project, and they are listening and taking notes.

The process takes place for an extended time, including the moment in which we are talking: it is a temporary activity.

The moment of speech is not the focus, but rather a longer period of time. The verb describes an activity rather than an on-going action.

Este año, **estoy escribiendo** mi tesis.   *This year, I am writing my thesis.*

FORM

The *presente progresivo* is formed with the *presente del indicativo* of *estar* followed by the *gerundio* form of the verb [202].

Presente progresivo = estar in presente + Verb in the gerundio.

	TRABAJAR *(to work)*
yo	estoy trabajando
tú	estás trabajando
él/ella/Ud.	está trabajando
nosotros/as	estamos trabajando
vosotros/as	estáis trabajando
ellos/ellas/Uds.	están trabajando

135

We can describe processes which occur in the immediate future. We then use the tense called *futuro inmediato*. To form the *futuro inmediato*, we use the auxiliary *ir* followed by the preposition *a* and the verb in the *infinitivo*. The English equivalent is the form *to be going to* + Verb.

Futuro inmediato = **ir** + **a** + **Verb in the** *infinitivo*

TRABAJAR
(to work)

yo	voy a trabajar
tú	vas a trabajar
él/ella/Ud.	va a trabajar
nosotros/as	vamos a trabajar
vosotros/as	vais a trabajar
ellos/ellas/Uds.	van a trabajar

The process takes place immediately after the moment in which we speak.

In this case, the auxiliary *ir* has to be conjugated in the *presente* [129].

Yo **voy a leer** este libro.	*I am going to read this book.*
Ana **va a ir** a Madrid.	*Ana is going to go to Madrid.*
Ellos **van a regresar** pronto.	*They are going to come back soon.*

The process takes place immediately after a specific moment in the past.

In this case, the auxiliary *ir* is conjugated in the *imperfecto* [145]. It is an immediate future with respect to a past.

Yo **iba a leer** este libro.	*I was going to read this book.*
Ana **iba a ir** a Madrid.	*Ana was going to go to Madrid.*
Ellos **iban a regresar** pronto.	*They were going to come back soon.*

136

We can describe processes which occur in the immediate past. We then use the tense called *pasado inmediato*. To form the *pasado inmediato,* we use the auxiliary *acabar* followed by the preposition *de* and the verb in the *infinitivo*. The English equivalent is the form *to have just* + Verb in the past participle.

Pasado inmediato = *acabar* + *de* + V in the *infinitivo*

TRABAJAR
(to work)

yo	acabo de trabajar
tú	acabas de trabajar
él/ella/Ud.	acaba de trabajar
nosotros/as	acabamos de trabajar
vosotros/as	acabáis de trabajar
ellos/ellas/Uds.	acaban de trabajar

The process takes place immediately before the moment in which we speak.

In this case, the auxiliary *acabar* has to be conjugated in the *presente* [128].

Yo **acabo de leer** este libro.   *I have just read this book.*
Ana **acaba de ir** a Madrid.   *Ana has just gone to Madrid.*
Ellos **acaban de regresar.**   *They have just come back.*

The process can also take place immediately before a specific moment in the past.

In this case, the auxiliary *acabar* is conjugated in the *imperfecto* [145]. It is an immediate past with respect to a past.

Yo **acababa de leer** este libro.   *I had just read this book.*
Ana **acababa de ir** a Madrid.   *Ana had just gone to Madrid.*
Ellos **acababan de regresar.**   *They had just come back.*

Before we can understand the uses of all the past tenses, it is important to understand how a story is built.

Blanca Nieves llega a una casita en el bosque. Como la puerta está abierta, ella entra en la casita. Hay siete sillas alrededor de la mesa y siete camas. Las sillas y las camas son pequeñas. Blanca Nieves, que es una muchacha muy aseada, se pone a limpiar el suelo porque está sucio. Después, prepara la cena y hace las camas. Más tarde, se acuesta y se duerme porque está muy cansada. Al anochecer, los enanitos regresan.

Snow White arrives to a little house in the woods. Since the door is open, she goes into the house. There are seven chairs around the table, and seven beds. The chairs and the beds are small. Snow White, who is a very tidy child, starts cleaning the floor because it is dirty. Afterwards, she prepares dinner and makes the beds. Later, she lies down and falls asleep because she is very tired. At sundown, the dwarfs come back.

There is a distinction between **what happened**, what we call the events of the story, and the **background circumstances**, the explanations and descriptions.

EVENTS	BACKGROUND
1. llega a una casita	
2. entra en la casita	2 a. está abierta
	2 b. hay siete sillas, son pequeñas
3. se pone a limpiar	3 a. es muy aseada
	3 b. está sucio
4. prepara la cena y	
5. hace las camas	
6. se acuesta y se duerme	6 a. está cansada
7. regresan	

The events are the backbone of every story; and the background is added as a setting.

The story is built around the sequence of events. If there are no events, we have no story. In a story we are interested in what happens. The background circumstances are given to highlight and explain the events, and put them in the focus of attention.

When the story is narrated in the past, the events are given in the *pretérito* [139-143], and the background, which takes place at the same time in the *imperfecto* [144-145].

138

The *pretérito* is the tense of **completed processes** in the past. A completed process is a process which has a beginning, some duration, and an end. These completed processes in the past are always understood as events.

The *pretérito* expresses a past process understood as an event.

¿Qué pasó?	*What happened?*

Accidente:
— Un avión **se estrelló** en la colina.   *A plane crashed in the hill.*

Sucesos:
— **Robaron** un cuadro en el museo.   *A painting was stolen from the museum.*

Deporte:
— Induráin **ganó** la "Vuelta a Francia".*Induráin won the "Tour de France."*

Cultura:
— **Se inauguró** un nuevo museo.   *A new museum was opened.*

Meteorología:
— **Llovió** en la capital.   *It rained in the capital.*

The *pretérito* narrates successive events in the past.

Él **entró** y **tomó** sus llaves.   *He came in and took his keys.*

Blanca Nieves **llegó** a una casita. . . ella **entró** en la casita. . . **Se puso** a limpiar el suelo. . . Después, **preparó** la cena e **hizo** las camas. . . . **se acostó** y **se durmió**. . . Al anochecer, los enanitos **regresaron** [138].

 Note that the *pretérito* has no connection with the moment of speech. Contrary to the *presente perfecto* [146 - 147], the *pretérito* has no connection with the moment of speech. It says nothing about now, and has no result or consequences on the present moment.

Ellas **llegaron** por la noche.
They arrived at night.

Ellas **han llegado** por la noche.
They have arrived at night.

This sentence doesn't say if they are still here.

This sentence implies that they are here now.

REGULAR VERBS

(1) Find the stem:

Take the *infinitivo* and delete the *infinitivo* ending (1st group -**ar**; 2nd group -**er**; and 3rd group -**ir**):

Infinitivo:	hablar	——	stem:	**habl-**	*(to speak)*
Infinitivo:	beber	——	stem:	**beb-**	*(to drink)*
Infinitivo:	vivir	——	stem:	**viv-**	*(to live)*

(2) Add the following endings:

1st group (-ar):	**é, aste, ó, amos, asteis, aron**
2nd and 3rd groups:	**í, iste, ió, imos, isteis, ieron**

	HABLAR	**BEBER**	**VIVIR**
yo	hablé	bebí	viví
tú	hablaste	bebiste	viviste
él/ella/Ud.	habló	bebió	vivió
nosotros/as	hablamos	bebimos	vivimos
vosotros/as	hablasteis	bebisteis	vivisteis
ellos/ellas/Uds.	hablaron	bebieron	vivieron

IRREGULAR VERBS

(1)   Four verbs are completely irregular.

	SER / IR	**DAR**	**VER**
yo	fui	di	vi
tú	fuiste	diste	viste
él/ella/Ud.	fue	dio	vio
nosotros/as	fuimos	dimos	vimos
vosotros/as	fuisteis	disteis	visteis
ellos/ellas/Uds.	fueron	dieron	vieron

(2) The following verbs change stem and endings.

√   The stems undergo various changes:

andar:	anduv-	*to walk*	poner:	pus-	*to put*
caber:	cup-	*to fit*	querer:	quis-	*to want*
estar:	estuv-	*to be*	saber:	sup-	*to know*
haber:	hub-	*to have*	tener:	tuv-	*to have*
hacer*:	hic-	*to do*	venir:	vin-	*to come*
poder:	pud-	*to be able to*			

* The 3rd person of the *pretérito* of hacer is hi**z**o.

For the verbs of the list above, the endings are:

Endings:	**e, iste, o, imos, isteis, ieron**

	ANDAR	PODER	VENIR
yo	anduve	pude	vine
tú	anduviste	pudiste	viniste
él/ella/Ud.	anduvo	pudo	vino
nosotros/as	anduvimos	pudimos	vinimos
vosotros/as	anduvisteis	pudisteis	vinisteis
ellos/ellas/Uds.	anduvieron	pudieron	vinieron

√   For the verbs **decir, producir** and **traer,** the stems are:

decir:	dij-	*to say*
producir	produj-	*to produce*
traer:	traj-	*to bring*

and the endings are:

Endings:	**e, iste, o, imos, isteis, eron**

	DECIR	PRODUCIR	TRAER
yo	dije	produje	traje
tú	dijiste	produjiste	trajiste
él/ella/Ud.	dijo	produjo	trajo
nosotros/as	dijimos	produjimos	trajimos
vosotros/as	dijisteis	produjisteis	trajisteis
ellos/ellas/Uds.	dijeron	produjeron	trajeron

(3) Some verbs have regular endings but the last vowel in the stem changes.

O becomes U in the 3rd persons singular and plural.

	DORMIR	*(to sleep)*
yo	dormí	
tú	dormiste	
él/ella/Ud.	d**u**rmió	
nosotros/as	dormimos	
vosotros/as	dormisteis	VERB LIKE DORMIR
ellos/ellas/Uds.	d**u**rmieron	morir

O becomes I in the 3rd persons singular and plural.

	REPETIR	*(to repeat)*
yo	repetí	VERBS LIKE REPETIR
tú	repetiste	advertir; arrepentirse; competir; conseguir;
él/ella/Ud.	rep**i**tió	convertir; corregir; despedir; divertirse;
nosotros/as	repetimos	elegir; freír; impedir; medir; mentir; pedir;
vosotros/as	repetisteis	perseguir; preferir; reír; reñir; seguir;
ellos/ellas/Uds.	rep**i**tieron	sentir; servir; sonreir; sugerir; vestirse

(4) Some verbs have spelling changes.

√ Here is a spelling rule that influences the spelling of certain verbs:

> Spelling rule:
> The sound [s]/[th] is spelled: **z** before **a** and **o** (**z**anahoria, **z**oo)
> **c** before **e** and **i** (**c**erca, **c**ien)

Because of this rule, certain verbs undergo the following change:

Z changes to C before E.

The first person singular ending in the pretérito is **-é.** As indicated in the rule above, the sound [s]/[th] is spelled **c.**

comenzar: yo comen**c**é   VERBS LIKE COMENZAR
All verbs ending in **-zar.**

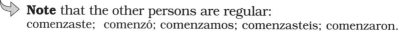 **Note** that the other persons are regular:
comenzaste; comenzó; comenzamos; comenzasteis; comenzaron.

142

√ Here is a rule that affects the letter **i.**

Change I to Y in the 3rd person singular and plural.

caer: él cayó; ellos cayeron
oir: él oyó; ellos oyeron

VERBS LIKE CAER
All **-er** and **-ir** verbs whose stem ends in a vowel, like: creer; leer; instruir; sustituir; etc.

√ Here are two rules of pronunciation which influence the spelling of certain verbs in the *pretérito* [see 134]:

Pronunciation of the letter C

The letter **c** is pronounced:
[s]/[th] before **e** and **i** (**ce**rca).
[k] before **o** and **a** (cer**ca**).

Pronunciation of the letter G

The letter **g** is pronounced:
[j] before **e** and **i** (**ge**ranio).
[g] before **o** and **a** (**go**l).

Because of this rule, we have the following change;

Because of this rule, we have the following change:

C changes to QU before E

Add U to G before E

The first person singular ending is **-é.** Verbs which have a **c** before the ending (bus**c**ar) raise a problem since, according to the rule above, the ending **-é** would change the pronunciation of the **c** from [k] to [s]/[th]. In order to avoid the change in pronunciation and to maintain the sound [k], we write **qu** instead of **c.**

The first person singular ending is **-é.** Verbs which have a **g** before the ending (ju**g**ar) raise a problem since, according to the rule above, the ending **-é** would change the pronunciation of **g** from [g] to [j]. In order to avoid this change in pronunciation and maintain the sound [g], we add **u** to the **g.**

buscar: yo bus**qu**é

jugar: yo jug**u**é

 Note that all the other persons are regular: buscaste; buscó, buscamos, buscasteis; buscaron

 Note that the other persons are regular: jugaste; jugó; jugamos; jugasteis; jugaron

VERBS LIKE BUSCAR
all verbs ending in **-car.**

VERBS LIKE JUGAR
all verbs ending in **-gar.**

143

The *imperfecto* describes an **incomplete process**. We call a process incomplete when we do not know when the process started, when (or if) it ended, or how many times it took place. We know that there was some duration, but there are no boundaries, the beginning and the end are irrelevant.

The *imperfecto* indicates the background information in a story.

It describes the circumstances in which some event occurred: description of the scenery, portrait of the characters and information on their feelings and emotions at the time of the events, explanations and additional information which can highlight the events.

> La puerta estaba abierta [description]. . . Había siete sillas alrededor de la mesa [description]. . . Las sillas y las camas eran pequeñas [description]. . . que era una muchacha aseada [portrait]. . . el suelo porque estaba sucio [explanation]. . . estaba muy cansada [explanation] [138].

The *imperfecto* expresses a habitual process.

It describes something that the subject used to do in the past. It is translated by the English *used to*. This habitual *imperfecto* can also serve as a background information in a story.

Íbamos a la playa todos los días.   *We used to go the beach every day.*

 Note that it has no connection with the moment of speech.
The *imperfecto* says nothing about the moment of speech. We do not know if the process is still true or still going on as we speak now.

El año pasado, él **tenía** un carro azul.   *Last year he had a blue car.*

We do not know whether he still has a blue car. The *imperfecto* does not indicate if the process of having a blue car ever ended.

144

REGULAR VERBS

(1) Find the stem.

Take the *infinitivo* and delete the *infinitivo* ending (1st group -**ar**; 2nd group -**er**; and 3rd group -**ir**):

Infinitivo: hablar	——	stem: **habl-**	*(to speak)*
Infinitivo: beber	——	stem: **beb-**	*(to drink)*
Infinitivo: vivir	——	stem: **viv-**	*(to live)*

(2) Add the following endings:

1st group (-ar):	**aba, abas, aba, ábamos, abais, aban**
2nd and 3rd groups:	**ía, ías, ía, íamos, íais, ían**

	HABLAR	BEBER	VIVIR
yo	hablaba	bebía	vivía
tú	hablabas	bebías	vivías
él/ella/Ud.	hablaba	bebía	vivía
nosotros/as	hablábamos	bebíamos	vivíamos
vosotros/as	hablabais	bebíais	vivíais
ellos/ellas/Uds.	hablaban	bebían	vivían

IRREGULAR VERBS

Three verbs are completely irregular.

	SER	IR	VER
yo	era	iba	veía
tú	eras	ibas	veías
él/ella/Ud.	era	iba	veía
nosotros/as	éramos	íbamos	veíamos
vosotros/as	erais	ibais	veíais
ellos/ellas/Uds.	eran	iban	veían

Uses of the *Presente Perfecto del Indicativo* √

The *presente perfecto* is a compound tense, formed with the auxiliary *haber* followed by the verb in the *participio*. Like all compound tenses, it is the tense of **completed actions**. A completed action is an action which has a beginning, a duration, and an end. We can show a completed action with the schema on the left, where two boundaries show the beginning and the end, and a straight line shows the duration.

The *presente perfecto* is used to describe a process completed before the moment of speech.

It started some time in the past, had a certain duration, and finished before now. It is related to the moment of speech: now we can see the result of this process.

Él **ha escrito** una carta.
(Now the letter is written.)
He has written a letter.

Juan **ha estado** enfermo.
(Now he is no longer sick, but we may be able to still see that he was.)
Juan has been sick.

El osito dijo: "Alguien **ha comido** mi sopa, **ha roto** mi silla y está durmiendo en mi cama."
Baby Bear said: "Someone has eaten my soup, has broken my chair, and is sleeping in my bed."

NOW

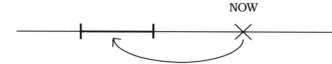

The *presente perfecto* describes a process started in the past and still going on now.

It usually comes with an adverb of time which indicates that the process is still going on or can still be repeated.

Siempre **he hecho** todo aquí.
I've always done everything here.
Siempre **he hecho** la tarea a tiempo.
I've always done my homework on time.

146

The *presente perfecto* is a **compound tense**. This means that the tense is formed with two words: the auxiliary or helping verb *haber*, and a special form of the verb called the *participio* [195].

To form the *presente perfecto,* we use the auxiliary *haber* in the *presente del indicativo* [129].

> *Presente perfecto* = ***haber* in the** *presente del indicativo* **+ Verb in the** *participio*

	CAMINAR *(to walk)*	**BEBER** *(to drink)*	**SALIR** *(to go out)*
yo	he caminado	he bebido	he salido
tú	has caminado	has bebido	has salido
él/ella/Ud.	ha caminado	ha bebido	ha salido
nosotros/as	hemos caminado	hemos bebido	hemos salido
vosotros/as	habéis caminado	habéis bebido	habéis salido
ellos/as/Uds.	han caminado	han bebido	han salido

La carta misteriosa

Ha abierto la puerta.
Se ha sentado en la silla.
Ha visto la carta.
Ha leído la carta.
Ha descubierto el secreto.
Ha escrito la repuesta.
Ha salido pronto de la casa.

USE

The *pasado perfecto* is a compound tense. Like all compound tenses, it is the tense of **completed actions,** actions which have a beginning, a duration, and an end [146].

> **The *pasado perfecto* is used to describe a process completed before a specific moment in the past.**

It started long ago in the past, had a certain duration, and finished before a specific moment in the past.

Él **había escrito** una carta.	*He had written a letter.*
Juan **había estado** enfermo.	*Juan had been sick.*
El osito dijo que alguien **había** comido su sopa, **había roto** su silla y estaba durmiendo en su cama.	*Baby Bear said that someone had eaten his soup, had broken his chair, and was sleeping in his bed.*

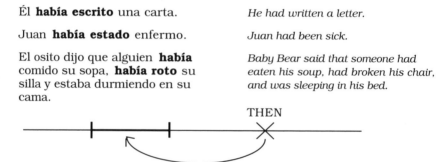

FORM

The *pasado perfecto* is a **compound tense.** It is formed with the auxiliary *haber* in the *imperfecto* [145] followed by the verb in the *participio* [195].

> *Pasado perfecto* = **haber** in the *imperfecto del indicativo* + **Verb in the** *participio*

	CAMINAR *(to walk)*	BEBER *(to drink)*	SALIR *(to go out)*
yo	había caminado	había bebido	había salido
tú	habías caminado	habías bebido	habías salido
él/ella/Ud.	había caminado	había bebido	había salido
nosotros/as	habíamos caminado	habíamos bebido	habíamos salido
vosotros/as	habíais caminado	habíais bebido	habíais salido
ellos/as/Uds.	habían caminado	habían bebido	habían salido

148

USE

The *pretérito perfecto* is a literary tense, rarely used in modern Spanish. It is explained here because you may encounter this tense in literary texts. It is a compound tense. Like all compound tenses, it is the tense of **completed actions,** actions which have a beginning, a duration, and an end [146].

> The *pretérito perfecto* **is used to describe a process completed before a specific moment in the past. It follows an expression of time, such as** *después que, cuando, en cuanto, luego que, tan pronto como...*

It started in the past, had a certain duration, and finished before a specific moment in the past.

> Desde que la gente hubo comido, mandé a Lope de Oviedo que...
> (*Naufragios*, Alvar Neuñez Cabeza de Vaca)
>
> *As soon as the company had eaten, I ordered Lope to....*

FORM

The *pretérito perfecto* is a **compound tense**. It is formed with the auxiliary *haber* in the *pretérito* [140 - 143] followed by the verb in the *participio* [195].

> *Pretérito perfecto* = *haber* **in the** *pretérito del indicativo* **+ Verb in the** *participio*

	CAMINAR *(to walk)*	**BEBER** *(to drink)*	**SALIR** *(to go out)*
yo	hube caminado	hube bebido	hube salido
tú	hubiste caminado	hubiste bebido	hubiste salido
él/ella/Ud.	hubo caminado	hubo bebido	hubo salido
nosotros/as	hubimos caminado	hubimos bebido	hubimos salido
vosotros/as	hubisteis caminado	hubisteis bebido	hubisteis salido
ellos/as/Uds.	hubieron caminado	hubieron bebido	hubieron salido

Uses of the *Futuro del Indicativo* √

> **The *futuro* is used to describe a process which will take place after the moment of speech.**

Yo **saldré** mañana.　　　　　*I will leave tomorrow.*
Si hace buen tiempo, yo **saldré.**　　*If the weather is nice, I'll go out.*

> **The *futuro* can express a possibility or probability.**

The *futuro* can also express probability. For instance, the speaker has reasons to assume that the process is taking place **now,** but is not sure about it. In English the words *maybe, probably* convey this meaning.

√　For verbs expressing a state *(estar, ser)*, we use the *futuro*:

Luis no está aquí; **estará** enfermo.　*Luis isn't here; he is probably sick.*

Luis usually misses classes when he is sick. Today Luis is not in class. So, we can assume that today he is sick.

¿Qué hora es? — **Serán** las nueve.　*What time is it? — It's probably 9 o'clock.*

√　For verbs expressing actions, we use the *futuro progresivo* [159] to express probability.

A esta hora, mi abuelo **estará**　　*At this time, my grandfather is probably*
jugando al dominó en el parque.　*playing dominoes in the park.*

> **The *futuro* can express a command.**

The *futuro* can be used to express a command, an absolute requirement.

Tomarás tus cosas y saldrás　　*You will pick up your things and get out*
de la casa.　　　　　　　　*of the house.*

Ud. **devolverá** el libro la semana　*You will return the book next week.*
próxima.

No **matarás.**　　　　　　　*You shall not kill.*

150

REGULAR VERBS

(1) Find the stem.

Take the *infinitivo:* the stem is the *infinitivo*.

1st group:	hablar
2nd group:	beber
3rd group:	vivir

(2) Add the endings.

The endings are those of *haber* in the *presente del indicativo* [129] with an accent on the vowel (except for *-emos).*

é, ás, á, emos, éis, án

	HABLAR	BEBER	VIVIR
yo	hablaré	beberé	viviré
tú	hablarás	beberás	vivirás
él/ella/Ud.	hablará	beberá	vivirá
nosotros/as	hablaremos	beberemos	viviremos
vosotros/as	hablaréis	beberéis	viviréis
ellos/ellas/Uds.	hablarán	beberán	vivirán

IRREGULAR VERBS

In the irregular forms, the stems change. However the endings are regular.

caber:	cabr–	*to fit*	poner:	pondr–	*to put*
decir:	dir–	*to say*	saber:	sabr–	*to know*
haber:	habr–	*to have*	salir:	saldr–	*to go out*
hacer:	har–	*to do*	tener:	tendr–	*to have*
querer:	querr–	*to want*	valer:	valdr–	*to cost*
poder:	podr–	*to be able to*	venir:	vendr–	*to come*

The *futuro perfecto* is a compound tense used for **completed processes.**

The *futuro perfecto* **is used to describe a process which is to be completed before some time in the future.**

It is equivalent to the English *will have* + Verb in the past participle.

Mañana a las 9, yo ya **habré hablado** con tu padre.	*Tomorrow at 9 o'clock, I will already have spoken with your father.*

The *futuro perfecto* **can express a completed possibility or probability.**

The *futuro perfecto* can also express probability. For instance, the speaker has reasons to assume that the process has taken place, but is not sure about it. In English the expressions *may have* + Verb in the past participle or *probably,* convey this meaning. It is not often used, however:

Luis no está aquí; no **habrá oído** el despertador esta mañana.	*Luis is not here; he probably did not hear his alarm clock this morning.*

Usually when Luis misses class, it's because he has not heard his alarm clock. Today he is not in class. So, we can assume that he has not heard his alarm clock. The *futuro perfecto* expresses this supposition.

The *futuro perfecto* **expresses a process completed at the moment of speech.**

With this meaning, it is used with an affective, emotional tone.

Este trabajo **habrá sido** mi mejor experiencia en Monterrey.	*This job will have been my best experience in Monterrey.*

152

The *futuro perfecto* is a compound tense. It is formed with the auxiliary *haber* in the *futuro* [151] followed by the verb in the *participio* form [195].

> ***Futuro perfecto* = *haber* in the *futuro* + Verb in the *participio***

	HABLAR	**BEBER**	**SALIR**
yo	habré hablado	habré bebido	habré salido
tú	habrás hablado	habrás bebido	habrás salido
él/ella/Ud.	habrá hablado	habrá bebido	habrá salido
nosotros/as	habremos hablado	habremos bebido	habremos salido
vosotros/as	habréis hablado	habréis bebido	habréis salido
ellos/ellas/Uds.	habrán hablado	habrán bebido	habrán salido

Regresaré a las cuatro.

A las cuatro, yo ya habré salido para la oficina.

> **The *futuro hipotético* (traditionally called *condicional*) is used to describe a process which took place after a specific moment in the past.**

The *futuro hipotético* describes a process which took place after a specific moment in the past. It has the meaning of a *futuro del pasado*.

Yo no pensaba que Luis **iría** al teatro sin avisarme.	*I didn't think that Luis would go to the theater without telling me.*
Margarita decía siempre que un día **sería** piloto de avión.	*Margarita always said that one day she would be a pilot.*

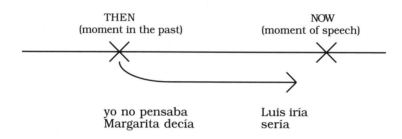

THEN
(moment in the past)

NOW
(moment of speech)

yo no pensaba
Margarita decía

Luis iría
sería

 Note that the *futuro hipotético (futuro del pasado)* does not have any connection with the moment of speech, with now.

Ricardo prometió que me **invitaría;** y me ha invitado.	*Ricardo promised that he would Invite me; and he did.*
Ricardo prometió que me **invitaría;** pero todavía no me ha invitado.	*Ricardo promised that he would invite me; but he has not done it yet.*

Whether or not the invitation has already occurred is not relevant for the use of the *futuro hipotético;* what is important is that the invitation was expected after the promise.

The first sentence says that the promise has been fulfilled and the invitation has already come. The second sentence, on the contrary, says that the invitation has not been done yet.

The *futuro hipotético* describes a process which depends on a condition.

The *futuro hipotético* describes a process which is not taking place now because it depends on some condition that is not being met.

> Si tuviera tiempo, **iría** de compras.   *If I had the time, I would go shopping.*

The process of going shopping depends on whether I have the time. Since this condition is not met (I do not have the time), the process of going shopping is not realized (I do not go shopping).

The condition is expressed by *si...*; but it can also be expressed in a different way:

> **Con tu ayuda,** yo lo conseguiría.   *With your help, I would succeed.*

The *futuro hipotético* can express a possibility or probability at a specific moment in the past.

The *futuro hipotético* can also express a probability. For instance, the speaker has reasons to assume that the process took place at a specific moment in the past (THEN), but is not sure about it. The English *may/ must have* + Verb in the past participle convey this meaning.

> Luis no estaba allá; **estaría** enfermo.   *Luis wasn't there; he was probably sick.*
>
> Eran las nueve ¿Dónde estaba Juan?   *It was nine o'clock. Where was Juan?*
> _ **Estaría** en su oficina.   _ *He must have been in his office.*

The *futuro hipotético* expresses a polite request.

> **Me gustaría** probarme estos zapatos.   *I would like to try these shoes on.*
> ¿**Podría** probarme estos zapatos?   *Could I try these shoes on?*

The uses of the *futuro hipotético* are parallel to those of the *futuro* [150].

155

REGULAR VERBS

(1) Find the stem.

The stem is the same as for the *futuro*: it is the *infinitivo*.

1st group:	hablar
2nd group:	beber
3rd group:	vivir

(2) Add the endings.

The endings are the endings of *haber* in the *imperfecto del indicativo* [145].

ía, ías, ía, íamos, íais, ían

	HABLAR	**BEBER**	**VIVIR**
yo	hablaría	bebería	viviría
tú	hablarías	beberías	vivirías
él/ella/Ud.	hablaría	bebería	viviría
nosotros/as	hablaríamos	beberíamos	viviríamos
vosotros/as	hablaríais	beberías	viviríais
ellos/ellas/Uds.	hablarían	beberían	vivirían

IRREGULAR VERBS

In the irregular forms, the stems change. However the endings are regular.

caber:	cabr-	*to fit*	poner:	pondr-	*to put*
decir:	dir-	*to say*	saber:	sabr-	*to know*
haber:	habr-	*to have*	salir:	saldr-	*to go out*
hacer:	har-	*to do*	tener:	tendr-	*to have*
querer:	querr-	*to want*	valer:	valdr-	*to cost*
poder:	podr-	*to be able to*	venir:	vendr-	*to come*

The *futuro hipotético perfecto* (traditionally called *condicional perfecto*) is a compound tense used for **completed processes**.

The *futuro hipotético perfecto* describes a completed process which depends on a condition.

The *futuro hipotético perfecto* describes a process which did not take place in the past because it depended on some condition that was not met.

Si hubiera tenido tiempo ayer, **habría ido** de compras.	*If I had had the time yesterday, I would have gone shopping.*

The shopping did not take place because the condition of having the time was not met (I did not have the time).

The condition is usually expressed by *si...*; but it can be expressed in other ways:

Sin tu ayuda, yo no habría podido terminar este trabajo.	*Without your help, I would not have been able to finish this work.*
Luis **habría venido;** pero no oyó el despertador esta mañana.	*Luis would have come; but he did not hear the alarm clock.*

Here the condition is not explicitly stated. We understand from the second part of the sentence that the condition is "if he had heard the alarm clock".

The *futuro hipotético perfecto* expresses a completed possibility or probability.

The *futuro hipotético perfecto* can also express a probability. For instance, the speaker has reasons to assume that the process took place, but is not sure about it. In English the expressions *may/must have* + Verb in the past participle convey this meaning.

Luis no vino; seguro que no **habría podido** alcanzar a tomar el tren.	*Luis is not here; he must not have been able to catch the train.*

The *futuro hipotético perfecto* is a compound tense. It is formed with the auxiliary *haber* in the *futuro hipotético* [156], followed by the verb in the *participio* [195].

Futuro hipotético perfecto =	**haber** in the *futuro hipotético* + **Verb** in the *participio*

	HABLAR	**BEBER**	**SALIR**
yo	habría hablado	habría bebido	habría salido
tú	habrías hablado	habrías bebido	habrías salido
él/ella/Ud.	habría hablado	habría bebido	habría salido
nosotros/as	habríamos hablado	habríamos bebido	habríamos salido
vosotros/as	habríais hablado	habríais bebido	habríais salido
ellos/ellas/Uds.	habrían hablado	habrían bebido	habrían salido

A process can be shown as an action in progress. We then use the progressive form. In Spanish, like in English, tenses have a regular and a progressive form. The progressive is formed with the auxiliary *estar* followed by the verb in the *gerundio* [202]. The English equivalent uses the auxiliary *to be* followed by the verb in the present participle.

Progressivo = *estar* + verb in the *gerundio*

SPANISH	ENGLISH
Estoy preparando la cena ahora mismo.	*I am preparing dinner right now.*
Estaba preparando la cena cuando anunciaron el acuerdo de paz en la radio.	*I was preparing dinner when they gave the news about the peace agreement on the radio.*
Mientras mis amigos paseaban por la plaza, yo **estuve preparando** la cena para la fiesta.	*While my friends were in the square taking a walk, I was preparing the holiday dinner.*
He estado preparando la cena desde las tres de la tarde.	*I have been preparing dinner since 3:00 P. M.*
Mañana a las seis de la tarde, **estaré preparando** la cena para la fiesta.	*Tomorrow at 6:00 P. M. I will be preparing the holiday dinner.*

 Note that the Spanish and English progressive forms are not always used in the exact same situations.

SPANISH uses the *presente*.   **ENGLISH** uses the progressive.

1. To give more strength to the statement of a future action or an intention to do something:

Mañana yo **me levanto** temprano.	*Tomorrow I am getting up early.*
Mañana **dejo** de fumar.	*Tomorrow I am quitting smoking.*

2. In situations when an on-going action is obvious and where the goal of this action is the focus; for instance, in letters, phone calls, etc.

Te **escribo** para decirte...	*I am writing you to tell you...*
Le **llamo** para informarle...	*I am calling you to inform you...*
Alzo mi copa en su honor.	*I am raising my glass in your honor.*

When we tell a story, we have to make a distinction between **the events** (what happened) and **background circumstances** (why, where, when, etc.). Building a story involves two steps:

(i) finding the sequence of events; and

(ii) adding information to highlight or explain these events. Here is an example of what to do.

Begin with a situation: the topic of your story.

We are surrounded by situations, in the news, in our everyday life, in everything we experience or read. Most of our communication deals with telling what happened. Accuracy in this important task is achieved through control of the two levels: events and background.

 Estrella brings home a frog she found on her way back from school.

Find the sequence of events.

1.	salir de la escuela	*get out of school*
2.	ver una rana debajo de un árbol.	*see a frog under a tree*
3.	tomar la rana en sus manos	*take the frog in her hands*
4.	correr a su casa	*run to her house*
5.	mostrar a su madre	*show it to her mother*
6.	su madre dice algo	*her mother says something*

All these events are in the *pretérito* [138 - 143].

> Estrella **salió** de la escuela / Ella **vio** una rana debajo de un árbol /
> **Tomó** la rana en sus manos / **Corrió** a su casa / **Mostró** la rana a su madre / Su madre le **dijo** algo.

Add the background.

We are going to enrich our story by adding a background to it. The background can come before the first event, interspersed with the events, and after the last event.

(1) Before the first event

A description of the scene will give the setting and prepare the reader for the coming events. For instance, we can start our story with a description of the beginning situation: when? where? who?, etc.

> Estrella **vivía** cerca de la escuela y le **gustaba** recoger piedras y flores cuando **regresaba** de la escuela. El martes, **hacía** fresco y el suelo **estaba** mojado. **Eran** las cuatro de la tarde.

The verbs above describe actions or states that are still going on during the events or that are habitual actions; therefore, the verbs are in the *imperfecto* [144 - 145].

(2) With each one of the events

We can provide explanations, clarifications, descriptions, and other background circumstances, which will help highlight the events of the story.

EVENTS	BACKGROUND
1. Salió de la escuela.	**estaba** contenta porque no **tenía** tarea
	√ *estaba* and *tenía* occur at the same time as *salió:* we use the *imperfecto.*
2. Vio una rana debajo del árbol	que su abuela **había plantado**
	√ *había plantado* took place before: we use the *pasado perfecto* [148]

161

EVENTS (continued)	**BACKGROUND** (continued)
3. Tomó la rana en sus manos	para **regalársela** a su madre y **pensando** que **estaría** muy alegre con el regalo

√ *regalar* follows the preposition *para:* we use the *infinitivo* [198];
√ *pensando* is an incomplete process and it has the same subject as *tomó:* we use the *gerundio* [200];
√ *estaría* will take place after: we use the *futuro hipotético* [154 - 156].

4. Corrió a su casa	porque **tenía** prisa

√ *tenía* takes place at the same time: we use the *imperfecto*.

5. Mostró la rana a su madre,	**apretándola** con sus dos manos

√ *apretándola* is an incomplete process and has the same subject as *mostró:* we use the *gerundio*.

6. Su madre dijo	que era un sapo

√ *era* adds identification: we use the *imperfecto*.

(3) At the end of the story

We can describe the ending situation.

Estrella **estaba** muy desilusionada porque su madre no **había apreciado** su regalo. La próxima vez le **iba a traer** flores.

√ *estaba* takes place at the same time as the last event: we use the *imperfecto;*
√ *había apreciado* took place before *estaba desilusionada:* we use the *pasado perfecto;*
√ *iba a traer* will take place in an immediate future with respect to this past situation because it tells us about her decision with respect to future gifts: we use the *futuro inmediato* in the past [136].

162

Wrap up your story.

Put all the sentences together into a cohesive text, adding transition words: expression of time, place, etc.

La rana que era un sapo

Estrella vivía cerca de la escuela y le gustaba recoger piedras y flores cuando regresaba de la escuela. El martes, hacía fresco y el suelo estaba mojado. Eran las cuatro de la tarde. Cuando Estrella salió de la escuela, estaba contenta porque no tenía tarea. Al cabo de un rato, ella vio una rana debajo del árbol que su abuela había plantado hacía años. Entonces, tomó la rana en sus manos para regalársela a su madre, pensando que estaría muy alegre con el regalo. Corrió rápidamente a su casa porque tenía prisa. Al llegar a su casa, le mostró la rana a su madre, apretándola

con sus dos manos. Al ver al animal, su madre le dijo que era un sapo. Estrella estaba muy desilusionada porque su madre no había apreciado su regalo. La próxima vez le iba a traer flores.

The frog that was a toad

Estrella lived close to the school and she liked to pick up stones and flowers on her way back from school. That Tuesday, the weather was chilly and the ground humid. It was four o'clock. When Estrella got out of school, she was happy because she had no homework. After a while she saw a frog under the tree that her grandmother had planted years ago. Then she took the frog in her hand to offer it to her mother, thinking that she would be happy with her present. She ran home fast because she was in a hurry. At home, she showed the frog to her mother, squeezing it in both hands. As soon as she saw the animal, her mother said that it was a toad. Estrella was very disappointed because her mother did not appreciate her present. Next time, she would bring her flowers.

163

THE SUBJUNTIVO

The *subjuntivo* is a mode which indicates the speaker's attitude towards the process described in the sentence [121 -122]. The *subjuntivo* presents the process, not as a statement of a situation which takes place in reality, but rather as the perspective of the speaker's subjective reaction to it. In a process described with the *subjuntivo*, what is important is not whether it happened or not, but what is the reaction in front of that process.

INDICATIVO	*SUBJUNTIVO*
Está lloviendo. *It is raining.*	Me alegro que **llueva.** *I am glad it's raining.*
The rain is presented as a true fact. One can check by looking outside if it is actually raining.	Whether it is actually raining or not is not relevant; what is important is my feeling about it, the fact that I am glad.

Because the *subjuntivo* always depends on a specific reaction, it will always be used in a subordinate clause: a clause which follows another clause and always begins with the word *que.*

1. The reality of the process in *subjuntivo* is irrelevant.
2. The *subjuntivo* always follows *que*.

Examples:

Siento que **hayas perdido** dinero.	*I am sorry that you lost money.*
Dudo que **hayas perdido** dinero.	*I doubt that you lost money.*
No creo que **pierdas** dinero.	*I don't think you'll lose money.*
¡Ojalá que no **pierdas** dinero!	*I wish you won't lose money.*
No es posible que **pierdas** dinero.	*It's not possible for you to lose money.*
Te presto mi bolsa para que no **pierdas** el dinero.	*I lend you my purse in order for you not to lose the money.*

In all these examples, the sentence does not focus on whether you lost or did not lose money, but rather on the different reactions to the possibility of losing money.

166

The conditions for the use of the *subjuntivo* are the following:

(i)   The *subjuntivo* is in **a subordinate clause** introduced by *que* or another specific conjunction.

(ii) The meaning of the verbs, adjectives, impersonal expressions, or conjunctions which trigger the *subjuntivo* involves a focus on the main clause (the clause which precedes *que*), more specifically on **the subject's reaction** to the process in the subordinate clause.

(iii) Whether **the process in the subordinate clause is real or not is irrelevant.**

We use the *subjuntivo* when the main clause carries the following meanings.

The first step in learning the *subjuntivo* consists in identifying the contexts which trigger the use of this mode. The following pages will give detailed lists of these contexts.

The Uses of the Subjuntivo √

┌─────────────────────────┐
│ **EXPRESSING FEELINGS** │
└─────────────────────────┘

Verbs:
alegrarse (de), celebrar, consolar, disgustar, doler, encantar, esperar, extrañarse, fastidiar, gustar, inquietarse, lamentar, molestar, odiar, quejarse, sentir, sorprenderse, temer, tener miedo.

Impersonal constructions:
es una lástima; es lamentable/extraño/justo/hora de que/ mejor/normal

Adjectives:
ser bueno/malo/magnífico/triste
estar alegre/contento/encantado/orgulloso/cansado/mal/ sorprendido

Conjunctions:
de miedo (de) que *(for fear that)*

Expression:
¡Lástima! *(it's a pity)*

 Pablo está enfermo.   *Pablo is sick.*

Yo siento que **esté** enfermo.   *I regret that he is sick.*

Sus padres temen que **sea** grave.   *His parents are afraid that his condition might be serious.*

¡Lástima que no **pueda** salir con sus amigos!   *It's a pity that he cannot go out with his friends.*

 Yo gané la lotería.   *I won the lottery.*

Mis amigos están contentos que yo **sea** rico.   *My friends are glad that I am rich.*

Unos esperan que yo les **dé** regalos.   *Some people expect me to give them presents.*

El director del banco se alegra de que yo **abra** una cuenta en su banco.   *The bank manager is happy that I am opening an account in his bank.*

168

EXPRESSING A WILL

(1) DESIRE, WISH

Verbs:
desear, esperar, oponerse, preferir, querer, tener ganas de

Conjunctions:
¡Ojalá que! *(I hope that)*; ¡Quién + Verb! *(How I wish...)*

Que   followed by a *subjuntivo* is also used to express a wish.

(2) NECESSITY

Verbs:
necesitar, tener

Impersonal constructions:
es necesario/preciso/importante; basta con; conviene; urge

(3) INTENTION, GOAL

Conjunctions:
para que *(in order that)*; a fin de que *(in order that)*; de forma/modo/manera que *(so that)*; antes de que *(before)*; en cuanto que *(as soon as)*; hasta que *(until)*

(4) SET EXPRESSIONS

¡Viva...!; ¡(Que) Dios te ayude/escuche/oiga!; ¡Que sea lo que sea! *(Come what may)*

 Hay una competición deportiva.   *There is a sports competition.*

¡Ojalá que **haga** buen tiempo!	*I wish the weather will be nice.*
¡Qué **gane** el mejor!	*May the best win!*
¡Quién **pudiera** ser campeón!	*I wish I could be a champion!*
¡Qué lo **pases** bien!	*I wish you have a good time.*

GIVING A COMMAND

(1) ADVICE, REQUEST, ORDER

Verbs:
aconsejar, animar a, decir, dejar, exigir, implorar, invitar, mandar, obligar, oponerse a, pedir, recomendar, rogar, sugerir, suplicar.

Que followed by a *subjuntivo* is used to express orders in the 3rd persons singular and plural *(ask her/him/them to +*Verb)

(2) PERMISSION

Verbs:
admitir, aprobar, autorizar, dejar, impedir, oponerse, permitir, prohibir, tolerar

 Una nueva estudiante llega a la escuela. El consejero habla con sus padres.

A new student comes to school.
A counselor speaks to her parents.

Les aconsejo que **consulten** con el director.

I advise you to discuss it with the principal.

El reglamento manda que los nuevos estudiantes **traigan** un certificado médico.

The regulations require that new students bring a medical certificate.

Se permite que **lleven** pantalones cortos.

It is permitted to wear shorts.

¡Digan a su hija que **venga** a verme!

Tell your daughter to come and see me.

 Un professor pregunta: "¿Qué debo decirle al nuevo estudiante?" El consejero responde.

A teacher asks:"What should I advise to the new student?"
The adviser answers.

¡Que **salga** temprano de la clase y me **traiga** su certificado médico!

Ask her to get out of class early and bring me her medical certificate!

¡Que **vaya** a la secretaría para recojer los libros!

Ask her to go to the secretary's office to pick up the books!

EXPRESSING NEGATION

(1) NEGATION, DENIAL

Verbs:
desmentir, negar, no demostrar, no querer decir

Conjunctions:
no sea que *(lest)*; sin que *(without)*

Impersonal constructions:
no es verdad; no hay nada/nadie/ningún/ninguna/quien

(2) OPPOSITION, CONCESSION, RESTRICTION

Conjunctions:
a menos que *(unless)*; a no ser que *(unless)*; a pesar de que *(in spite of)*; aunque *(although)*; aun cuando *(even though)*; basta (con) que *(it is enough)*

Construction doubling the verb:
hagan lo que hagan *(whatever they do)* [All verbs can be used in this construction.]

 Esta noche, dos ladrones han asaltado un banco. La policía ha detenido a un sospechoso, llamado Ruiz Rubio.

Last night, two burglars broke into a bank. The police has arrested a suspect named Ruiz Rubio.

Ruiz Rubio niega que **haya participado** en el asalto.

Ruiz Rubio denies that he has taken part in the hold-up.

Su parecido con el ladrón no prueba que **sea** él.

The fact that he resembles the burglar does not prove that he is the one.

No hay nadie que **pueda** identificarle.

There is nobody who can identify him.

Tendrá problemas, a menos que **pruebe** su inocencia.

He will have problems unless he proves his innocence.

EXPRESSING DOUBT

(1) DOUBT

Verbs:
dudar, ignorar, no creer, no pensar

Adverbs:
acaso *(perhaps)*; quizá(s) *(maybe)*; posiblemente *(possibly)*; tal vez *(perhaps)*

Impersonal construction:
es difícil

(2) POSSIBILITY

Impersonal constructions:
es (im)posible/(im)probable; puede (ser)

(3) CONDITION, SUPPOSITION

Conjunctions:
a condición de que *(on condition that)*; a menos que *(unless)*; a no ser que *(unless)*; como *(if)*; como no *(if... not)*; con tal (de) que *(on condition that)*; cuando *(whenever)*; (en) caso (de) que *(in case)*; no sea que *(in case)*; suponiendo que *(assuming that)*; **si (see the following pages)**; siempre cuando *(provided that)*

 Un turista ha desaparecido en la visita a las pirámides.

A tourist has disappeared during a visit to the pyramides.

Es posible que **se haya perdido.**

It is possible that he got lost.

Tal vez **regrese** directamente al hotel.

Maybe he will go directly to the hotel.

Él ignoraba que **fuera** peligroso dejar al grupo y andar solo.

He did not know that it was dangerous to leave the group and go by himself.

The Uses of the Subjuntivo with "Si" √

> **The word *si* is used with the *subjuntivo* to introduce a hypothesis.**

A hypothesis is a condition which has not been met. A sentence expressing a hypothesis usually contains two parts: the condition and the consequence. The consequence depends on whether the condition really takes place. In a hypothetical sentence, both condition and consequence are not accomplished.

Si...

Si yo fuera rico,...
Si yo tuviera suerte,...
Si yo pudiera volar,...
Si hubiera nacido en la Edad de Piedra,...
Si hubiéramos comprendido,...

CONDITION

Si yo **fuera** rico,
If I were rich,

Si yo **tuviera** suerte,
If I were lucky,

Si yo **pudiera** volar,
If I could fly,

Si **hubiera nacido** en la Edad de Piedra,
If I had been born in the Stone Age,

Si **hubiéramos comprendido** el problema,

If we had understood the problem,

CONSEQUENCE

viajaría por el mundo.
I would travel around the world.

ganaría la lotería.
I would win the lottery.

viviría con las águilas.
I would live with the eagles.

habría vivido en cuevas.
I would have lived in caves.

habríamos encontrado la solución.
we would have found the solution.

Three cases are possible, depending on when the condition and the consequence take place.

Si + *Imperfecto del subjuntivo* [182 - 183]	***Futuro hipotético*** [154 - 156]
The condition is not met now, or is highly improbable in the future.	The consequence is not realized now, nor later, because the condition is not met.

Si **fuera** rico, **viajaría** a todos los países del mundo. — *If I were rich, I would travel all over the world.*

This sentence means: I am not rich; therefore, I do not travel all over the world.

Si **hablaras** lenguas extranjeras, **tendrías** un trabajo más interesante. — *If you spoke foreign languages, you would have a more interesting job.*

This sentence means: you do not speak foreign languages; therefore, you don't have a more interesting job now.

Si + *Pasado perfecto del subjuntivo* [184 - 185]	***Futuro hipotético perfecto*** [157 - 158]
The condition was not met in the past.	The consequence was not accomplished in the past because the condition was not met.

Si Mozart no **hubiera muerto** tan joven, **habría compuesto** muchas más óperas. — *If Mozart had not died so young, he would have composed many more operas.*

This sentence means: Mozart died young; therefore, he did not write many more operas.

Si **hubiera tenido** dinero el año pasado, **habría ido** a Chile. — *If I had had money last year, I would have gone to Chile.*

This sentence means: last year I had no money; therefore, I did not go to Chile.

 Note that this sentence has no connection with my situation today. It does not say whether or not I have money or I am traveling today.

174

Si + *Pasado perfecto del subjuntivo* [184 - 185]	*Futuro hipotético* [154 - 156]
The condition was not met in the past.	The consequence is not accomplished now because the condition was not met then.

Si **hubiera estudiado** en mi juventud, yo ahora **sería** un gran académico.	*If I had studied in my youth, I would now be a great scholar.*

This sentence means: when I was young, I did not study; therefore, now, I am not a great scholar. In this sentence the condition was not met in the past; but the consequence is in the present.

Si **hubieras comprado** un buen carro, ahora no **estarías** en la carretera con avería.	*If you had bought a good car, you would not be stuck now on the road with a breakdown.*

This sentence means: you did not buy a good car; therefore, now, you are stuck with a breakdown.

The expression *como si* is followed by the *imperfecto* or *pasado perfecto del subjuntivo* and means *as if*.

After the expression *como si (as if)*, we use:

(1) the *imperfecto del subjuntivo* for a process which takes place at the same time as the main process:

Habla/habló como si **fuera** médico.	*He speaks/spoke as if he were a doctor.*

(2) the *pasado perfecto del subjuntivo* for a process which has been completed before the main process.

Habla/habló como si **hubiera recibido** un mensaje secreto.	*He speaks/spoke as if he had received a secret message.*

175

The *subjuntivo* **has four tenses.**

The use of the tenses of the *subjuntivo* depends on two factors:

(i) the tense of the main verb;

(ii) the relationship of the verb in the *subjuntivo* to the main verb: before, at the same time, or after the process expressed by the main verb.

We use the *presente del subjuntivo* **in the following situation:**

If the main verb is in	**and if the process in the**
√ the *presente* √ or in any other tense related to the moment of speech (*presente perfecto, futuro,* *futuro perfecto,* or *imperativo*)	*subjuntivo* is located at the same time or after the main process.

Then the verb is in the *presente del subjuntivo.*

 Luisa se prepara para ir de vacaciones la semana próxima. Su amiga le habla.

Luisa is going on a vacation trip next week. Her friend talks to her.

Deseo que **hagas** un buen viaje y que me **compres** muchos regalos.

I wish you have a good trip and that you buy me a lot of presents.

Isabel ha pedido que la **recojas** en el hotel.

Isabel asked that you pick her up at the hotel.

Regaré las flores hasta que **regreses.**

I will water the flowers until you come back.

Es importante que no **olvides** tu pasaporte.

It is important that you do not forget your passport.

176

REGULAR VERBS

(1) Find the stem.

Take the *presente del indicativo,* 1st person singular, and delete the ending.

presente indicativo:	hablo	——	stem:	**habl-**
presente indicativo:	bebo	——	stem:	**beb-**
presente indicativo:	vivo	——	stem:	**viv-**

(2) Add the following endings:

1rst group (-ar)	**e, es, e, emos, éis, en**
2nd group (-er)	**a, as, a, amos, áis, an**
3rd group (-ir)	**a, as, a, amos, áis, an**

	HABLAR	**BEBER**	**VIVIR**
yo	hable	beba	viva
tú	hables	bebas	vivas
él/ella/Ud.	hable	beba	viva
nosotros/as	hablemos	bebamos	vivamos
vosotros/as	habléis	bebáis	viváis
ellos/ellas/Uds.	hablen	beban	vivan

IRREGULAR VERBS

(1) -ar and -er verbs which have stem vowel changes in the *presente del indicativo* follow the same irregularities in the *presente del subjuntivo.*

PRESENTE INDICATIVO		PRESENTE SUBJUNTIVO	
pienso	pensamos	piense	pensemos
piensas	pensáis	pienses	penséis
piensa	piensan	piense	piensen

177

(2) -ir verbs which have stem vowel changes in the *presente del indicativo* have an additional irregularity.

Presente del indicativo	*Presente del subjuntivo*
E becomes **IE** in all persons except *nosotros/vosotros (sentir* [129]).	(i) same change and (ii) **E** becomes **I** for *nosotros/vosotros.*

sie nto	sentimos	sie nta	si ntamos
sie ntes	sentís	sie ntas	si ntáis
sie nte	sie nten	sie nta	sie ntan

Presente del indicativo	*Presente del subjuntivo*
O becomes **UE** in all persons except *nosotros/vosotros (dormir* [130]).	(i) same change and (ii) **O** becomes **U** for *nosotros/vosotros.*

due rmo	dormimos	due rma	du rmamos
due rmes	dormís	due rmas	du rmáis
due rme	due rmen	due rma	due rman

Presente del indicativo	*Presente del subjuntivo*
E becomes **I** in all persons except *nosotros/vosotros (repetir* [130]).	**E** becomes **I** (all persons)

repi to	repetimos	repi ta	repi tamos
repi tes	repetís	repi tas	repi táis
repi te	repi ten	repi ta	repi tan

(3) **Some verbs are irregular in the** *presente del subjuntivo.*

HABER	IR	ESTAR	SER
haya	vaya	esté	sea
hayas	vayas	estés	seas
haya	vaya	esté	sea
hayamos	vayamos	estemos	seamos
hayáis	vayáis	estéis	seáis
hayan	vayan	estén	sean

DAR	SABER	CABER
dé	sepa	quepa
des	sepas	quepas
dé	sepa	quepa
demos	sepamos	quepamos
deis	sepáis	quepáis
den	sepan	quepan

Here are some examples:

El presidente:

Estoy optimista a pesar de que los problemas del país **sean** numerosos.

I am optimistic although the problems in the country are numerous.

El profesor:

Yo quiero que cada estudiante **repita** las frases, las **escriba** en su cuaderno, **vaya** a casa para revisarlas y **sepa** la lección perfectamente.

I want each student to repeat the sentences, write them down in the notebook, go home to review, and know the lesson perfectly.

El estudiante:

Me gustaría que el profesor me **dé** una buena nota.

I would like the teacher to give me a good grade.

We use the *presente perfecto del subjuntivo* **to express a completed process in the following situation:**

If the main verb is in √ the *presente* √ or in any other tense related to the moment of speech *(presente perfecto, futuro,* *futuro perfecto,* or *imperativo)*	**and if the process in the** *subjuntivo* has been completed before the main process.

Then the verb is in the *presente perfecto del subjuntivo.*

 Luisa está de regreso de vacaciones. Su amiga le habla.

Luisa is back from her vacation. Her friend talks to her.

Me alegro que **hayas hecho** un buen viaje y que me **hayas comprado** muchos regalos.

I am glad that you had a good trip and that you bought me a lot of presents.

¿Comó es posible que no **hayas encontrado** a mi amigo Fernando?

How is it possible that you have not seen my friend Fernando?

¡No estés decepcionada de que no **hayas podido** visitar muchos museos!

Don't be disappointed that you have not been able to visit a lot of museums.

Espero que **hayas tomado** muchas fotos.

I hope you have taken many pictures.

Iré a verte en cuanto **hayas descansado** del viaje.

I will go and visit you as soon as you have rested from your trip.

The Forms of the *Presente Perfecto del Subjuntivo* √

The *presente perfecto del subjuntivo* is a compound tense formed with the auxiliary *haber* in the *presente del subjuntivo* [179] followed by the *participio* [195].

> *Presente perfecto del subjuntivo* = ***haber*** **in the** *presente del subjuntivo* + **Verb in the** *participio*

	HABLAR	**BEBER**	**SALIR**
yo	haya hablado	haya bebido	haya salido
tú	hayas hablado	hayas bebido	hayas salido
él/ella/Ud.	haya hablado	haya bebido	haya salido
nosotros/as	hayamos hablado	hayamos bebido	hayamos salido
vosotros/as	hayáis hablado	hayáis bebido	hayáis salido
ellos/ellas/Uds.	hayan hablado	hayan bebido	hayan salido

 Note that the *presente perfecto del subjuntivo* **and the** *presente perfecto del indicativo* **are similar in form and meaning.**

(1) Both are formed in the same way:

> *Presente perfecto subj.* = *Haber* in *pres. subj.* + Verb in *participio*
> *Presente perfecto indic.* = *Haber* in *pres. indic.* + Verb in *participio*

(2) Both express a process which has been completed before a specific moment (moment of speech).

 Note also that the *presente perfecto del subjuntivo* **and** *the presente perfecto del indicativo* **are used in different contexts.**

The difference is in the main verb or the conjunction: the *indicativo* and the *subjuntivo* are connected to different types of verbs and conjunctions.

Siento que **haya llegado** tarde.   *I regret that he came late.*
Te aseguro que **ha llegado** tarde.   *I assure you that he came late.*

In both sentences *llegar* is a completed process. But *sentir* requires the *subjuntivo* whereas *asegurar* requires the *indicativo*.

We use the *imperfecto del subjuntivo* in the following situations:

The main verb is related to a past moment and the process in *subjuntivo* takes place at the same time.

If the main verb is in	and if the process in the
√ the *pretérito, imperfecto* √ or in any other tense related to a past moment (*pasado perfecto, futuro hipotético, futuro hipotético perfecto*)	*subjuntivo* is located at the same time or after the main process.

Then the verb is in the *imperfecto del subjuntivo*.

 Picasso pintó el cuadro "Guernica" durante la Guerra Civil española (1936-1939).

Picasso painted "Guernica" during the Spanish Civil War.

El deseaba que el cuadro **sirviera** de testimonio.

He wished his painting to serve as a testimony.

El quería que el público **sintiera** el horror de la guerra y **reaccionara** contra el fascismo.

He wanted the public to feel the horror brought about by war and to react against fascism.

The *imperfecto del subjuntivo* is used after *si* in sentences expressing hypothesis [173 - 174] and after *como si* [175].

Si Picasso **estuviera** vivo hoy, tendría más de cien años.

If Picasso were alive today, he would be more than 100 years old.

Sonia hablaba del cuadro como si **fuera** un crítico de arte.

Sonia was speaking about the painting as though she was an art critic.

The *imperfecto del subjuntivo* is used to express an event in the past.

Siento que no **vinieras** al partido.

I regret that you didn't come to the game.

182

To form the *imperfecto del subjuntivo:*

(1) Find the stem.

Take the 3rd person plural of the *pretérito del indicativo,* and delete the ending **-on.**

pretérito indicativo: hablaron	——	stem:	**hablar-**
pretérito indicativo: bebieron	——	stem:	**bebier-**
pretérito indicativo: vivieron	——	stem:	**vivier-**
pretérito indicativo: dijeron	——	stem:	**dijer-**
pretérito indicativo: tuvieron	——	stem:	**tuvier-**

(2) Add the following endings:

a, as, a, amos, ais, an

The first person plural takes an accent on the last syllable of the stem: **habláramos, bebiéramos, viviéramos**

	HABLAR	BEBER	VIVIR
yo	hablara	bebiera	viviera
tú	hablaras	bebieras	vivieras
él/ella/Ud.	hablara	bebiera	viviera
nosotros/as	habláramos	bebiéramos	viviéramos
vosotros/as	hablarais	bebierais	vivierais
ellos/ellas/Uds.	hablaran	bebieran	vivieran

 Note that there is another form of the *imperfecto del subjuntivo,* which is a rarely used, a literary form. To form this tense, change **ra** to **se.** Here is the conjugation:

	HABLAR	BEBER	VIVIR
yo	hablase	bebiese	viviese
tú	hablases	bebieses	vivieses
él/ella/Ud.	hablase	bebiese	viviese
nosotros/as	hablásemos	bebiésemos	viviésemos
vosotros/as	hablaseis	bebieseis	vivieseis
ellos/ellas/Uds.	hablasen	bebiesen	viviesen

The Uses of the *Pasado Perfecto del Subjuntivo* √

We use the *pasado perfecto del subjuntivo* **to express a completed process in the following situation:**

If the main verb is in	**and if the process in the**
√ the *pretérito, imperfecto*	*subjuntivo* has been completed
√ or in any other tense	before the main process.
related to a past moment	
(pasado perfecto, futuro hipotético,	
futuro hipotético perfecto)	

Then the verb is in the *pasado perfecto del subjuntivo.*

 Luisa fue a estudiar a Quito el año pasado.

Luisa went to study in Quito last year.

Al llegar a Quito, Luisa **se** alegró de que su profesor le **hubiera recomendado** este viaje.

When she arrived in Quito, she was glad that her professor had recommended her this trip.

Sentía que su amigo no **hubiera venido.**

She regretted that her friend had not come.

The *pasado perfecto del subjuntivo* **is used after** *si* **in sentences expressing hypothesis [173 - 174] and after** *como si* **[175].**

Si el científico **hubiera conocido** el uso de su invento, no lo habría revelado.

If the scientist had known how his invention would be used, he would not have revealed it.

Sonia hablaba del cuadro como si **hubiera estudiado** arte toda su vida.

Sonia spoke about the painting as though she had studied art all her life.

184

The *pasado perfecto del subjuntivo* is a compound tense formed with the auxiliary *haber* in the *imperfecto del subjuntivo* [183] followed by the *participio* [195].

> *Pasado perfecto del subjuntivo* = **haber** in the *imperfecto del subjuntivo* + **Verb in the** *participio*

	HABLAR	**BEBER**	**SALIR**
yo	hubiera hablado	hubiera bebido	hubiera salido
tú	hubieras hablado	hubieras bebido	hubieras salido
él/ella/Ud.	hubiera hablado	hubiera bebido	hubiera salido
nosotros/as	hubiéramos hablado	hubiéramos bebido	hubiéramos salido
vosotros/as	hubierais hablado	hubierais bebido	hubierais salido
ellos/ellas/Uds.	hubieran hablado	hubieran bebido	hubieran salido

The second form of the *imperfecto del subjuntivo* of *haber* can also be used: hubiese, hubieses, hubiese, hubiésemos, hubieseis, hubiesen.

 Note that the *pasado perfecto del subjuntivo* **and the** *pasado perfecto del indicativo* **are similar in form and meaning.**

(1) Both are formed in the same way:

> *Pasado perfecto subj.* = *Haber* in *imperfecto subj.* + Verb in *participio*
> *Pasado perfecto indic.* = *Haber* in *imperfecto indic.* + Verb in *participio*

(2) Both express a process which has been completed before a moment in the past.

 Note also that the *pasado perfecto del subjuntivo* **and the** *pasado perfecto del indicativo* **are used in different contexts.**

The difference is in the main verb or the conjunction: the *indicativo* and the *subjuntivo* are connected to different types of verbs and conjunctions.

Sentí que **hubiera llegado** tarde.	*I regretted that he had come late.*
Estaba seguro de que **había llegado** tarde.	*I was sure that he had come late.*

In both sentences *llegar* is a completed process. But *sentir* requires the *subjuntivo* whereas *estar seguro* requires the *indicativo*.

185

In clauses which begin with *que*, we can find the *subjuntivo* or the *indicativo*. The environments that require the *subjuntivo* are subjective (the truth of the process in the *subjuntivo* is not relevant) whereas the environments that require the *indicativo* imply that the process is true.

SUBJUNTIVO	*INDICATIVO*
√ **SUBJECTIVE EXPRESSIONS:** feelings, desire, will, order, permission, request, doubt, necessity, possibility, negation, intention, goal, opposition, concession, supposition, condition.	√ **VERBS OF COMMUNICATION:** afirmar, asegurar, contar, declarar, decir, explicar, pretender √ **VERBS OF INTELLECT AND JUDGMENT:** concluir, deducir, estimar, juzgar, notar, observar, saber
√ **no creer/pensar +** *subjuntivo* (imply a doubt) No creo que Ana venga. *I don't think that Ana will come.*	√ **creer/pensar +** *indicativo* (imply judgment) Creo que Ana vendrá. *I think that Ana will come.*
√ **decir +** *subjuntivo* *(to command)* Te digo que vengas pronto. *I ask you to come soon.*	√ **decir +** *indicativo* *(to say, to tell)* Te digo que él vendrá pronto. *I tell you that he'll come soon.*
√ **comprender +** *subjuntivo* *(to understand or emphasize)* En esta situación, comprendo que esté Ud. enojado. *In this situation, I understand that you would be angry.*	√ **comprender +** *indicativo* *(to understand, realize)* Al verle a Ud., comprendí que estaba enojado. *When I saw you, I realized that you were angry.*

IN A RELATIVE CLAUSE

A **relative clause** is a clause that is related to a noun [96]. Some relative clauses can contain either the *subjuntivo* or the *indicativo*, depending on their meaning.

(1) The relative clause follows a superlative or an expression that selects one individual or thing among others: *el primer(o), el último, el único, el mejor, el peor, el más* + Adjective. The verb in the relative clause is in the *subjuntivo* when it emphasizes the superlative, and in the *indicativo* when it states a fact.

> **The *subjuntivo* emphasizes the superlative; the *indicativo* describes a fact.**

Es el mejor libro que **se haya publicado** jamás.	*It is the best book that was ever published.*

This sentence is pronounced with a stress on *el mejor*, and usually contains an expression like *jamás* to emphasize the superlative. Compare with:

Es el mejor libro que se **ha publicado** este año.	*It is the best book published this year.*

(2) The relative clause follows verbs such as *buscar, querer,* or negative and interrogative constructions which indicate an intention or a doubt. The verb in the relative clause is in the *subjuntivo* to emphasize the intention, or in the *indicativo* to state a fact.

> **The *subjuntivo* emphasizes the intention; the *indicativo* describes something which does exist.**

Yo busco un secretario que **hable** tres lenguas.	*I am looking for a secretary who can speak three languages.*

This means that it is my intention to find such a secretary; but I do not know if there is such a person on the job market. Compare with:

Yo busco al secretario que **habla** tres lenguas.	*I am looking for the secretary who speaks three languages.*

This means: I know that there is such a person in the office and I'm looking for that person.

187

MAIN CLAUSE

presente	espero
presente perfecto	he esperado
futuro	esperaré
futuro perfecto	habrá esperado
imperativo	¡espera!

COMPLETED BEFORE

presente perfecto del subjuntivo
que Juan haya aprobado
that Juan has passed the exam
que se haya ocupado de la casa
that he took care of the house

INCOMPLETE: AT THE SAME TIME OR AFTER

presente del subjuntivo
que Juan apruebe
that Juan passes the exam
que se ocupe de la casa
that he takes care of the house

MAIN CLAUSE

pretérito	esperé
imperfecto	esperaba
pasado perfecto	había esperado
futuro hipotético	esperaría
futuro hipotético perfecto	habría esperado

COMPLETED BEFORE

pasado perfecto del subjuntivo
que Juan hubiera aprobado
that Juan had passed the exam
que se hubiera ocupado de la casa
that he had taken care of the house

INCOMPLETE: AT THE SAME TIME OR AFTER

imperfecto del subjuntivo
que Juan aprobara
that Juan passes the exam
que se ocupara de la casa
that he takes care of the house

188

THE IMPERATIVO

USE

The *imperativo* expresses a request or command.

Like the *subjuntivo*, the **imperativo** expresses the speaker's desire or will. This is done in the form of a request or a command.

¡**Sal** antes de que yo regrese!   *Go out before I come back!*
¡**Dáme** el libro!   *Give me the book!*

FORMS OF REQUEST

The *imperativo* is used only for *tú, Ud., nosotros/as, vosotros/as, Uds.*

Since the *imperativo* is a form for requests, it will be used only in the persons to whom the subject can address a request: the listener or listeners.

tú, Ud.	for the singular
vosotros, Uds.	for the plural
nosotros/as	for the group including the speaker and the listeners

We can address an indirect request to a 3rd person.

The 3rd person is the person who is not participating in the conversation. The speaker can express his/her desire for that person to do something. In this case the form ***que + subjuntivo*** is used.

¡**Que venga**!   *Ask him to come!*
¡**Que salgan** inmediatamente!   *Ask them to leave immediately!*

The *imperativo* is conjugated without the subject pronouns.

We will therefore write the pronouns in parenthesis in the conjugation charts.

190

REGULAR CONJUGATION

The affirmative forms are the following.

tú:	Delete the final **-s** of the 2nd pers. sing. of the *presente del indicativo*.
vosotros:	Change the final **-r** of the *infinitivo* into **-d**.
Ud./Uds./nosotros:	Same as the *presente del subjuntivo*.

	COMPRAR	**BEBER**	**SUBIR**
(tú)	compra	bebe	sube
(Ud.)	compre	beba	suba
(nosotros/as)	compremos	bebamos	subamos
(vosotros/as)	comprad	bebed	subid
(Uds.)	compren	beban	suban

The negative forms of the *imperativo* are the same as the forms of the *presente del subjuntivo*.

	COMPRAR	**BEBER**	**SUBIR**
(tú)	no compres	no bebas	no subas
(Ud.)	no compre	no beba	no suba
(nosotros/as)	no compremos	no bebamos	no subamos
(vosotros/as)	no compréis	no bebáis	no subáis
(Uds.)	no compren	no beban	no suban

IRREGULAR AFFIRMATIVE IMPERATIVO

√ The following verbs are irregular in the second person singular, **tú:**

decir:	**di**	*say*		salir:	**sal**	*go out*
hacer:	**haz**	*do*		ser:	**sé**	*know*
ir:	**ve**	*go*		tener:	**ten**	*have*
poner:	**pon**	*put*		venir:	**ven**	*come*

√ The verb *ir* is irregular in the first person plural, **nosotros/as:**

ir: **vamos** *let's go*

Vamos also means *let's* when used before a verb, as in *vamos a cantar (let's sing)*.

191

PLACEMENT OF REFLEXIVE PRONOUNS

> In the *imperativo*, the reflexive pronouns are attached to the verb endings in the affirmative form; but they come before the verb in the negative form.

Affirmative *imperativo*:	levántate, levántese	*get up*
Negative *imperativo*:	no te levantes, no se levante	*do not get up*

CHANGES IN THE FORMS OF THE *IMPERATIVO* DUE TO THE PRONOUNS

(1) **In the 1st and 2nd persons plural (*nosotros/as* and *vosotros/as*),** the **-s** and **-d** endings are deleted before the reflexive pronoun in the affirmative *imperativo*.

Nosotros/as	Delete **-s** ending before reflexive pronoun
Vosotros/as	Delete **-d** ending before reflexive pronoun

Affirmative *imperativo*:	preparémonos; preparáos	*let's get ready*
Negative *imperativo* : (undergoes no change)	no nos preparemos, no os preparéis	

(2) **In the 2nd persons plural (*vosotros/as*),** the *infinitivo* ending **-r** is sometimes used before the reflexive pronoun: prepara**r**os.

PREPARARSE

	AFFIRMATIVE	NEGATIVE
(tú)	prepárate	no te prepares
(Ud.)	prepárese	no se prepare
(nosotros/as)	preparémonos	no nos preparemos
(vosotros/as)	prepara(r)os	no os preparéis
(Uds.)	prepárense	no se preparen

THE NON-CONJUGATED MODES

The *participio* is a form of the verb which is not conjugated. There are three main uses of the *participio*.

The *participio* is the form of the verb which comes after auxiliary *haber*.

The *participio* is the form of the verb which is used to form all compound tenses. It comes after the auxiliary *haber* [107].

Yo he **recibido** dinero.	*I received money.*
No había **olvidado** la llave.	*He had not forgotten the key.*
No habría **venido** sin tí.	*I wouldn't have come without you.*

The *participio* is used as an adjective after the verb *estar*.

It can be used after the verb *estar* as an adjective to describe a person or a thing.

Si no duermes, estarás **cansado.**	*If you don't sleep, you'll be tired.*
La puerta está **abierta.**	*The door is open.*
El río estaba **contaminado.**	*The river was contaminated.*

The *participio* is used in passive sentences after the auxiliary *ser*.

In passive sentences, the *participio* follows the passive auxiliary *ser*. It is just like the English passive where the past participle follows the passive auxiliary *to be*.

Esta casa fue **renovada** hace diez años.	*This house was renovated ten years ago.*
Mi carta será **publicada** en el periódico.	*My letter will be published in the newspaper.*
Los resultados del concurso serán **anunciados** por la radio.	*The results of the competition will be announced on the radio.*

REGULAR FORMS

(1) Find the stem.

Take the *infinitivo* and delete the *infinitivo* ending (1st group -**ar**; 2nd group -**er**; and 3rd group -**ir**):

Infinitivo:	hablar	——	stem:	**habl-**	*(to speak)*
Infinitivo:	beber	——	stem:	**beb-**	*(to drink)*
Infinitivo:	vivir	——	stem:	**viv-**	*(to live)*

(2) Add the following endings:

Verbs in -**ar**: -**ado**	Verbs in -**er**: -**ido**	Verbs in -**ir**: -**ido**
hablado	bebido	pedido
lavado	creído	salido
preparado	ofrecido	vivido

IRREGULAR FORMS

In the irregular forms the stem and the ending change. Here is a list of the most frequently used *participios*, in alphabetical order:

abrir:	**abierto**	*to open*
cubrir:	**cubierto**	*to cover*
decir:	**dicho**	*to say*
descubrir:	**descubierto**	*to discover*
describir:	**descrito**	*to describe*
devolver:	**devuelto**	*to return, give back*
disponer:	**dispuesto**	*to dispose*
encubrir:	**encubierto**	*to hide*
envolver:	**envuelto**	*to wrap up*
escribir:	**escrito**	*to write*
freir:	**frito**	*to fry*
hacer:	**hecho**	*to do*
morir:	**muerto**	*to die*
poner:	**puesto**	*to put*
resolver:	**resuelto**	*to solve*
romper:	**roto**	*to break*
ver:	**visto**	*to see*
volver:	**vuelto**	*to return*

The *infinitivo* is a form of the verb which is not conjugated. It is the name of the verb, the form we find in the dictionary.

The *infinitivo* can be used as the subject of a sentence.

Dormir es necesario.
Bostezar en público es grosero.

Sleeping is necessary.
To yawn in public is ill-mannered.

The *infinitivo* can be used as the object of a verb.

√ **The *infinitivo* immediately follows the verb:**

Yo creo **comprender.**
Decidimos **ir** juntos a la playa.

I think I understand
We decided to go together to the beach.

√ **The *infinitivo* comes after the conjunction *que*** in the expressions
hay que (it is necessary that), and *tener que (to have to).*

Hay que **leer** el periódico.
Tengo que **salir** inmediatamente.

It is necessary to read the newspaper.
I must leave immediately.

√ **With verbs expressing movement from one place to another,** we use
a* + *infinitivo to express the goal *(in order to):* ir, bajar, entrar,
pasar, salir, subir, venir, volver [231].

¡Pasa a **charlar** un rato con nosotros! *Come and have a chat with us!*
Elsa vino a **tomar** su maleta. *Elsa came to take her suitcase.*

The *infinitivo* is used in commands.

The *infinitivo* is used to express an obligation, especially in slogans and specific formulas, road signs and other signs.

No **fumar** en el edificio. *Do not smoke in the building.*
En caso de incendio, **sonar** la alarma. *In case of fire, ring the alarm.*

The *infinitivo* can follow the preposition *a* to express a command in the first person plural. The English equivalent is *let's* + V.

¡A pasear! *Let's take a walk!*

Cuando llegue el equipo, todos a
gritar " ¡Viva los ganadores! "

When the team arrives, let's
shout "Hurray for the winners!"

196

The *infinitivo* is used after prepositions.

The *infinitivo* comes after prepositions: *a, cabe, con, contra, de, desde, hasta, para, por, sin, sobre, tras, además de, a pesar de, antes de,* etc. The English translation uses the present participle.

SPANISH	ENGLISH
Preposition + *infinitivo*	**Preposition + present part.**
Yo tengo una máquina **de coser.**	*I have a sewing machine.*
Yo terminaré **antes de salir.**	*I will finish before leaving.*
Yo leo **sin comprender.**	*I read without understanding.*

The *infinitivo* takes a special meaning after certain prepositions.

√ **Al +** *infinitivo* has a temporal meaning, sometimes accompanied by a sense of causality (*upon* + Verb in the present participle; *when*). This construction is very often used in Spanish.

Al salir de casa, encontré a Juan.   *Upon going out, I met Juan.*

Al oír la noticia, se puso triste.   *When she heard the news, she became sad.*

√ **De +** *infinitivo* has a conditional meaning (*if*). This construction is not often used.

De haber sabido, habría venido.   *If I had known, I would have come.*

√ **Por +** *infinitivo* indicates an action yet to be completed:

Quedan dos capítulos **por estudiar.**   *There are two chapters left to study.*

Hay tres kilómetros **por recorrer.**   *There are three more kilometers to cover.*

197

The *infinitivo* has two forms: the *infinitivo simple* and the *infinitivo perfecto.*

The *infinitivo simple* is used to express incomplete processes.

The *infinitivo simple* expresses processes which take place at the same time or after the moment indicated by the main verb. It corresponds to the English infinitive: *hablar (to speak); comer (to eat); salir (to go out).* It is formed by adding the following endings to the stem:

1st Group: **-ar**	2nd Group: **-er**	3rd Group: **-ir**

Está contenta de **viajar.**	*She is happy to travel.*
Estaba contenta de **viajar.**	*She was happy to travel.*
Estará contenta de **viajar.**	*She will be happy to travel.*

Viajar and *estar contenta* occur at the same time.

The *infinitivo perfecto* is used to express completed processes.

The *infinitivo perfecto* expresses processes which were completed before the moment indicated by the main verb. The English equivalent is the infinitive perfect: *haber hablado (to have spoken), haber comido (to have eaten), haber salido (to have gone out).*

The *infinitivo perfecto* is a compound tense formed with the auxiliary *haber* in the *infinitivo simple* followed by the *participio* of the verb [195].

Infinitivo perfecto =	**haber** in the *Infinitivo simple* + **Verb in the** *participio*

Está contenta de **haber terminado** su trabajo.	*She is happy to have finished her work.*
Estaba contenta de **haber terminado** su trabajo.	*She was happy to have finished her work.*
Estará contenta de **haber terminado** su trabajo.	*She will be happy to have finished her work.*

The ***gerundio*** is a form of the verb which is not conjugated. There are four main uses of the *gerundio*.

The *gerundio* expresses an on-going process, a process in progress.

The *gerundio* follows a verb which indicates the continuation of a process.

√ ***Estar / quedarse / seguir / continuar / andar*** + *gerundio* are used to indicate a process in progress. It is similar to the English *be / keep on / still be / continue* + Verb in the present participle.

Cuando llegamos, Juan estaba **hablando** por teléfono.	*When we arrived, Juan was talking on the phone.*
Mientras comíamos con Eva, Juan se quedó **hablando** por teléfono.	*While we were eating with Eva, Juan continued talking on the phone.*

√ ***Llevar*** + *gerundio* also indicate the continuation of a process. This construction always comes with a time expression and means *for.*

Llevo tres años **viviendo** en Santa Fe.	*I have been living in Santa Fe for three years.*

The *gerundio* expresses the first or the last in a sequence of processes.

√ ***Empezar / Comenzar*** + *gerundio* are used to indicate the first in a sequence of processes. It is similar to the English *begin by* + Verb in the present participle. But, contrary to the English equivalent construction, the *gerundio* never follows a preposition.

El director empezó **dando** los resultados del examen.	*The principal began by giving the results of the exam.*

√ ***Acabar / Terminar*** + *gerundio* are used to indicate the last in a sequence of processes. It is similar to the English *finish by* + Verb in the present participle.

El director acabó/terminó **dando** los premios a los mejores.	*The principal finished by giving the awards to the best ones.*

199

The *gerundio* expresses a circumstance.

The *gerundio* comes without a subject of its own: it is connected to the subject (or sometimes the object) of the main verb to indicate a circumstance, telling when, how, or why the main process takes place.

√ **Simultaneity.** The process in the *gerundio* takes place at the same time as the main process.

Siempre estudio **escuchando** música.

I always study while listening to music.

√ **Manner.** The process in the *gerundio* explains how the main process takes place.

Corremos **respirando** profundamente.

We run breathing deeply.

√ **Condition.** The process in the *gerundio* also indicates the condition.

Trabajando mucho se logra el éxito.

Working hard, one reaches success.

√ **Cause.** The *gerundio* expresses the cause, the reason why the main process takes place.

Corriendo de esta manera, te vas a cansar desde el comienzo de la carrera.

If you run in this way, you are going to get tired from the beginning of the race.

No **sabiendo** la respuesta, prefirió permanecer callado.

Not knowing the answer, he preferred to remain silent.

√ **Consequence.** The *gerundio* expresses a process that occurs as a result of the main process.

El agua hierve a 100 grados, **desprendiendo** vapor.

Water boils at 100 degrees, emitting vapor.

The *gerundio* is used with verbs of perception.

√ **Verbs of perception** are verbs that indicate the way our senses perceive the world: *oír (to hear), escuchar (to listen), ver (to see), mirar (to look).* The *gerundio* is used with verbs of perception to indicate what the object of the perception is doing. English also uses the present participle with verbs of perception.

La vi **cruzando** la calle.
I saw her crossing the street.

Desde aquí, podemos oír a la soprano **cantando** "Carmen".
From here we can hear the soprano singing "Carmen."

√ **Other verbs like perception verbs** are: *encontrar (to find), hallar (to find), recordar (to remember).* These verbs have a meaning similar to verbs of perception. The *gerundio* is also used with these verbs.

Recuerdo a mi abuelo **contando** historias sobre la vida en la frontera.
I remember my grandfather telling stories about life on the border.

Está haciendo pompas.

Lo vi jugando al vóleibol.

The *gerundio* is a mode which is not conjugated. The *gerundio* has two forms: the **gerundio simple** and the **gerundio perfecto**.

The *gerundio simple* **expresses incomplete processes.**

The *gerundio simple* is used to express an incomplete process which takes place at the same time or after the main process. English uses the equivalent form called present participle: *hablando (speaking), comiendo (eating), saliendo (going out)*. This is how to form the *gerundio*:

(1) Find the stem.

Take the *infinitivo* and delete the *infinitivo* ending.

1st group:	hablar	——	stem:	**habl-**
2nd group:	beber	——	stem:	**beb-**
3rd group:	salir	——	stem:	**sal-**

(2) Add the following endings:

Verbs in **-ar: ando**	Verbs in **-er: iendo**	Verbs in **-ir: iendo**

Juan iba a casa **saltando** y **corriendo**.   *Juan went home jumping and running.*

Me rompí la mano **boxeando**.   *I broke my hand boxing.*

The *gerundio perfecto* **expresses completed processes.**

The *gerundio perfecto* expresses processes which were completed before the moment indicated by the main verb. The English has an equivalent form: *habiendo hablado (having spoken), habiendo comido (having eaten), habiendo salido (having gone out)*.

The *gerundio perfecto* is a compound tense formed with the auxiliary *haber* in the *gerundio simple* followed by the *participio* of the verb [195].

Gerundio perfecto = **haber** in *gerundio simple* + **Verb in** *participio*

Habiendo comprendido que Julieta estaba muerta, Romeo se suicidó.   *Having realized that Juliet was dead, Romeo committed suicide.*

THE ADVERB

Adverbs are words which tell us **where, when,** and **how** the process takes place:

 Antonio hizo viajes de negocios a Miami.

Antonio made business trips to Miami.

Antonio fue a Miami y se quedará **allá** dos meses.

Antonio went to Miami and he will stay there two months.

Había viajado a Miami **a menudo,** pero **nunca** había podido quedarse mucho tiempo.

He had often been to Miami, but he had never been able to stay long.

En los dos meses, Antonio pudo explorar **detenidamente** las posibilidades de exportación a América Latina.

During the two months, Antonio could carefully explore the prospects to export to Latin America.

Adverbs also tell us about **the degree** or **the intensity** of the quality or attributes expressed by an adjective or another adverb.

Su viaje fue **muy** productivo.

His trip was very productive.

Tras la firma del contrato, Antonio regresará a Miami **muy** a menudo.

After closing the business deal, he will return to Miami very often.

Adverbs are very frequently used, and provide clarity and precision in communication. It is therefore important to know how to use them. We frequently use several adverbs in one single sentence.

Como viajo **mucho, siempre** compro un buen libro en la estación para leer mientras espero el tren. Ese día, **especialmente,** estaba leyendo una novela policíaca **muy** llena de acción. Un  tren entró **lentamente** por el andén número 8. Yo estaba **tan** concentrado en la lectura que **apenas** me di cuenta que el tren **ya** había llegado. De un salto, recogí **rápidamente** mis cosas de **alrededor** y subí **pronto** al tren. Cuando el tren salió me di cuenta que no era el que debía haber tomado.

Since I travel a lot, I always buy a good book at the station to read while waiting for the train. On that day, especially, I was reading an action-packed detective story. A train slowly pulled in on platform 8. I was so deeply concentrated in my reading that I hardly realized that the train had arrived. In a rush, I pick up my things around me, and I got on the train quickly. When the train left, I realized that this was not the one I should have taken.

204

Adverbs can be classified into different classes, depending on their meanings.

Adverbs of place tell where the process takes place.

The adverbs of place are:

acá/allá/acullá (Latin America)	*here/there/there*
aquí/ahí/allí (Spain)	*here/there/there*
alrededor	*around*
enfrente	*in front*
arriba ≠ abajo	*above, up ≠ below/down*
cerca ≠ lejos	*close ≠ far*
delante ≠ detrás	*in front ≠ behind*
debajo ≠ encima	*below, undeneath ≠ above*
dentro ≠ fuera	*inside ≠ outside*

 Note that the adverbs *acá/allá/acullá* and *aquí/ahí/allí* can come before other adverbs or prepositions:

acá arriba/allá arriba...	*up here/there*
acá dentro/allá dentro...	*in here/there*
acá mismo/allá mismo...	*right here/there*

 Note also that the adverbs *acá...* or *aquí...* can come after other adverbs:

más acá/más allá...	*closer/further away*
hasta acá/hasta allá...	*up to/as far as*
por acá/por allá...	*round here/there*

Other expressions indicating place are:

a la derecha ≠ a la izquierda	*on the right ≠ on the left*
al lado	*close by/near*
en el centro	*in the center*
en la parte superior ≠ inferior	*on the top part/the bottom part*

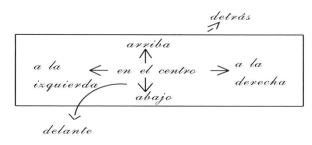

Adverbs of time tell when the process takes place.

The adverbs of time are:

a menudo	*very often*	jamás	*never*
ahora	*now*	luego	*after*
anoche	*last night*	mañana	*tomorrow*
anteayer	*the day before yesterday*	nunca	*never*
		pronto	*soon*
antes	*before*	siempre	*always*
ayer	*yesterday*	tarde	*late*
después	*after*	temprano	*early*
hoy	*today*	ya	*already*

Other expressions of time, see also [223 - 229]

de aquí en adelante	*from now on*
de aquí a un mes	*in a month*
dentro de poco	*soon*
de vez en cuando	*sometimes*
en el futuro	*in the future*

Adverbs of quantity tell about the intensity of the process.

The adverbs of quantity are:

además	*besides*	medio	*half*
algo	*somewhat*	menos	*less*
apenas	*hardly*	mucho	*a lot*
bastante	*enough*	poco	*a little*
casi	*almost*	sólo	*only*
demasiado	*too much*	tanto	*as/so*
más	*more*		

Other expressions of quantity

al menos	*at least*	más o menos	*more or less*
al por mayor	*wholesale*	poco a poco	*little by little*
al por menor	*retail*	poco más o menos	*more or less*

Quien mucho abarca poco aprieta.
You can bite off more than you can chew.

Adverbs of manner tell how the process is done.

The adverbs of manner are:

bien/mal	*well, right/badly*
mejor/peor	*better/worse*
despacio/aprisa	*slowly/fast*
all the adverbs in **-mente** (see below)	

Some expressions also describe the manner, but are not adverbs:

a la americana/española/etc.	*in the American/Spanish way*
a pie/a caballo	*on foot/on horseback*
a mano	*by hand*

√ Formation of Adverbs in *-mente*

Adverbs ending in **-mente** come from adjectives and describe the way in which the action is done. For example, for the adjective *serio (serious),* the adverb *seriamente (seriously)* means "in a serious way." The English corresponding form is the **-ly** ending added to adjectives *(serious/seriously).*

> **To form an adverb from an adjective, we add the suffix *-mente* to the feminine of the adjective.**

ADJ. (Masc.)	ADJ. (Fem.)	ADVERB	ENGLISH
alegre	alegre	alegremente	*joyfully*
final	final	finalmente	*finally*
lento	lenta	lentamente	*slowly*
serio	seria	seriamente	*seriously*
loco	loca	locamente	*madly*
profundo	profunda	profundamente	*deeply*
prudente	prudente	prudentemente	*prudently*
moderado	moderada	moderadamente	*moderately*

Most adjectives have a corresponding **-mente** adverb.

 Note that when two or more adverbs in **-mente** are conjoined, the **-mente** ending is omitted on all except the last adverb.

Ella habla **lenta** y **seriamente**.   *She speaks slowly and seriously.*

Adverbs of affirmation, negation and doubt

√   The adverbs used in affirmative (≠ negative) contexts are:

sí ≠ no	*yes ≠ no*
también ≠ tampoco	*also ≠ neither*

¡Trae la mochila y **también** tu saco de dormir!	*Bring your backpack and also your sleeping bag!*
Yo no vi la película, ¿y tú? — Yo **tampoco.**	*I did not see the movie, and you? — Me neither.*

√   The adverbs expressing doubt are:

acaso	*perhaps*
quizá(s)	*maybe*
tal vez	*perhaps*

Other expressions with affirmative and negative meaning:

a lo mejor	*at best*	en absoluto	*absolutely not*
claro que no	*of course not*	¿comó no?	*why not?*
de ninguna manera	*in no way*	¡qué va!	*non sense!*

ADVERBS VS. PREPOSITIONS

Some words can be used as adverbs as well as prepositions, for instance: *antes (before), delante (in front), depués (after).* There is a difference, however, in the way these words are used.

√   When they are used as prepositions they are followed by *de* + a noun or a verb in the *infinitivo* [59 - 71]:

El ascensor está **delante de** la puerta.	*The elevator is in front of the door.*

√   When they are used as adverbs, they stand by themselves, and have no complement.

Cuando va al cine, siempre se sienta **delante.**	*When he goes to the movies, he always sits in the front.*

208

The place of the adverb √

The position of adverbs in the sentence depends on the category of the word modified by the adverb.

Adverbs modifying a verb come after the verb.

Yo leo **mucho,** pero él lee **más.**	*I read a lot, but he reads more.*
Hay que comer **lentamente.**	*One has to eat slowly.*
Hemos comido **bien.**	*We ate well.*
¡Maneja **prudentemente!**	*Drive carefully!*
Puso **cuidadosamente** las flores en la mesa.	*He carefully put the flowers on the table.*

Contrary to English, the adverb never comes between the auxiliary and the *participio* in compound tenses.

He dicho **finalmente** la verdad.	*I have finally told the truth.*
Había tenido **siempre** buen gusto.	*He had always had good taste.*
Hemos considerado **ya** su caso.	*We have already considered his case.*

Adverbs modifying an adjective, a *participio* used as adjective, or another adverb, come before.

Estoy **tan** contento.	*I am so happy.*
Viven **muy** lejos.	*They live very far away.*
Esta casa ha sido **especialmente** construida para él.	*This house was built especially for him.*

Adverbs modifying a whole sentence can come in several places in the sentence.

Quizás, tú tengas razón.	*You may be right.*
Juan, **evidentemente,** volvió a ganar.	*Juan, obviously, won again.*

209

TYPES OF SENTENCES

A declarative sentence is a sentence which makes a statement. Spanish declarative sentence structures are different from those of English in two respects:

(i)   the omission of the subject
(ii) the word order

OMISSION OF THE SUBJECT

We have explained that, contrary to English, the subject can be omitted in Spanish [78]. The general principle that applies is the following: omit the subject as much as possible when it is understood from the context.

Ese año pasaron muchas cosas en este país. Entre otras, Andrés y yo nos casamos. Lo **conocí** en un café de los portales. . . . Entonces él tenía más de treinta años y yo menos de quince. **Estaba** con mis hermanas y sus novios cuando lo **vimos** acercarse. **Dijo** su nombre y **se sentó** a conversar entre nosotros. Me **gustó.** (Angeles Mastreta, ¡Arráncame la vida!)

That year many things happened in this country. Among other things, Andres and I got married. I met him in a café in the arcades. . . . Then, he was more than thirty years old and I less than fifteen. I was with my sisters and their fiancés when we saw him approach us. He said his name and sat down to speak with us. I liked him.

In this text, as soon as the characters are known, the subjects are omitted in Spanish, because they are not needed to understand the situation.

The subject is present only when it is presented for the first time in the story *(Andrés, yo)*, or for contrast *(él. . . yo).*

___ *¡Toma!*
Es   para ti.

___ *Gracias. Es*
muy   bonita.

WORD ORDER

Sentences can begin with the verb, the subject, or the object, depending on what the speaker is talking about, what we call the topic. The topic always comes at the beginning of the sentence.

√ Sentences which focus on processes or present events begin with the verb.

¿Qué pasó?	*What happened?*
— **Se desplomó** el puente y murieron varios transeúntes.	*— The bridge collapsed and several pedestrians were killed.*
¿Qué noticias trae la prensa hoy?	*What's the news in the press today?*
— No sé. **No llegó** el periódico.	*— I don't know. The newspaper did not arrive.*
Cada día **suena** la campana a las doce.	*Every day the bell rings at noon.*

√ Sentences which focus on the subject and give information about it begin with the subject.

Dos motoristas se cayeron del puente.	*Two motorcyclists fell from the bridge.*
Mi amigo Juan me envió una postal de Caracas.	*My friend Juan sent me a postcard from Caracas.*

√ We can also focus on the object. The sentence will then begin with the object. In this case, the object is repeated with a pronoun.

Este poema lo escribió mi hija.	*This poem was written by my daughter.*
A Eva le dieron el premio.	*They gave the prize to Eva.*

 Luis y Eva están en el restaurante.   *Luis and Eva are in the restaurant.*

When they are ordering, focus is put on each person:

Luis ha pedido calamares y Eva jamón.	*Luis has ordered squid and Eva ham.*

When the dishes arrive, focus is put on the dishes:

Los calamares los ha pedido Luis, y el jamón lo ha pedido Eva.	*The squid was ordered by Luis, and the ham by Eva.*

√   Questions are formed by placing the subject after the verb. We write an inverted question mark at the beginning of the sentence and a regular question mark at the end.

¿Hiciste tú esta escultura?   *Did you do this sculpture?*
¿Ha llegado el correo?   *Did the mail arrive?*

 Note that in spoken informal Spanish, it is possible to use the declarative structure, without changing the word order; it is then pronounced with a rising intonation:

¿Tú hablas español?   *Do you speak Spanish?*
¿Juan va con nosotros?   *Is Juan going with us?*

√   When asking for a specific piece of information, a question word is placed at the beginning of the sentence [see 100, repeated here]:

Information	Question Word	English
a person	quién/quiénes	who/whom
a thing	qué	what
a choice among people/things	cuál/cuáles	which one
place	dónde	where
time	cuándo	when
manner	cómo	how
quantity	cuánto	how much
	cuánto/a/os/as	how much/many
cause	por qué	why

¿Por qué hay tanta gente allá?   *Why are there so many people there?*
¿Cuándo sales del trabajo?   *When do you get off work?*
¿Cuál de estas películas prefieres?   *Which one of these movies do you prefer?*
¿Cuál es tu número de teléfono?   *What is your phone number?*
¿Qué película preferiste?   *Which movie did you prefer?*
¿Qué prefieres?   *What do you prefer?*

 Note that the question word can be preceded by a preposition:

¿De dónde eres?   *Where are you from?*
¿Hasta cuándo debemos esperar?   *Until when do we have to wait?*
¿Con quién hablaste?   *With whom did you speak?*
¿Para quién compraste este regalo?   *For whom did you buy this present?*

Some idiomatic questions

¿Cómo te llamas?
— Me llamo Isabel.

What's your name?
— My name is Isabel.

¿Cuántos años tienes?
— Tengo doce años.

How old are you?
— I am twelve years old.

¿Cómo estás?
— Muy bien, gracias.

How are you?
— Very well, thank you.

¿Quién es?
— Es Juana Lopez.

Who is this?
— This is Juana Lopez.

¿De qué color es tu bolsa?
— Es azul.

What color is your purse?
— It is blue.

¿Qué hora es?
— Son las cinco.

What time is it?
— It is five o' clock.

A qué hora empieza el examen?
— A las nueve y media.

At what time does the exam begin?
— At nine thirty.

¿Qué tiempo hace?
— Hace frío.

What's the weather like?
— It is cold.

¿A dónde vas este fin de semana?
— A San Juan.

Where are you going this week-end?
— To San Juan.

¿Qué pasa?
— Hubo un accidente.

What is going on?
— There was an accident.

Indirect questions

An indirect question is a question which is reported as a statement. It has the following properties:
(i) It has the form of a direct question.
(ii) It is introduced by a specific verb *(preguntar,* etc.).

Juan preguntó dónde trabajo.
No sé porqué se fue tan pronto.

Juan asked where I work.
I don't know why he left so early.

Note that when the corresponding direct question is a yes/no question, i. e., does not begin with a question word, the indirect question is introduced by the word **si** *(if, whether):*

Juan preguntó si había comido.

Juan asked if I had eaten.

215

Negative sentences √

√ In Spanish, **negative sentences** are formed by placing the word **no** before the verb:

No he visto esta película.	*I have not seen this movie.*
Mi hermano **no** vendrá.	*My brother will not come.*

 Note that when there are pronouns before the verb, the negative word **no** comes before all the object pronouns, but after the subject pronoun:

Esta película **no** la he visto.	*I have not seen this movie.*
El libro **no** me lo dieron.	*They did not give me the book.*
Yo **no** se lo devolví.	*I did not return it.*
A Juan **no** le gustan las bromas.	*Juan does not like jokes.*

√ **No** can be used in correlation with the following negative elements [94-95; 208]: *jamás (never), nada (nothing), nadie (nobody), ni (neither), ninguno (no one), nunca (never), tampoco (neither/either).*

No como jamás queso.	*I never eat cheese.*
No hay nada que hacer.	*There is nothing to do.*
No vino nadie a la reunión.	*Nobody came to the meeting.*
No quiero ni verle.	*I don't even want to see him.*
No fumo tampoco.	*I don't smoke either.*

 Note that when the negation is at the beginning of the sentence, **no** is omitted.

Jamás como queso.	*I never eat cheese.*
Nada vale tanto como una buena educación.	*Nothing is better than a good education.*
Nadie vino a la reunión.	*Nobody came to the meeting.*
Tampoco fumo.	*I don't smoke either.*
Ni viene ni llama por teléfono.	*He neither comes nor calls.*

√ It is possible to use several negative elements in the same sentence:

No he dicho **nada** a **nadie.**	*I have not said anything to anybody.*
No lee **jamás nada.**	*He never reads anything.*
Nadie le ha dicho **nunca** la verdad.	*Nobody ever told him the truth.*
A **nadie** le importa **nada.**	*No one really cares.*

216

Exclamatory sentences are used for special emphasis to express the following: order, command, surprise, admiration, indignation. We write an inverted exclamation mark at the beginning of the sentence and a regular exclamation mark at the end.

√ To emphasize ideas expressed by a noun, an adjective or an adverb, the exclamatory word **qué** is used. It is translated to English by *what a* and *how.*

¡Qué hamburguesa!	*What a hamburger!*
¡Qué calor!	*How hot it is!*
¡Qué bonito/feo!	*How pretty/ugly it is!*
¡Qué bonita es tu casa!	*What a nice house you have!*
¡Qué bonita casa!	*What a nice house!*
¡Qué magnífica vista!	*What a wonderful view!*
¡Qué rápido manejas!	*How fast you drive!*
¡Qué lejos está la playa!	*How far the beach is!*

 Note that when an adjective follows a noun, we add **más** or **tan** before the adjective:

¡Qué día más bonito!	*What a nice day!*
¡Qué pianista tan extraordinario!	*What an extraordinary pianist!*

√ To emphasize quantity or intensity, the exclamatory word **cuánto/ os/a/as** is used before a noun or a verb.

¡Cuántas flores!	*What a lot of flowers!*
¡Cuánta pobreza en este país!	*How much poverty in this country!*
¡Cuánto me alegra su llegada!	*I am so glad she is coming!*
¡Cuánto he dormido!	*I slept a lot!*

Idiomatic exclamations

¡Qué bueno!	*How nice!*
¡Qué padre! (Mexico and Southwest US)	*Wow!*

217

Imperative sentences are sentences that give commands or requests. The *imperativo* is used in these sentences [190 - 192].

¡Levántate!   *Get up!*
¡No olvides tu paraguas!   *Don't forget your umbrella!*

Other ways of making commands are:

√ Use of the *futuro* [150]:

¡Para mañana, harán los ejercicios!   *For tomorrow, you will do the exercises!*

√ Use of the *infinitivo* [196], or *a* + *infinitivo* [61]:

A estudiar!   *Study!*

En caso de incendio, no tomar el ascensor!   *In case of fire, do not take the elevator.*

√ Formulas for general orders and interdictions:

Prohibido estacionar.   *Do not park.*

Se ruega guardar silencio en el hospital.   *Please keep silent in the hospital.*

√ Polite forms of request:

Cierra la ventana, por favor.   *Please close the window.*

√ Questions containing the *futuro hipotético*:

¿Podrías cerrar la ventana?   *Could you close the window?*
¿Sería Ud. tan amable de cerrar la ventana?   *Would you be so kind as to close the window?*

√ Use of specific verbs and expressions followed by the *subjuntivo* to reinforce orders:

Te pido que bajes el volumen del televisor.   *I ask you to lower the volume of the TV.*

Te mando que limpies el cañon.   *I order you to clean the cannon.*

Te prohibo que me hables con ese tono.   *I forbid you to talk to me in that tone.*

218

When a process involves an agent (the one who performs the action) and a recipient of the action, there are two ways to express it, depending on whether we want to emphasize the performer or the recipient.

√ In active sentences, the focus is on the performer; and it is therefore presented at the beginning of the sentence: it is the subject of the verb:

Diego de Rivera pintó esos murales. *Diego de Rivera painted those murals.*

√ In passive sentences, the focus is on the recipient of the action; and it therefore becomes the subject of the verb.

Esos murales fueron pintados por Diego de Rivera. *Those murals were painted by Diego de Rivera.*

FORMATION OF PASSIVE SENTENCES

In Spanish, like in English, there is a correlation between active and passive sentences: (i) the direct object of the active sentence is the subject of its passive counterpart; (ii) the subject of the active sentence comes after the preposition **por** *(by)* in the passive; and (iii) the auxiliary **ser** *(to be)* is added before the verb, in the passive sentence. *Ser* comes in the **same tense** as the verb in the active sentence, and the verb in the passive sentence comes in the *participio*.

El viento arrancó un árbol. *The wind pulled out a tree.*

Un árbol **fue** arrancado **por** el viento. *A tree was pulled out by the wind.*

ACTIVE SENTENCE

el viento: subject (performer of the action)
arrancó: verb in the *pretérito*
un árbol: direct object (recipient of the action)

PASSIVE SENTENCE

el viento: follows **por**
fue: passive auxiliary in the *pretérito*
arrancado: *participio*
un árbol: subject (recipient of the action)

219

Pay special attention to the fact that the tense of the passive sentence is carried by the auxiliary *ser*, which is the same tense as the verb in the active counterpart:

Un millonario **ha comprado** el cuadro.	*A millionaire has bought the painting.*
El cuadro **ha sido** comprado por un millonario.	*The painting has been bought by a millionaire.*
El leñador **abandona** a Pulgarcito.	*The woodcutter abandons Tom Thumb.*
Pulgarcito **es** abandonado por el leñador.	*Tom Thumb is abandoned by the woodcutter.*

 Note that, contrary to English, only direct objects can become subjects of passive sentences. Indirect objects cannot. Therefore, there is no Spanish passive equivalent for the English passive: *John was given a book.*

 Note that the agent (the phrase following **por**) in the passive sentence can be omitted when it is not important for the message or when it is an unknown agent.

La nueva autopista ha sido inaugurada en mayo.	*The new highway was inaugurated in May.*

 The passive meaning can also be expressed by the pronoun **se** [84]. This is the most widely used construction; it is used when we speak about things rather than people and when the agent is irrelevant.

Se construyó una carretera.	*A road was built.*
Este año, se han construido muchas casas.	*This year, many houses have been built.*

Luis López construyó esta casa.

Esta casa fue construida por Luis López

EXPANDED SENTENCES

Luis tuvo un accidente ayer.	TIME
Luis patinó porque había gravilla en la carretera.	CAUSE
Luis se hizo tanto daño que no podrá participar en la próxima carrera.	CONSEQUENCE

Luis fue al hospital para hacer una radiografía.	GOAL
Si Luis está bien, podrá participar en la próxima carrerra.	CONDITION
Si no hubiera habido gravilla, Luis no hubiera patinado.	HYPOTHESIS
Al contrario de sus compañeros, Luis no pudo terminar la etapa.	OPPOSITION
A pesar del accidente, volverá a correr.	CONCESSION

A process always occurs in time. Time is a crucial dimension in our perception of the world around us, of our life, and of every process that forms the core of communication. In the section on verb tenses, we explained the relationship between the tense of a verb and the time when the process takes place. We can also expand sentences to give more specific information on time.

In this section, we will present the different ways to express time when we communicate in Spanish. We will focus on the various aspects of what we call time. The following diagram shows the different ways in which we can conceive of time:

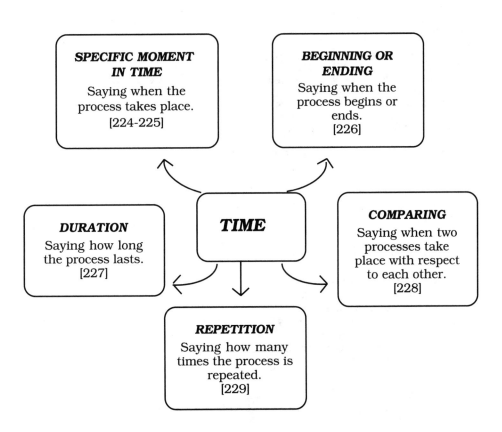

There are expressions which identify a specific moment in time, indicating when a process takes place.

Before NOW	NOW	After NOW
antes *before* **ayer** *yesterday* **ayer por la mañana** *yesterday morning* **anteayer** *the day before yesterday* **hace 5 días** *5 days ago* **la semana pasada** *last week* **el mes pasado** *last month* **el año pasado** *last year* **la última vez** *last time* **antiguamente** *in the past*	**ahora** *now* **hoy** *today* **esta mañana** *this morning* **esta semana** *this week* **este mes** *this month* **este año** *this year* **esta vez** *this time* **hoy en día** *at present*	**después** *after* **mañana** *tomorrow* **mañana por la mañana** *tomorrow morning* **pasado mañana** *the day after tomorrow* **dentro de 5 días** *in 5 days* **la semana próxima** *next week* **el mes próximo** *next month* **el año próximo** *next year* **la próxima vez** *next time* **en el futuro** *in the future* ↳ We can use the expression **que viene** *(coming)* instead of *próximo:* la semana/el mes/el año que viene.

La semana pasada fui a ver a mi abuela que no había visto desde **el año pasado.** Me dijo que va a terminar de bordar una mantilla que empezó **hace veinte años** y me la regalará **la próxima vez** que la visite.

Last week I went to see my grandmother, that I had not seen since last year. She told me that she is going to finish embroidering a mantilla which she began 20 years ago, and that she will offer it to me next time I visit her.

¡Hasta mañana!   ¡Adiós!

Expressions of time can also indicate when a process takes place with respect to a specific moment in the past (THEN).

Before THEN	THEN	After THEN
antes *before* **un momento antes** *a moment before* **la víspera** *the day before, the eve* **unos días antes** *a few days before* **la semana antes** *the week before* **hacía 5 días** *5 days before* **el año antes** *the previous year* **la vez antes** *the time before*	**entonces** *then* **en ese momento** *at that moment* **ese día** *on that day* **esa semana** *on that week* **ese año** *that year* **esa vez** *that time* We can use **aquel/aquella...** instead of ese/esa...	**después** *after* **un momento después** *a moment later* **al día siguiente** *the day after* **unos días después** *a few days after* **la semana después/ siguiente** *the week after/the following week* **5 días más tarde/después** *5 days later* **el año después/siguiente** *the year after/the following year* **la vez después/siguiente** *the next time/the following time*

Aquella semana fui a ver a mi abuela que no había visto desde **hacía un año.** Me dijo que iba a terminar de bordar una mantilla que había empezado **hacía veinte años** y que me la regalaría **la próxima vez** que la visitara.

That week I went to see my grandmother, that I had not seen since the previous year. She told me that she was going to finish embroidering a mantilla which she had begun 20 years before, and that she would offer it to me the next time I would visit her.

There are expressions that say when a process began or ended.

√ If a process is still going on, or was still going on at a specific moment in the past, we can indicate when it began by using the expression *desde (since)*:

Tenemos el mismo gobierno **desde** el año 1984.

We have had the same government since 1984.

Tenemos el mismo gobierno **desde que** yo nací.

We have had the same government since I was born.

These sentences answer the question:

¿**Desde cuándo** tienen este gobierno?

Since when have you had this government?

Expressions:

desde entonces — *since then*
desde niño/joven — *from childhood/youth*
desde que el mundo es mundo — *since the world began*

√ To indicate that a process ends, we use *hasta (until)*.

Estaré en la oficina **hasta** las cinco.

I'll be in the office until 5 o'clock.

Estaré en casa **hasta que** regreses.

I'll be home until you come back.

Estudió **hasta** la madrugada.

He studied until dawn.

Estudió **hasta que** no pudo más.

He studied until he could not study any more.

These sentences answer the questions:

¿**Hasta cuándo/que hora** estarás en la oficina?

Until when/what time will you be in the office?

¿**Hasta cuándo** estudió Juan?

Until when did Juan study?

Expression:

¡Hasta la vista!

See you later!

226

There are expressions that indicate the duration of a process.

√ If the process is still going on now, or was still going on at a specific moment in the past, we indicate the duration of the process with *desde hace, desde hacía* [64], *hace, hacía* [110 - 111].

Hace 2 años **que** dirige la orquesta.
Dirige la orquesta **desde hace** 2 años.

She has conducted the orchestra for 2 years.

Note that she is still conducting the orchestra now.

Hacía 2 años **que** dirigía la orquesta.
Dirigía la orquesta **desde hacía** 2 años.

She had conducted the orchestra for 2 years.

Note that she was still conducting the orchestra at a specific moment in the past.

These sentences answer the questions:

¿Cuánto tiempo hace que dirige la orquesta?
¿Cuánto tiempo hacía que dirigía la orquesta?

How long has/had she conducted the orchestra?

√ If the process is completed or was completed, we use the expressions: *de... a, desde... hasta, por, durante, en* [59 - 71].

Estuve en Cuernavaca **de** mayo **a** julio/
desde mayo **hasta** julio.

I stayed in Cuernavaca from May to July.

Estuve en Cuernavaca **por/durante** 2 meses.

I stayed in Cuernavaca for 2 months

Puedo hacer este trabajo **en** 2 horas.

I can do this work in 2 hours.

Note that **por** and **durante** can be omitted:

Estuve en Cuernavaca dos meses.

I stayed 2 months in Cuernavaca.

These sentences answer the questions:

¿Cuánto tiempo estuviste en Cuernavaca?

How long have you been in Cuernavaca?

There are expressions that indicate when two processes take place with respect to each other.

√ To indicate that a process takes place **before** another process, we use the following:

antes de + V in the *infinitivo*	*before* + V in the **-ing** form
antes (de) que + clause in the *subjuntivo*	*before* + clause
desde (que) + clause in the *indicativo*	*since* + clause

√ To indicate that a process takes place **after** another process, we use the following:

después de + V in the *infinitivo*	*after* + V in the **-ing** form
después de que + clause	*after* + clause
apenas + clause. . . que	*just . . . that*
hasta que + clause	*until* + clause
tan pronto como + clause	*as soon as*
en cuanto + clause	*once, as soon as*

 Note that these conjunctions can be followed by a clause in the *indicativo* or in the *subjuntivo*.

INDICATIVO
It usually refers to past or present processes, interpreted as facts.

Me quedé en la biblioteca hasta que cerraron.
I stayed in the library until they closed.

SUBJUNTIVO
It usually refers to future processes, with a nuance of intention.

Me quedaré en la biblioteca hasta que vengas.
I'll stay in the library until you come.

√ To indicate that a process takes place **at the same time** as another process, we use the following;

al + V in the *infinitivo*	*when, upon*
siempre que/cada vez que + clause	*each time*
cuando + clause	*when*
mientras (tanto) que + clause	*while*
a medida que + clause	*as*
entretanto + clause	*meanwhile*

There are expressions that indicate the repetition of the process.

√ To indicate that a process takes place several times (or never), we use:

algunas veces	*sometimes*
a menudo	*often*
a veces/muchas veces	*at times/many times*
cada + expression of time	each + expression of time
(cada vez/hora/día/noche/semana/	*each time/hour/day/night/*
mes/semestre/año, etc.)	*week/month/semester/year*
frecuentemente	*frequently*
todos/as + determiner + expression of time	
(todas las veces/horas/noches/	*every time/hour/night/*
semanas, etc.)	*week*
(todos los días/semestres, etc.)	*every day/semester*
siempre ≠ jamás/nunca	*always ≠ never*

 Note that **cada** is always followed by the noun in the singular, whereas **todos/as** is always followed by a determiner and a noun in the plural.

Cada día me paseo por el parque.   *Each day I take a walk in the park.*
Todos los días me paseo por el parque.   *Every day I take a walk in the park.*

 Note also that these expressions are not always used with the *imperfecto*, although they can come with this tense. A repeated process can be expressed in the *pretérito* or the *imperfecto*, depending on the number of repetitions.

PRETÉRITO

If we know the number of times a process was repeated and if the the repetition of the process has stopped, we use the *pretérito*:

Fui al zócalo cada día.
I went to the town square every day.

Siempre regó las flores.
He always watered the flowers.
(But he does not do it anymore.)

IMPERFECTO

If the process was repeated as a habit, with no limitation on the number of repetitions, then we use the *imperfecto*.

Iba al zócalo cada día.
I used to go to the town square every day.

Siempre regaba las flores.
He used to water the flowers.
(He may still be doing it.)

229

Expressions of cause tell why the process takes place.

The cause is expressed in the following way:

a causa de	*because of*
a falta de	*for lack of*
a fuerza de	*driven by*
como	*since*
dado que/ya que + clause in the *indicativo*	*since, given that*
de tanto + V in the *infinitivo*	V in the -**ing** form
debido a	*due to*
debido a que + clause in the *indicativo*	*due to*
gracias a	*thanks to*
por	*by*
porque	*because*
puesto que	*since*

 Note that **como** puts a strong emphasis on the cause and always comes in the beginning of the sentence:

Como se le estropeó el carro, tuvo que tomar el autobús.	*Since his car broke down, he had to take the bus.*

 Un carro se estrelló contra un árbol.

A car ran into a tree.

El conductor perdió el control del volante **porque** los frenos no funcionaron.	*The driver lost control of the steering wheel because the brakes did not work.*
El carro patinó **a causa de** la lluvia.	*The car slid because of the rain.*
Como la curva era muy cerrada, el conductor no vio el tractor que atravesaba la carretera.	*Since the curve was very sharp, the driver did not see the tractor which was crossing the road.*
El conductor se salvó **gracias al** cinturón de seguridad.	*The driver was safe thanks to the seatbelt.*
Debido a que han ocurrido varios accidentes en esta parte de la carretera, se decidió poner una señal de tráfico en el lugar.	*Due to the fact that there were various accidents in this part of the road, it was decided to put a roadsign there.*

230

The goal is the purpose of the process.

The goal is expressed with the following:

a + V in the *infinitivo*	*in order to*
a fin de/con el fin de + V in the *infinitivo*	*in order to*
a fin de que + clause in the *subjuntivo*	*so that, in such a way that*
con objeto de + V in the *infinitivo*	*with the aim of*
de manera/de forma + que	*in such a way that/order to*
+ clause in the *subjuntivo*	
para + V in the *infinitivo*	*in order to*
para que + clause in the *subjuntivo*	*in order to*

 Note that the first structure, **a** + V in the *infinitivo* is used with verbs expressing movement from one place to another [196]:

Fueron **a inspeccionar** la fábrica.
Sacó el perro **a pasear.**

They went to inspect the factory.
He took out the dog for a walk.

 El Señor Ruiz piensa abrir una pensión en un barrio residencial de la ciudad.

Mr. Ruiz is planning to open a bed and breakfast in a residential area of town.

La comisión del ayuntamiento se reune:

1. **para** discutir el proyecto del Sr. Ruiz,

2. **a fin de** conocer la opinión de los vecinos,

3. **con objeto de** tomar una decisión sobre el caso,

4. **para que** el Sr. Ruiz pueda explicar sus planes,

5. **de manera que** todos los interesados puedan expresarse.

The town committee will meet:

1. in order to discuss Mr. Ruiz's project

2. in order to know the neighbors' opinion,

3. with the aim of making a decision on the case,

4. in order for Mr. Ruiz to explain his plan,

5. in order for the interested parties to express themselves.

231

The consequence is the outcome of the process.

The outcome can be due to different aspects of the process. The consequence will then be introduced by different expressions.

√   If the consequence is the general outcome of the process, we use the following:

entonces	*therefore*
por eso/por lo tanto	*so/therefore*
por consiguiente	*consequently*

√   If the consequence has to do with the way the process was done, we use the following:

así que	*so that*
de forma/de manera/de modo + que	*so/in such a way that*
+ clause in the *indicativo*	
de tal forma/de tal modo + que	*in such a way that*
+ clause in the *indicativo*	

 Note that the expressions *de forma que,* etc., can also be used to express a goal [231]. The difference between goal and consequence is that the goal is expressed with the clause in the *subjuntivo* whereas the consequence is in the *indicativo*:

GOAL (*subjuntivo*)	**CONSEQUENCE** (*indicativo*)
Escribió en un estilo sencillo **de forma que** todos pudieran comprender.	Escribió en un estilo sencillo, **de forma que** todos comprendieron.
She wrote in a simple style so that they would all understand.	*She wrote in a simple style, in such a way that they all understood.*
El actor estudió y practicó el flamenco **de manera que** le dieran el papel principal en la película.	El actor estudió y bailó el flamenco perfectamente, **de manera que** obtuvo el papel principal.
The actor studied and practiced the flamenco in such a way that they would give him the main role in the picture.	*The actor studied and danced the flamenco in such a way that he got the main part.*

232

√ If the consequence is due to the intensity of the process, we use the following:

tal/tales + noun. . . *que*	such. . . that
tan + Adj/Adv. . . *que*	so much. . . that
Verb + *tanto* + *que*	so much. . . that
tanto/os/a/as + Noun + *que*	so much/many. . . that

All these expressions are followed by a clause in the *indicativo*.

Un grupo de arqueólogos descubrió dos momias debajo de la nieve, en los Andes.

A group of archaeologists found two mummies under the snow, in the Andes.

El jeep no podía subir;

The jeep could not go up the mountain;

1. **entonces** decidieron emplear el transporte local.

1. therefore they decided to use local transportation.

2. **por consiguiente** tuvieron que usar lamas.

2. Consequently, they had to use lamas.

3. **por eso** se quedaron varios días en el pueblo.

3. So they stayed several days in the village.

El camino era **tan** largo **que** tardaron cinco días en llegar al lugar.

The road was so long that it took them five days to arrive at the site.

Hacía **tanto** frío **que** tuvieron que interrumpir la búsqueda.

It was so cold that they had to interrupt the search.

Cuando hallaron la momias, éstas estaban **tan** bien conservadas **que** permitirán conocer mejor la historia de la región.

When they found the mummies, these were so well preserved that they will enable us to know the history of that region better.

233

When we express the **condition** under which a process will occur, we use specific expressions and specific tenses.

√ We can express the condition with **si**:

Si has leído el libro, podrás responder a las preguntas.	*If you have read the book, you will be able to answer the questions.*
Si llueve hoy, saldrán las flores.	*If it rains today, the flowers will bloom.*
Si tienes tiempo, ven con nosotros a la playa.	*If you have time, come with us to the beach.*

√ The other expressions of condition are the following:

a condición de que	*on condition that*
con que	*providing that*
con tal (de) que	*provided that*
en caso de que	*in case*
siempre y cuando	*provided that*

All these expressions are followed by a clause in the *subjuntivo*.

El grupo de ventas discute la exportación de un nuevo producto para el mercado latino americano.	*The marketing group is discussing about the export of a new product to the Latin American market.*
El nuevo producto será aceptado **a condición que** se haga bien la publicidad.	*The new product will be accepted on condition that the advertizing is well done.*
Tendremos éxito **siempre y cuando** el producto mantenga una calidad superior.	*We will be successful, provided that our product maintains a superior quality.*

Hypothesis is a condition which has not been met [173 - 175]. A hypothetical sentence contains two parts: a condition, and a process which depends on this condition. Since the condition has not been met, the process has not occurred. The basic rules for tense agreement are repeated here:

CONDITION	CONSEQUENCE
Si + *Imperfecto del subjuntivo*	*Futuro hipotético*
The condition is not met now, or is highly improbable in the future.	The consequence is not realized now, nor later, because the condition is not met.
Si + *Pasado perfecto del subjuntivo*	*Futuro hipotético perfecto*
The condition was not met in the past.	The consequence was not accomplished in the past because the condition was not met.
Si + *Pasado perfecto del subjuntivo*	*Futuro hipotético perfecto*
The condition was not met in the past.	The consequence is not accomplished now because the condition was not met then.

 Una escritora famosa

A Famous Writer

Si no hubiera estado débil de salud, no habría viajado al campo; **si** no hubiera viajado al campo, no habría conocido el mundo fantástico de la infancia; **si** no hubiera conocido el mundo fantástico de la infancia, no habría sido escritora, ni habría escrito cuentos, ni sería famosa; **si** no fuera famosa, no sabríamos que se llama Ana María Matute.

If she had not had poor health, she would not have gone to the country; if she had not gone to the country, she would not have known the fantastic world of childhood; if she had not known the fantastic world of childhood, she would not have been a writer, she would not have written tales, and she would not be famous; if she were not famous, we would not know that her name is Ana María Matute.

235

We call **opposition** a situation in which two opposite processes take place. We can express opposition with the following:

al contrario de	*contrary to*
por el contrario	*on the contrary*
en lugar de + V in the *infinitivo*	*instead of*
mientras que + clause in the *subjuntivo*	*while*
pero	*but*
por muy + Adj. + **que** + clause in the *subjuntivo*	*however* Adj.
por mucho/os/a/as + noun + **que** + clause	*however much, despite*
sin + V in the *infinitivo*	*without*
sin que + clause in the *subjuntivo*	*without*

El ayuntamiento aceptó la instalación de un vertedero regional en las afueras de la ciudad.

Town Hall accepted the installation of a regional dumping site in the outskirts of the city.

La comisión municipal aceptó la instalación de un vertedero regional **sin** consultar con los vecinos.

The town committee accepted the installation of a regional dumping site without consulting with the neighbors.

Por mucha oposición que hubo, se decidió hacerlo.

Despite the opposition, they decided to do it.

El ingeniero especialista en la materia explicó el bajo nivel de contaminación, **pero** el público no está convencido.

The expert engineer explained that the pollution level would be low, but the public is not convinced.

El público piensa que no se puede decidir sobre el caso **sin que** todos los interesados tengan la oportunidad de votar.

The public thinks that a decision cannot be made in that matter without giving the interested parties the opportunity to vote.

Expressing Concession √

We call **concession** a situation in which one process should prevent the other one from taking place. However both take place. We can express concession with the following:

a pesar de	*in spite of*
aun cuando	*in spite of*
***aunque/bien que* + Clause in the** *subjuntivo*	*although*
incluso si	*even though*
no obstante	*however*
***quienquiera+ que* + clause in the** *subjuntivo*	*whoever*
sin embargo	*however*

 Note that we can also express a concession by using the *subjuntivo* in a construction where the verb is repeated [171]:

Digas lo que digas...	*Whatever you say...*
Hagas lo que hagas...	*Whatever you do...*

 Los estudiantes detenidos fueron condenados.

The students who were arrested were condemned.

Los estudiantes detenidos fueron condenados	*The students arrested were condemned.*
1. **a pesar de** la opinión internacional;	*1. in spite of international opinion;*
2. **aunque** solo querían la libertad de expresión;	*2. although they only wanted freedom of speech;*
3. **aun cuando** todo indica que la mayoría de la población quiere un cambio.	*3. in spite of the fact that the majority of the population wants change.*
Quienquiera que proteste será encarcelado.	*Whoever protests will be incarcerated.*
Sin embargo, todo parece indicar que habrá un cambio de régimen.	*However, there are indications that there will be a change of regime.*

237

When we communicate, we put our ideas together and join them according to their importance. In order to join two ideas of the same importance, we use **coordinating conjunctions.**
The coordinating conjunctions are: *y (and), o (or), pero (but), ni (nor), pues (for).*

y

The conjunction **y** joins words, phrases, or sentences:

Esta casa es grande **y** bonita.	*This house is big and nice.*
Voy a comer un pastel **y** beber café.	*I'm going to eat a piece of cake and drink coffee.*
Después de la ceremonia, Luisa regresó a su casa **y** Pedro se quedó un rato más.	*After the ceremony, Luisa went back home and Pedro stayed a little longer.*

 Note that **y** becomes **e** if the following word begins with the vowel **i** (or **hi**):

Luisa **e** Isabel son buenas amigas.	*Luisa and Isabel are good friends.*
Bailó **e** hizo mucho ruido.	*He danced and made a lot of noise.*

o

The conjunction **o** indicates an alternative or a choice between two things:

¿Quieres fresa **o** chocolate?	*Do you want strawberry or chocolate?*
Puedes ir al cine **o** venir conmigo a la alberca.	*You can go to the movies or come with me to the swimming pool.*

 Note that **o** becomes **u** if the following word begins with the vowel **o** (or **ho**):

Juan **u** Octavio manejará el autobús.	*Juan or Octavio will drive the bus.*
Tengo siete **u** ocho rosales en el jardín.	*I have seven or eight rosebushes.*

238

pero

The conjunction **pero** conveys the meaning of opposition.

Me gustaría ir al concierto de
guitarra clásica, **pero** no puedo.

*I would like to go to the classical guitar
concert, but I cannot.*

ni

The conjunction **ni** is the negative counterpart of **y.**

No compré leche **ni** pan.
Ni escribe **ni** llama por teléfono.

I didn't buy milk nor bread.
He neither writes nor calls.

pues

The conjunction **pues** is very frequently used. Its meaning conveys the sense that the speaker can relate to the preceding message and link his or her response to it. It is therefore an important transition word.

— Me gusta ver películas en español.
— **Pues** nuestra tienda de video tiene una buena selección.

— *I like to see movies in Spanish.*
— *Well, our video store has a good selection.*

Pues si estás enfermo, no salgas con este frío.

Well, if you are sick, don't go out in this cold.

Explanatory Conjunctions

Some coordinating expressions are used for explanatory purposes.

a saber	*namely*
dicho, sea de paso	*by the way*
dicho de otra manera	*in other words*
digámoslo así	*so to speak*
en otros términos	*in other words*
es decir	*that is to say*
esto es	*that is*
mejor dicho	*rather*
por ejemplo	*for instance*

WORD FORMS
AND
MEANINGS

241

Stress and Marked Accent √

The stress is the intensity with which we pronounce a specific syllable in a word. When we pronounce a word, we give a special force to a syllable and pronounce its vowel louder. In Spanish, like in English, the stress is important because it can be contrastive, i.e., it can differentiate between meanings (the stressed syllables are in bold):

English: **re**cord (noun meaning 'disc') vs. re**cord** (verb, as in *I record music*)

Spanish: **pa**pa *(potato)* vs. pa**pá** *(dad)*
          canto *(I sing)* vs. can**tó** *(she/he sang)*

There are rules that determine on which syllable the stress falls. These rules are presented in the table below, in the left column. All the exceptions to these rules have to be learned individually, and will be **marked,** in writing, by an **accent** on the vowel.

WITHOUT MARKED ACCENT (Regular cases: the stress is pronounced, but there is no written accent.)	WITH MARKED ACCENT (Exceptions: the stressed vowel must carry a written accent.)
Rule 1 Words ending in a **consonant** other than **n** or **s**: *the last syllable is stressed:* ca**lor**, ha**cer**, pa**pel**, pa**red**, universi**dad**	*Exceptions to rule 1* **ár**bol, **cón**sul, **lá**piz
Rule 2 Words ending in **n** or **s,** or a **vowel**: *the syllable before last is stressed:* exa**men**, **Car**los, **to**mas, se**gun**da, **gen**te, **co**mo	*Exceptions to rule 2* al**gún**, Co**lón**, fran**cés** ca**fé**, a**quí**, co**mí**, to**mó**, bam**bú**
Rule 3 There are cases in which the stress falls on other syllables. But these cases are all exceptional and have to be memorized. See opposite column. ⟶	There is always a marked accent: **cán**taro, **cír**culo, **có**moda, **má**quina, **dí**gamelo, mate**má**ticas, **rá**pido

242

WORDS CONTAINING TWO VOWELS IN CONTACT

In order to know which syllable in a word carries the (oral) stress or bears a marked (written) accent, we apply the basic rules given in [242]. When these rules identify a syllable which contains two vowels, we have to determine which one of the two vowels will do the job. For that purpose, we distinguish between two sets of vowels: the open vowels (**e, a, o**), and the closed vowels (**i, u**).

√ If an open vowel (**e, a, o**) comes in contact with a closed vowel (**i, u**), stress the open vowel:

pu**e**rta, ci**e**rra, b**a**ile, b**o**ina, cami**ó**n

But if the closed vowel is exceptionally stressed, always put a marked accent on it:

cre**í**do, Mar**í**a, r**í**o, le**í**do, Ra**ú**l, o**í**r

√ If a closed vowel (**i, u**) comes in contact with another closed vowel, stress the second vowel:

r u**i**do, bu**i**tre, vi**u**do

√ If an open vowel (**e, a, o**) comes in contact with another open vowel, the two vowels count as two syllables, and the stress falls according to the basic rules [242]:

re**a**l, ro**er**, ca**er**	(rule 1)
creo, **cre**as, ma**es**tro	(rule 2)

 Examples of marked accents involving two vowels in contact.

boina   Rule 2 [242] identifies the syllable *boi*. This syllable contains an open vowel (**o**) and a closed one (**i**). Stress the open one: the word is pronounced with a stress on **o**.

cami**ón**   This is an exception to rule 2 [242] because the stress falls on the last syllable although the word ends in **n**.
Since it is an exception, we have to write a marked accent on the vowel.
Which vowel? The syllable has an open vowel and a closed one: the marked accent falls on the open vowel (**ó**).

243

PAIRS OF HOMONYMS

One-syllable words do not have a marked accent, except to distinguish between homonyms: *dé (give!)* vs. *de (of)*.

The following table includes **one- and two-syllable words** which have an important grammatical function and for which the marked accent indicates a difference in meaning.

WORDS	WITHOUT MARKED ACCENT	WITH MARKED ACCENT
aun	[Adv] *even* **Aun** su prima lejana de San Agustín vino a la boda. *Even her cousin from San Agùstin came to the wedding.*	[Adv] *still, yet* El novio no ha llegado **aún.** *The groom has not yet arrived.*
de	[Preposition] *of, from* Este es el recibo **del** agua. *This is the receipt of the water bill.*	[Verb] *to give* ¡**Dé** un recibo a cada uno! *Give a receipt to each one!*
el	[Article] *the* Este es **el** paquete. *This is the parcel.*	[Pronoun] *he* Este paquete es para **él.** *This parcel is for him.*
hacia	[Preposition] *towards* Vamos **hacia** el pueblo. *We are going towards the village.*	[Verb] *to do* **Hacía** 1 hora que andaba. *I had been walking for 1 hour.*
mas	[Conjunction] *but* Hubiera venido, **mas** no pude. *I would have come, but I could not.*	[Adv] *more* Quiere **más** mercancía. *He wants more merchandize.*
mi	[Possessive] *my* Esta es **mi** guitarra. *This is my guitar.*	[Pronoun] *me/myself* La guitarra es para **mí.** *The guitar is for me.*
si	[Conjunction] *if* **Si** viajo a Oaxaca tomaré fotos. *If I go to Oaxaca, I'll take pictures.*	[Adv] *yes* **Sí,** le gusta la biología. *Yes, he likes biology.* [Pronoun] *him/herself* Toma fotos para **sí** mismo. *He takes pictures for himself.*

WORDS	WITHOUT MARKED ACCENT	WITH MARKED ACCENT
se	[Pronoun] *himself/herself* En el nordeste de América **se** habla francés. *In north-eastern America, they speak French.*	[Verb] *to know* Yo **sé** que la provincia del Quebec es francohablante. *I know that Quebec is a French-speaking province.*
solo	[Adj] *single, alone* Todo lo hace **solo.** *He does everything alone.*	[Adv] *only, solely* **Sólo** trabaja por la mañana. *He works only in the morning.*
te	[Pronoun] *you* ¿**Te** apetece tomar algo? *Would you like to drink something?*	[Noun] *tea* Tengo **té** y café. *I have tea and coffee.*
tu	[Possessive] *your* **Tu** ciudad es muy bonita. *Your town is very nice.*	[Pronoun] *you* **Tú** vives en una ciudad bonita. *You live in a nice town.*
porque	[Conjunction] *because/since* No se le ve **porque** está enfermo. *We don't see him because he is sick.*	[Question word] *why* ¿**Por qué** no vino? *Why didn't he come?* [Noun] *cause* No sabemos el **porqué** de su enfermedad. *We don't know the cause of his sickness.*
este **ese** **aquel**	[Demonstrative Det.] *this/that* **Este** video es de mala calidad. *This video tape is bad.*	[Demonstrative pron.] ¡Dáme **éste!** *Give me this one!*
o	[Conjunction] *or* ¿Te gustaría café **o** té? *Would you like coffee or tea?*	[Conjunction] *or* It is used only between two numbers to avoid confusion with 0 (zero). Tengo 2 **ó** 3 dólares. *I have 2 or 3 dollars.*
que **donde** **quien** **cuanto**	[Relative Pronouns] El libro que he leído El pueblo donde nació El hombre a quien llamé Te he dicho cuanto sabía.	[Question} [Exclamation] ¿Qué? ¡Qué! ¿Dónde? ¡Dónde! ¿Quién? ¡Quién! ¿Cuánto? ¡Cuánto!

SINGULAR AND PLURAL

The stress always falls on the same syllable in the singular and the plural forms of the words:

pa**pel**/pa**pe**les *(paper)*; **ár**bol/**ár**boles *(tree)*; **má**quina/**má**quinas *(machine)*

Exceptions:
ca**rác**ter/caracte**res** *(character)*; **ré**gimen/re**gí**menes *(régime)*

 Note that because of this rule, some words will undergo a change in the marked accent:

joven	(rule 2)	*young*
jóvenes	(rule 3: stress on the first syllable does not follow from the first two rules; therefore we add a marked accent.)	
fran**cés**	(exception to rule 2)	*French*
fran**ce**ses	(rule 2)	

PRONOUNS

When one or two pronouns are attached to the ending of a verb in the *imperativo* and the *gerundio* [88], the oral stress does not change. As a consequence, we will add a marked accent to maintain the oral stress.

¡**Sa**ca la muela! (rule 2)		*Extract the molar!*
¡**Sá**cala!	(rule 3)	
Estoy to**man**do el examen. (rule 2)		*I am taking the exam.*
Estoy to**mán**dolo.		*I am taking it.*

ADVERBS IN -MENTE

Adverbs in **-mente** come from adjectives [207]. For adverbs in **-mente** the stress falls on the first syllable of the suffix, **men** [rule 2], and the adjective loses its original stress.

loca/loca**men**te   *crazy/crazily*

However, when the adjective carries a marked accent, the adverb keeps it and ends up with two stresses.

cor**tés**/cor**tés**mente; **fá**cil/**fá**cil**men**te   *courteous/courteously; easy/easily*

246

The Spanish alphabet is:

A	B	C	Ch	D	E	F	G	H	I
[a]	[be]	[ce]	[che]	[de]	[e]	[efe]	[ge]	[hache]	[i]

J	K	L	Ll	M	N	Ñ	O	P	Q
[jota]	[ka]	[ele]	[elle]	[eme]	[ene]	[eñe]	[o]	[pe]	[ku]

R	S	T	U	V	W		X	Y	Z
[erre]	[ese]	[te]	[u]	[uve]	[uve doble] [doble u (Mexico)] [doble ve (Argentina)]		[equis]	[I griega]	[zeta]

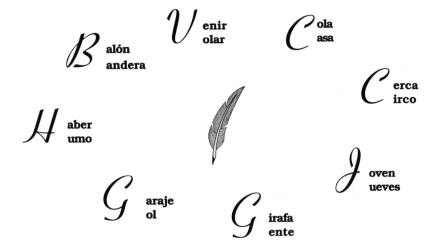

The main difficulties in Spanish spelling have to do with the following letters:

b/v

The letters **b** and **v** are both pronounced [b] in Spanish. It may therefore be difficult to know which letter to write when you spell a word that contains the sound [b]. Here are some useful generalizations.

The sound [b] is spelled *b* in:

√ words that begin with the prefix **al-**, immediately following the prefix: albaricoque *(apricot)*; albóndiga *(meatball)*

√ some prefixes:
ab- *(not)*: abnormal *(abnormal)*
bene- *(good)*: beneficio *(benefit)*; benigno *(benign)*
bio- *(life)*: biografía *(biography)*; biología *(biology)*
bi- *(two)*: bilingüe *(bilingual)*; bifurcarse *(to fork)*
sub- *(under)*: subconsciente *(subconscious)*; subcultura *(subculture)*

√ some suffixes:
able/ible (indicate a quality): amable *(kind)*; increíble *(incredible)*
abilidad/ibilidad: capabilidad *(capability)*; amabilidad *(kindness)*

√ *imperfecto* endings of **-ar** verbs: aba, abas, etc. [145]; and the *imperfecto* of the verb **ir**: iba, ibas, etc. [145]

√ after letter **m**; tambor *(drum)*
before letters **l** and **r**: abrazo *(hug)*; blanco *(white)*

The sound [b] is spelled *v* in:

√ the stem of the following irregular verbs in the *pretérito*: andar/andu**v**-; estar/estu**v**-; and tener/tu**v**- [141].

 Note that, in many cases, English can help us decide on the spelling of the sound [b], because many Spanish and English words have a common origin, and their form and spelling will therefore exhibit similarities. Here are some examples:

a**v**entura	*adventure*	o**b**stáculo	*obstacle*
inhi**b**ición	*inhibition*	**v**alor	*value*

However, you have to pay attention to some rare exceptions:

apro**b**ar	*approve*	pro**b**ar	*prove*
go**b**ernar	*govern*	reci**b**ir	*receive*

248

h

Contrary to English, the letter **h** in Spanish is mute; this means that it is not pronounced. It may therefore be difficult to know when to write it. Most words containing **h** have to be learned together with their spelling.

√   It is important to remember that the verbs **haber** and **hacer** begin with **h** in all their various tenses and forms. More specifically, remember that all the forms of the auxiliary which precede the *participio* begin with **h.**

     Ha viajado.   *She has traveled.*

     The **ha** in this sentence is the *presente del indicativo* of the auxiliary *haber;* and it precedes the *participio,* **viajado.** This should not be confused with the preposition **a** (similar in sound), which precedes the *infinitivo*:

     Va **a** viajar.   *She is going to travel.*

√   Another pair which has to be carefully differentiated is **hecho** *(done, made)* and **echo** *(I pour).*

     He **hecho** un buen plato.   *I made a good dish.*
     Echo sal en el plato.   *I put salt in the dish.*

   Note that, in most cases, referring to the English words which have the same origin, will help us find the correct spelling in Spanish. Here are some examples:

herencia	*heritage*	**h**umano	*human*
hospital	*hospital*	**h**uésped	*host*

     and all the words using prefixes, such as **hecto-**: hectolitro, *(hectoliter);* **hidr-**: hidroplano *(hydroplane);* hidráulica *(hydraulics);* **hiper-**: hipermercado *(hypermarket);* hipersensible *(hypersensitive);* **hipo-**: hipótesis *(hypothesis);* **homo-**: homónimo *(homonymous).*

Te echo de menos. I miss you.

g / j

The letter **j** is always pronounced [j], as in *pájaro*. But the sound [j] is sometimes spelled **g** (followed by **e** or **i**). It may therefore be difficult to know which letter to write when you spell a word that contains the sound [j] followed by letters **e** or **i**. Here are some useful remarks.

√ When the sound [j] is followed by **a, o,** or **u,** it is always spelled **j:**
jamón *(ham);* ajo *(garlic);* julio *(July).*

√ When the sound [j] is followed by **e** or **i,** it is written:

g in verbs ending in **-ger** and **-gir:** escoger *(choose);* elegir *(elect)*
in the prefix **geo-:** geografía *(geography)*
in the suffix **-gía:** biología *(biology)*
in words ending in **-gente:** agente *(agent);* vigente *(prevailing)*

j the words containing the letter **j** have to be learned individually.

PRONUNCIATION OF THE LETTER G

The letter **g** corresponds to two different sounds, depending on the letters following it. Here are the rules for pronouncing **g:**

√ ***g* is pronounced [g] :**

before **a, o, u:**   gato *(cat);* gorra *(cap);* legumbre *(vegetable)*
before **ue, ui:**   llegué *(I arrived);* guiñar *(to wink)*
before consonants: inglés *(English);* gramática *(grammar);* ignorante *(ignorant)*

√ ***g* is pronounced [j]:**

before **e** and **i:** general *(general);* girar *(to turn)*

Note that these two rules of pronunciation are important because they affect the spelling of certain verbs; see [134; 143].

√ ***g* followed by *üe* or *üi* is pronounced [gwe] or [gwi]:**
vergüenza *(shame);* pingüino *(penguin)*

√ ***g* followed by *ua* or *uo* is pronounced [gwa] ot [gwo]:**
lenguage *(language);* averiguo *(I guess)*

250

c / z / s

The three letters **c, z,** and **s** have the following properties:

Spanish spoken in Latin America, the US, Andalucia, and the Canary Isles	Castilian Spanish
The letters **s, z** and **c** followed by **e** or **i** are pronounced [s]. It is therefore important to pay careful attention when spelling this sound.	The letter **s** is pronounced [s]; and the letters **c** and **z** are pronounced [th], like the beginning sound of the English word *thin*.

Here are some useful remarks:

√ The words containing the letter **s** have to be learned individually.

√ The sounds [s]/[th] are spelled:

a. with the letter **z**:
  before the letters **a, o, u:** zapato *(shoe)*; zorro *(fox)*; azúcar *(sugar)*
  in the augmentative suffix **-azo/a:** ojazos *(big eyes)*
  in the suffix **-eza** (quality): aspereza *(roughness)*; belleza *(beauty)*
  in the suffix **-izar:** armonizar *(to harmonize)*; socializar *(to socialize)*
  in the suffix **-anza:** esperanza *(hope)*

b. with the letter **c,** before **e** and **i** in:
  the suffix **-ción:** atención *(attention)*; dirección *(direction)*
  the diminutive suffix **-cito/a:** florecita *(small flower)*
  the plural of words ending in **z:** *pez/peces (fish)*

PRONUNCIATION OF THE LETTER C

The letter **c** corresponds to two different sounds, depending on the letters following it.

√ *c* **is pronounced [k]:**

  before **a, o, u:** casa *(house)*; comer *(to eat)*; cuna *(cradle)*
  before consonants: clase *(class)*; crimen *(crime)*; acto *(act)*

√ *c* **is pronounced [s]/[th]:**

  before **e, i:** cerca *(near)*; vecino *(neighbor)*

 Note that the rules for pronouncing **z** before **a, o, u,** and **c** before **e** and **i,** [s]/[th] affect the spelling of certain verbs; see [134; 142; 143].

Capitalization √

Spanish has a simple system of capitalization. The following table shows the similarities and the differences between Spanish and English.

	SIMILARITIES SPANISH, LIKE ENGLISH, USES CAPITALS IN THE FOLLOWING CASES:	
The first letter of the first word in a sentence	**E**l diccionario está en la mesa.	*The dictionary is on the table.*
Proper nouns	**A**dina de **Z**avala **U**niversidad de **T**exas	*Adina de Zavala* *University of Texas*
Titles	el **R**ey Juan Carlos **P**rofesor Castro	*King Juan Carlos* *Professor Castro*

	DIFFERENCES	
	SPANISH **NO** **CAPITALIZATION**	**ENGLISH** **CAPITALIZATION**
Names of days and months	lunes, martes, viernes enero, febrero, marzo	*Monday, Tuesday, Friday* *January, February, March*
First person subject pronoun	yo	*I*
Names of languages	inglés, francés	*English, French*
Nouns and adjectives of nationality	los peruanos un ciudadano peruano	*the Peruvians* *a Peruvian citizen*
Nouns and adjectives of religion	budista, católico, judío, musulmán	*Buddhist, Catholic,* *Jewish, Muslim*
Titles of books, major works	**C**ien años de soledad	*A Hundred Years of Solitude*

Punctuation marks are the same in English and in Spanish, although some differ in their uses.

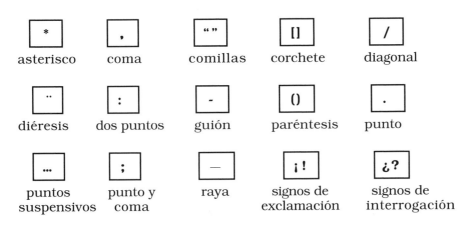

*	,	" "	[]	/
asterisco	coma	comillas	corchete	diagonal
··	:	-	()	.
diéresis	dos puntos	guión	paréntesis	punto
...	;	—	¡!	¿?
puntos suspensivos	punto y coma	raya	signos de exclamación	signos de interrogación

Punctuation marks the pauses in a sentence, indicates the structure of the sentence, and therefore helps the reader construct meaning. For instance, read the following sentence, which has two meanings, depending on its punctuation.

Estos campesinos, dijeron los soldados, son perezosos.

These peasants, said the soldiers, are lazy.

Estos campesinos dijeron: "los soldados son perezosos".

These peasants said: "the soldiers are lazy."

Here are the main uses of the most frequently used punctuation signs.

¡! and ¿? Signos de exclamación y de interrogación

In Spanish, inverted exclamation and question marks are placed at the beginning of the exclamation or question, and regular exclamation and question marks come at the end.

¡Dámelo!
¿Vienes al concierto?

Give it to me!
Are you coming to the concert?

These marks always frame exclamations and questions even if these constitute only part of a whole sentence:

Si no te gusta la música, ¿por qué vas al concierto?

If you don't like music, why are you going to the concert?

Coma

In Spanish, like in English, the comma is used in the following cases:

√ between two clauses linked by a coordinating conjunction [238 - 239]. The comma is placed after the first clause, before the conjunction:

Sylvia salió para Honduras, pero Luis se quedó en Miami.	*Sylvia left for Honduras, but Luis stayed in Miami.*
Luis lanzó el balón, y Eva lo agarró.	*Luis threw the ball, and Eva caught it.*

√ to set apart additional information; the comma comes before and after the phrase:

Manuel, que siempre está en la luna, no se enteró de la noticia.	*Manuel, who always has his head in the clouds, did not hear the news.*
Puerto Rico, refiriéndonos al marco histórico, es una isla con muchos lugares para visitar.	*Puerto Rico, from a historical point of view, is an island with a lot of places to visit.*
Luis Gonzales, el maestro de mi hermano, hará una presentación sobre la cultura caribeña.	*Luis Gonzales, my brother's teacher, will give a talk on Caribbean culture.*

√ to set apart connectives, such as *a menudo (often), en cambio (on the other hand), en fin (finally), en realidad (actually), es decir (that is to say), no obstante (nevertheless), por consiguiente (consequently), por ejemplo (for example), por último (finally), sin duda (undoubtedly), sin embargo (however),* etc.

Espero, sin embargo, que puedas participar en el concurso.	*I hope, however, that you will be able to participate in the contest.*
En realidad, no cuesta mucho viajar por América Latina.	*Actually, it does not cost much to travel in Latin America.*
Mi hermana, por ejemplo, visitó varios países con muy poco dinero.	*My sister, for instance, visited various countries with very little money.*

254

√ when a circumstantial clause precedes the main clause, a comma separates the two clauses:

Cuando yo regresé de la excursión, dormí 12 horas.	*When I came back from the trip, I slept 12 hours.*
Para estar en forma, hay que hacer ejercicio todos los días.	*To be in good shape, one must exercise every day.*
Corriendo en el parque, me encontré con un antiguo compañero de escuela.	*Jogging in the park, I met an old schoolmate.*

Like English, Spanish uses commas to separate the items in a series; but, unlike English, there is no comma between the last two items, which are separated only by the coordinating conjunction **y**.

Tiene en su bolsa libros, lápices, estampillas **y** otras cosas.	*In her bag, she has books, pencils, stamps, and other things.*

 Comillas

√ The quotation marks are used to enclose direct quotations in your own text. Punctuation marks that punctuate the quotation are inside, and those that punctuate your sentence are outside of the quotation marks.

Me acordé del viejo proverbio "donde fueres, haz lo que vieres", pero no lo seguí.	*I remembered the old proverb "when in Rome, do as the Romans do", but I didn't follow it.*

 Note that, when both the quoted piece and your sentence are punctuated, the punctuation mark is placed outside.

Me acordé del viejo proverbio "donde fueres, haz lo que vieres".	*I remembered the old proverb "when in Rome, do as the Romans do."*

√ The quotation marks are also used to frame quoted titles, to put emphasis on an element or to signal foreign words:

Vi la serie televisiva "Los gitanos".	*I watched the TV series "Los Gitanos."*
Mi gato es "el rey" de la casa.	*My cat is "the king" of the house.*
Es el típico "yuppy" de los ochenta.	*He is the typical yuppy of the 80's.*

Diminutives √

In Spanish, several suffixes are used to express the size. To describe something little, we use the diminutive suffixes **-ito/ita, -cito/cita,** and **-ico/ica/ín.**

Words ending in a vowel other than *e* take *-ito/ita.*

casa	casita	*house*
silla	sillita	*chair*
perro	perrito	*dog*
vaso	vasito	*glass*
Pablo	Pablito	*Little Pablo*

Words ending in a consonant, or *e* take *-cito/cita* .

noche	nochecita	*night*
parque	parquecito	*park*
pan	panecito	*bread*
flor	florecita	*flower*
Carmen	Carmencita	*Little Carmen*

The diminutive is usually associated with an affective nuance: small is viewed as nice, charming, or emotionally engaging:

Pobrecito, este niñito, que le duele *Poor little boy, he has a headache.*
la cabecita.

This affective nuance is also clear in the use of diminutives with adverbs, especially in spoken Latin-American Spanish.

ahora	ahorita	*now*	despacio	despacito	*slowly*
aprisa	aprisita	*fast*	junto	juntito	*together*
arriba	arribita	*up*	lejos	lejitos	*far*
cerca	cerquita	*close*	luego	lueguito	*soon*

 Note that other suffixes are also used: **-ín** *(pequeñín, small)* and **-illo/illa** *(chiquilla, small girl).*

To describe something big, we use the augmentative suffixes **-azo/aza, -ón/ona,** and **-ote/ota.** There are no specific rules for the selection of the augmentative suffixes. Here are some examples:

-azo/a

perro	perrazo	*dog*
gato	gatazo	*cat*
dedo	dedazo	*finger*
hombre	hombrazo	*man*
bigote	bigotazo	*mustache*
jefe	jefazo	*boss*

-ón/ona

casa	casona	*house*
mujer	mujerona	*woman*

-ote /ota

grande	grandote	*big*
muchacho	muchachote	*child*
nariz	narizota	*nose*

Most augmentatives have a depreciative meaning: things that are bigger than expected are viewed as disproportionate.

 Note that there are a number of words ending with augmentative suffixes, but which take a different meaning. *Orejón* refers to a person with big ears and *llorón*, to a person who cries a lot.

Some suffixes are always and clearly derogatory: **-ucho/ucha, aco/aca, -uzo/uza, -zuelo/zuela...**

-ucho/ucha

casa	casucha	*shack*
feo	feucho	*ugly*
pálido	paliducho	*pale*

-aco/a

pájaro	pajarraco	*big ugly bird*

-uzo/uza

gente	gentuza	*mob*

-zuelo/zuela

rey	reyezuelo	*petty king*

APPENDIX

SELF-CORRECTION

You will become an independent learner.

This section will help you master the Spanish language and become an independent learner. Being able to find your own mistakes, and to correct them will enable you to be your own master, independent, confident and competent. In the learning process, teachers and tutors are helpful to explain and guide you; but you will achieve knowledge and gain satisfaction when you can rely on your own abilities. Then the relation with the learning environment will be more productive, and therefore more exciting and motivating.

You will achieve grammatical accuracy.

In this section you will find a system which helps you **check and correct** your written and oral work. The goal is to achieve grammatical accuracy, and to speak and write correctly in Spanish. When preparing for a written essay or an oral presentation, you will follow the steps described in this section:

(1) Production: writing or speaking.
(2) Verification and self-correction: using self-correction techniques.

You will use the self-correction system.

The self-correction techniques are the same for written and oral assignments. However, there are specific ways to use them in writing or speaking.

Page 263   presents specific strategies for written assignments.
Pages 264 - 265   presents specific strategies for oral assignments.
Pages 266 - 270   present the self-correction strategies common to
                    both writing and speaking.

Write your essay.

First write your essay, following the general strategies for writing a composition:

1. **Search** for information in magazines, catalogues, newspapers, books, encyclopedias. Select the materials which are relevant to your topic and read them carefully, taking notes and highlighting key words.

2. **Organize** your ideas, using diagrams and maps, and then write an outline which shows the different parts of your essay.

3. **Write** your essay and revise it as many times as needed to make it clear and effective.

When all these tasks are completed, you can start verification and self-correction of your essay, using the self-correction techniques given in [266 - 270] in the way explained below.

Verify and correct the language in your essay.

The general principle that you will use is the following: **check one sentence at a time**, focusing on one element at a time and following the guidelines given in the self-correction section [266 - 270]. They will help you find your errors. The page numbers given next to each point identify the page or pages in which you will find the correct forms.

Follow the self-correction guidelines.

You will use the self-correction guidelines to check and correct your essay. Do not forget to also check the spelling and punctuation [247 - 255] as well as the accents [242 - 246].

Record your oral presentation.

When you have an oral presentation to make in front of a group of people, it is helpful to follow the preparation strategy given here.

1. Search for information as you would do for a written assignment.

2. Organize your ideas: structuring your presentation will make it coherent and more interesting. You may write an outline which shows the different parts of your presentation.

3. Plan to use hand-outs, visuals, and any document which might be helpful to support your presentation: pictures, graphics, recordings. These documents are important to illustrate and clarify your points. They will also help divert the listeners' attention from the speaker to the materials and therefore alleviate the speaker's "stage fright."

4. Use a tape recorder and record your speech without writing it in advance. You can write a number of expressions which you plan to use; but never write the complete text of your presentation. Oral presentations do not consist of reading a written text, but rather presenting your ideas clearly.

When all these tasks are completed, you can start verification and self-correction of your presentation, using the self-correction techniques given in [266 - 270], in the way explained below.

Follow the self-correction guidelines.

The general principle that you will use is the following: **check one sentence at a time**, focusing on one element at a time and following the guidelines given in the self-correction section. They will help you find your errors. The page numbers given next to each point identify the page or pages in which you will find the correct forms.

Begin with short oral presentations. One-minute presentations have proved to provide a reasonable amount of material, easy to handle at the beginning stages of independent work.

Verify and correct the language of your presentation.

The sentence-by-sentence correction has to be done **orally:**

(a) Listen carefully to the first sentence, apply the self-correction technique to find out if you have made mistakes. When you do find a mistake, look for the correct form in the appropriate sections of the grammar, and repeat it several times.

(b) Move on to the next sentence and apply the same strategy. Then move on to the next sentence, and so on, until the end of your recorded oral presentation.

(c) Record your speech a second time, again without writing it.

(d) Start a second self-correction. Repeat the process as many times as needed.

The various recordings do not have to be identical. Since you do not write the text of your presentation, it is expected that there may be differences between the first recording and the second, and so on. This is acceptable. What is important is that this technique enables you to work systematically on improving your speech, rather than memorizing a single oral assignment. What is crucial is **the process of learning through independent self-correction.**

You will use the self-correction guidelines to check and correct your presentation.

Do not forget to work on pronunciation and intonation.

265

Verify the verb phrase.

Verification of the verb phrase is the most important because the verb is the core element of the sentence. Four aspects of the verb phrase should be verified for all sentences:

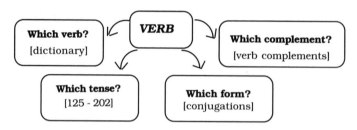

Verify the noun phrase.

Verification of the noun phrase involves the elements that accompany the noun and the elements which can replace the noun phrase: the pronouns.

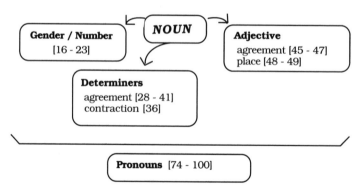

Verify the whole sentence.

Verification of the whole sentence involves word order [213], sentence structure [212 - 220], and sentence expansion [223 - 239].

266

Check the verb phrase.

Using the following sentence as an example of text to check out, we will now follow the self-correction system and check the verb phrase:

> Mi amigo italiano aprende a tocar la guitarra.
> *My Italian friend learns how to play the guitar.*

√ **Which verb?** Find the verb that expresses exactly what you want to communicate. The two verbs needed to express this message are:

aprender *(learn)* and

tocar *(play an instrument).*

√ **Which tense?** Find the tense appropriate to the situation you are describing. The tenses to be used in this situation are:

the *presente* [127] for the main verb, *aprender.*

the *infinitivo* [197] for the second verb, *tocar,* because it follows a preposition *(a).*

√ **Which form?** Find the proper form of the verb, in agreement with the subject, i.e., check the conjugation:

aprende	The subject *mi amigo* is 3rd person singular. The verb is an **-er** verb. In the *presente*, 3rd person singular, the form is **aprende** [128, or see *verb conjugations*].
tocar	The second verb is in the *infinitivo*, which is not conjugated in Spanish.

√ **Which complement?** Find the complement required by the verb [see the section *Verb Complements*].

aprender:	**aprender + a + Verb in the** *infinitivo*
tocar:	**tocar + noun phrase (an instrument)**

267

Check the noun phrase.

Having checked the verb or verbs in the sentence, we now focus on each noun, its determiner, and its modifiers.

Our sentence *"Mi amigo italiano aprende a tocar la guitarra"* contains two nouns.

√ **Gender / Number** Check the gender and number of the nouns.

mi amigo italiano:	**amigo** is masculine singular.
la guitarra:	**guitarra** is feminine singular.

√ **Determiners** Check agreement of the determiners.

mi amigo italiano:	**mi** is the possessive determiner used for masculine [40].
la guitarra:	**la** is the definite article used for the feminine singular [36].

√ **Adjectives**

(a) Check agreement:

mi amigo italiano:	**italiano** is the masculine singular [44 - 45].
la guitarra:	There is no adjective.

(b) Check place of adjectives:

mi amigo italiano:	**italiano** is an adjective of nationality and comes after the noun [48].
la guitarra:	There is no adjective.

Check the pronouns.

You now have to check the pronouns. Since there are no pronouns in our sentence, we will give a specific example for each kind of pronoun.

√ **Personal pronouns**   Check their form and place [76 - 91].

Ellos me telefonean cada mañana para despertarme.

They phone me every morning to wake me up.

ellos   It is the 3rd person plural masculine subject pronoun [77]. It comes in the beginning, before other pronouns [78].

me   It is the 1st person singular object pronoun [80]. It comes before the conjugated verb [88].

me   It is the 1st person singular object pronoun [80]. It is attached to the end of the verb in the *infinitivo* [88].

√ **Reflexive pronouns**   Check their form and place [83; 88 - 90].

Me he peinado y quiero verme en el espejo.

I combed my hair and I want to see myself in the mirror.

me   It is the 1st person singular reflexive [83], and comes before the conjugated verb *peino* [88].

me   It is the same reflexive, but attaches to the *infinitivo ver* [88].

√ **Demonstrative pronouns**   Check their form [92].

Mi camisa es barata, pero ésta es cara.

My shirt is inexpensive, but this one is expensive.

ésta   It is the demonstrative pronoun used for feminine singular, near to the speaker [92].

√ **Check the possessive pronouns**   Check their form [93].

Mi casa es más grande que la tuya.

My house is bigger than yours.

la tuya It is the possessive pronoun used for feminine singular, belonging to you [93].

269

Check the sentence.

When you have checked the verbs, the nouns, the pronouns in a specific sentence, it is now time to check the whole sentence and its structure. We will check the following sentence:

¿Por qué no visitaste más museos en Madrid el año pasado?

Why didn't you visit more museums in Madrid last year?

√ **Check the negative sentences** [216].

no   It is the negative word and comes before the verb.

√ **Check the question form** [214 - 215].

por qué   It is the question word and comes at the beginning [214].

Spanish uses a reversed question mark before the sentence [214].

√ **Check comparative and superlative forms** [50 - 58].

más   It is the higher degree of comparison which comes before nouns [53].

Check the circumstances.

en Madrid expresses the place where the process took place.

el año pasado expresses the time when the process took place [224].

por qué   indicates that the speaker wants to know the cause, why the process took place [214].

VERB CONJUGATIONS

This section contains the complete conjugation of 54 verbs. Each conjugation chart is followed by a list of the most frequently used verbs conjugated according to the same pattern (292 irregular and 3 regular verbs in total). The complete list of verbs is given in the index. These charts are helpful for finding the forms quickly, without referring to the rules. If rules are needed, see [127 - 202].

This section does not contain:

(a) the second form of the *imperfecto del subjuntivo* [183] because it is always predictable. The form is based on the one given in the charts, with the following change: **Ra** is replaced by **se**:

Example

First form	Second form
almorza**ra**	almorza**se**
almorza**ras**	almorza**ses**
almorza**ra**	almorza**se**
almorzá**ramos**	almorzá**semos**
almorza**rais**	almorza**seis**
almorza**ran**	almorza**sen**

(b) the second form of the *pasado perfecto del subjuntivo* [185]. It is formed with the *imperfecto del subjuntivo* of *haber* followed by the *participio* of the verb.

Example

First form	Second form
hubiera almorzado	hubiese almorzado
hubieras almorzado	hubieses almorzado
hubiera almorzado	hubiese almorzado
hubiéramos almorzado	hubiésemos almorzado
hubierais almorzado	hubieseis almorzado
hubieran almorzado	hubiesen almorzado

(c) the complete conjugation of pronominal verbs [116]. Their conjugation is similar to the non-pronominal counterparts, with the following changes: It comes with a pronoun before the verb in conjugated tenses, and it is attached at the end of the verb in non-conjugated forms with an accent added in the *gerundio* and the affirmative *imperativo*:

me lavo, **te** lavas, **se** lava, **nos** lavamos, **os** laváis, **se** lavan

lavar**se**, lavándo**se;** láva**te**, láve**se**, lavémo**nos**, lava**os**, láven**se**

INDICATIVO

Presente	Presente perfecto	Imperfecto	Pasado perfecto
almuerzo	he almorzado	almorzaba	había almorzado
almuerzas	has almorzado	almorzabas	habías almorzado
almuerza	ha almorzado	almorzaba	había almorzado
almorzamos	hemos almorzado	almorzábamos	habíamos almorzado
almorzáis	habéis almorzado	almorzabais	habíais almorzado
almuerzan	han almorzado	almorzaban	habían almorzado

Futuro	Futuro perfecto	Fut. hip.	Fut. perf. hip.
almorzaré	habré almorzado	almorzaría	habría almorzado
almorzarás	habrás almorzado	almorzarías	habrías almorzado
almorzará	habrá almorzado	almorzaría	habría almorzado
almorzaremos	habremos almorzado	almorzaríamos	habríamos almorzado
almorzaréis	habréis almorzado	almorzaríais	habríais almorzado
almorzarán	habrán almorzado	almorzarían	habrían almorzado

Pretérito	Pretérito perf.
almorcé	hube almorzado
almorzaste	hubiste almorzado
almorzó	hubo almorzado
almorzamos	hubimos almorzado
almorzasteis	hubisteis almorzado
almorzaron	hubieron almorzado

IMPERATIVO

Afirmativo	Negativo
almuerza (tú)	no almuerces
almuerce (Ud.)	no almuerce
almorcemos	no almorcemos
almorzad	no almorcéis
almuercen	no almuercen

SUBJUNTIVO

Presente	Presente perfecto	Imperfecto	Pasado perfecto
almuerce	haya almorzado	almorzara	hubiera almorzado
almuerces	hayas almorzado	almorzaras	hubieras almorzado
almuerce	haya almorzado	almorzara	hubiera almorzado
almorcemos	hayamos almorzado	almorzáramos	hubiéramos almorzado
almorcéis	hayáis almorzado	almorzarais	hubierais almorzado
almuercen	hayan almorzado	almorzaran	hubieran almorzado

INFINITIVO   PARTICIPIO   GERUNDIO

Simple	Perfecto		Simple	Perfecto
almorzar	haber almorzado	almorzado	almorzando	habiendo almorzado

Another verb: avergonzar**se***
* **avergonzarse** is conjugated like **almorzar,** with the following changes: (i) it is a
pronominal verb [272]; (ii) the diaeresis is added on the **u** before **e**: avergüénzate, etc.

INDICATIVO

Presente	Presente perfecto	Imperfecto	Pasado perfecto
ando	he andado	andaba	había andado
andas	has andado	andabas	habías andado
anda	ha andado	andaba	había andado
andamos	hemos andado	andábamos	habíamos andado
andáis	habéis andado	andabais	habíais andado
andan	han andado	andaban	habían andado

Futuro	Futuro perfecto	Fut. hip.	Fut. perf. hip.
andaré	habré andado	andaría	habría andado
andarás	habrás andado	andarías	habrías andado
andará	habrá andado	andaría	habría andado
andaremos	habremos andado	andaríamos	habríamos andado
andaréis	habréis andado	andaríais	habríais andado
andarán	habrán andado	andarían	habrían andado

Pretérito	Pretérito perfecto
anduve	hube andado
anduviste	hubiste andado
anduvo	hubo andado
anduvimos	hubimos andado
anduvisteis	hubisteis andado
anduvieron	hubieron andado

IMPERATIVO

Afirmativo	Negativo
anda (tú)	no andes
ande (Ud.)	no ande
andemos	no andemos
andad	no andéis
anden	no anden

SUBJUNTIVO

Presente	Presente perfecto	Imperfecto	Pasado perfecto
ande	haya andado	anduviera	hubiera andado
andes	hayas andado	anduvieras	hubieras andado
ande	haya andado	anduviera	hubiera andado
andemos	hayamos andado	anduviéramos	hubiéramos andado
andéis	hayáis andado	anduvierais	hubierais andado
anden	hayan andado	anduvieran	hubieran andado

INFINITIVO   PARTICIPIO   GERUNDIO

Simple	Perfecto		Simple	Perfecto
andar	haber andado	andado	andando	habiendo andado

INDICATIVO

Presente	Presente perfecto	Imperfecto	Pasado perfecto
quepo	he cabido	cabía	había cabido
cabes	has cabido	cabías	habías cabido
cabe	ha cabido	cabía	había cabido
cabemos	hemos cabido	cabíamos	habíamos cabido
cabéis	habéis cabido	cabíais	habíais cabido
caben	han cabido	cabían	habían cabido

Futuro	Futuro perfecto	Fut. hip.	Fut. perf. hip.
cabré	habré cabido	cabría	habría cabido
cabrás	habrás cabido	cabrías	habrías cabido
cabrá	habrá cabido	cabría	habría cabido
cabremos	habremos cabido	cabríamos	habríamos cabido
cabréis	habréis cabido	cabríais	habríais cabido
cabrán	habrán cabido	cabrían	habrían cabido

Pretérito	Pretérito perfecto
cupe	hube cabido
cupiste	hubiste cabido
cupo	hubo cabido
cupimos	hubimos cabido
cupisteis	hubisteis cabido
cupieron	hubieron cabido

IMPERATIVO

Afirmativo	Negativo
cabe (tú)	no quepas
quepa (Ud.)	no quepa
quepamos	no quepamos
cabed	no quepáis
quepan	no quepan

SUBJUNTIVO

Presente	Presente perfecto	Imperfecto	Pasado perfecto
quepa	haya cabido	cupiera	hubiera cabido
quepas	hayas cabido	cupieras	hubieras cabido
quepa	haya cabido	cupiera	hubiera cabido
quepamos	hayamos cabido	cupiéramos	hubiéramos cabido
quepáis	hayáis cabido	cupierais	hubierais cabido
quepan	hayan cabido	cupieran	hubieran cabido

INFINITIVO | PARTICIPIO | GERUNDIO

Simple	Perfecto		Simple	Perfecto
caber	haber cabido	cabido	cabiendo	habiendo cabido

275

INDICATIVO

Presente	Presente perfecto	Imperfecto	Pasado perfecto
cuezo	he cocido	cocía	había cocido
cueces	has cocido	cocías	habías cocido
cuece	ha cocido	cocía	había cocido
cocemos	hemos cocido	cocíamos	habíamos cocido
cocéis	habéis cocido	cocíais	habíais cocido
cuecen	han cocido	cocían	habian cocido

Futuro	Futuro perfecto	Fut. hip.	Fut. perf. hip.
coceré	habré cocido	cocería	habría cocido
cocerás	habrás cocido	cocerías	habrías cocido
cocerá	habrá cocido	cocería	habría cocido
coceremos	habremos cocido	coceríamos	habríamos cocido
coceréis	habréis cocido	coceríais	habríais cocido
cocerán	habrán cocido	cocerían	habrían cocido

Pretérito	Pretérito perf.
cocí	hube cocido
cociste	hubiste cocido
coció	hubo cocido
cocimos	hubimos cocido
cocisteis	hubisteis cocido
cocieron	hubieron cocido

IMPERATIVO

Afirmativo	Negativo
cuece (tú)	no cuezas
cueza (Ud.)	no cueza
cozamos	no cozamos
coced	no cozáis
cuezan	no cuezan

SUBJUNTIVO

Presente	Presente perfecto	Imperfecto	Pasado perfecto
cueza	haya cocido	cociera	hubiera cocido
cuezas	hayas cocido	cocieras	hubieras cocido
cueza	haya cocido	cociera	hubiera cocido
cozamos	hayamos cocido	cociéramos	hubiéramos cocido
cozáis	hayáis cocido	cocierais	hubierais cocido
cuezan	hayan cocido	cocieran	hubieran cocido

INFINITIVO
Simple	Perfecto
cocer	haber cocido

PARTICIPIO
cocido

GERUNDIO
Simple	Perfecto
cociendo	habiendo cocido

Another verb: torcer

276

INDICATIVO

Presente	Presente perfecto	Imperfecto	Pasado perfecto
cuelgo	he colgado	colgaba	había colgado
cuelgas	has colgado	colgabas	habías colgado
cuelga	ha colgado	colgaba	había colgado
colgamos	hemos colgado	colgábamos	habíamos colgado
colgáis	habéis colgado	colgabais	habíais colgado
cuelgan	han colgado	colgaban	habían colgado

Futuro	Futuro perfecto	Fut. hip.	Fut. perf. hip.
colgaré	habré colgado	colgaría	habría colgado
colgarás	habrás colgado	colgarías	habrías colgado
colgará	habrá colgado	colgaría	habría colgado
colgaremos	habremos colgado	colgaríamos	habríamos colgado
colgaréis	habréis colgado	colgaríais	habríais colgado
colgarán	habrán colgado	colgarían	habrían colgado

Pretérito	Pretérito perf.
colgué	hube colgado
colgaste	hubiste colgado
colgó	hubo colgado
colgamos	hubimos colgado
colgasteis	hubisteis colgado
colgaron	hubieron colgado

IMPERATIVO

Afirmativo	Negativo
cuelga (tú)	no cuelgues
cuelgue (Ud.)	no cuelgue
colguemos	no colguemos
colgad	no colguéis
cuelguen	no cuelguen

SUBJUNTIVO

Presente	Presente perfecto	Imperfecto	Pasado perfecto
cuelgue	haya colgado	colgara	hubiera colgado
cuelgues	hayas colgado	colgaras	hubieras colgado
cuelgue	haya colgado	colgara	hubiera colgado
colguemos	hayamos colgado	colgáramos	hubiéramos colgado
colguéis	hayáis colgado	colgarais	hubierais colgado
cuelguen	hayan colgado	colgaran	hubieran colgado

INFINITIVO / PARTICIPIO / GERUNDIO

INFINITIVO Simple	Perfecto	PARTICIPIO	GERUNDIO Simple	Perfecto
colgar	haber colgado	colgado	colgando	habiendo colgado

Another verb: rogar

277

INDICATIVO

Presente	Presente perfecto	Imperfecto	Pasado perfecto
comienzo	he comenzado	comenzaba	había comenzado
comienzas	has comenzado	comenzabas	habías comenzado
comienza	ha comenzado	comenzaba	había comenzado
comenzamos	hemos comenzado	comenzábamos	habíamos comenzado
comenzáis	habéis comenzado	comenzabais	habíais comenzado
comienzan	han comenzado	comenzaban	habían comenzado

Futuro	Futuro perfecto	Fut. hip.	Fut. perf. hip.
comenzaré	habré comenzado	comenzaría	habría comenzado
comenzarás	habrás comenzado	comenzarías	habrías comenzado
comenzará	habrá comenzado	comenzaría	habría comenzado
comenzaremos	habremos comenzado	comenzaríamos	habríamos comenzado
comenzaréis	habréis comenzado	comenzaríais	habríais comenzado
comenzarán	habrán comenzado	comenzarían	habrían comenzado

Pretérito	Pretérito perf.
comencé	hube comenzado
comenzaste	hubiste comenzado
comenzó	hubo comenzado
comenzamos	hubimos comenzado
comenzasteis	hubisteis comenzado
comenzaron	hubieron comenzado

IMPERATIVO

Afirmativo	Negativo
comienza (tú)	no comiences
comience (Ud.)	no comience
comencemos	no comencemos
comenzad	no comencéis
comiencen	no comiencen

SUBJUNTIVO

Presente	Presente perfecto	Imperfecto	Pasado perfecto
comience	haya comenzado	comenzara	hubiera comenzado
comiences	hayas comenzado	comenzaras	hubieras comenzado
comience	haya comenzado	comenzara	hubiera comenzado
comencemos	hayamos comenzado	comenzáramos	hubiéramos comenzado
comencéis	hayáis comenzado	comenzarais	hubierais comenzado
comiencen	hayan comenzado	comenzaran	hubieran comenzado

INFINITIVO
Simple comenzar **Perfecto** haber comenzado

PARTICIPIO
comenzado

GERUNDIO
Simple comenzando **Perfecto** habiendo comenzado

Other verbs: empezar, tropezar

278

INDICATIVO

Presente	Presente perfecto	Imperfecto	Pasado perfecto
como	he comido	comía	había comido
comes	has comido	comías	habías comido
come	ha comido	comía	había comido
comemos	hemos comido	comíamos	habíamos comido
coméis	habéis comido	comíais	habíais comido
comen	han comido	comían	habían comido

Futuro	Futuro perfecto	Fut. hip.	Fut. perf. hip.
comeré	habré comido	comería	habría comido
comerás	habrás comido	comerías	habrías comido
comerá	habrá comido	comería	habría comido
comeremos	habremos comido	comeríamos	habríamos comido
comeréis	habréis comido	comeríais	habríais comido
comerán	habrán comido	comerían	habrían comido

Pretérito	Pretérito perf.
comí	hube comido
comiste	hubiste comido
comió	hubo comido
comimos	hubimos comido
comisteis	hubisteis comido
comieron	hubieron comido

IMPERATIVO

Afirmativo	Negativo
come (tú)	no comas
coma (Ud.)	no coma
comamos	no comamos
comed	no comáis
coman	no coman

SUBJUNTIVO

Presente	Presente perfecto	Imperfecto	Pasado perfecto
coma	haya comido	comiera	hubiera comido
comas	hayas comido	comieras	hubieras comido
coma	haya comido	comiera	hubiera comido
comamos	hayamos comido	comiéramos	hubiéramos comido
comáis	hayáis comido	comierais	hubierais comido
coman	hayan comido	comieran	hubieran comido

INFINITIVO   PARTICIPIO   GERUNDIO

Simple	Perfecto		Simple	Perfecto
comer	haber comido	comido	comiendo	habiendo comido

* **romper** is regular except for the *participio*: roto

279

INDICATIVO

Presente	Presente perfecto	Imperfecto	Pasado perfecto
concluyo	he concluido	concluía	había concluido
concluyes	has concluido	concluías	habías concluido
concluye	ha concluido	concluía	había concluido
concluimos	hemos concluido	concluíamos	habíamos concluido
concluís	habéis concluido	concluíais	habíais concluido
concluyen	han concluido	concluían	habían concluido

Futuro	Futuro perfecto	Fut. hip.	Fut. perf. hip.
concluiré	habré concluido	concluiría	habría concluido
concluirás	habrás concluido	concluirías	habrías concluido
concluirá	habrá concluido	concluiría	habría concluido
concluiremos	habremos concluido	concluiríamos	habríamos concluido
concluiréis	habréis concluido	concluiríais	habríais concluido
concluirán	habrán concluido	concluirían	habrían concluido

Pretérito	Pretérito perf.
concluí	hube concluido
concluiste	hubiste concluido
concluyó	hubo concluido
concluimos	hubimos concluido
concluisteis	hubisteis concluido
concluyeron	hubieron concluido

IMPERATIVO

Afirmativo	Negativo
concluye (tú)	no concluyas
concluya (Ud.)	no concluya
concluyamos	no concluyamos
concluid	no concluyáis
concluyan	no concluyan

SUBJUNTIVO

Presente	Presente perfecto	Imperfecto	Pasado perfecto
concluya	haya concluido	concluyera	hubiera concluido
concluyas	hayas concluido	concluyeras	hubieras concluido
concluya	haya concluido	concluyera	hubiera concluido
concluyamos	hayamos concluido	concluyéramos	hubiéramos concluido
concluyáis	hayáis concluido	concluyerais	hubierais concluido
concluyan	hayan concluido	concluyeran	hubieran concluido

INFINITIVO

Simple	Perfecto
concluir	haber concluido

PARTICIPIO

concluido

GERUNDIO

Simple	Perfecto
concluyendo	habiendo concluido

Other verbs: all verbs ending in **-uir,** such as construir, contribuir, destruir, influir, huir, etc.

INDICATIVO

Presente	Presente perfecto	Imperfecto	Pasado perfecto
conozco	he conocido	conocía	había conocido
conoces	has conocido	conocías	habías conocido
conoce	ha conocido	conocía	había conocido
conocemos	hemos conocido	conocíamos	habíamos conocido
conocéis	habéis conocido	conocíais	habíais conocido
conocen	han conocido	conocían	habían conocido

Futuro	Futuro perfecto	Fut. hip.	Fut. perf. hip.
conoceré	habré conocido	conocería	habría conocido
conocerás	habrás conocido	conocerías	habrías conocido
conocerá	habrá conocido	conocería	habría conocido
conoceremos	habremos conocido	conoceríamos	habríamos conocido
conoceréis	habréis conocido	conoceríais	habríais conocido
conocerán	habrán conocido	conocerían	habrían conocido

Pretérito	Pretérito perf.
conocí	hube conocido
conociste	hubiste conocido
conoció	hubo conocido
conocimos	hubimos conocido
conocisteis	hubisteis conocido
conocieron	hubieron conocido

IMPERATIVO

Afirmativo	Negativo
conoce (tú)	no conozcas
conozca (Ud.)	no conozca
conozcamos	no conozcamos
conoced	no conozcáis
conozcan	no conozcan

SUBJUNTIVO

Presente	Presente perfecto	Imperfecto	Pasado perfecto
conozca	haya conocido	conociera	hubiera conocido
conozcas	hayas conocido	conocieras	hubieras conocido
conozca	haya conocido	conociera	hubiera conocido
conozcamos	hayamos conocido	conociéramos	hubiéramos conocido
conozcáis	hayáis conocido	conocierais	hubierais conocido
conozcan	hayan conocido	conocieran	hubieran conocido

INFINITIVO   PARTICIPIO   GERUNDIO

Simple	Perfecto	Simple	Perfecto
conocer	haber conocido	conocido	conociendo	habiendo conocido

<u>Other verbs:</u>   agradecer, complacer, crecer, desconocer, desobedecer, florecer, merecer, nacer, obedecer, ofrecer, parecer**(se)**, pertenecer, reconocer.

INDICATIVO

Presente	Presente perfecto	Imperfecto	Pasado perfecto
convenzo	he convencido	convencía	había convencido
convences	has convencido	convencías	habías convencido
convence	ha convencido	convencía	había convencido
convencemos	hemos convencido	convencíamos	habíamos convencido
convencéis	habéis convencido	convencíais	habíais convencido
convencen	han convencido	convencían	habían convencido

Futuro	Futuro perfecto	Fut. hip.	Fut. perf. hip.
convenceré	habré convencido	convencería	habría convencido
convencerás	habrás convencido	convencerías	habrías convencido
convencerá	habrá convencido	convencería	habría convencido
convenceremos	habremos convencido	convenceríamos	habríamos convencido
convenceréis	habréis convencido	convenceríais	habríais convencido
convencerán	habrán convencido	convencerían	habrían convencido

Pretérito	Pretérito perf.
convencí	hube convencido
convenciste	hubiste convencido
convenció	hubo convencido
convencimos	hubimos convencido
convencisteis	hubisteis convencido
convencieron	hubieron convencido

IMPERATIVO

Afirmativo	Negativo
convence (tú)	no convenzas
convenza (ud.)	no convenza
convenzamos	no convenzamos
convenced	no convenzáis
convenzan	no convenzan

SUBJUNTIVO

Presente	Presente perfecto	Imperfecto	Pasado perfecto
convenza	haya convencido	convenciera	hubiera convencido
convenzas	hayas convencido	convencieras	hubieras convencido
convenza	haya convencido	convenciera	hubiera convencido
convenzamos	hayamos convencido	convenciéramos	hubiéramos convencido
convenzáis	hayáis convencido	convencierais	hubierais convencido
convenzan	hayan convencido	convencieran	hubieran convencido

INFINITIVO
Simple convencer **Perfecto** haber convencido

PARTICIPIO
convencido

GERUNDIO
Simple convenciendo **Perfecto** habiendo convencido

Another verb: vencer

282

INDICATIVO

Presente	Presente perfecto	Imperfecto	Pasado perfecto
corrijo	he corregido	corregía	había corregido
corriges	has corregido	corregías	habías corregido
corrige	ha corregido	corregía	había corregido
corregimos	hemos corregido	corregíamos	habíamos corregido
corregís	habéis corregido	corregíais	habíais corregido
corrigen	han corregido	corregían	habían corregido

Futuro	Futuro perfecto	Fut. hip.	Fut. perf. hip.
corregiré	habré corregido	corregiría	habría corregido
corregirás	habrás corregido	corregirías	habrías corregido
corregirá	habrá corregido	corregiría	habría corregido
corregiremos	habremos corregido	corregiríamos	habríamos corregido
corregiréis	habréis corregido	corregiríais	habríais corregido
corregirán	habrán corregido	corregirían	habrían corregido

Pretérito	Pretérito perf.
corregí	hube corregido
corregiste	hubiste corregido
corrigió	hubo corregido
corregimos	hubimos corregido
corregisteis	hubisteis corregido
corrigieron	hubieron corregido

IMPERATIVO

Afirmativo	Negativo
corrige (tú)	no corrijas
corrija (Ud.)	no corrija
corrijamos	no corrijamos
corregid	no corrijáis
corrijan	no corrijan

SUBJUNTIVO

Presente	Presente perfecto	Imperfecto	Pasado perfecto
corrija	haya corregido	corrigiera	hubiera corregido
corrijas	hayas corregido	corrigieras	hubieras corregido
corrija	haya corregido	corrigiera	hubiera corregido
corrijamos	hayamos corregido	corrigiéramos	hubiéramos corregido
corrijáis	hayáis corregido	corrigierais	hubierais corregido
corrijan	hayan corregido	corrigieran	hubieran corregido

INFINITIVO

Simple	Perfecto
corregir	haber corregido

PARTICIPIO

corregido

GERUNDIO

Simple	Perfecto
corrigiendo	habiendo corregido

<u>Other verbs</u>: elegir, regir

INDICATIVO

Presente	Presente perfecto	Imperfecto	Pasado perfecto
doy	he dado	daba	había dado
das	has dado	dabas	habías dado
da	ha dado	daba	había dado
damos	hemos dado	dábamos	habíamos dado
dais	habéis dado	dabais	habíais dado
dan	han dado	daban	habían dado

Futuro	Futuro perfecto	Fut. hip.	Fut. perf. hip.
daré	habré dado	daría	habría dado
darás	habrás dado	darías	habrías dado
dará	habrá dado	daría	habría dado
daremos	habremos dado	daríamos	habríamos dado
daréis	habréis dado	daríais	habríais dado
darán	habrán dado	darían	habrían dado

Pretérito	Pretérito perf.
di	hube dado
diste	hubiste dado
dio	hubo dado
dimos	hubimos dado
disteis	hubisteis dado
dieron	hubieron dado

IMPERATIVO

Afirmativo	Negativo
da (tú)	no des
dé (Ud.)	no dé
demos	no demos
dad	no déis
den	no den

SUBJUNTIVO

Presente	Presente perfecto	Imperfecto	Pasado perfecto
dé	haya dado	diera	hubiera dado
des	hayas dado	dieras	hubieras dado
dé	haya dado	diera	hubiera dado
demos	hayamos dado	diéramos	hubiéramos dado
deis	hayáis dado	dierais	hubierais dado
den	hayan dado	dieran	hubieran dado

INFINITIVO | PARTICIPIO | GERUNDIO

Simple	Perfecto		Simple	Perfecto
dar	haber dado	dado	dando	habiendo dado

284

INDICATIVO

Presente	Presente perfecto	Imperfecto	Pasado perfecto
digo	he dicho	decía	había dicho
dices	has dicho	decías	habías dicho
dice	ha dicho	decía	había dicho
decimos	hemos dicho	decíamos	habíamos dicho
decís	habéis dicho	decíais	habíais dicho
dicen	han dicho	decían	habían dicho

Futuro	Futuro perfecto	Fut. hip.	Fut. perf. hip.
diré	habré dicho	diría	habría dicho
dirás	habrás dicho	dirías	habrías dicho
dirá	habrá dicho	diría	habría dicho
diremos	habremos dicho	diríamos	habríamos dicho
diréis	habréis dicho	diríais	habríais dicho
dirán	habrán dicho	dirían	habrían dicho

Pretérito	Pretérito perf.
dije	hube dicho
dijiste	hubiste dicho
dijo	hubo dicho
dijimos	hubimos dicho
dijisteis	hubisteis dicho
dijeron	hubieron dicho

IMPERATIVO

Afirmativo	Negativo
di (tú)	no digas
diga (Ud.)	no diga
digamos	no digamos
decid	no digáis
digan	no digan

SUBJUNTIVO

Presente	Presente perfecto	Imperfecto	Pasado perfecto
diga	haya dicho	dijera	hubiera dicho
digas	hayas dicho	dijeras	hubieras dicho
diga	haya dicho	dijera	hubiera dicho
digamos	hayamos dicho	dijéramos	hubiéramos dicho
digáis	hayáis dicho	dijerais	hubierais dicho
digan	hayan dicho	dijeran	hubieran dicho

INFINITIVO / PARTICIPIO / GERUNDIO

Infinitivo Simple	Perfecto	Participio	Gerundio Simple	Perfecto
decir	haber dicho	dicho	diciendo	habiendo dicho

* **maldecir** is conjugated like **decir**, except in the *futuro (maldeciré, maldecirás, maldecirá, maldeciremos, maldeciréis, maldecirán)*, the *futuro hipotético (maldeciría, maldecirías, maldeciría, maldeciríamos, maldeciríais, maldecirían)*, the second person *imperativo (maldice)*, and the *participio (maldecido)*.
* **bendecir** is like **maldecir**.

INDICATIVO

Presente	Presente perfecto	Imperfecto	Pasado perfecto
dirijo	he dirigido	dirigía	había dirigido
diriges	has dirigido	dirigías	habías dirigido
dirige	ha dirigido	dirigía	había dirigido
dirigimos	hemos dirigido	dirigíamos	habíamos dirigido
dirigís	habéis dirigido	dirigíais	habíais dirigido
dirigen	han dirigido	dirigían	habían dirigido

Futuro	Futuro perfecto	Fut. hip.	Fut. perf. hip.
dirigiré	habré dirigido	dirigiría	habría dirigido
dirigirás	habrás dirigido	dirigirías	habrías dirigido
dirigirá	habrá dirigido	dirigiría	habría dirigido
dirigiremos	habremos dirigido	dirigiríamos	habríamos dirigido
dirigiréis	habréis dirigido	dirigiríais	habríais dirigido
dirigirán	habrán dirigido	dirigirían	habrían dirigido

Pretérito	Pretérito perf.
dirigí	hube dirigido
dirigiste	hubiste dirigido
dirigió	hubo dirigido
dirigimos	hubimos dirigido
dirigisteis	hubisteis dirigido
dirigieron	hubieron dirigido

IMPERATIVO

Afirmativo	Negativo
dirige (tú)	no dirija
dirija (Ud.)	no dirija
dirijamos	no dirijamos
dirigid	no dirijáis
dirijan	no dirijan

SUBJUNTIVO

Presente	Presente perfecto	Imperfecto	Pasado perfecto
dirija	haya dirigido	dirigiera	hubiera dirigido
dirijas	hayas dirigido	dirigieras	hubieras dirigido
dirija	haya dirigido	dirigiera	hubiera dirigido
dirijamos	hayamos dirigido	dirigiéramos	hubiéramos dirigido
dirijáis	hayáis dirigido	dirigierais	hubierais dirigido
dirijan	hayan dirigido	dirigieran	hubieran dirigido

INFINITIVO   PARTICIPIO   GERUNDIO

Simple	Perfecto		Simple	Perfecto
dirigir	haber dirigido	dirigido	dirigiendo	habiendo dirigido

Other verbs: exigir, surgir

286

INDICATIVO

Presente	Presente perfecto	Imperfecto	Pasado perfecto
distingo	he distinguido	distinguía	había distinguido
distingues	has distinguido	distinguías	habías distinguido
distingue	ha distinguido	distinguía	había distinguido
distinguimos	hemos distinguido	distinguíamos	habíamos distinguido
distinguís	habéis distinguido	distinguíais	habíais distinguido
distinguen	han distinguido	distinguían	habían distinguido

Futuro	Futuro perfecto	Fut. hip.	Fut. perf. hip.
distinguiré	habré distinguido	distinguiría	habría distinguido
distinguirás	habrás distinguido	distinguirías	habrías distinguido
distinguirá	habrá distinguido	distinguiría	habría distinguido
distinguiremos	habremos distinguido	distinguiríamos	habríamos distinguido
distinguiréis	habréis distinguido	distinguiríais	habríais distinguido
distinguirán	habrán distinguido	distinguirían	habrían distinguido

Pretérito	Pretérito perf.
distinguí	hube distinguido
distinguiste	hubiste distinguido
distinguió	hubo distinguido
distinguimos	hubimos distinguido
distinguisteis	hubisteis distinguido
distinguieron	hubieron distinguido

IMPERATIVO

Afirmativo	Negativo
distingue (tú)	no distingas
distinga (Ud.)	no distinga
distingamos	no distingamos
distinguid	no distingáis
distingan	no distingan

SUBJUNTIVO

Presente	Presente perfecto	Imperfecto	Pasado perfecto
distinga	haya distinguido	distinguiera	hubiera distinguido
distingas	hayas distinguido	distinguieras	hubieras distinguido
distinga	haya distinguido	distinguiera	hubiera distinguido
distingamos	hayamos distinguido	distinguiéramos	hubiéramos distinguido
distingáis	hayáis distinguido	distinguierais	hubierais distinguido
distingan	hayan distinguido	distinguieran	hubieran distinguido

INFINITIVO   PARTICIPIO   GERUNDIO

Simple	Perfecto	Simple	Perfecto
distinguir	haber distinguido	distinguido · distinguiendo	habiendo distinguido

287

DORMIR

INDICATIVO

Presente	Presente perfecto	Imperfecto	Pasado perfecto
duermo	he dormido	dormía	había dormido
duermes	has dormido	dormías	habías dormido
duerme	ha dormido	dormía	había dormido
dormimos	hemos dormido	dormíamos	habíamos dormido
dormís	habéis dormido	dormíais	habíais dormido
duermen	han dormido	dormían	habían dormido

Futuro	Futuro perfecto	Fut. hip.	Fut. perf. hip.
dormiré	habré dormido	dormiría	habría dormido
dormirás	habrás dormido	dormirías	habrías dormido
dormirá	habrá dormido	dormiría	habría dormido
dormiremos	habremos dormido	dormiríamos	habríamos dormido
dormiréis	habréis dormido	dormiríais	habríais dormido
dormirán	habrán dormido	dormirían	habrían dormido

Pretérito	Pretérito perf.
dormí	hube dormido
dormiste	hubiste dormido
durmió	hubo dormido
dormimos	hubimos dormido
dormisteis	hubisteis dormido
durmieron	hubieron dormido

IMPERATIVO

Afirmativo	Negativo
duerme (tú)	no duermas
duerma (Ud.)	no duerma
durmamos	no durmamos
dormid	no durmáis
duerman	no duerman

SUBJUNTIVO

Presente	Presente perfecto	Imperfecto	Pasado perfecto
duerma	haya dormido	durmiera	hubiera dormido
duermas	hayas dormido	durmieras	hubieras dormido
duerma	haya dormido	durmiera	hubiera dormido
durmamos	hayamos dormido	durmiéramos	hubiéramos dormido
durmáis	hayáis dormido	durmierais	hubierais dormido
duerman	hayan dormido	durmieran	hubieran dormido

INFINITIVO
Simple dormir **Perfecto** haber dormido

PARTICIPIO
dormido

GERUNDIO
Simple durmiendo **Perfecto** habiendo dormido

Another verb: morir (except for the *participio*: *muerto)

288

INDICATIVO

Presente	Presente perfecto	Imperfecto	Pasado perfecto
envío	he enviado	enviaba	había enviado
envías	has enviado	enviabas	habías enviado
envía	ha enviado	enviaba	había enviado
enviamos	hemos enviado	enviábamos	habíamos enviado
enviáis	habéis enviado	enviabais	habíais enviado
envían	han enviado	enviaban	habían enviado

Futuro	Futuro perfecto	Fut. hip.	Fut. perf. hip.
enviaré	habré enviado	enviaría	habría enviado
enviarás	habrás enviado	enviarías	habrías enviado
enviará	habrá enviado	enviaría	habría enviado
enviaremos	habremos enviado	enviaríamos	habríamos enviado
enviaréis	habréis enviado	enviaríais	habríais enviado
enviarán	habrán enviado	enviarían	habrían enviado

Pretérito	Pretérito perf.
envié	hube enviado
enviaste	hubiste enviado
envió	hubo enviado
enviamos	hubimos enviado
enviasteis	hubisteis enviado
enviaron	hubieron enviado

IMPERATIVO

Afirmativo	Negativo
envía (tú)	no envíes
envíe (Ud.)	no envíe
enviemos	no enviemos
enviad	no enviéis
envíen	no envíen

SUBJUNTIVO

Presente	Presente perfecto	Imperfecto	Pasado perfecto
envíe	haya enviado	enviara	hubiera enviado
envíes	hayas enviado	enviaras	hubieras enviado
envíe	haya enviado	enviara	hubiera enviado
enviemos	hayamos enviado	enviáramos	hubiéramos enviado
enviéis	hayáis enviado	enviarais	hubierais enviado
envíen	hayan enviado	enviaran	hubieran enviado

INFINITIVO / PARTICIPIO / GERUNDIO

INFINITIVO		PARTICIPIO	GERUNDIO	
Simple	Perfecto		Simple	Perfecto
enviar	haber enviado	enviado	enviando	habiendo enviado

Other verbs: continuar, fiar, guiar

289

INDICATIVO

Presente	Presente perfecto	Imperfecto	Pasado perfecto
escojo	he escogido	escogía	había escogido
escoges	has escogido	escogías	habías escogido
escoge	ha escogido	escogía	había escogido
escogemos	hemos escogido	escogíamos	habíamos escogido
escogéis	habéis escogido	escogíais	habíais escogido
escogen	han escogido	escogían	habían escogido

Futuro	Futuro perfecto	Fut. hip.	Fut. perf. hip.
escogeré	habré escogido	escogería	habría escogido
escogerás	habrás escogido	escogerías	habrías escogido
escogerá	habrá escogido	escogería	habría escogido
escogeremos	habremos escogido	escogeríamos	habríamos escogido
escogeréis	habréis escogido	escogeríais	habríais escogido
escogerán	habrán escogido	escogerían	habrían escogido

Pretérito	Pretérito perf.
escogí	hube escogido
escogiste	hubiste escogido
escogió	hubo escogido
escogimos	hubimos escogido
escogisteis	hubisteis escogido
escogieron	hubieron escogido

IMPERATIVO

Afirmativo	Negativo
escoge (tú)	no escojas
escoja (Ud.)	no escoja
escojamos	no escojamos
escoged	no escojáis
escojan	no escojan

SUBJUNTIVO

Presente	Presente perfecto	Imperfecto	Pasado perfecto
escoja	haya escogido	escogiera	hubiera escogido
escojas	hayas escogido	escogieras	hubieras escogido
escoja	haya escogido	escogiera	hubiera escogido
escojamos	hayamos escogido	escogiéramos	hubiéramos escogido
escojáis	hayáis escogido	escogierais	hubierais escogido
escojan	hayan escogido	escogieran	hubieran escogido

INFINITIVO — PARTICIPIO — GERUNDIO

Simple	Perfecto		Simple	Perfecto
escoger	haber escogido	escogido	escogiendo	habiendo escogido

Other verbs: coger, encoger, proteger, recoger

INDICATIVO

Presente	Presente perfecto	Imperfecto	Pasado perfecto
esparzo	he esparcido	esparcía	había esparcido
esparces	has esparcido	esparcías	habías esparcido
esparce	ha esparcido	esparcía	había esparcido
esparcimos	hemos esparcido	espacíamos	habíamos esparcido
esparcís	habéis esparcido	esparcíais	habíais esparcido
esparcen	han esparcido	esparcían	habian esparcido

Futuro	Futuro perfecto	Fut. hip.	Fut. perf. hip.
esparciré	habré esparcido	esparciría	habría esparcido
esparcirás	habrás esparcido	esparcirías	habrías esparcido
esparcirá	habrá esparcido	esparciría	habría esparcido
esparciremos	habremos esparcido	esparciríamos	habríamos esparcido
esparciréis	habréis esparcido	esparciríais	habríais esparcido
esparcirán	habrán esparcido	esparcirían	habrían esparcido

Pretérito	Pretérito perf.
esparcí	hube esparcido
esparciste	hubiste esparcido
esparció	hubo esparcido
esparcimos	hubimos esparcido
esparcisteis	hubisteis esparcido
esparcieron	hubieron esparcido

IMPERATIVO

Afirmativo	Negativo
esparce (tú)	no esparzas
esparza (Ud.)	no esparza
esparzamos	no esparzamos
esparcid	no esparzáis
esparzan	no esparzan

SUBJUNTIVO

Presente	Presente perfecto	Imperfecto	Pasado perfecto
esparza	haya esparcido	esparciera	hubiera esparcido
esparzas	hayas esparcido	esparcieras	hubieras esparcido
esparza	haya esparcido	esparciera	hubiera esparcido
esparzamos	hayamos esparcido	esparciéramos	hubiéramos esparcido
esparzáis	hayáis esparcido	esparcierais	hubierais esparcido
esparzan	hayan esparcido	esparcieran	hubieran esparcido

INFINITIVO · PARTICIPIO · GERUNDIO

Simple	Perfecto		Simple	Perfecto
esparcir	haber esparcido	esparcido	esparciendo	habiendo esparcido

INDICATIVO

Presente	Presente perfecto	Imperfecto	Pasado perfecto
estoy	he estado	estaba	había estado
estás	has estado	estabas	habías estado
está	ha estado	estaba	había estado
estamos	hemos estado	estábamos	habíamos estado
estáis	habéis estado	estabais	habíais estado
están	han estado	estaban	habían estado

Futuro	Futuro perfecto	Fut. hip.	Fut. perf. hip.
estaré	habré estado	estaría	habría estado
estarás	habrás estado	estarías	habrías estado
estará	habrá estado	estaría	habría estado
estaremos	habremos estado	estaríamos	habríamos estado
estaréis	habréis estado	estaríais	habríais estado
estarán	habrán estado	estarían	habrían estado

Pretérito	Pretérito perf.
estuve	hube estado
estuviste	hubiste estado
estuvo	hubo estado
estuvimos	hubimos estado
estuvisteis	hubisteis estado
estuvieron	hubieron estado

IMPERATIVO

Afirmativo	Negativo
está (tú)	no estés
esté (Ud.)	no esté
estemos	no estemos
estad	no estéis
estén	no estén

SUBJUNTIVO

Presente	Presente perfecto	Imperfecto	Pasado perfecto
esté	haya estado	estuviera	hubiera estado
estés	hayas estado	estuvieras	hubieras estado
esté	haya estado	estuviera	hubiera estado
estemos	hayamos estado	estuviéramos	hubiéramos estado
estéis	hayáis estado	estuvierais	hubierais estado
estén	hayan estado	estuvieran	hubieran estado

INFINITIVO

Simple	Perfecto
estar	haber estado

PARTICIPIO

estado

GERUNDIO

Simple	Perfecto
estando	habiendo estado

INDICATIVO

Presente	Presente perfecto	Imperfecto	Pasado perfecto
he		había	
has		habías	
ha (hay)	(ha habido)	había	(había habido)
hemos		habíamos	
habéis		habíais	
han (hay)	(han habido)	habían	(habían habido)

Futuro	Futuro perfecto	Fut. hip.	Fut. perf. hip.
habré		habría	
habrás		habrías	
habrá	(habrá habido)	habría	(habría habido)
habremos		habríamos	
habréis		habríais	
habrán	(habrán habido)	habrían	(habrían habido)

Pretérito	Pretérito perf.
hube	
hubiste	
hubo	(hubo habido)
hubimos	
hubisteis	
hubieron	(hubieron habido)

IMPERATIVO
Afirmativo   Negativo

There is no *imperativo*.

SUBJUNTIVO

Presente	Presente perfecto	Imperfecto	Pasado perfecto
haya		hubiera	
hayas		hubieras	
haya	(haya habido)	hubiera	(hubiera habido)
hayamos		hubiéramos	
hayáis		hubierais	
hayan	(hayan habido)	habieran	(hubieran habido)

INFINITIVO
Simple	Perfecto
haber	haber habido

PARTICIPIO
habido

GERUNDIO
Simple	Perfecto
habiendo	(habiendo habido)

√ The simple tenses of **haber** serve to form all the compound tenses in Spanish.

√ **Haber** can also be used with the meaning *"there is/are"* (hay), and in the impersonal *"it is necessary"* (hay que). With these meanings, it comes in all tenses, simple and compound (given in parenthesis).

INDICATIVO

Presente	Presente perfecto	Imperfecto	Pasado perfecto
hablo	he hablado	hablaba	había hablado
hablas	has hablado	hablabas	habías hablado
habla	ha hablado	hablaba	había hablado
hablamos	hemos hablado	hablábamos	habíamos hablado
habláis	habéis hablado	hablabais	habíais hablado
hablan	han hablado	hablaban	habían hablado

Futuro	Futuro perfecto	Fut. hip.	Fut. perf. hip.
hablaré	habré hablado	hablaría	habría hablado
hablarás	habrás hablado	hablarías	habrías hablado
hablará	habrá hablado	hablaría	habría hablado
hablaremos	habremos hablado	hablaríamos	habríamos hablado
hablaréis	habréis hablado	hablaríais	habríais hablado
hablarán	habrán hablado	hablarían	habrían hablado

Pretérito	Pretérito perf.
hablé	hube hablado
hablaste	hubiste hablado
habló	hubo hablado
hablamos	hubimos hablado
hablasteis	hubisteis hablado
hablaron	hubieron hablado

IMPERATIVO

Afirmativo	Negativo
habla (tú)	no hables
hable (Ud.)	no hable
hablemos	no hablemos
hablad	no habléis
hablen	no hablen

SUBJUNTIVO

Presente	Presente perfecto	Imperfecto	Pasado perfecto
hable	haya hablado	hablara	hubiera hablado
hables	hayas hablado	hablaras	hubieras hablado
hable	haya hablado	hablara	hubiera hablado
hablemos	hayamos hablado	habláramos	hubiéramos hablado
habléis	hayáis hablado	hablarais	hubierais hablado
hablen	hayan hablado	hablaran	hubieran hablado

INFINITIVO   PARTICIPIO   GERUNDIO

Simple	Perfecto	Simple	Perfecto
hablar	haber hablado	hablado	hablando	habiendo hablado

* **averiguar** is conjugated like **hablar,** except with the **-e** endings; then **u** takes a diaeresis (**ü**). This occurs in the 1st person *pretérito (averigüé),* the *presente del subjuntivo (averigüe, averigües, averigüe, averigüemos, averigüéis, averigüen),* the *imperativo* for Ud. *(averigüe),* Uds. *(averigüen),* nosotros *(averigüemos),* and in the negative *imperativo (no averigües, no averigüe, no averigüemos, no averigüéis, no averigüen).*

294

INDICATIVO

Presente	Presente perfecto	Imperfecto	Pasado perfecto
hago	he hecho	hacía	había hecho
haces	has hecho	hacías	habías hecho
hace	ha hecho	hacía	había hecho
hacemos	hemos hecho	hacíamos	habíamos hecho
hacéis	habéis hecho	hacíais	habíais hecho
hacen	han hecho	hacían	habían hecho

Futuro	Futuro perfecto	Fut. hip.	Fut. perf. hip.
haré	habré hecho	haría	habría hecho
harás	habrás hecho	harías	habrías hecho
hará	habrá hecho	haría	habría hecho
haremos	habremos hecho	haríamos	habríamos hecho
haréis	habréis hecho	haríais	habríais hecho
harán	habrán hecho	harían	habrían hecho

Pretérito	Pretérito perf.
hice	hube hecho
hiciste	hubiste hecho
hizo	hubo hecho
hicimos	hubimos hecho
hicisteis	hubisteis hecho
hicieron	hubieron hecho

IMPERATIVO

Afirmativo	Negativo
haz (tú)	no hagas
haga (Ud.)	no haga
hagamos	no hagamos
haced	no hagáis
hagan	no hagan

SUBJUNTIVO

Presente	Presente perfecto	Imperfecto	Pasado perfecto
haga	haya hecho	hiciera	hubiera hecho
hagas	hayas hecho	hicieras	hubieras hecho
haga	haya hecho	hiciera	hubiera hecho
hagamos	hayamos hecho	hiciéramos	hubiéramos hecho
hagáis	hayáis hecho	hicierais	hubierais hecho
hagan	hayan hecho	hicieran	hubieran hecho

INFINITIVO   PARTICIPIO   GERUNDIO

Simple	Perfecto		Simple	Perfecto
hacer	haber hecho	hecho	haciendo	habiendo hecho

Other verbs: deshacer, satisfacer.

INDICATIVO

Present	Presente perfecto	Imperfecto	Pasado perfecto
voy	he ido	iba	había ido
vas	has ido	ibas	habías ido
va	ha ido	iba	había ido
vamos	hemos ido	íbamos	habíamos ido
vais	habéis ido	ibais	habíais ido
van	han ido	iban	habían ido

Futuro	Futuro perfecto	Fut. hip.	Fut. perf. hip.
iré	habré ido	iría	habría ido
irás	habrás ido	irías	habrías ido
irá	habrá ido	iría	habría ido
iremos	habremos ido	iríamos	habríamos ido
iréis	habréis ido	iríais	habríais ido
irán	habrán ido	irían	habrían ido

Pretérito	Pretérito perf.
fui	hube ido
fuiste	hubiste ido
fue	hubo ido
fuimos	hubimos ido
fuisteis	hubisteis ido
fueron	hubieron ido

IMPERATIVO

Afirmativo	Negativo
ve (tú)	no vayas
vaya (Ud.)	no vaya
vayamos	no vayamos
id	no vayáis
vayan	no vayan

SUBJUNTIVO

Presente	Presente perfecto	Imperfecto	Pasado perfecto
vaya	haya ido	fuera	hubiera ido
vayas	hayas ido	fueras	hubieras ido
vaya	haya ido	fuera	hubiera ido
vayamos	hayamos ido	fuéramos	hubiéramos ido
vayáis	hayáis ido	fuerais	hubierais ido
vayan	hayan ido	fueran	hubieran ido

INFINITIVO

Simple	Perfecto	PARTICIPIO	GERUNDIO Simple	Perfecto
ir	haber ido	ido	yendo	habiendo ido

INDICATIVO

Presente	Presente perfecto	Imperfecto	Pasado perfecto
juego	he jugado	jugaba	había jugado
juegas	has jugado	jugabas	habías jugado
juega	ha jugado	jugaba	había jugado
jugamos	hemos jugado	jugábamos	habíamos jugado
jugáis	habéis jugado	jugabais	habíais jugado
juegan	han jugado	jugaban	habían jugado

Futuro	Futuro perfecto	Fut. hip.	Fut. perf. hip.
jugaré	habré jugado	jugaría	habría jugado
jugarás	habrás jugado	jugarías	habrías jugado
jugará	habrá jugado	jugaría	habría jugado
jugaremos	habremos jugado	jugaríamos	habríamos jugado
jugaréis	habréis jugado	jugaríais	habríais jugado
jugarán	habrán jugado	jugarían	habrían jugado

Pretérito	Pretérito perf.
jugué	hube jugado
jugaste	hubiste jugado
jugó	hubo jugado
jugamos	hubimos jugado
jugasteis	hubisteis jugado
jugaron	hubieron jugado

IMPERATIVO

Afirmativo	Negativo
juega (tú)	no juegues
juegue (Ud.)	no juegue
juguemos	no juguemos
jugad	no juguéis
jueguen	no jueguen

SUBJUNTIVO

Presente	Presente perfecto	Imperfecto	Pasado perfecto
juegue	haya jugado	jugara	hubiera jugado
juegues	hayas jugado	jugaras	hubieras jugado
juegue	haya jugado	jugara	hubiera jugado
juguemos	hayamos jugado	jugáramos	hubiéramos jugado
juguéis	hayáis jugado	jugarais	hubierais jugado
jueguen	hayan jugado	jugaran	hubieran jugado

INFINITIVO   PARTICIPIO   GERUNDIO

Simple	Perfecto		Simple	Perfecto
jugar	haber jugado	jugado	jugando	habiendo jugado

297

INDICATIVO

Presente	Presente perfecto	Imperfecto	Pasado perfecto
lanzo	he lanzado	lanzaba	había lanzado
lanzas	has lanzado	lanzabas	habías lanzado
lanza	ha lanzado	lanzaba	había lanzado
lanzamos	hemos lanzado	lanzábamos	habíamos lanzado
lanzáis	habéis lanzado	lanzabais	habíais lanzado
lanzan	han lanzado	lanzaban	habían lanzado

Futuro	Futuro perfecto	Fut. hip.	Fut. perf. hip.
lanzaré	habré lanzado	lanzaría	habría lanzado
lanzarás	habrás lanzado	lanzarías	habrías lanzado
lanzará	habrá lanzado	lanzaría	habría lanzado
lanzaremos	habremos lanzado	lanzaríamos	habríamos lanzado
lanzaréis	habréis lanzado	lanzaríais	habríais lanzado
lanzarán	habrán lanzado	lanzarían	habrían lanzado

Pretérito	Pretérito perf.
lancé	hube lanzado
lanzaste	hubiste lanzado
lanzó	hubo lanzado
lanzamos	hubimos lanzado
lanzasteis	hubisteis lanzado
lanzaron	hubieron lanzado

IMPERATIVO

Afirmativo	Negativo
lanza (tú)	no lances
lance (Ud.)	no lance
lancemos	no lancemos
lanzad	no lancéis
lancen	no lancen

SUBJUNTIVO

Presente	Presente perfecto	Imperfecto	Pasado perfecto
lance	haya lanzado	lanzara	hubiera lanzado
lances	hayas lanzado	lanzaras	hubieras lanzado
lance	haya lanzado	lanzara	hubiera lanzado
lancemos	hayamos lanzado	lanzáramos	hubiéramos lanzado
lancéis	hayáis lanzado	lanzarais	hubierais lanzado
lancen	hayan lanzado	lanzaran	hubieran lanzado

INFINITIVO

Simple	Perfecto
lanzar	haber lanzado

PARTICIPIO

lanzado

GERUNDIO

Simple	Perfecto
lanzando	habiendo lanzado

Other verbs: abrazar(se), adelgazar, amenazar, aplazar, aterrizar, avanzar, bostezar, cazar, cristalizar, cruzar, descalzar, destrozar, disfrazar, economizar, embarazar, encabezar, endulzar, garantizar, gozar, izar, organizar, rezar, rechazar, trazar, utilizar

INDICATIVO

Presente	Presente perfecto	Imperfecto	Pasado perfecto
leo	he leído	leía	había leído
lees	has leído	leías	habías leído
lee	ha leído	leía	había leído
leemos	hemos leído	leíamos	habíamos leído
leéis	habéis leído	leíais	habíais leído
leen	han leído	leían	habían leído

Futuro	Futuro perfecto	Fut. hip.	Fut. perf. hip.
leeré	habré leído	leería	habría leído
leerás	habrás leído	leerías	habrías leído
leerá	habrá leído	leería	habría leído
leeremos	habremos leído	leeríamos	habríamos leído
leeréis	habréis leído	leeríais	habríais leído
leerán	habrán leído	leerían	habrían leído

Pretérito	Pretérito perf.
leí	hube leído
leíste	hubiste leído
leyó	hubo leído
leímos	hubimos leído
leísteis	hubisteis leído
leyeron	hubieron leído

IMPERATIVO

Afirmativo	Negativo
lee (tú)	no leas
lea (ud.)	no lea
leamos	no leamos
leed	no leáis
lean	no lean

SUBJUNTIVO

Presente	Presente perfecto	Imperfecto	Pasado perfecto
lea	haya leído	leyera	hubiera leído
leas	hayas leído	leyeras	hubieras leído
lea	haya leído	leyera	hubiera leído
leamos	hayamos leído	leyéramos	hubiéramos leído
leáis	hayáis leído	leyerais	hubierais leído
lean	hayan leído	leyeran	hubieran leído

INFINITIVO / PARTICIPIO / GERUNDIO

Simple	Perfecto	PARTICIPIO	Simple	Perfecto
leer	haber leído	leído	leyendo	habiendo leído

Other verbs: creer, poseer, *proveer (conjugated like leer; but the *participio* is **provisto**)

INDICATIVO

Presente	Presente perfecto	Imperfecto	Pasado perfecto
muevo	he movido	movía	había movido
mueves	has movido	movías	habías movido
mueve	ha movido	movía	había movido
movemos	hemos movido	movíamos	habíamos movido
movéis	habéis movido	movíais	habíais movido
mueven	han movido	movían	habían movido

Futuro	Futuro perfecto	Fut. hip.	Fut. perf. hip.
moveré	habré movido	movería	habría movido
moverás	habrás movido	moverías	habrías movido
moverá	habrá movido	movería	habría movido
moveremos	habremos movido	moveríamos	habríamos movido
moveréis	habréis movido	moveríais	habríais movido
moverán	habrán movido	moverían	habrían movido

Pretérito	Pretérito perf.
moví	hube movido
moviste	hubiste movido
movió	hubo movido
movimos	hubimos movido
movisteis	hubisteis movido
movieron	hubieron movido

IMPERATIVO

Afirmativo	Negativo
mueve (tú)	no muevas
mueva (Ud.)	no mueva
movamos	no movamos
moved	no mováis
muevan	no muevan

SUBJUNTIVO

Presente	Presente perfecto	Imperfecto	Pasado perfecto
mueva	haya movido	moviera	hubiera movido
muevas	hayas movido	movieras	hubieras movido
mueva	haya movido	moviera	hubiera movido
movamos	hayamos movido	moviéramos	hubiéramos movido
mováis	hayáis movido	movierais	hubierais movido
muevan	hayan movido	movieran	hubieran movido

INFINITIVO

Simple	Perfecto
mover	haber movido

PARTICIPIO

movido

GERUNDIO

Simple	Perfecto
moviendo	habiendo movido

Other verbs: absolver*, conmover, desenvolver*, devolver *, disolver*, doler (conjugated in the 3rd pers. sing. and plural only), envolver, llover (conjugated in the 3rd pers. sing. only), moler, morder, promover, remover, revolver*, soler, volver*
* The verbs containing **solver** and **volver** have an irregular *participio:*
absolver *(absuelto),* disolver *(disuelto),* desenvolver *(desenvuelto),* devolver *(devuelto),* revolver *(revuelto),* and volver *(vuelto).*

INDICATIVO

Presente	Presente perfecto	Imperfecto	Pasado perfecto
niego	he negado	negaba	habia negado
niegas	has negado	negabas	habías negado
niega	ha negado	negaba	habia negado
negamos	hemos negado	negábamos	habíamos negado
negáis	habéis negado	negábais	habíais negado
niegan	han negado	negaban	habían negado

Futuro	Futuro perfecto	Fut. hip.	Fut. perf. hip.
negaré	habré negado	negaría	habría negado
negarás	habrás negado	negarías	habrías negado
negará	habrá negado	negaría	habría negado
negaremos	habremos negado	negaríamos	habríamos negado
negaréis	habréis negado	negaríais	habríais negado
negarán	habrán negado	negarían	habrían negado

Pretérito	Pretérito perf.
negué	hube negado
negaste	hubiste negado
negó	hubo negado
negamos	hubimos negado
negasteis	hubisteis negado
negaron	hubieron negado

IMPERATIVO

Afirmativo	Negativo
niega (tú)	no niegues
niegue (Ud.)	no niegue
neguemos	no neguemos
negad	no neguéis
nieguen	no nieguen

SUBJUNTIVO

Presente	Presente perfecto	Imperfecto	Pasado perfecto
niegue	haya negado	negara	hubiera negado
niegues	hayas negado	negaras	hubieras negado
niegue	haya negado	negara	hubiera negado
neguemos	hayamos negado	negáramos	hubiéramos negado
neguéis	hayáis negado	negarais	hubierais negado
nieguen	hayan negado	negaran	hubieran negado

INFINITIVO / PARTICIPIO / GERUNDIO

Simple	Perfecto	PARTICIPIO	Simple	Perfecto
negar	haber negado	negado	negando	habiendo negado

Other verbs: fregar, regar, segar

301

INDICATIVO

Presente	Presente perfecto	Imperfecto	Pasado perfecto
oigo	he oído	oía	había oído
oyes	has oído	oías	habías oído
oye	ha oído	oía	había oído
oímos	hemos oído	oíamos	habíamos oído
oís	habéis oído	oíais	habíais oído
oyen	han oído	oían	habían oído

Futuro	Futuro perfecto	Fut. hip.	Fut. perf. hip.
oiré	habré oído	oiría	habría oído
oirás	habrás oído	oirías	habrías oído
oirá	habrá oído	oiría	habría oído
oiremos	habremos oído	oiríamos	habríamos oído
oiréis	habréis oído	oiríais	habríais oído
oirán	habrán oído	oirían	habrían oído

Pretérito	Pretérito perf.
oí	hube oído
oíste	hubiste oído
oyó	hubo oído
oímos	hubimos oído
oísteis	hubisteis oído
oyeron	hubieron oído

IMPERATIVO

Afirmativo	Negativo
oye (tú)	no oigas
oiga (Ud.)	no oiga
oigamos	no oigamos
oíd	no oigáis
oigan	no oigan

SUBJUNTIVO

Presente	Presente perfecto	Imperfecto	Pasado perfecto
oiga	haya oído	oyera	hubiera oído
oigas	hayas oído	oyeras	hubieras oído
oiga	haya oído	oyera	hubiera oído
oigamos	hayamos oído	oyéramos	hubiéramos oído
oigáis	hayáis oído	oyerais	hubierais oído
oigan	hayan oído	oyeran	hubieran oído

INFINITIVO / PARTICIPIO / GERUNDIO

INFINITIVO		PARTICIPIO	GERUNDIO	
Simple	Perfecto		Simple	Perfecto
oír	haber oído	oído	oyendo	habiendo oído

302

INDICATIVO

Presente	Presente perfecto	Imperfecto	Pasado perfecto
huelo	he olido	olía	había olido
hueles	has olido	olías	habías olido
huele	ha olido	olía	había olido
olemos	hemos olido	olíamos	habíamos olido
oléis	habéis olido	olíais	habíais olido
huelen	han olido	olían	habían olido

Futuro	Futuro perfecto	Fut. hip.	Fut. perf. hip.
oleré	habré olido	olería	habría olido
olerás	habrás olido	olerías	habrías olido
olerá	habrá olido	olería	habría olido
oleremos	habremos olido	oleríamos	habríamos olido
oleréis	habréis olido	oleríais	habríais olido
olerán	habrán olido	olerían	habrían olido

Pretérito	Pretérito perf.
olí	hube olido
oliste	hubiste olido
olió	hubo olido
olimos	hubimos olido
olisteis	hubisteis olido
olieron	hubieron olido

IMPERATIVO

Afirmativo	Negativo
huele (tú)	no huelas
huela (Ud.)	no huela
olamos	no olamos
oled	no oláis
huelan	no huelan

SUBJUNTIVO

Presente	Presente perfecto	Imperfecto	Pasado perfecto
huela	haya olido	oliera	hubiera olido
huelas	hayas olido	olieras	hubieras olido
huela	haya olido	oliera	hubiera olido
olamos	hayamos olido	oliéramos	hubiéramos olido
oláis	hayáis olido	olierais	hubierais olido
huelan	hayan olido	olieran	hubieran olido

INFINITIVO / **PARTICIPIO** / **GERUNDIO**

Simple	Perfecto		Simple	Perfecto
oler	haber olido	olido	oliendo	habiendo olido

INDICATIVO

Presente	Presente perfecto	Imperfecto	Pasado perfecto
pago	he pagado	pagaba	había pagado
pagas	has pagado	pagabas	habías pagado
paga	ha pagado	pagaba	había pagado
pagamos	hemos pagado	pagábamos	habíamos pagado
pagáis	habéis pagado	pagabais	habíais pagado
pagan	han pagado	pagaban	habían pagado

Futuro	Futuro perfecto	Fut. hip.	Fut. perf. hip.
pagaré	habré pagado	pagaría	habría pagado
pagarás	habrás pagado	pagarías	habrías pagado
pagará	habrá pagado	pagaría	habría pagado
pagaremos	habremos pagado	pagaríamos	habríamos pagado
pagaréis	habréis pagado	pagaríais	habríais pagado
pagarán	habrán pagado	pagarían	habrían pagado

Pretérito	Pretérito perf.
pagué	hube pagado
pagaste	hubiste pagado
pagó	hubo pagado
pagamos	hubimos pagado
pagasteis	hubisteis pagado
pagaron	hubieron pagado

IMPERATIVO

Afirmativo	Negativo
paga (tú)	no pagues
pague (Ud.)	no pague
paguemos	no paguemos
pagad	no paguéis
paguen	no paguen

SUBJUNTIVO

Presente	Presente perfecto	Imperfecto	Pasado perfecto
pague	haya pagado	pagara	hubiera pagado
pagues	hayas pagado	pagaras	hubieras pagado
pague	haya pagado	pagara	hubiera pagado
paguemos	hayamos pagado	pagáramos	hubiéramos pagado
paguéis	hayáis pagado	pagarais	hubierais pagado
paguen	hayan pagado	pagaran	hubieran pagado

INFINITIVO   PARTICIPIO   GERUNDIO

Simple	Perfecto		Simple	Perfecto
pagar	haber pagado	pagado	pagando	habiendo pagado

Other verbs: apagar, cargar, despegar(se), entregar(se), juzgar, llegar, obligar, pegar, tragar, vengar

INDICATIVO

Presente	Presente perfecto	Imperfecto	Pasado perfecto
pienso	he pensado	pensaba	había pensado
piensas	has pensado	pensabas	habías pensado
piensa	ha pensado	pensaba	había pensado
pensamos	hemos pensado	pensábamos	habíamos pensado
pensáis	habéis pensado	pensábais	habíais pensado
piensan	han pensado	pensaban	habían pensado

Futuro	Futuro perfecto	Fut. hip.	Fut. perf. hip.
pensaré	habré pensado	pensaría	habría pensado
pensarás	habrás pensado	pensarías	habrías pensado
pensará	habrá pensado	pensaría	habría pensado
pensaremos	habremos pensado	pensaríamos	habríamos pensado
pensaréis	habréis pensado	pensaríais	habríais pensado
pensarán	habrán pensado	pensarían	habrían pensado

Pretérito	Pretérito perf.
pensé	hube pensado
pensaste	hubiste pensado
pensó	hubo pensado
pensamos	hubimos pensado
pensasteis	hubisteis pensado
pensaron	hubieron pensado

IMPERATIVO

Afirmativo	Negativo
piensa (tú)	no pienses
piense (Ud.)	no piense
pensemos	no pensemos
pensad	no penséis
piensen	no piensen

SUBJUNTIVO

Presente	Presente perfecto	Imperfecto	Pasado perfecto
piense	haya pensado	pensara	hubiera pensado
pienses	hayas pensado	pensaras	hubieras pensado
piense	haya pensado	pensara	hubiera pensado
pensemos	hayamos pensado	pensáramos	hubiéramos pensado
penséis	hayáis pensado	pensarais	hubierais pensado
piensen	hayan pensado	pensaran	hubieran pensado

INFINITIVO / PARTICIPIO / GERUNDIO

Simple	Perfecto	PARTICIPIO	Simple	Perfecto
pensar	haber pensado	pensado	pensando	habiendo pensado

Other verbs: acertar, alentar, apretar, arrendar, atravesar, calentar, cerrar, confesar, despertar, encerrar, enterrar, errar*, gobernar, helar*, manifestar, merendar, nevar*, recomendar, reventar, sembrar, sentar(se)

* **helar** and **nevar** are conjugated only in the 3rd person singular.
* **errar** takes **y** instead of **i**: yerro, yerras, yerra, yerran; and yerre, yerres, yerre, yerren

305

INDICATIVO

Presente	Presente perfecto	Imperfecto	Pasado perfecto
pierdo	he perdido	perdía	había perdido
pierdes	has perdido	perdías	habías perdido
pierde	ha perdido	perdía	había perdido
perdemos	hemos perdido	perdíamos	habíamos perdido
perdéis	habéis perdido	perdíais	habíais perdido
pierden	han perdido	perdían	habían perdido

Futuro	Futuro perfecto	Fut. hip.	Fut. perf. hip.
perderé	habré perdido	perdería	habría perdido
perderás	habrás perdido	perderías	habrías perdido
perderá	habrá perdido	perdería	habría perdido
perderemos	habremos perdido	perderíamos	habríamos perdido
perderéis	habréis perdido	perderíais	habríais perdido
perderán	habrán perdido	perderían	habrían perdido

Pretérito	Pretérito perf.
perdí	hube perdido
perdiste	hubiste perdido
perdió	hubo perdido
perdimos	hubimos perdido
perdisteis	hubisteis perdido
perdieron	hubieron perdido

IMPERATIVO

Afirmativo	Negativo
pierde (tú)	no pierdas
pierda (Ud.)	no pierda
perdamos	no perdamos
perded	no perdáis
pierdan	no pierdan

SUBJUNTIVO

Presente	Presente perfecto	Imperfecto	Pasado perfecto
pierda	haya perdido	perdiera	hubiera perdido
pierdas	hayas perdido	perdieras	hubieras perdido
pierda	haya perdido	perdiera	hubiera perdido
perdamos	hayamos perdido	perdiéramos	hubiéramos perdido
perdáis	hayáis perdido	perdierais	hubierais perdido
pierdan	hayan perdido	perdieran	hubieran perdido

INFINITIVO / PARTICIPIO / GERUNDIO

INFINITIVO		PARTICIPIO	GERUNDIO	
Simple	Perfecto		Simple	Perfecto
perder	haber perdido	perdido	perdiendo	habiendo perdido

Other verbs: ascender, atender, defender, descender, encender, entender.

306

INDICATIVO

Presente	Presente perfecto	Imperfecto	Pasado perfecto
puedo	he podido	podía	había podido
puedes	has podido	podías	habías podido
puede	ha podido	podía	había podido
podemos	hemos podido	podíamos	habíamos podido
podéis	habéis podido	podíais	habíais podido
pueden	han podido	podían	habían podido

Futuro	Futuro perfecto	Fut. hip.	Fut. perf. hip.
podré	habré podido	podría	habría podido
podrás	habrás podido	podrías	habrías podido
podrá	habrá podido	podría	habría podido
podremos	habremos podido	podríamos	habríamos podido
podréis	habréis podido	podríais	habríais podido
podrán	habrán podido	podrían	habrían podido

Pretérito	Pretérito perf.
pude	hube podido
pudiste	hubiste podido
pudo	hubo podido
pudimos	hubimos podido
pudisteis	hubisteis podido
pudieron	hubieron podido

IMPERATIVO

Afirmativo	Negativo
puede (tú)	no puedas
pueda (Ud.)	no pueda
podamos	no podamos
poded	no podáis
puedan	no puedan

SUBJUNTIVO

Presente	Presente perfecto	Imperfecto	Pasado perfecto
pueda	haya podido	pudiera	hubiera podido
puedas	hayas podido	pudieras	hubieras podido
pueda	haya podido	pudiera	hubiera podido
podamos	hayamos podido	pudiéramos	hubiéramos podido
podáis	hayáis podido	pudierais	hubierais podido
puedan	hayan podido	pudieran	hubieran podido

INFINITIVO PARTICIPIO GERUNDIO

Simple	Perfecto		Simple	Perfecto
poder	haber podido	podido	pudiendo	habiendo podido

INDICATIVO

Presente	Presente perfecto	Imperfecto	Pasado perfecto
pongo	he puesto	ponía	había puesto
pones	has puesto	ponías	habías puesto
pone	ha puesto	ponía	había puesto
ponemos	hemos puesto	poníamos	habíamos puesto
ponéis	habéis puesto	poníais	habíais puesto
ponen	han puesto	ponían	habían puesto

Futuro	Futuro perfecto	Fut. hip.	Fut. perf. hip.
pondré	habré puesto	pondría	habría puesto
pondrás	habrás puesto	pondrías	habrías puesto
pondrá	habrá puesto	pondría	habría puesto
pondremos	habremos puesto	pondríamos	habríamos puesto
pondréis	habréis puesto	pondríais	habríais puesto
pondrán	habrán puesto	pondrían	habrían puesto

Pretérito	Pretérito perf.
puse	hube puesto
pusiste	hubiste puesto
puso	hubo puesto
pusimos	hubimos puesto
pusisteis	hubisteis puesto
pusieron	hubieron puesto

IMPERATIVO

Afirmativo	Negativo
pon (tú)	no pongas
ponga (Ud.)	no ponga
pongamos	no pongamos
poned	no pongáis
pongan	no pongan

SUBJUNTIVO

Presente	Presente perfecto	Imperfecto	Pasado perfecto
ponga	haya puesto	pusiera	hubiera puesto
pongas	hayas puesto	pusieras	hubieras puesto
ponga	haya puesto	puisiera	hubiera puesto
pongamos	hayamos puesto	pusiéramos	hubiéramos puesto
pongáis	hayáis puesto	pusierais	hubierais puesto
pongan	hayan puesto	pusieran	hubieran puesto

INFINITIVO
Simple	Perfecto
poner	haber puesto

PARTICIPIO
puesto

GERUNDIO
Simple	Perfecto
poniendo	habiendo puesto

Other verbs: verbs ending in -poner: componer, disponer, exponer, imponer, oponer, proponer, reponer, suponer, etc.

308

INDICATIVO

Presente	Presente perfecto	Imperfecto	Pasado Perfecto
prefiero	he preferido	prefería	había preferido
prefieres	has preferido	preferías	habías preferido
prefiere	ha preferido	prefería	había preferido
preferimos	hemos preferido	preferíamos	habíamos preferido
preferís	habéis preferido	preferíais	habíais preferido
prefieren	han preferido	preferían	habían preferido

Futuro	Futuro perfecto	Fut. hip.	Fut. perf. hip.
preferiré	habré preferido	preferiría	habría preferido
preferirás	habrás preferido	preferirías	habrías preferido
preferirá	habrá preferido	preferiría	habría preferido
preferiremos	habremos preferido	preferiríamos	habríamos preferido
preferiréis	habréis preferido	preferiríais	habríais preferido
preferirán	habrán preferido	preferirían	habrían preferido

Pretérito	Pretérito perf.
preferí	hube preferido
preferiste	hubiste preferido
prefirió	hubo preferido
preferimos	hubimos preferido
preferisteis	hubisteis preferido
prefirieron	hubieron preferido

IMPERATIVO

Afirmativo	Negativo
prefiere (tú)	no prefieras
prefiera (Ud.)	no prefiera
prefiramos	no prefiramos
preferid	no prefiráis
prefieran	no prefieran

SUBJUNTIVO

Presente	Presente perfecto	Imperfecto	Pasado perfecto
prefiera	haya preferido	prefiriera	hubiera preferido
prefieras	hayas preferido	prefirieras	hubieras preferido
prefiera	haya preferido	prefiriera	hubiera preferido
prefiramos	hayamos preferido	prefiriéramos	hubiéramos preferido
prefiráis	hayáis preferido	prefirierais	hubierais preferido
prefieran	hayan preferido	prefirieran	hubieran preferido

INFINITIVO / PARTICIPIO / GERUNDIO

Infinitivo Simple	Perfecto	Participio	Gerundio Simple	Perfecto
preferir	haber preferido	preferido	prefiriendo	habiendo preferido

Other verbs: adherir, adquirir, advertir, arrepentirse, convertir, digerir, divertir, herir, hervir, invertir, referir

INDICATIVO

Presente	Presente perfecto	Imperfecto	Pasado perfecto
quiero	he querido	quería	había querido
quieres	has querido	querías	habías querido
quiere	ha querido	quería	había querido
queremos	hemos querido	queríamos	habíamos querido
queréis	habéis querido	queríais	habíais querido
quieren	han querido	querían	habían querido

Futuro	Futuro perfecto	Fut. hip.	Fut. perf. hip.
querré	habré querido	querría	habría querido
querrás	habrás querido	querrías	habrías querido
querrá	habrá querido	querría	habría querido
querremos	habremos querido	querríamos	habríamos querido
querréis	habréis querido	querríais	habríais querido
querrán	habrán querido	querrían	habrían querido

Pretérito	Pretérito perf.
quise	hube querido
quisiste	hubiste querido
quiso	hubo querido
quisimos	hubimos querido
quisisteis	hubisteis querido
quisieron	hubieron querido

IMPERATIVO

Afirmativo	Negativo
quiere (tú)	no quieras
quiera (Ud.)	no quiera
queramos	no queramos
quered	no queráis
quieran	no quieran

SUBJUNTIVO

Presente	Presente perfecto	Imperfecto	Pasado perfecto
quiera	haya querido	quisiera	hubiera querido
quieras	hayas querido	quisieras	hubieras querido
quiera	haya querido	quisiera	hubiera querido
queramos	hayamos querido	quisiéramos	hubiéramos querido
queráis	hayáis querido	quisierais	hubierais querido
quieran	hayan querido	quisieran	hubieran querido

INFINITIVO

Simple	Perfecto
querer	haber querido

PARTICIPIO

querido

GERUNDIO

Simple	Perfecto
queriendo	habiendo querido

310

INDICATIVO

Presente	Presente perfecto	Imperfecto	Pasado perfecto
río	he reído	reía	había reído
ríes	has reído	reías	habías reído
ríe	ha reído	reía	había reído
reímos	hemos reído	reíamos	habíamos reído
reís	habéis reído	reíais	habíais reído
ríen	han reído	reían	habían reído

Futuro	Futuro perfecto	Fut. hip.	Fut. perf. hip.
reiré	habré reído	reiría	habría reído
reirás	habrás reído	reirías	habrías reído
reirá	habrá reído	reiría	habría reído
reiremos	habremos reído	reiríamos	habríamos reído
reiréis	habréis reído	reiríais	habríais reído
reirán	habrán reído	reirían	habrían reído

Pretérito	Pretérito perf.
reí	hube reído
reíste	hubiste reído
rió	hubo reído
reímos	hubimos reído
reísteis	hubisteis reído
rieron	hubieron reído

IMPERATIVO

Afirmativo	Negativo
ríe (tú)	no rías
ría (Ud.)	no ría
riamos	no riamos
reíd	no riáis
rían	no rían

SUBJUNTIVO

Presente	Presente perfecto	Imperfecto	Pasado perfecto
ría	haya reído	riera	hubiera reído
rías	hayas reído	rieras	hubieras reído
ría	haya reído	riera	hubiera reído
riamos	hayamos reído	riéramos	hubiéramos reído
riáis	hayáis reído	rierais	hubierais reído
rían	hayan reído	rieran	hubieran reído

INFINITIVO | PARTICIPIO | GERUNDIO

Simple	Perfecto	PARTICIPIO	Simple	Perfecto
reír	haber reído	reído	riendo	habiendo reído

Other verbs: freír, sonreír

INDICATIVO

Presente	Presente perfecto	Imperfecto	Pasado perfecto
repito	he repetido	repetía	había repetido
repites	has repetido	repetías	habías repetido
repite	ha repetido	repetía	había repetido
repetimos	hemos repetido	repetíamos	habíamos repetido
repetís	habéis repetido	repetíais	habíais repetido
repiten	han repetido	repetían	habían repetido

Futuro	Futuro perfecto	Fut. hip.	Fut. perf. hip.
repetiré	habré repetido	repetiría	habría repetido
repetirás	habrás repetido	repetirías	habrías repetido
repetirá	habrá repetido	repetiría	habría repetido
repetiremos	habremos repetido	repetiríamos	habríamos repetido
repetiréis	habréis repetido	repetiríais	habríais repetido
repetirán	habrán repetido	repetirían	habrían repetido

Pretérito	Pretérito perf.
repetí	hube repetido
repetiste	hubiste repetido
repitió	hubo repetido
repetimos	hubimos repetido
repetisteis	hubisteis repetido
repitieron	hubieron repetido

IMPERATIVO

Afirmativo	Negativo
repite (tú)	no repitas
repita (Ud.)	no repita
repitamos	no repitamos
repetid	no repitáis
repitan	no repitan

SUBJUNTIVO

Presente	Presente perfecto	Imperfecto	Pasado perfecto
repita	haya repetido	repitiera	hubiera repetido
repitas	hayas repetido	repitieras	hubieras repetido
repita	haya repetido	repitiera	hubiera repetido
repitamos	hayamos repetido	repitiéramos	hubiéramos repetido
repitáis	hayáis repetido	repitierais	hubierais repetido
repitan	hayan repetido	repitieran	hubieran repetido

INFINITIVO
Simple	Perfecto
repetir	haber repetido

PARTICIPIO
repetido

GERUNDIO
Simple	Perfecto
repitiendo	habiendo repetido

Other verbs: competir, despedir, impedir, medir, pedir, reñir, servir, vestir

312

INDICATIVO

Presente	Presente perfecto	Imperfecto	Pasado perfecto
sé	he sabido	sabía	había sabido
sabes	has sabido	sabías	habías sabido
sabe	ha sabido	sabía	había sabido
sabemos	hemos sabido	sabíamos	habíamos sabido
sabéis	habéis sabido	sabíais	habíais sabido
saben	han sabido	sabían	habían sabido

Futuro	Futuro perfecto	Fut. hip.	Fut. perf. hip.
sabré	habré sabido	sabría	habría sabido
sabrás	habrás sabido	sabrías	habrías sabido
sabrá	habrá sabido	sabría	habría sabido
sabremos	habremos sabido	sabríamos	habríamos sabido
sabréis	habréis sabido	sabríais	habríais sabido
sabrán	habrán sabido	sabrían	habrían sabido

Pretérito	Pretérito perf.
supe	hube sabido
supistes	hubiste sabido
supo	hubo sabido
supimos	hubimos sabido
supisteis	hubisteis sabido
supieron	hubieron sabido

IMPERATIVO

Afirmativo	Negativo
sabe (tú)	no sepas
sepa (Ud.)	no sepa
sepamos	no sepamos
sabed	no sepáis
sepan	no sepan

SUBJUNTIVO

Presente	Presente perfecto	Imperfecto	Pasado perfecto
sepa	haya sabido	supiera	hubiera sabido
sepas	hayas sabido	supieras	hubieras sabido
sepa	haya sabido	supiera	hubiera sabido
sepamos	hayamos sabido	supiéramos	hubiéramos sabido
sepáis	hayáis sabido	supierais	hubierais sabido
sepan	hayan sabido	supieran	hubieran sabido

INFINITIVO — PARTICIPIO — GERUNDIO

INFINITIVO		PARTICIPIO	GERUNDIO	
Simple	Perfecto		Simple	Perfecto
saber	haber sabido	sabido	sabiendo	habiendo sabido

313

INDICATIVO

Presente	Presente perfecto	Imperfecto	Pasado perfecto
saco	he sacado	sacaba	había sacado
sacas	has sacado	sacabas	habías sacado
saca	ha sacado	sacaba	había sacado
sacamos	hemos sacado	sacábamos	habíamos sacado
sacáis	habéis sacado	sacábais	habíais sacado
sacan	han sacado	sacaban	habían sacado

Futuro	Futuro perfecto	Fut. hip.	Fut. perf. hip.
sacaré	habré sacado	sacaría	habría sacado
sacarás	habrás sacado	sacarías	habrías sacado
sacará	habrá sacado	sacaría	habría sacado
sacaremos	habremos sacado	sacaríamos	habríamos sacado
sacaréis	habréis sacado	sacaríais	habríais sacado
sacarán	habrán sacado	sacarían	habrían sacado

Pretérito	Pretérito perf.
saqué	hube sacado
sacaste	hubiste sacado
sacó	hubo sacado
sacamos	hubimos sacado
sacasteis	hubisteis sacado
sacaron	hubieron sacado

IMPERATIVO

Afirmativo	Negativo
saca (tú)	no saques
saque (Ud.)	no saque
saquemos	no saquemos
sacad	no saquéis
saquen	no saquen

SUBJUNTIVO

Presente	Presente perfecto	Imperfecto	Pasado perfecto
saque	haya sacado	sacara	hubiera sacado
saques	hayas sacado	sacaras	hubieras sacado
saque	haya sacado	sacara	hubiera sacado
saquemos	hayamos sacado	sacáramos	hubiéramos sacado
saquéis	hayáis sacado	sacarais	hubierais sacado
saquen	hayan sacado	sacaran	hubieran sacado

INFINITIVO

Simple	Perfecto
sacar	haber sacado

PARTICIPIO

sacado

GERUNDIO

Simple	Perfecto
sacando	habiendo sacado

Other verbs: acercar, aparcar, aplicar, arrancar, atacar, buscar, colocar, comunicar, criticar, chocar, edificar, equivocar(**se**), explicar, indicar, marcar, perjudicar, pescar, practicar, provocar, publicar, secar(**se**), suplicar, tocar, volcar

INDICATIVO

Presente	Presente perfecto	Imperfecto	Pasado perfecto
salgo	he salido	salía	había salido
sales	has salido	salías	habías salido
sale	ha salido	salía	había salido
salimos	hemos salido	salíamos	habíamos salido
salís	habéis salido	salíais	habíais salido
salen	han salido	salían	habían salido

Futuro	Futuro perfecto	Fut. hip.	Fut. perf. hip.
saldré	habré salido	saldría	habría salido
saldrás	habrás salido	saldrías	habrías salido
saldrá	habrá salido	saldría	habría salido
saldremos	habremos salido	saldríamos	habríamos salido
saldréis	habréis salido	saldríais	habríais salido
saldrán	habrán salido	saldrían	habrían salido

Pretérito	Pretérito perf.
salí	hube salido
saliste	hubiste salido
salió	hubo salido
salimos	hubimos salido
salisteis	hubisteis salido
salieron	hubieron salido

IMPERATIVO

Afirmativo	Negativo
sal (tú)	no salgas
salga (Ud.)	no salga
salgamos	no salgamos
salid	no salgáis
salgan	no salgan

SUBJUNTIVO

Presente	Presente perfecto	Imperfecto	Pasado perfecto
salga	haya salido	saliera	hubiera salido
salgas	hayas salido	salieras	hubieras salido
salga	haya salido	saliera	hubiera salido
salgamos	hayamos salido	saliéramos	hubiéramos salido
salgáis	hayáis salido	salierais	hubierais salido
salgan	hayan salido	salieran	hubieran salido

INFINITIVO / PARTICIPIO / GERUNDIO

Simple	Perfecto	PARTICIPIO	Simple	Perfecto
salir	haber salido	salido	saliendo	habiendo salido

Other verbs: sobresalir, and verbs ending in **-alir** and **-aler**

315

INDICATIVO

Presente	Presente perfecto	Imperfecto	Pasado perfecto
sigo	he seguido	seguía	había seguido
sigues	has seguido	seguías	habías seguido
sigue	ha seguido	seguía	había seguido
seguimos	hemos seguido	seguíamos	habíamos seguido
seguís	habéis seguido	seguíais	habíais seguido
siguen	han seguido	seguían	habían seguido

Futuro	Futuro perfecto	Fut. hip.	Fut. perf. hip.
seguiré	habré seguido	seguiría	habría seguido
seguirás	habrás seguido	seguirías	habrías seguido
seguirá	habrá seguido	seguiría	habría seguido
seguiremos	habremos seguido	seguiríamos	habríamos seguido
seguiréis	habréis seguido	seguiríais	habríais seguido
seguirán	habrán seguido	seguirían	habrían seguido

Pretérito	Pretérito perf.
seguí	hube seguido
seguiste	hubiste seguido
siguió	hubo seguido
seguimos	hubimos seguido
seguisteis	hubisteis seguido
siguieron	hubieron seguido

IMPERATIVO

Afirmativo	Negativo
sigue (tú)	no sigas
siga (Ud.)	no siga
sigamos	no sigamos
seguid	no sigáis
sigan	no sigan

SUBJUNTIVO

Presente	Presente perfecto	Imperfecto	Pasado perfecto
siga	haya seguido	siguiera	hubiera seguido
sigas	hayas seguido	siguieras	hubieras seguido
siga	haya seguido	siguiera	hubiera seguido
sigamos	hayamos seguido	siguiéramos	hubiéramos seguido
sigáis	hayáis seguido	siguierais	hubierais seguido
sigan	hayan seguido	siguieran	hubieran seguido

INFINITIVO   PARTICIPIO   GERUNDIO

Simple	Perfecto		Simple	Perfecto
seguir	haber seguido	seguido	siguiendo	habiendo seguido

Other verbs: conseguir, perseguir

316

INDICATIVO

Presente	Presente perfecto	Imperfecto	Pasado perfecto
siento	he sentido	sentía	había sentido
sientes	has sentido	sentías	habías sentido
siente	ha sentido	sentía	había sentido
sentimos	hemos sentido	sentíamos	habíamos sentido
sentís	habéis sentido	sentíais	habíais sentido
sienten	han sentido	sentían	habían sentido

Futuro	Futuro perfecto	Fut. hip.	Fut. perf. hip.
sentiré	habré sentido	sentiría	habría sentido
sentirás	habrás sentido	sentirías	habrías sentido
sentirá	habrá sentido	sentiría	habría sentido
sentiremos	habremos sentido	sentiríamos	habríamos sentido
sentiréis	habréis sentido	sentiríais	habríais sentido
sentirán	habrán sentido	sentirían	habrían sentido

Pretérito	Pretérito perf.
sentí	hube salido
sentiste	hubiste salido
sintió	hubo salido
sentimos	hubimos salido
sentisteis	hubisteis salido
sintieron	hubieron salido

IMPERATIVO

Afirmativo	Negativo
siente (tú)	no sientas
sienta (Ud.)	no sienta
sintamos	no sintamos
sentid	no sintáis
sientan	no sientan

SUBJUNTIVO

Presente	Presente perfecto	Imperfecto	Pasado perfecto
sienta	haya sentido	sintiera	hubiera sentido
sientas	hayas sentido	sintieras	hubieras sentido
sienta	haya sentido	sintiera	hubiera sentido
sintamos	hayamos sentido	sintiéramos	hubiéramos sentido
sintáis	hayáis sentido	sintierais	hubierais sentido
sientan	hayan sentido	sintieran	hubieran sentido

INFINITIVO
Simple sentir **Perfecto** haber sentido

PARTICIPIO
sentido

GERUNDIO
Simple sintiendo **Perfecto** habiendo sentido

Other verbs: asentir, concernir, conferir, consentir, deferir, desmentir, disentir, inferir, mentir, pervertir, presentir, proferir, resentir

INDICATIVO

Presente	Presente perfecto	Imperfecto	Pasado perfecto
soy	he sido	era	había sido
eres	has sido	eras	habías sido
es	ha sido	era	había sido
somos	hemos sido	éramos	habíamos sido
sois	habéis sido	erais	habíais sido
son	han sido	eran	habían sido

Futuro	Futuro perfecto	Fut. hip.	Fut. perf. hip.
seré	habré sido	sería	habría sido
serás	habrás sido	serías	habrías sido
será	habrá sido	sería	habría sido
seremos	habremos sido	seríamos	habríamos sido
seréis	habréis sido	seríais	habríais sido
serán	habrán sido	serían	habrían sido

Pretérito	Pretérito perf.
fui	hube sido
fuiste	hubiste sido
fue	hubo sido
fuimos	hubimos sido
fuisteis	hubisteis sido
fueron	hubieron sido

IMPERATIVO

Afirmativo	Negativo
sé (tú)	no seas
sea (Ud.)	no sea
seamos	no seamos
sed	no seáis
sean	no sean

SUBJUNTIVO

Presente	Presente perfecto	Imperfecto	Pasado perfecto
sea	haya sido	fuera	hubiera sido
seas	hayas sido	fueras	hubieras sido
sea	haya sido	fuera	hubiera sido
seamos	hayamos sido	fuéramos	hubiéramos sido
seáis	hayáis sido	fuerais	hubierais sido
sean	hayan sido	fueran	hubieran sido

INFINITIVO   PARTICIPIO   GERUNDIO

Simple	Perfecto		Simple	Perfecto
ser	haber sido	sido	siendo	habiendo sido

INDICATIVO

Presente	Presente perfecto	Imperfecto	Pasado perfecto
sueño	he soñado	soñaba	había soñado
sueñas	has soñado	soñabas	habías soñado
sueña	ha soñado	soñaba	había soñado
soñamos	hemos soñado	soñábamos	habíamos soñado
soñáis	habéis soñado	soñabais	habíais soñado
sueñan	han soñado	soñaban	habían soñado

Futuro	Futuro perfecto	Fut. hip.	Fut. perf. hip.
soñaré	habré soñado	soñaría	habría soñado
soñarás	habrás soñado	soñarías	habrías soñado
soñará	habrá soñado	soñaría	habría soñado
soñaremos	habremos soñado	soñaríamos	habríamos soñado
soñaréis	habréis soñado	soñaríais	habríais soñado
soñarán	habrán soñado	soñarían	habrían soñado

Pretérito	Pretérito perf.
soñé	hube soñado
soñaste	hubiste soñado
soñó	hubo soñado
soñamos	hubimos soñado
soñasteis	hubisteis soñado
soñaron	hubieron soñado

IMPERATIVO

Afirmativo	Negativo
sueña (tú)	no sueñes
sueñe (Ud.)	no sueñe
soñemos	no soñemos
soñad	no soñéis
sueñen	no sueñen

SUBJUNTIVO

Presente	Presente perfecto	Imperfecto	Pasado perfecto
sueñe	haya soñado	soñara	hubiera soñado
sueñes	hayas soñado	soñaras	hubieras soñado
sueñe	haya soñado	soñara	hubiera soñado
soñemos	hayamos soñado	soñáramos	hubiéramos soñado
soñéis	hayáis soñado	soñarais	hubierais soñado
sueñen	hayan soñado	soñaran	hubieran soñado

INFINITIVO   PARTICIPIO   GERUNDIO

Simple	Perfecto		Simple	Perfecto
soñar	haber soñado	soñado	soñando	habiendo soñado

Other verbs: acordar**(se)**, acostar**(se)**, apostar, comprobar, contar, consolar, costar, demostrar, encontrar, mostrar, probar, recordar, renovar, soltar, sonar, volar

INDICATIVO

Presente	Presente perfecto	Imperfecto	Pasado perfecto
subo	he subido	subía	había subido
subes	has subido	subías	habías subido
sube	ha subido	subía	había subido
subimos	hemos subido	subíamos	habíamos subido
subís	habéis subido	subíais	habíais subido
suben	han subido	subían	habían subido

Futuro	Futuro perfecto	Fut. hip.	Fut. perf. hip.
subiré	habré subido	subiría	habría subido
subirás	habrás subido	subirías	habrías subido
subirá	habrá subido	subiría	habría subido
subiremos	habremos subido	subiríamos	habríamos subido
subiréis	habréis subido	subiríais	habríais subido
subirán	habrán subido	subirían	habrían subido

Pretérito	Pretérito perf.
subí	hube subido
subiste	hubiste subido
subió	hubo subido
subimos	hubimos subido
subisteis	hubisteis subido
subieron	hubieron subido

IMPERATIVO

Afirmativo	Negativo
sube (tú)	no subas
suba (Ud.)	no suba
subamos	no subamos
subid	no subáis
suban	no suban

SUBJUNTIVO

Presente	Presente perfecto	Imperfecto	Pasado perfecto
suba	haya subido	subiera	hubiera subido
subas	hayas subido	subieras	hubieras subido
suba	haya subido	subiera	hubiera subido
subamos	hayamos subido	subiéramos	hubiéramos subido
subáis	hayáis subido	subierais	hubierais subido
suban	hayan subido	subieran	hubieran subido

INFINITIVO   PARTICIPIO   GERUNDIO

Simple	Perfecto		Simple	Perfecto
subir	haber subido	subido	subiendo	habiendo subido

This is the regular conjugation for **-ir** verbs.

The verbs **abrir, cubrir,** and **descubrir** are regular except in the *participio*: *abierto, cubierto, descubierto.*

INDICATIVO

Presente	Presente perfecto	Imperfecto	Pasado perfecto
tengo	he tenido	tenía	había tenido
tienes	has tenido	tenías	habías tenido
tiene	ha tenido	tenía	había tenido
tenemos	hemos tenido	teníamos	habíamos tenido
tenéis	habéis tenido	teníais	habíais tenido
tienen	han tenido	tenían	habían tenido

Futuro	Futuro perfecto	Fut. hip.	Fut. perf. hip.
tendré	habré tenido	tendría	habría tenido
tendrás	habrás tenido	tendrías	habrías tenido
tendrá	habrá tenido	tendría	habría tenido
tendremos	habremos tenido	tendríamos	habríamos tenido
tendréis	habréis tenido	tendríais	habríais tenido
tendrán	habrán tenido	tendrían	habrían tenido

Pretérito	Pretérito perf.
tuve	hube tenido
tuviste	hubiste tenido
tuvo	hubo tenido
tuvimos	hubimos tenido
tuvisteis	hubisteis tenido
tuvieron	hubieron tenido

IMPERATIVO

Afirmativo	Negativo
ten (tú)	no tengas
tenga (Ud.)	no tenga
tengamos	no tengamos
tened	no tengáis
tengan	no tengan

SUBJUNTIVO

Presente	Presente perfecto	Imperfecto	Pasado perfecto
tenga	haya tenido	tuviera	hubiera tenido
tengas	hayas tenido	tuvieras	hubieras tenido
tenga	haya tenido	tuviera	hubiera tenido
tengamos	hayamos tenido	tuviéramos	hubiéramos tenido
tengáis	hayáis tenido	tuvierais	hubierais tenido
tengan	hayan tenido	tuvieran	hubieran tenido

INFINITIVO / PARTICIPIO / GERUNDIO

Simple	Perfecto	PARTICIPIO	Simple	Perfecto
tener	haber tenido	tenido	teniendo	habiendo tenido

Other verbs: contener, detener, entretener, obtener

INDICATIVO

Presente	Presente perfecto	Imperfecto	Pasado perfecto
traduzco	he traducido	traducía	había traducido
traduces	has traducido	traducías	habías traducido
traduce	ha traducido	traducía	había traducido
traducimos	hemos traducido	traducíamos	habíamos traducido
traducis	habéis traducido	traducíais	habíais traducido
traducen	han traducido	traducían	habían traducido

Futuro	Futuro perfecto	Fut. hip.	Fut. perf. hip.
traduciré	habré traducido	traduciría	habría traducido
traducirás	habrás traducido	traducirías	habrías traducido
traducirá	habrá traducido	traduciría	habría traducido
traduciremos	habremos traducido	traduciríamos	habríamos traducido
traduciréis	habréis traducido	traduciríais	habríais traducido
traducirán	habrán traducido	traducirían	habrían traducido

Pretérito	Pretérito perf.
traduje	hube traducido
tradujiste	hubiste traducido
tradujo	hubo traducido
tradujimos	hubimos traducido
tradujisteis	hubisteis traducido
tradujeron	hubieron traducido

IMPERATIVO

Afirmativo	Negativo
traduce (tú)	no traduzcas
traduzca (Ud.)	no traduzca
traduzcamos	no traduzcamos
traducid	no traduzcáis
traduzcan	no traduzcan

SUBJUNTIVO

Presente	Presente perfecto	Imperfecto	Pasado perfecto
traduzca	haya traducido	tradujera	hubiera traducido
traduzcas	hayas traducido	tradujeras	hubieras traducido
traduzca	haya traducido	tradujera	hubiera traducido
traduzcamos	hayamos traducido	tradujéramos	hubiéramos traducido
traduzcáis	hayáis traducido	tradujerais	hubierais traducido
traduzcan	hayan traducido	tradujeran	hubieran traducido

INFINITIVO   PARTICIPIO GERUNDIO

Simple	Perfecto		Simple	Perfecto
traducir	haber traducido	traducido	traduciendo	habiendo traducido

Other verbs: conducir, introducir, producir, reducir, reproducir, seducir

322

INDICATIVO

Presente	Presente perfecto	Imperfecto	Pasado perfecto
traigo	he traído	traía	había traído
traes	has traído	traías	habías traído
trae	ha traído	traía	había traído
traemos	hemos traído	traíamos	habíamos traído
traéis	habéis traído	traíais	habíais traído
traen	han traído	traían	habían traído

Futuro	Futuro perfecto	Fut. hip.	Fut. perf. hip.
traeré	habré traído	traería	habría traído
traerás	habrás traído	trerías	habrías traído
traerá	habrá traído	traería	habría traído
traeremos	habremos traído	traeríamos	habríamos traído
traeréis	habréis traído	traeríais	habríais traído
traerán	habrán traído	traerían	habrían traído

Pretérito	Pretérito perf.
traje	hube traído
trajiste	hubiste traído
trajo	hubo traído
trajimos	hubimos traído
trajisteis	hubisteis traído
trajeron	hubieron traído

IMPERATIVO

Afirmativo	Negativo
trae (tú)	no traigas
traiga (Ud.)	no traiga
traigamos	no traigamos
traed	no traigáis
traigan	no traigan

SUBJUNTIVO

Presente	Presente perfecto	Imperfecto	Pasado perfecto
traiga	haya traído	trajera	hubiera traído
traigas	hayas traído	trajeras	hubieras traído
traiga	haya traído	trajera	hubiera traído
traigamos	hayamos traído	trajéramos	hubiéramos traído
traigáis	hayáis traído	trajerais	hubierais traído
traigan	hayan traído	trajeran	hubieran traído

INFINITIVO   PARTICIPIO   GERUNDIO

Simple	Perfecto		Simple	Perfecto
traer	haber traído	traído	trayendo	habiendo traído

Other verbs: abstraer, atraer, contraer, distraer, extraer, retraer, sustraer

* **Caer** is conjugated like **traer** except in the following tenses:

(i) *pretérito:* caí, caíste, cayó, caímos, caísteis, cayeron

(ii) *imperfecto del subjuntivo:* cayera, cayeras, cayera, cayéramos, cayerais, cayeran

INDICATIVO

Presente	Presente perfecto	Imperfecto	Pasado perfecto
valgo	he valido	valía	había valido
vales	has valido	valías	habías valido
vale	ha valido	valía	había valido
valemos	hemos valido	valíamos	habíamos valido
valéis	habéis valido	valíais	habíais valido
valen	han valido	valían	habían valido

Futuro	Futuro perfecto	Fut. hip.	Fut. perf. hip.
valdré	habré valido	valdría	habría valido
valdrás	habrás valido	valdrías	habrías valido
valdrá	habrá valido	valdría	habría valido
valdremos	habremos valido	valdríamos	habríamos valido
valdréis	habréis valido	valdríais	habríais valido
valdrán	habrán valido	valdrían	habrían valido

Pretérito	Pretérito perf.
valí	hube valido
valiste	hubiste valido
valió	hubo valido
valimos	hubimos valido
valisteis	hubisteis valido
valieron	hubieron valido

IMPERATIVO

Afirmativo	Negativo
val (tú)	no valgas
valga (Ud.)	no valga
valgamos	no valgamos
valed	no valgáis
valgan	no valgan

SUBJUNTIVO

Presente	Presente perfecto	Imperfecto	Pasado perfecto
valga	haya valido	valiera	hubiera valido
valgas	hayas valido	valieras	hubieras valido
valga	haya valido	valiera	hubiera valido
valgamos	hayamos valido	valiéramos	hubiéramos valido
valgáis	hayáis valido	valierais	hubierais valido
valgan	hayan valido	valieran	hubieran valido

INFINITIVO

Simple	Perfecto
valer	haber valido

PARTICIPIO

valido

GERUNDIO

Simple	Perfecto
valiendo	habiendo valido

INDICATIVO

Presente	Presente perfecto	Imperfecto	Pasado perfecto
vengo	he venido	venía	había venido
vienes	has venido	venías	habías venido
viene	ha venido	venía	había venido
venimos	hemos venido	veníamos	habíamos venido
venís	habéis venido	veníais	habíais venido
vienen	han venido	venían	habían venido

Futuro	Futuro perfecto	Fut. hip.	Fut. perf. hip.
vendré	habré venido	vendría	habría venido
vendrás	habrás venido	vendrías	habrías venido
vendrá	habrá venido	vendría	habría venido
vendremos	habremos venido	vendríamos	habríamos venido
vendréis	habréis venido	vendríais	habríais venido
vendrán	habrán venido	vendrían	habrían venido

Pretérito	Pretérito perf.
vine	hube venido
viniste	hubiste venido
vino	hubo venido
vinimos	hubimos venido
vinisteis	hubisteis venido
vinieron	hubieron venido

IMPERATIVO

Afirmativo	Negativo
ven (tú)	no vengas
venga (Ud.)	no venga
vengamos	no vengamos
venid	no vengáis
vengan	no vengan

SUBJUNTIVO

Presente	Presente perfecto	Imperfecto	Pasado perfecto
venga	haya venido	viniera	hubiera venido
vengas	hayas venido	vinieras	hubieras venido
venga	haya venido	viniera	hubiera venido
vengamos	hayamos venido	viniéramos	hubiéramos venido
vengáis	hayáis venido	vinierais	hubierais venido
vengan	hayan venido	vinieran	hubieran venido

INFINITIVO / PARTICIPIO / GERUNDIO

Infinitivo Simple	Perfecto	Participio	Gerundio Simple	Perfecto
venir	haber venido	venido	viniendo	habiendo venido

Other verbs: intervenir, prevenir

325

INDICATIVO

Presente	Presente perfecto	Imperfecto	Pasado perfecto
veo	he visto	veía	había visto
ves	has visto	veías	habías visto
ve	ha visto	veía	había visto
vemos	hemos visto	veíamos	habíamos visto
veis	habéis visto	veíais	habíais visto
ven	han visto	veían	habían visto

Futuro	Futuro perfecto	Fut. hip.	Fut. perf. hip.
veré	habré visto	vería	habría visto
verás	habrás visto	verías	habrías visto
verá	habrá visto	vería	habría visto
veremos	habremos visto	veríamos	habríamos visto
veréis	habréis visto	veríais	habríais visto
verán	habrán visto	verían	habrían visto

Pretérito	Pretérito perf.
vi	hube visto
viste	hubiste visto
vio	hubo visto
vimos	hubimos visto
visteis	hubisteis visto
vieron	hubieron visto

IMPERATIVO

Afirmativo	Negativo
ve (tú)	no veas
vea (Ud.)	no vea
veamos	no veamos
ved	no veáis
vean	no vean

SUBJUNTIVO

Presente	Presente perfecto	Imperfecto	Pasado perfecto
vea	haya visto	viera	hubiera visto
veas	hayas visto	vieras	hubieras visto
vea	haya visto	viera	hubiera visto
veamos	hayamos visto	viéramos	hubiéramos visto
veáis	hayáis visto	vierais	hubierais visto
vean	hayan visto	vieran	hubieran visto

INFINITIVO

Simple	Perfecto
ver	haber visto

PARTICIPIO

visto

GERUNDIO

Simple	Perfecto
viendo	habiendo visto

326

VERB COMPLEMENTS

This section contains a list of the most frequent verbs with their complements, i.e., the structure which usually follows them. An example is given for each verb complement, and the English translation of the verb is provided.
The following abbreviations will be used to describe the complements:

ø

The verb does not require any complement.

dormir   *ø*   El bebé está durmiendo.   *to sleep*

adj

The verb is followed by an adjective.

estar   *adj*   El televisor está roto.   *to be*

adv

The verb is followed by an adverb.

comportarse *adv*   Tienes que comportarte bien.   *to behave*

exp

The abbreviation **exp** (expressions) indicates special uses and idiomatic meanings.

aguantar *exp*   No aguantar más.   *(I, you...) can't bear it any more*

ger

The verb is followed by a verb in the *gerundio*.

acabar   *ger*   Juan acabó dejando su trabajo.   *to end up*

imp

The verb is used in the impersonal form: 3rd person singular.

convenir *imp*   Conviene llevar un paraguas.   *it is advisable*

inf

The verb is followed by a verb in the *infinitivo*.

querer   *inf*   Quiero ir a la playa.   *to want*

328

When the verb is followed by a preposition and **inf,**
the preposition is specified.

empezar *a inf*   Empezó a llover.   *to start*

que ind

The verb is followed by **que** and a sentence in the
indicativo.

decir   *que ind*   Juan dice que su hermano   *to say*
                          tiene mucho dinero.

que sub

The verb is followed by **que** and a sentence in the
subuntivo.

esperar *que sub*   Juan espera que su hermano   *to hope*
                          tenga dinero

quest

The verb is followed by an indirect question.

adivinar *quest*   ¿Adivina quién viene esta noche?   *to guess*

uno/alg

The verb is directly followed by a noun phrase: **uno**
(somebody) or **alg** (something). This noun phrase is the
direct object of the verb.

comer   *alg*   Yo como un pastel.   *to eat*

The direct object is preceded by **a,** when it names a
human being and is specific. We will then write **(a) uno/alg.**
This abbreviation stands for **a uno** or **alg.**

ver   *(a) uno/alg* Veo la foto.   *to see*
                          Veo a María en la foto.   *to see*

When the verb requires a preposition, the preposition is
specified. The noun phrase is then an indirect (**a uno/alg**)
or prepositional object (other prepositions).

telefonear *a uno*   David telefonea a la doctora.   *to phone*
hablar   *de uno/alg* Marcos habla de su trabajo.   *to speak*
dar   *alg a uno* Leona dio dinero a su hijo.   *to give*

When the complement refers to a specific concept, such
as place or time, this will be indicated in brackets.

pasar   [time]   Pasé el fin de semana en la cama.   *to spend*

329

a

abalanzarse	*sobre uno/alg*	Todos se abalanzaron sobre la mesa.	*to rush at*
		Los fans se abalanzaron sobre el cantante y le rompieron la camisa.	*to hurl upon*
	hacia [place]	Todos se abalanzaron hacia la salida.	*to rush toward*
abandonar	*(a) uno/alg*	La gente abandonó la plaza.	*to desert, leave*
		Isabel abandonó a su amigo.	*to abandon*
	exp	*abandonar el cargo*	*to give up the post*
abarcar	*alg* [time/ space]	El libro abarca todo el siglo.	*to contain*
	exp	*Quien mucho abarca poco aprieta.* / You	*can bite off more than you can chew.*
abarrotar	*alg*	Ha abarrotado la casa de antigüedades.	*to overfill*
		La cantante abarrotó la sala.	*to overcrowd*
abarrotarse	*de alg*	Luis se abarrotó de pasteles.	*to be stuffed*
abastecer	*a uno/alg*	La casa Martico abastece a los hoteles.	*to supply*
abatir	*(a) uno/alg*	Los leñadores abatieron el árbol.	*to cut down*
		La artillería abatió un avión enemigo.	*to shot down*
		Las noticias de la guerra me abaten.	*to sadden, depress*
abatirse	*sobre uno/alg*	Los niños se abatieron sobre el helado.	*to swoop on*
abdicar	*ø*	El Ministro de Economía abdicó.	*to abdicate*
	a alg	Don Carlos addicó al trono.	*to abdicate*
ablandar	*a uno*	Se mostró muy enojado, pero su nieta consiguió ablandarle.	*to appease*
abochornar	*(a) uno*	Su conducta me abochorna.	*to embarrass*
abochornarse	*(de) inf*	Me abochorna de ver su conducta.	*to get embarrassed about*
abofetear	*(a) uno*	Su novia lo abofeteó delante de todos.	*to slap*
abogar	*por/a (en) favor de*	El partido aboga por la causa indígena.	*to advocate*
abolir	*alg*	El Gobierno decidió abolir el impuesto de autopistas.	*to abolish*
abominar	*alg*	Abomino las mentiras y las calumnias.	*to abominate*

330

abonar	*alg*	Aboné mucho dinero para los estudios.	*to pay*
	(a) uno	Abonamos el candidato a la presidencia.	*to support*
abonarse	*a alg*	Me aboné a una nueva revista.	*to subscribe*
abordar	*a uno*	Al salir del teatro abordé al actor.	*to accost*
	alg	El conferenciante abordó bien el tema.	*to approach*
aborrecer	*(a) uno/alg*	Aborrece las playas del este.	*to detest*
	inf	Aborrezco tener que esperar al bus.	*to detest*
abortar	*ø*	No tuvo otro remedio que abortar.	*to have an abortion*
		La nueva propuesta de ley abortó.	*to fail*
	exp	*hacerse abortar*	*to have an abortion*
abotonar	*alg*	¡Abotona tu abrigo porque hace frío!	*to button*
abrasar	*alg*	El sol abrasa las plantas.	*to burn*
abrasarse	*exp*	*abrasarse de calor / to be dying on the heat*	
abrazar	*(a) uno*	Es un gato tan lindo que todos lo abrazan.	*to hug*
	alg [idea]	El partido abrazó la causa ecologista.	*to adopt, embrace*
abrazarse	*ø*	Al firmar la paz, los Presidentes se abrazaron.	*to embrace*
	a uno/alg	Como tenía miedo del perro, Luisito se abrazó a su madre.	*to cling to*
abreviar	*alg*	Tienes que abreviar tu texto.	*to shorten*
	exp	*bueno, para abreviar / well, to make a long story short*	
abrigar	*ø*	Esta chamarra me abriga muy bien.	*to keep warm*
	exp	*abrigar malas intenciones / to have bad intention*	
abrigarse	*de alg*	Nos abrigamos de la lluvia en la plaza.	*to take shelter*
abrir	*ø*	El gimnasio abre a las nueve.	*to open*
	alg a uno	¡Ábreme la puerta!	*to open*
	exp	*en un abrir y cerrar de ojos / in the twinkling of an eye*	
abrirse	*a uno/alg*	Es tan tímido que no se abre ni siquiera a sus mejores amigos.	*to confide in*
abrochar	*alg*	¡Abrochen el cinturón para el aterrizaje!	*to fasten*
abrocharse	*alg*	¡Abróchate la chamarra!	*to button*
abrumar	*a uno*	Le abruma la tarea que le queda.	*to overwhelm*
absolver	*(a) uno*	Tras deliberación, el jurado absolvió al acusado.	*to acquit*
	de alg	El reo quedó absuelto de los cargos.	*to acquit*

331

absorber	*alg*	La tierra ha absorbido todo el agua.	*to absorb*
	exp	*estar absorbido en alg / to be absorbed in*	
abstenerse	*ø*	20% de los votantes se abstuvieron.	*to abstain*
	de alg	Le recomendó abstenerse del alcohol.	*to abstain from*
	de inf	Me abstengo de dar mi opinión.	*to abstain from*
	exp	*En la duda, ¡abstente! / When in doubt, don't.*	
abstraerse	*de alg*	No podemos abstraernos de la realidad.	*to leave aside*
abundar	*ø*	Los restaurantes abundan en la ciudad.	*to abound*
	de uno/alg	El campo abunda de flores.	*to abound*
aburrir	*(a) uno*	La película aburrió a todos.	*to bore*
aburrirse	*ø*	Me aburrí en esta fiesta.	*to be bored*
	de inf	Me aburrí de esperarle.	*to become bored*
	exp	*aburrirse como una ostra / tobe bored to tears*	
		aburrirse de no hacer nada / to be bored of doing nothing	
abusar	*de uno/alg*	Abusó de mi paciencia.	*to take advantage*
		Es perjudicial abusar del alcohol.	*to take too much*
		Abusar de los niños es un gran crimen.	*to abuse*
acabar	*alg*	Acabé mi tarea.	*to finish*
	con uno/alg	Hay que acabar con este juego.	*to put an end*
		El escándalo acabó con él.	*to be the end of*
		El granizo acabó con la cosecha.	*to destroy*
	de alg	Iba a ser jefa pero acabó de secretaria.	*to end up by Ving*
	de inf	El autobús acaba de salir.	*I/you... have just*
	por inf	Acabó por dejar la universidad.	*to end up Ving*
	ger	Acabé leyendo la novela.	*to finish Ving*
acabarse	*ø*	El concierto se acabó a las diez.	*to end*
	alg	Se me acabó el papel.	*to run out of*
	exp	*¡Se acabó!*	*It's all over.*
acaecer	*ø*	En el Pais de las Maravillas, siempre acaece algo inesperado.	*to happen*
	que ind	El pueblo vivía feliz; pero acaeció que una plaga de ratas invadió los campos.	*to happen*
acalorarse	*ø*	Se acalora cuando hablan de política.	*to get worked up*
	con alg	Se acaloraron con la discusión.	*to get angry*
acallar	*(a) uno/alg*	Las amenazas del director acallaron a los manifestantes.	*to silence*
acaparar	*alg*	Ellos acaparan los mejores puestos.	*to monopolize*
		Acaparó las miradas de los invitados.	*to absorb*
acariciar	*(a) uno* [body]		
		Para consolarle, le acarició el cabello.	*to caress*
	alg	Acaricia la idea de dar la vuelta al mundo.	*to cherish*

acarrear	*alg*	Sus camiones acarrean la mercancía por las autopistas.	*to transport*
	con uno/alg	Su madre acarrea con todo el trabajo.	*to bear the burden*
acatarrarse	*ø*	Debido al cambio de temperatura, me acatarré.	*to catch a cold*
acceder	*a alg*	Consiguió acceder al nuevo puesto.	*to be promoted*
	a inf	Accedieron a aumentar los salarios.	*to agree to*
acelerar	*a* [speed]	Aceleró a 140 km por hora.	*to accelerate*
	alg	Se decidió acelerar el plan económico.	*to speed up*
acentuar	*alg*	Hay que acentuar las palabras esdrújulas.	*to stress*
aceptar	*(a) uno/alg*	No acepté su regalo.	*to accept*
		Aceptaron a mi hijo en la universidad.	*to accept*
		El gobierno aceptó el nuevo plan.	*to approve*
	inf	Nunca aceptaré actuar contra mi propia conciencia.	*to accept V*
		Aceptaron pagar el resto de la cuenta.	*to agree to*
	que sub	Acepto que tengas tu propia opinión, pero no acepto que me la impongas.	*to accept*
	exp	*aceptar a alguien por esposo(a)* / *to accept as a spouse*	
acercar	*alg (a alg)*	¡Acerca la silla (a la mesa)!	*to bring closer*
acercarse	*ø*	Cuando se acercó, reconoció al herido.	*to come closer*
		Se acercan las Navidades.	*to approach*
	a uno/alg	Se acercó a Luis y le saludó.	*to get close to*
		Se acercó a la ventanilla del banco.	*to get close to*
	a inf	Me acerqué a ver lo que había pasado.	*to get close in order to*
acertar	*ø*	Tiró diez piedras, pero ninguna acertó.	*to hit*
		Si aciertas, te doy un premio.	*to guess correctly*
	(a) uno/alg	El campeón de tiro acertó todos los discos.	*to hit*
	en uno/alg	La flecha acertó en medio de la diana.	*to hit*
	con alg	No aciertan con su enfermedad.	*to find*
	alg	El concursante acertó todas las preguntas y ganó un millón de dólares.	*to guess correctly*
	a inf	No acertó a encontrar la casa.	*to manage*
aclamar	*(a) uno*	El público aclamó al orador.	*to applaud*
	(a) uno alg	Lo aclamaron Rey del Rock.	*to acclaim as*
aclarar	*alg*	Es necesario aclarar la situación.	*to clarify*
aclararse	*exp*	*No se aclara.* / *He can't work it out; he is confused.*	
acoger	*(a) uno*	Nuestro país acoge a los exiliados.	*to harbor*
		Acogieron al nuevo maestro con respeto.	*to receive*

333

acogerse	*a uno/alg*	En caso de conflicto, hay que acorgerse a la ley internacional.	*to have recourse to*
		Si tienes un problema en el extranjero, ¡acógete al cónsul!	*to ask for sb's help*
acometer	*alg*	Debemos acometer la empresa.	*to undertake*
	contra uno	El jugador acometió contra el árbitro.	*to attack*
	exp	*Me acometió la duda/el miedo/ el sueño...*	*I was overcome with...*
acomodar	*ø*	Acomodó la recámara para Luis y Eva.	*to arrange*
acomodarse	*exp*	*¡Acomódese a su gusto! / Make yourself comfortable!*	
acompañar	*(a) uno/alg*	Acompañó a los estudiantes a Veracruz.	*to accompany*
		Acompaño esta carta con un cheque.	*to enclose*
	exp	*acompañar a uno en el sentimiento / to offer condoleances*	
aconsejar	*(a) uno*	Hoy he aconsejado diez estudiantes.	*to counsel*
		Aconsejo también a las familias.	*to counsel*
	alg a uno	Aconsejamos esta clase a todos los nuevos estudiantes.	*to recommend*
	inf	Aconsejo llevar paraguas.	*to advise*
	a uno que sub		
		Él me aconsejó que tomara manzanilla.	*to advise uno to*
aconsejarse	*con uno*	Fui a aconsejarme con mi abogado.	*to consult*
acordar	*alg a uno*	A mi amigo, le acordaron una beca.	*to grant*
	alg	Hemos acordado la fecha de la boda.	*to decide*
	inf	Todos acordaron reunirse por la tarde.	*to agree*
	que sub	Hemos acordado que Luis lo haga.	*to agree*
acordarse	*de uno/alg*	Me acuerdo de mi infancia en El Paso.	*to remember*
		¿Te acuerdas de Fernando?	*to remember*
	de inf	Acuérdate de saludar a mi primo.	*to remember*
	exp	*si mal no me acuerdo / if my memory serves me right*	
		¡Te acordarás de ésta! / I will teach you!	
acortar	*alg*	Por la ruta 9 acortamos la distancia.	*to shorten*
acostar	*(a) uno*	¡Acuesta a los niños a las nueve!	*to put to bed*
acostarse	*ø*	Ayer me acosté temprano.	*to go to bed*
	con uno	No te diré con quién se acuesta.	*to sleep with*
acostumbrar	*inf*	Él acostumbra acostarse temprano.	*to be accustomed to*
acostumbrarse			
	a alg	No se acostumbra a la vida de este país.	*to get used*
	a inf	¡Acostúmbrate a cerrar la puerta!	*to get used*

acribillar	**exp**	*acribillar a balazos / to riddle with bullets*	
		acribillar a preguntas / to pester with questions	
actuar	**ø**	¿Quiénes actúan en la película?	*to perform*
	de alg	En esta situación, actuaré de árbitro.	*to act as*
acudir	**a uno/alg**	Lo esperamos, pero no acudió a la cita.	*to turn up*
		Mi abuela se encuentra tan mal que	*to go*
		habrá que acudir al hospital.	
	a inf	Mucha gente acudió a recibirlo.	*to come to*
acumular	**alg**	José Borda acumuló una gran fortuna	*to accumulate*
		con sus minas de plata.	
acusar	**(a) uno**	Yo no acuso a nadie.	*to accuse*
	(a) uno de alg	Lo acusan de negligencia.	*to accuse*
	(a) uno de inf	Lo acusaron de cometer el crimen.	*to accuse*
	alg	El precio del gas ha acusado una subida.	*to undergo*
	exp	*acusar recibo / to acknowledge receipt*	
acusarse	**de alg**	Se acusa del crimen cometido ayer.	*to confess*
	de inf	Se acusa de haber robado un banco.	*to confess*
achacar	**exp**	*achacar la culpa a alguien*	*to lay the blame*
adaptar	**alg**	Adaptó la camioneta a sus necesidades.	*to adapt*
adaptarse	**a alg**	No logré adaptarme a la gran ciudad.	*to adapt*
adelantar	**ø**	El país ha adelantado mucho.	*to advance*
	(a) uno/alg	Adelanté todos los vehiculos.	*to pass*
	exp	*prohibido adelantar*	*no pass*
		Mi reloj adelanta.	*to be fast*
adelantarse	**a uno/alg**	Pérez se adelantó al resto de su equipo.	*to go ahead*
adelgazar	**ø**	Voy a hacer ejercicio para adelgazar.	*to lose weight*
	alg [weight]	Este mes he adelgazado varios kilos.	*to lose weight*
adentrarse	**en alg**	Se adentró en el fondo de la selva.	*to get into*
aderezar	**con alg**	La ensalada está aderezada con aceite	*to dress*
		de oliva, vinagre y sal.	
adherir	**alg**	No logro adherir este cartel.	*to stick*
	a alg	Rosa no adhiere a la opinión de la	*to join*
		mayoría	
adherirse	**a alg**	Rosa se adhirió al Partido Demócrata.	*to join*
adivinar	**alg**	Puedo adivinar todo lo que piensas.	*to guess*
	quest	¿Adivina quién viene esta noche?	*to guess*

adjudicar	*alg a uno*	Le adjudicaron una tarea muy difícil.	*to assign*
adjudicarse	*alg*	Se adjudicó todo el mérito del trabajo.	*to appropriate*
administrar	*alg*	Administró bien las finanzas del país.	*to administer*
administrarse	*ø*	Me administro muy bien con mi sueldo.	*to manage*
admirar	*(a) uno/alg*	Admiro a Elvira por su voluntad.	*to admire*
		Admiro su entusiasmo.	*to admire*
	a uno [like **gustar**]		
		A mí, me admira su franqueza.	*to astonish*
admitir	*(a) uno/alg*	El club no admite la entrada sin corbata.	*to admit*
	a uno en [place]		
		Me admitieron en la UDLA.	*to accept*
	inf	Admitió haber mentido.	*to admit to*
	que ind	Hay que admitir que Juan es el mejor jugador.	*it must be admitted that*
	que sub	No admito que toquen mis cosas.	*to admit*
adoptar	*(a) uno/alg*	Mia Farrow adoptó varios niños.	*to adopt*
		Vargas Llosa es un escritor peruano que ha adoptado la nacionalidad española.	*to adopt*
adormecer	*ø*	La televisión me adormece.	*to make sleepy*
adormecerse	[body]	Se me adormeció la pierna.	*to go numb*
adornar	*alg*	Le gusta adornar la casa con cuadros.	*to decorate*
	de/con alg	Adorno el altar con flores blancas.	*to embellish*
adquirir	*alg*	El anuncio dice que se puede adquirir un diploma de Maestría en dos veranos.	*to acquire*
adueñarse	*de uno/alg*	No dejes que se adueñen de ti.	*to take possession*
		La familia García se adueño del pueblo.	
advertir	*a uno*	Advertí a Juan pero no me hizo caso.	*to warn*
	en uno/alg	No advirtió en la nueva decoración.	*to notice*
	que alg	Advertí que mucha gente pide limosna.	*to notice*
	a uno que ind	Le advertí que el examen sería difícil.	*to advise/warn*
	a uno que sub	Le advirtieron que no se paseara sólo.	*to advise/warn*
afanarse	*por inf*	Se afanó por dejar la casa arreglada.	*to strive*
afectar	*a uno/alg*	Le afectó la muerte de su madre.	*to affect*
		Las nuevas medidas nos afectan a todos.	*to encumber*
afeitarse	*ø*	Se afeitaba con maquinilla eléctrica.	*to shave*
	alg	Pancho se afeitó el bigote.	*to shave*
aferrarse	*a uno/alg*	Se aferró a la escalera para no caerse.	*to grapple*

336

aficionarse	*a alg*	Se aficionó a las carreras de caballos.	*to get fond of*
		Está aficionado a la buena vida.	*to get used to*
	a inf	Te estás aficionando a jugar a las cartas.	*to get fond of*
afiliarse	*a alg*	Se afilió al nuevo partido.	*to join*
afirmar	*que ind*	Afirmó que tomará medidas drásticas.	*to affirm*
agarrar	*alg*	¡Agarra el balón!	*to catch*
	(a) uno/alg	Agarró su perro y salió para el bosque.	*to grasp*
	a uno de/por alg		
		Le agarré por la camisa.	*to grasp*
	exp	*agarrarla con alguien*	*to have sth against*
agarrarse	*a uno/alg*	¡Agárrate a mí que giramos a la derecha!	*to hold*
agitar	*(a) uno/alg*	Agitó los obreros a la huelga.	*to agitate*
		¡Agite el frasco antes de tomar!	*to shake*
		La señorita agitaba el abanico con salero.	*to wave*
agradar [like **gustar**]	*a uno*	Me agrada la nueva orquesta.	*to be pleased*
		Me agrada pasearme por las tardes.	*to be pleased*
agradecer	*alg*	Agradezco tu ayuda.	*to be grateful for*
	a uno	Le agradezco por su amabilidad.	*to be thankful for*
	a uno que sub	Le agradecería que me respondiera.	*to thank*
agravarse	*ø*	La situación se agrava cada día.	*to become worse*
agregar	*alg*	¡Agrega dos cucharas de aceite!	*to add*
aguantar	*(a) uno/alg*	Bernarda es tan soberbia que no hay quien la aguante.	*to bear. stand*
	sin inf	Aguantó tres días sin beber.	*to endure*
	exp	*No aguanto más. / I/you... can't bear it any more.*	
aguantarse	*alg*	La Poncia se aguantó las ganas de decir lo que pensaba.	*to restrain*
	exp	¡Aguántate!	*too bad for you*
aguardar	*ø*	Aguardaremos hasta que llegue el tren.	*to wait*
	(a) uno/alg	Aguardamos el tren más de dos horas.	*to wait for*
	a que sub	Aguardamos a que suba el dólar.	*to wait for*
ahogarse	*en* [place]	Dos personas se ahogaron en el mar.	*to drown*
ahondar	*en alg*	Le gusta ahondar en todas las tareas.	*to go deeply into*
ahorrar	*alg*	Ha logrado ahorrar bastante dinero.	*to save*
	exp	*ahorrarse la molestia*	*to spare the effort*
ajustar	*alg*	Siempre ajusta las cuerdas de la guitarra antes de tocar.	*to tune*

337

ajustarse	*alg*	Se ajustó la corbata para hablar.	*to tighten*
	a alg	Es difícil ajustarse al nuevo horario.	*to get adjusted*
	exp	*ajustarse a las reglas*	*to abide by the rules*
alabar	*(a) uno/alg*	Las tenistas españolas han ganado tantos premios que la prensa las alaba.	*to praise*
alabarse	*de alg*	Le gusta alabarse de su éxito.	*to boast*
alcanzar	*alg*	El cantante ha alcanzado gran éxito.	*to reach*
	a uno	Tuve que correr para alcanzar a Luis.	*to catch*
	a inf	No alcancé a terminar a tiempo.	*to manage*
alegrarse	*de alg*	Nos alegramos de su visita.	*to be glad*
	de inf	Me alegro de conocerle.	*to be glad*
	(de) que sub	Me alegro de que vengas con nosotros.	*to be glad*
alejarse	*de uno/alg*	Nos estamos alejando del problema.	*to go away from*
alentar	*a uno*	Alentaron al equipo con aplausos.	*to encourage*
	a uno a inf	Para alentarle a estudiar, le prometieron un buen regalo.	*to encourage*
alimentar	*(a) uno/alg*	Mi trabajo es alimentar los animales.	*to feed*
		Trabaja para alimentar a su familia.	*to support*
alimentarse	*de alg*	Se alimenta de frutas tropicales.	*to live on*
almorzar	*ø*	Regreso a mi casa para almorzar.	*to have lunch*
alojarse	*en* [place]	Yo me alojo en el Hotel Cortés.	*to be lodged at*
alquilar	*alg*	Alquilé este coche por una semana.	*to rent*
	exp	*Se alquila.*	*for rent*
alternar	*con uno*	Le gusta alternar con sus amigos.	*to go around*
alternarse	*ø*	Los dos amigos se alternaron al volante.	*to take turns*
alzar	*alg*	Alzó la copa para brindar por el equipo.	*to elevate*
alzarse	*con alg*	Raquel se alzó con el primer premio.	*to carry off*
	contra uno	El pueblo se alzó contra el tirano.	*to revolt*
amar	*(a) uno/alg*	Amo mucho mi ciudad.	*to love*
amarse	*ø*	Pepita y Julián se aman.	*to love*
amarrar	*alg*	Joselito no sabe amarrar sus zapatos.	*to fasten*
amenazar	*a uno con inf*	Amenazó a los obreros con despedirlos.	*to threaten to*
amontonar	*alg*	Logró amontonar una buena fortuna.	*to gather*

amontonarse	ø	La gente se amontonó a la entrada del baile.	*to crowd*
	a uno	Se me amontonó el trabajo.	*to pile up*
amparar	*(a) uno*	Hay que amparar a los necesitados.	*to help*
ampararse	*a alg*	Se ampararon a la ley internacional.	*to have recourse to*
analizar	*alg*	Hay que analizar la situación política.	*to analyze*
andar	ø	Yo siempre voy al trabajo andando.	*to walk*
	tras uno/alg	Ando tras mi perro, que se escapó.	*to go after*
	ger	Anda contando que le robaron.	*to be Ving*
	exp	*andar por aquí*	*to be around here*
		andar mal/bien de salud	*to be (health)*
		andar en los 40/50...	*to be (age)*
		andar tras alguien	*to court*
		andar a pie/a caballo/en bicicleta...	*to ride*
		andar en problemas / to run into problems	
		Hay que andar con cuidado. / One must go carefully.	
animar	*a uno a inf*	Animó a Elisa a continuar los estudios.	*to encourage*
	a uno a que sub		*to encourage*
		Me animó a que enviara mis cuentos al concurso Max Aub.	
antojarse [like **gustar**]	*a uno*	¿Se te antoja un pastelillo?	*to want*
		Se me antojó pasear con mis amigos.	*to feel like*
anunciar	*alg*	Anunciaron los resultados en la TV.	*to announce*
anunciarse	*alg*	El festival se anuncia un éxito.	*to promise to be*
añadir	*(a) uno/alg*	Cuando el aceite está caliente, ¡añade el pollo!	*to add*
apagar	*alg*	Los bomberos apagaron el fuego.	*to extinguish*
		¡No olvides de apagar el televisor!	*to switch off*
aparecer	*alg*	Aparecieron unas nubes en el horizonte.	*to appear*
	exp	¡Ya apareció!	*to show up*
aparecerse	*a uno*	La hada se apareció a Cenicienta.	*to appear*
aparcar	ø	En la calle se puede aparcar de 8 a 6.	*to park*
apartar	*(a) uno/alg*	Hay que apartar las manzanas podridas para que no pudran el resto.	*to take away*
apartarse	ø	Los esposos se apartaron, pero permanecieron amigos.	*to part*
	a inf	Después de ganar la lotería, se apartaron a vivir a un barrio rico.	*to move*
	de uno/alg	¡Apártate de la mala compañía!	*to move away from*

339

apasionar [like **gustar**]	*a uno*	A Juana le apasionan los viajes.	*to get excited about*
apegarse	*a uno/alg*	Me apegué a mis nuevos amigos.	*to become attached*
apenarse	*alg*	Me apena mucho lo que le pasó.	*to be distressed*
apercibirse	*de alg*	Él no se apercibe de lo que está pasando en su propia casa.	*to notice*
aplaudir	*alg* *(a) uno*	Aplaudo su valentía. Aplaudimos a la directora de la orquesta.	*to applaud* *to applaud*
aplazar	*alg*	Tuvieron que aplazar el viaje debido a la enfermedad de Felipe.	*to postpone*
aplicar	*alg*	Hay que aplicar la crema una vez por día.	*to apply*
aplicarse	*en alg*	Es un carpintero que se aplica mucho en su trabajo.	*to devote oneself*
apoderarse	*de alg*	Esta familia se apoderó del pueblo.	*to take possession*
aportar	*alg*	El turismo aporta grandes beneficios.	*to bring*
apostar	*por* *a uno a que ind*	Apuesto por el caballo de Osborne. Te apuesto a que no llegamos a la hora.	*to bet* *to bet that*
apostarse	*ø* *exp*	Un soldado se apostó en la torre. *¿Qué te apuestas a que + Ind?*	*to post* *to bet*
apoyar	*alg en alg* *(a) uno*	Apoyó la cabeza en el hombro de Eva. Todos apoyan al nuevo candidato.	*to lean* *to support*
apoyarse	*en alg* *exp*	¡No te apoyes en mi hombro! *¿En qué te apoyas para decirlo?*	*to lean* *to base*
apreciar	*alg* [possession] *(a) uno/alg* *exp*	El banco apreció la casa en un millón. Le gusta apreciar el silencio del campo. Aprecia mucho a su profesor. *Se aprecia/puede apreciarse* [concept]	*to value* *to appreciate* *to esteem* *One can tell the difference*
aprender	*alg* *a inf* *alg de uno* *exp*	Aún no ha aprendido la lección. María aprendió a tocar la guitarra. Lo aprendí de mi abuela. *Todos los días se aprende algo nuevo.*	*to learn* *to learn (how) to* *to learn* *to learn*
apresar	*(a) uno* *alg*	Lo apresaron cuando saltaba el muro. Apresaron un cargamento de droga.	*to capture* *to seize*
apresurar	*alg*	Tuvo que apresurar su regreso.	*to hurry*

apresurarse	*a inf*	Se apresuró a mandar la carta.	*to hasten to*
	por inf	No te apresures por devolvérmelo.	*to hurry*
apretar	*alg*	Apretó los tornillos de la rueda.	*to tighten*
	a uno	Estos zapatos me aprietan demasiado.	*to pinch*
aprobar	*alg*	Aprobó todas las materias.	*to pass* [a course]
		Aprobaron el nuevo tratado comercial.	*to approve*
	que sub	Aprobó que se vendiera la Compañía.	*to approve*
apropiarse	*(de) alg*	Se apropió de mi idea.	*to appropriate*
aprovechar	*(de) alg*	Aprovecha sus viajes para estudiar lenguas.	*to take advantage of*
		Aproveché los restos para el gazpacho.	*to make good use*
aprovecharse	*de uno/alg*	¡No te aproveches de mí!	*to take advantage*
apuntar	*(a) uno/alg*	En su discurso, el Ministro de Economía apuntó las causas de la crisis.	*to point out*
	alg	Félix apunta lo que dice el profesor.	*to take notes*
apuntarse	*a alg*	Irene se apuntó a la Marina.	*to join*
apurar	*alg*	Apuró el vaso de un trago.	*to drink up*
apurarse	*por alg*	Díle que no se apure por la situación.	*to worry*
	por inf	Se apuró por llegar a la hora.	*to hurry*
arder	*alg*	Ayer ardieron dos montes en la sierra.	*to burn*
arrancar	*alg*	Me arrancaron una muela del juicio.	*to extract*
	de alg	La idea arranca del Siglo de Las Luces.	*to originate in*
	a inf	Pepe arrancó a correr al ver al perro.	*to start*
arrastrar	*(a) uno/alg*	Un caballo arrastró todos los troncos.	*to drag*
	con alg	El huracán arrastró con todo.	*to sweep*
arreglar	*alg*	José arregló la sala para la recepción.	*to arrange*
		Arreglamos la recámara para el niño.	*to fix*
arreglarse	*ø*	Después de varios años de discusiones, por fin se arreglaron.	*to come to terms*
	con uno	Se arregla muy bien con su suegra.	*to get by*
	exp	*No sé cómo te (las) arreglas para...*	*to manage to*
arrendar	*alg*	Hemos arrendado un apartamento en el centro de la ciudad.	*to rent*
arrepentirse	*de inf*	Se arrepiente de haber salido al mar.	*to regret*
	de alg	Me arrepiento de mis errores.	*to be sorry for*
arriesgarse	*a inf*	Si escalas el Everest, te arriesgas a tener un accidente grave.	*to risk*

arrojar	*alg*	Arrojó los trastos a la basura. Este fin de semana, las carreteras arrojaron 120 muertos.	*to throw* *to leave*
arrojarse	*a/sobre alg*	Se quitó la camisa y se arrojó al agua.	*to jump into*
arrugarse	*ø*	Se me arrugó el traje durante el viaje.	*to winckle*
ascender	*a* [place] *a uno* *a alg* [number]	Para ver bien el panorama, hay que ascender a lo alto de la colina. Le ascendieron en el trabajo. Mi cuenta de hotel asciende a 400 $.	*to go up* *to promote* *to amount to*
asegurar	*alg contra alg* *a uno que ind*	Aseguró su casa contra incendios. Te aseguro que cumpliremos la palabra.	*to insure* *to affirm*
asegurarse	*de que sub*	¡Asegúrate de que todos estén bien!	*to make sure*
asemejarse	*a uno*	Luisa se asemeja a su hermana.	*to be alike*
asentir	*exp*	*Asentir con la cabeza*	*to nod*
asignar	*alg*	Le asignaron el puesto de Director.	*to assign*
asistir	*a alg* *a uno*	Asistí a todas las clases del Doctor Rey. Asistieron a Pepe en el Hospital Central.	*to attend* *to assist*
asociarse	*con uno/ alg*	Se asociaron con una empresa chilena.	*to associate*
asomarse	*a alg*	¡Asómate al balcón para ver el desfile!	*to look out of*
asombrar [like **gustar**]	*a uno /alg*	Me asombraron los museos de París.	*to be astonished*
asombrarse	*de inf*	Me asombré de ver tantos museos.	*to be astonished*
aspirar	*alg* *a inf*	Estamos aspirando un aire muy nocivo. Ella aspira a ser Senadora.	*to breathe* *to aspire to V*
asustar [like **gustar**]	*a uno*	Me asustó el ruido que hacía el viento. Le asusta caminar sólo por la ciudad.	*to scare* *to scare*
asustarse	*al inf*	Me asusté al entrar en la cueva.	*to be frightened*
atacar	*(a) uno* *alg*	Dos ladrones atacaron al gerente del banco cuando iba a su casa. Hay que atacar fuerte este trabajo.	*to attack* *to press hard*
atajar	*(a) uno/alg*	No me gusta que me atajen. Debo atajar mi artículo pues es largo. Es necesario atajar el virus.	*to interrupt* *to cut off* *to put an end*
atar	*alg*	¡Ata el saco con una cuerda!	*to tie*

atarse	*alg*	¡Átense los cinturones, por favor!	*to fasten*
atender	*a uno*	En el hotel nos atendieron muy bien.	*to attend*
	a alg	¡Atiende bien a lo que te digan!	*to pay attention*
atenerse	*a uno/alg*	Se atiene a las instrucciones recibidas.	*to abide by*
	exp	*¡Atente a las consecuencias! / Bear the consequences!*	
		No sabe a qué atenerse. / He doesn't know what to expect.	
atentar	*a/contra alg*	Atentaron contra la vida del presidente.	*to attempt*
aterrizar	*ø*	El avión acaba de aterrizar.	*to land*
atorarse	*ø*	Tuve que darle agua porque se le atoró la comida.	*to choke*
		Javier es tan tímido que se atoró.	*to get tongue-tied*
atracar	*(a) uno/alg*	Ayer, dos ladrones atracaron un banco.	*to hold up*
	ø [boat]	El buque "El Sol" atracó en el puerto.	*to dock*
atracarse	*de alg*	Los niños se atracaron de chocolate.	*to stuff oneself*
atraer	*(a) uno/alg*	San Antonio atrae a muchos turistas.	*to attract*
atraerse	*alg*	Alberto se atrajo la antipatía de todos.	*to attract*
atravesar	*alg*	La ancianita atravesó la calle.	*to cross*
	alg a uno	Lo llevaron al hospital, porque un clavo le atravesó la mano.	*to pass through*
atreverse	*a inf*	No se atreve a salir por la noche.	*to dare to do*
aumentar	*ø*	Ha aumentado el número de viviendas.	*to increase*
	alg	Si trabajas bien, te aumentaré el sueldo.	*to increase*
autorizar	*alg*	No autorizan la entrada de menores.	*to authorize*
	a uno inf	Nos autorizaron contruir un Hotel.	*to license*
	a uno que sub	Le autorizaron que visite a sus hijos.	*to grant permission*
avanzar	*ø*	No hemos avanzado en este trabajo.	*to move forward*
	alg [money]	El Banco avanzó una buena cantidad.	*to advance*
	a uno	A Federico le avanzaron en su trabajo.	*to promote*
aventurarse	*a inf*	Si juegas a la ruleta, te aventuras a perder mucho dinero.	*to risk to*
avergonzarse			
	de/por alg	Se avergüenza de su conducta.	*to be ashamed of*
	de inf	Me avergüenzo de no haber hecho nada.	*to be ashamed of*
averiguar	*alg*	No he logrado averiguar los horarios.	*to find out*
	quest	Hay que averiguar dónde está María.	*to find out*

343

avisar	*a uno*	Al ver al herido, avisé al médico.	*to call*
		Es la segunda vez que te aviso.	*to warn*
	que ind	Avisé que llegaría tarde al trabajo.	*to notify*
ayudar	*a uno con/en alg*		
		Ayudé a mi hermano con la tarea.	*to help*
	a uno a inf	Me ayudó a cortar el pasto de mi casa.	*to help*

b

bailar	*ø*	Ivan bailó con Elena toda la noche.	*to dance*
	alg [dance]	Pablo baila bien el pasodoble.	*to dance*
bajar	*ø*	El precio de la carne ha bajado.	*to fall*
	a [place]	Bajó al sótano a buscar unas fotos.	*to go down*
bajarse	*a inf*	No se baja a pedir perdón.	*to lower oneself to*
bañarse	*ø*	Me voy a bañar con este jabón.	*to bathe*
barrer	*alg*	Los barrenderos barrieron la plaza.	*to sweep*
	(a) uno	El equipo contrario nos barrió.	*to beat*
basarse	*en alg*	¿En qué te basas?	*to base*
bastar	*a uno*	¿Te bastan 5 dólares para ir al cine?	*to be enough*
	con alg	Para ir al cine, basta con 5 dólares.	
	con inf	Basta con darle 5 dólares de propina.	*to be enough*
	para inf	Con esta información, basta para llegar.	*to be enough*
	exp	¡Basta de + inf.!	Enough + gerund
		¡Basta!	Enough!
bastarse	*con alg*	Mi abuelita se basta con muy poco.	*to be self-sufficient*
batallar	*con uno/alg*	Pasa el día batallando con su hermano.	*to fight*
	por uno/alg	Batallan por los derechos de los obreros.	*to struggle*
batir	*alg*	Hay que batirlo todo con el tenedor.	*to mix*
	a uno	El Betis batió al Barcelona tres a uno.	*to beat*
batirse	*ø*	Nuestro equipo se batió hasta el final.	*to fight*
beber	*ø*	Yo sé que mi prima bebe.	*to drink*
	alg	Siempre bebo vino con la cena.	*to drink*
	exp	¡Bebamos por el éxito de la empresa!	*to raise a toast*
bendecir	*(a) uno/alg*	Antes de comer, bendijo los alimentos.	*to bless*
	exp	¡Dios te/le bendiga!	God bless you!
beneficiarse *de alg*		Nos beneficiamos de la nueva ley.	*to benefit*

besar	*(a) uno/alg*	Besó a sus hijos y se despidió.	*to kiss*
besarse	*ø*	Los novios se besan en los bancos.	*to kiss*
bloquear	*(a) uno/alg*	Los zapatistas bloquearon el camino.	*to obstruct*
bordear	*con alg* *alg*	La casa bordea con la carretera. Se limitan a bordear el tema.	*to border* *to skirt around*
borrar	*alg* *(a) uno*	Al terminar la clase, borró la pizarra. Lo borraron de la lista de los invitados.	*to erase* *to delete*
borrarse	*alg* *de alg*	Con el tiempo se borró el mural. Me borré de la exursión del domingo.	*to erase* *to cancel*
bostezar	*ø*	La conferencia era tan aburrida que no paré de bostezar.	*to yawn*
botar	*ø* *alg* *(a) uno*	El balón de fútbol botó en la portería. Antonio botó su colección a la basura. A Roberto lo botaron del trabajo.	*to bounce* *to throw* *to fire*
brillar	*ø* *exp*	Le gusta que sus zapatos brillen. *¡Brilla por su ausencia!* / to be conspicuos by one's absence	*to shine*
brincar	*alg* *de* [feeling]	El caballo brincó la valla. Al oir su nombre brincó de emoción.	*to jump* *to jump for*
brindar	*alg a uno* *a alg* *por uno/alg*	La beca me brindó la oportunidad de conocer los países del Cono Sur. ¡Brindemos a la salud de todos! ¡Brindemos por el campeón!	*to offer* *to drink to* *to drink to*
brindarse	*a alg*	Este clima no se brinda bien al juego.	*to lend itself*
bromear	*ø* *con uno*	Juan tiene buen humor y le gusta bromear. Siempre está bromeando con su novio.	*to joke* *to kid*
broncearse	*ø*	Se asaron dos días en la playa de Acapulco, bronceándose.	*to sunbathe*
brotar	*alg* [plant] *ø*	En abril, brotaron los tulipanes. Aquí, han brotado casos de cólera.	*to sprout* *to appear*
bucear	*ø*	Va a Cozumel para bucear en el mar.	*to scuba dive*
bullir	*alg*	Siempre bulle los instrumentos para desinfectarlos.	*to boil*
burlar	*(a) uno*	El delantero centro burló a la defensa y metió un gol.	*to trick*

345

burlarse	*de uno*	¡No te burles de ese pobre hombre!	*to make fun of*
buscar	*(a) uno/alg*	Busco un libro sobre la época colonial.	*to look for*
	exp	*buscar tres pies al gato*	*to split hairs*

c

caber	*en alg*	La silla no cabe en el baúl del carro.	*to fit*
		En el baúl caben dos sillas.	*there's room for*
	a [quantity]	Veintitrés entre tres caben a siete y sobran dos.	*to give*
	exp	*cabe destacar que* + ind	*It should be pointed that*
caer	*ø*	Sólo cayeron unas gotas de agua.	*to fall*
	de [place]	Una maceta cayó de la ventana.	*to fall*
	de [body]	Fue terrible porque cayó de cabeza.	*to fall*
	en [time]	El Año Nuevo cae en jueves.	*to fall*
	exp	*El nuevo director me cae bien/mal.*	*to like*
		No caigo.	*I don't get it.*
caerse	*de* [place]	Luisito se cayó de la escalera y se rompió la clavícula.	*to fall*
calarse	*ø*	Como no tenía paraguas me calé.	*to get soaked*
calcular	*ø*	No sabe calcular.	*to calculate*
	que ind	Calculo que no vendrá mucha gente.	*to anticipate*
calentar	*alg*	En cuanto se levanta, calienta la leche.	*to warm*
calentarse	*ø*	El atleta comienza por calentarse.	*to warm up*
		Ramón se calienta en cuanto hablan de su tierra.	*to get angry*
calificar	[exams]	Es duro a la hora de calificar exámenes.	*to grade*
calzar	[number]	Yo calzo el número 40.	*to wear* [shoes]
callar	*ø*	En tales ocasiones lo mejor es callar.	*to say nothing*
	exp	*Quien calla otorga. / Silence gives consent.*	
callarse	*ø*	Es mejor que te calles.	*to shut up*
	exp	¡Cállate!	*Shut up!*
cambiar	*alg por alg*	Cambió su bicicleta por una colección de estampillas.	*to exchange*
	[money]*en*	Cambié 100 dólares en pesos.	*to change*
	de alg	Tengo que cambiar de butaca para ver.	*to change*

cambiarse	*ø*	¡Un momento!, tengo que cambiarme.	*to change*
	de alg/uno	Al llegar a casa se cambió de camisa.	*to change*
caminar	*en/por* [place]	Le gusta caminar por el pueblo.	*to walk*
	[distance]	Cada día, camina 10 kilómetros.	*to walk*
cansarse	*ø*	Pablo camina mucho pero no se cansa.	*to get tired*
	de inf	No se cansa de repetir lo mismo.	*to get tired of*
cantar	*ø*	Mi hermana canta estupendamente.	*to sing*
	alg	Le gusta cantar rancheras.	*to sing*
captar	*alg*	No consigue captar la gravedad del caso.	*to grasp*
		Con esta antena capto Univisión.	*to tune in*
carecer	*de alg*	La ciudad carece de interés histórico.	*to lack*
cargar	*alg*	¡Vamos a cargar las maletas en el bus!	*to load*
	con alg	Nosotros cargamos con el escritorio.	*to carry*
	alg de/con	Cargaron el camión de gallinas.	*to load*
	a uno con alg	A Eva le cargaron con la reponsabilidad.	*to charge*
cargarse	*a uno*	Se cargaron al guardia de la fábrica.	*to kill*
casar	*a uno*	Casó muy bien a todos sus hijos.	*to marry*
	con alg	El papel no casa con el estilo de la casa.	*to match*
casarse	*con uno*	Magdalena se casó con José.	*to marry*
	exp	*no casarse con nadie*	*to be independent*
castigar	*(a) uno*	Lo castigó su papá por insolente.	*to punish*
causar	*alg*	El león causó el pánico en la ciudad.	*to cause*
		La maestra causó buena impresión.	*to make*
cazar	*alg*	Salieron al campo a cazar conejos.	*to hunt*
	a uno	Cazaron al niño del vecino robando cerezas.	*to catch*
	exp	*cazarlas al vuelo*	*to be pretty sharp*
ceder	*alg a uno*	Cedió el asiento a una anciana.	*to yield*
		Luisa cedió sus derechos a su hija.	*to transfer*
	ø	Por más que insistan no cederá.	*to give up*
	exp	*ceder el paso*	*to yield*
cegar	*a uno* [light]	Le cegaron los faros del automóvil.	*to blind*
	alg	Cegaron el orificio con piedras.	*to block up*
cegarse	*de alg*	Bernarda se cegó de orgullo y no pudo ver lo que pasaba en su casa.	*to become blinded*
cejar	*exp*	*No ceja en su empeño/propósito.*	*to keep on*

347

celebrar	*alg*	Vamos a celebrar su cumpleaños.	*to celebrate*
		Se celebró la reunión de escritores.	*to hold*
	que sub	Celebro que te nombraran director.	*to be glad to*
	exp	*Lo celebro.*	*I'm very glad.*
cenar	*ø*	Ayer cenamos en el Hotel Santa Fé.	*to have supper*
cepillarse	*alg*	Me cepillo los dientes tres veces al día.	*to brush*
cerrar	*ø*	La puerta de la calle no cierra bien.	*to close*
	alg	¡Cierra la ventana!	*to close*
cerrarse	*a alg*	Se cierra a todo intento de diálogo.	*to close oneself*
cesar	*ø*	Por fin, cesó la lluvia.	*to stop*
	(a) uno	Lo cesaron en su cargo de coordinador.	*to dismiss*
	de inf	Los vecinos cesaron de hacer ruido.	*to stop*
clasificarse	*en alg*	Ana Ruiz se clasificó en segundo lugar.	*to rank*
cobrar	[quantity] *por alg*		
		¿Cuánto te cobraron por los anteojos?	*to charge*
	alg	Hoy cobré mi paga mensual.	*to get*
cocer	*alg*	Cocer las verduras en una cacerola.	*to cook*
		¡Coce la leche antes de beberla!	*to boil*
cocinar	*alg*	Voy a cocinar un plato poblano.	*to cook*
coger	*a uno*	La policía ha cogido al presunto ladrón.	*to cath*
	alg	No logramos coger el autobús de la una.	*to cath*
	de alg	Salieron cogidos de las manos.	*to hold*
	alg [illness]	Me descubrí y cogí un catarro.	*to catch*
	exp	*coger desprevenido*	*to take by surprise*
		coger cariño	*to take a liking to*
cohibirse	*exp*	*Sentirse cohibido por...*	*to feel inhibited*
coincidir	*con uno/alg*	Coincidé con ella en el Congreso.	*to agree*
	en que ind	Coincidemos en que debemos votar.	*to agree that*
cojear	*ø*	Tras el accidente, cojea.	*to limp*
	exp	*Sabemos/sé de qué pié cojea. /*	*to know his/her weakness*
colar	*ø*	Siempre que llueve, el agua cuela por el tejado de mi casa.	*to filter through*
colarse	*ø*	Siempre se cuela para entrar al teatro.	*to slip in*
	en alg	Se coló en la discoteca sin pagar.	*to sneak in*
colgar	*alg*	Al llegar a casa, colgó su abrigo.	*to hang*
	de alg	Los jamones cuelgan del techo.	*to hang from*
	en alg	Dos hilos cuelgan en el techo.	*to hang on*
	(a) uno	Lo condenaron y lo colgaron en la plaza.	*to hang*
	exp	*Le colgaron con la culpa.*	*to pin the blame*

colmar	*alg*	Colmaron los vasos de vino.	*to fill up*
	exp	*Lo colmaron de honores.*	*to shower honours*
		Lo colmaron de alabanzas.	*to heap praises on*
colocar	*alg*	Coloqué las fotos en el armario.	*to place*
	(a) uno de alg	Lo colocaron de director de Marketing.	*to place in a job*
colocarse	*en alg*	El equipo se colocó en segundo lugar.	*to place oneself*
	de alg	Se colocó de camarero.	*to place oneself*
columpiarse *ø*		A sus niños les gusta columpiarse en los columpios del parque.	*to swing*
combatir	*alg*	Supo combatir la enfermedad con valor.	*to fight*
	por alg	Zapata combatió por la justicia.	*to fight*
	uno contra uno		
		El equipo de Perú combate contra Chile.	*to oppose*
combinar	*alg*	Tiene buen gusto combinando colores.	*to combine*
	con alg	Esta corbata no combina con la camisa.	*to match*
combinarse *para inf*		Nos combinamos para lavar la ropa.	*to take it in turns*
comentar	*alg*	Estábamos comentando lo sucedido.	*to comment on*
comenzar	*alg*	Hemos comenzado las clases ayer.	*to start*
	con/por alg	¡Comencemos con una canción!	*to start*
	a inf	Mi niña comenzó a andar a los 2 años.	*to begin to*
	por inf	El presidente comenzó por felicitarnos.	*to begin by Ving*
comer	*alg*	Me gusta comer camarones.	*to eat*
	exp	*Come como una fiera.*	*to eat like a horse*
		ser de buen comer	*to have a hearty appetite*
comerse	*alg*	Tenía tanta hambre que se comió media docena de hamburguesas.	*to eat up*
	exp	*Cuando habla, se come las palabras.*	*to mumble*
comerciar	*con uno*	Texas comercia mucho con México.	*to do business*
cometer	*alg*	Julio ha cometido varios errores.	*to make*
compadecerse *de uno*		Se compadece de todos los condenados.	*to be sorry for*
compaginar *con alg*		El vestido no compagina con los zapatos.	*to fit with*
	con uno	No compagino muy bien con Roberto.	*to get along with*
comparar	*alg*	Comparó los resultados de las escuelas.	*to compare*
	alg a alg	Comparó la escuela a una familia unida.	*to compare*
compartir	*alg*	Teresa y Eva comparten el dormitorio.	*to share*
	alg con uno	Compartí mi comida con Roberto.	*to share with*

compensar	*ø*	Trabajar dos horas más no compensa.	*to compensate*
	a uno con alg	Le compensaron con tres millones.	*to compensate with*
competir	*con uno*	Nuestro equipo compite con el de Miami.	*to rival*
	por alg	Compiten por el primer puesto.	*to compete for*
	en alg	Las dos ciudades compiten en belleza.	*to compete in*
complacer	*inf*	La selva me complace más que el mar.	*to please*
[like **gustar**]	*exp*	¿En qué puedo complacerles? / *What can I do for you?*	
complacerse *en inf*		Se complace en hacer sufrir a todos.	*to take pleasure in*
componer	*alg*	Le gusta mucho componer canciones.	*to compose*
componerse	*ø*	¡Espera un momento! que termine de componerme.	*to put make up*
	de alg	El libro se compone de seis capítulos.	*to be composed of*
	exp	*componérselas como* + sub	*to manage*
		componérselas para + inf	
comportarse *adv*		Tienes que comportarte bien.	*to behave*
comprar	*alg*	Los Rodríguez compraron una casa.	*to buy*
	exp	*comprar a crédito*	*to buy on credit*
comprender	*alg*	El precio comprende hotel y transporte.	*to include*
		Aunque hablaba rápido, comprendí.	*to understand*
	exp	¿Comprendes?	*Understand?*
		¡Comprendido!	*All right!*
comprimir	*alg*	Comprime la maleta para que todo entre.	*to squeeze*
	exp	*No pude comprimir la risa/las lágrimas*	*to control*
comprobar	*alg*	¿Comprobaste el nivel del aceite?	*to check*
	que ind	Como me temía, comprobé que no quedan fondos en la cuenta.	*to confirm*
	quest	Hay que comprobar si dice la verdad.	*to check*
comprometer *(a) uno*		La declaración de la alcaldesa compromete al nuevo concejal.	*to implicate*
comprometerse			
	ø	Luis y María se comprometieron.	*to get engaged*
	a inf	Se comprometió a terminar en marzo.	*to make a commitment*
	en alg	Yo no me comprometo en ese asunto.	*to get involved*
comunicar	*alg*	Acaban de comunicar en las noticias la elección del nuevo presidente.	*to communicate*
	con uno/alg	La torre comunica con el palacio.	*to connect*
comunicarse *con uno*		Desearía comunicarme con el Sr. Prim.	*to speak to*

concebir	*alg*	El urbanista concibió la ciudad del futuro.	*to conceive*
	[neg]*que sub*	No concibo que no haya seguro médico.	*I cannot understand*
conceder	*alg*	Su mamá le concede todo lo que pide.	*to concede*
	que ind	Concedo que no debí decirlo.	*to admit*
concentrar	*(a) uno/alg*	Concentraron todas las fuerzas militares en la frontera.	*to concentrate*
concentrarse	*ø*	Con este ruido no logro concentrarme.	*to concentrate*
	en alg	No logro concentrame en la lección.	*to concentrate*
concernir	*alg*	A mí no me concierne este asunto.	*to concern*
concertar	*inf*	Concertaron verse en la reunión de abril.	*to agree to*
concertarse	*para inf*	Se concertaron para expulsar a Antonio.	*to conspire*
conciliar	*alg*	Intentó conciliar sus ideas con su vida.	*to harmonize*
	exp	*No logré conciliar el sueño.*	*to get to sleep*
conciliarse	*con uno*	Por fin se concilió con sus padres.	*to reconcile*
concluir	*ø*	Acaba de concluir el partido de fútbol.	*to finish*
	alg	La compañía concluyó la construcción de la autopista.	*to finish*
	con alg	El conferenciante concluyó con una cita de Unamuno.	*to end in*
	de inf	El presidente concluyó de hablar.	*to finish*
	ger	Concluyó aceptando el nuevo contrato.	*to end up by*
	exp	*y para concluir...*	*and to finish*
		¡Hemos concluido!	*It's all over.*
concurrir	*en* [place]	Todas las calles concurren en una plaza.	*to meet*
	a [place]	Muchas personas concurrieron a la fiesta.	*to attend*
	a alg	Las críticas concurrieron a su derrota.	*to contribute*
	en inf	Los pronósticos concurren en señalar a Peralta como el nuevo Gobernador.	*to concur in*
condenar	*(a) uno a alg*	Condenaron al reo a 40 años de cárcel.	*to sentence*
	alg	La Iglesia Católica condena el aborto.	*to condemn*
	a uno a inf	Le condenaron a pagar una gran multa.	*to sentence*
conducir	*(a) uno/alg*	Zaragoza condujo el ejército a la victoria.	*to lead*
	(a) uno	Me condujo por las calles de Toledo.	*to guide*
	adv	Ese taxista conducía muy mal.	*to drive*
	exp	*¿A qué conduce?*	*What's the point?*
conducirse	*adv*	Darío se condujo muy mal en la fiesta.	*to behave*
conectar	*alg con alg*	Conecté el TV con el equipo video.	*to connect*

conectarse	*con uno*	No logré conectarme con el Cónsul.	*to communicate*
confesar	*alg*	El técnico confesó su error.	*to admit*
		El penitente fue a la iglesia y confesó sus pecados al sacerdote.	*to confess*
confiar	*alg a uno*	Le confiaron la dirección de la empresa.	*to entrust*
	en uno/alg	Tras el accidente, no confía en el carro.	*to trust*
	en que ind	Confío en que el barco nos llevará.	*to rely on*
	de uno/alg	No confía de las intenciones de su socio.	*to trust*
conformarse	*con alg*	Se conforma con el dinero que gana.	*to be content with*
	con inf	Si no tenemos mucho tiempo, nos conformaremos con pasar dos días en la playa.	*to content oneself of*
confundir	*alg con alg*	¡No confundas el descanso con la pereza!	*to confuse*
confundirse	*de uno/alg*	Llegué tarde porque me confundí de calle.	*to take the wrong street*
	con uno/alg	El grupo se confundió con la gente.	*to mingle*
conmover	*alg*	El terremoto conmovió la capital.	*to shake*
conmoverse	*por alg*	Se conmueve por cualquier cosa.	*to be moved*
conocer	*(a) uno/alg*	¿Conoce el restaurante "La India Bonita"?	*to be familiar with*
		Conozco bien a la familia de Rosita.	
		Conoció a su esposa en Boston.	*to meet*
		No la conocí en esta foto.	*to recognize*
	alg de alg	No conozco nada de toros.	*to know about*
	(a) uno por alg		
		Lo conocí por su voz.	*to know by*
	exp	*dar a conocer*	*to present*
conquistar	*alg*	Conquistó el número uno en el mercado.	*to win*
	[place]	Conquistaron el país sin resistencia.	*to conquer*
	a uno	Lo conquistó en una discoteca de Roma.	*to win in attracting*
consagrar	*alg*	Consagró su vida a la investigación.	*to devote*
consagrarse	*a inf*	El especialista se consagró a investigar la civilización maya.	*to devote oneself*
conseguir	*alg*	Consiguió una beca para sus estudios.	*to obtain*
	inf	No consiguió ganar la carrera.	*to manage*
	que sub	Consiguieron que David fuera elegido.	*to manage*
consentir	*en inf*	El seguro consintió en pagar los gastos del accidente.	*to agree*
	que sub	No voy a consentir que me traten así.	*to allow*
	exp	*No se puede consentir.*	*We can't allow that.*

conservar	*alg*	Con el frío se consevan bien los tomates.	*to preserve*
conservarse	*adv*	Se conserva muy bien para su edad.	*to keep well*
consistir	*en alg*	El pueblo consiste en varias casas, una plaza y una iglesia.	*to be composed of*
	en inf	La dificultad consiste en enviarlo ahora.	*to lie in*
consolar	*a uno*	Fueron a consolar a la familia Ramírez porque se quemó su casa.	*to comfort*
	a uno que sub		
		Me consuela que no haya heridos.	*to find consolation*
consolarse	*con alg/inf*	Se consuela con el tercer puesto.	*to content oneself*
constar	*ø*	En la lista de invitados consta su nombre.	*to be included*
	de alg	La tesis consta de siete capítulos.	*to consist of*
	exp	*me consta que...*	*I know for sure*
		que conste...	*for the record*
constituir	*alg*	Decidimos constituir un comité para tratar el problema del tráfico.	*to form*
		La informática constituye la ciencia del futuro.	*to constitute*
construir	*alg*	A la salida del pueblo han construido un puente.	*to construct*
consultar	*alg*	Tengo que consultar mi agenda.	*to look up*
	(alg) con uno	Debo consultarlo con mi esposa.	*to discuss*
	exp	*consultar con la almohada*	*to sleep on it*
consumir	*alg*	En Texas se consume mucha carne.	*to consume*
contar	*alg*	Contó la historia de Caperucita Roja.	*to tell*
		He contado el número de banderas.	*to count*
	con uno/alg	Nosotros contamos con tu ayuda.	*to rely upon*
contener	*alg*	Esta botella contiene dos litros.	*to contain*
		Fue imposible contener el agua del río que desbordó por el campo.	*to hold*
contenerse	*ø*	Estaba muy enfadado pero me contuve.	*to restraint*
contentar	*a uno (con)*	Contentaron a su papá con un regalo.	*to please*
contentarse	*con alg*	Se contenta con poca cosa en la vida.	*to be satisfied with*
	con que sub	Me contento con que limpien el piso.	*to be satisfied with*
	con inf	Me contento con descansar una hora.	*to be satisfied with*
contestar	*ø*	Lo llamé varias veces, pero no contesta.	*to answer*
	a uno/ alg	Contestó bien a todas las preguntas.	*to answer*

continuar	*ø*	Ha continuado la subida del dólar.	*to continue*
	con uno/alg	Continúo con dolor de cabeza.	*to still have*
	adj	El restaurante continúa cerrado desde el mes pasado.	*to be still*
	ger	Beatriz continúa practicando el kárate.	*to be still doing*
contraer	*alg*	Debes contraer el texto a 14 páginas.	*to condense*
		¿Cuándo habrá un remedio para los que contraen el SIDA?	*to contract*
contribuir	*a alg (con alg)*		
		Hemos contribuido a la campaña con una buena donación.	*to contribute*
convencer	*a uno de que sub*		
		El director me ha convencido de que continúe mis estudios.	*to convince*
convencerse	*(de) que ind*	Espero que se convenza de que necesita perfeccionar la lengua.	*to be convinced*
	exp	¡Convéncete!	*Believe it!*
convenir	*en inf*	Convinieron en llamarse por teléfono.	*to agree to*
	<u>*impersonal uses:*</u>		
	inf	Conviene llevar un paraguas.	*it is advisable to*
	(a) uno inf	Nos conviene regresar al campamento.	*to be good for*
	que sub	Conviene que estemos preparados.	*it is important*
converger	*en* [place]	Los tres caminos convergen en la plaza.	*to converge*
conversar	*ø*	Su afición preferida es conversar.	*to talk*
	con uno	Todos los días converso con mi abuelita.	*to talk to*
	de alg	Le gusta conversar de su familia.	*to talk about*
convertir	*alg en alg*	Convirtieron el estadio en un basurero.	*to turn*
convertirse	*a* [religion]	La cantante se convirtió al catolicismo.	*to convert*
	en alg	Se convirtió en una gran señora.	*to change*
convidar	*a uno a alg*	Hoy estoy de salida porque me han convidado a la fiesta.	*to invite*
	a uno a inf	Me convidaron a pasar con ellos la fiesta.	*to invite*
convocar	*a uno/alg*	Convocaron a todos los ministros.	*to summon*
corregir	*alg*	Corregí los errores de mi composición.	*to correct*
corregirse	*ø*	Este niño ha logrado corregirse.	*to reform*
correr	*ø*	Yo corro rápido.	*to run*
	alg [distance]	Ayer corrí 10 millas.	*to run*
	alg	¡Corre la mesita para aquí!	*to push along*
	exp	*correr con los gastos*	*to pay*
		¡Cómo corre el tiempo!	*Time flies.*

corresponder
a uno	Le corresponde a Ruiz hacer el discurso.	*to correspond*
con alg	Le correspondió con un bonito regalo.	*to reciprocate with*
exp	*A quién corresponda.* / *To whom it may concern.*	

cortar
alg	Tienes que cortar la carne en trocitos.	*to cut*

costar
alg	¿Cuánto te costó la maleta de cuero?	*to cost*
a uno inf	Le cuesta comprender la lección.	*to find it hard to*
exp	*costar mucho/poco*	*it's difficult/easy*

crecer
ø	Este niño ha crecido mucho.	*to grow*
exp	*dejarse crecer el bigote/la barba...*	*to grow alg*

creer
en uno/alg	Como ateo, no cree en la otra vida.	*to believe*
que ind	Creo que Luisito no hizo la tarea.	*to think*
[negative] *que sub*		
	No creo que este verano pueda ir a visitar a mi familia en Colorado.	*not to believe; to doubt*

creerse
alg	Ramona se cree todo lo que le cuentan.	*to believe*
exp	*No me lo creo.*	*I don't believe it.*
	¿Qué se ha creído? / *Who does he thinks he is?*	

criticar
(a) uno/alg	En su artículo, critica la actitud del gobierno ante la cuestión indígena.	*to criticize*

cruzar
alg	Cruzó la calle sin mirar a los lados.	*to cross*

cruzarse
con uno	Me crucé con Alfonso en la calle.	*to pass sb*

cubrir
alg	Pepe ha cubierto el piso con alfombra.	*to cover*

cuidar
(a) uno	Andrés se quedó a cuidar a los niños.	*to take care of*

cuidarse
de uno/alg	Me cuidaré de los taxistas.	*to be careful of*
de inf	¡Cuídate de revelar tus opiniones!	*to be careful to*

culpar
a uno	No quiero culpar a nadie de lo sucedido.	*to blame*

cultivar
alg	Los campesinos cultivan maíz desde tiempos remotos.	*to cultivate*
	Los dos poetas cultivaron una amistad de muchos años.	*to cultivate*

cumplir
con alg	Mi mamá cumplió con su palabra.	*to fulfil*
alg [age]	Sofia Luna cumplió hoy sesenta años.	*to have a birthday*

curar
(a) uno/alg	Esta medicina cura el dolor de estómago.	*to cure*

curarse
ø	Si no tomas la medicina, no te curarás.	*to be cured*
con alg	Me curé con la receta de mi abuela.	*to recover*

ch

charlar	con uno	Se pasa el día charlando con Pepita.	*to chat*
	de/sobre alg	Le gusta charlar de su viaje a la India.	*to talk about*
	exp	*charlar por los codos*	*to talk incessantly*
chiflar	ø	No sé chiflar.	*to whistle*
	a uno/alg	El público se enojó y chifló al árbitro.	*to whistle*
chismear	ø	Mi vecino no para de chismear.	*to gossip*
chocar	con/contra	El camión chocó contra un árbol.	*to crah into*
	a uno	Esta costumbre choca a los turistas.	*to shock*
chupar	alg	La esponja chupa el agua.	*to absorb*
		Me gusta chupar el limón.	*to suck*
chuparse	exp	chuparse el dedo / to suck one's finger	

d

dar	alg a uno	¡Dále este paquete a tu madre!	*to give*
	con uno/alg	Dimos con Juan en la conferencia.	*to find*
	por/en inf	A Lupe le dio por escribir poemas.	*to decide*
	[time]	En nochevieja empezamos a comer las doce uvas cuando el reloj da las doce de la noche.	*to strike*
	exp	*dar a luz*	*to give birth*
		dar de alta	*to discharge sb*
		dar de baja	*to dismiss sb*
		dar de cabeza	*to fall on one's head*
		dar de narices	*to fall flat on one's face*
		dar la bienvenida	*to welcome*
		dar la cara	*to confront*
		dar la mano	*to shake hands*
		Lo mismo da. / It makes no difference.	
darse	a alg	Se dio al estudio sin descanso.	*to devote*
	exp	*Se la dio. / He (she) fooled him(her).*	
		darse cuenta de que + ind	*to realize*
deber	alg a uno	Francisca me debe 100 dólares.	*to owe*
	(de) inf	Debo salir a las ocho de la mañana.	*to have to*
decidir	inf	Decidió continuar sus estudios.	*to decide*
decidirse	por alg	Se decidió por la casa de piedra.	*to choose*

decir	*alg*	Yo le dije: "¡Deja de molestarme!"	*to say*
	que ind	Dijo que vendría a la reunión.	*to say*
	a uno que sub	Te digo que tengas cuidado.	*to advise*
	quest	No dijo cuándo debemos entregarlo.	*to say*
	imp	Se dice que fue a vivir a Brasil	*it is said*
	exp	*¿Cómo se dice en español...? / What's the Spanish for...?*	
		dicho sea de paso / by the way	
		es un decir / if I may use the expression	
decretar	*alg*	Decretó la estatización de la banca.	*to decree*
dedicar	*alg*	Dedica varias horas a estudiar francés.	*to dedicate*
dedicarse	*a alg/inf*	En los ratos libres, se dedica a pintar.	*to devote oneself*
defender	*(a) uno/alg*	El abogado defendió al acusado.	*to defend*
defenderse	*ø*	Me defiendo en francés y portugués.	*to manage*
	exp	*Me defiendo.*	*I can manage.*
dejar	*a uno inf*	Su mamá no le deja salir a jugar.	*to allow to*
	de inf	¡Deja de pensar en Beatriz!	*to stop Ving*
	que sub	¡Deja que lo haga ella primero!	*to let*
	exp	*dejar constancia*	*to place on record*
dejarse	*alg*	Me dejé mis libros en la oficina.	*to forget*
	inf	No se deja engañar por nadie.	*to let oneself be*
demostrar	*quest*	Nos demostró cómo se hace la paella.	*to show*
	alg/que ind	El concursante demostró que conocía la historia universal.	*to prove that*
denunciar	*(a) uno/alg*	Denunció el robo de su cartera.	*to report*
depender	*de alg/uno*	La decisión no depende de mí.	*to depend on*
	lo que sub	Depende de lo que diga Margarita.	*it depends on*
	exp	*Depende.*	*It all depends.*
derivar	*de alg*	La palabra "álgebra" deriva del árabe.	*to derive from*
	en alg	La discusión derivó en una riña.	*to degenerate into*
	hacia alg	Derivó la conversación hacia otro asunto.	*to divert to*
derramar	*alg*	Derramó el vaso sobre el nuevo mantel.	*to spill*
derribar	*alg*	Derribaron el antiguo edificio para construir un nuevo estacionamiento.	*to knock down*
derrotar	*(a) uno*	El equipo de Orlando derrotó a Georgia.	*to defeat*
derrumbarse	*ø*	Durante el sismo se derrumbaron varios puentes y edificios.	*to collapse*
desafiar	*a uno a inf*	Me desafió a comer 10 hamburguesas.	*to challenge*

357

desahogarse	*con uno/alg*	Le gusta desahogarse con sus amigos.	*to relieve stress*
desalojar	*(a) uno*	La ley no permite desalojar inquilinos durante el invierno.	*to eject*
	alg [place]	Tengo que desalojar el departamento.	*to move out*
descalzarse	*ø*	Marisa se descalza al llegar a casa.	*to take off one's shoes*
descansar	*ø*	Al llegar a casa, necesito descansar.	*to rest*
	en [place]	Descanso en el salón media hora.	*to rest*
	sobre alg	El techo descansa sobre tres columnas.	*to lean on*
	exp	¡Descanse en paz!	*Rest in peace!*
descender	*alg*	Vamos a descender las escaleras.	*to go down*
	hasta [place]	El funicular desciende hasta la playa.	*to get down*
	de uno	Marisa desciende de una familia rusa que emigró a la Argentina en 1885.	*to descend from*
descomponerse	*ø*	Se me descompuso el carro.	*to break down*
descubrir	*alg*	Colón descubrió América.	*to discover*
	exp	*descubrir la cabeza / to bare one's head*	
descuidar	*(a) uno/alg*	Con tanto trabajo he descuidado mi casa.	*to neglect*
	exp	¡Descuida!	*Don't worry!*
descuidarse	*ø*	Si te descuidas, te robarán la cartera.	*to be negligent*
desear	*a uno alg*	Le deseo un buen viaje por Andalucía.	*to wish*
	inf	Deseaba regresar a su tierra.	*to desire*
	que sub	El agricultor desea que llueva.	*to desire*
desempeñar	*alg* [job]	Desempeña el cargo de Delegado.	*to occupy*
desgajar	*alg*	El viento desgajó muchas ramas.	*to tear off*
desgarrar	*alg*	La muerte de su hijo desgarró su corazón.	*to break*
deshacer	*alg*	Hay que deshacer el paquete.	*to undo*
		La tormenta deshizo la cosecha.	*to ruin*
deshacerse	*de alg/uno*	Van a deshacerse del viejo perro.	*to get rid of*
desistir	*de alg*	Desistió de su loca idea.	*to desist from*
deslizar	*alg por/en*	Deslizó la carta por debajo de la puerta.	*to slide*
deslizarse	*en* [place]	Se deslizaron en la discoteca sin pagar.	*to slip unnoticed*
desmentir	*que sub*	El gobierno desmiente que haya vendido armas a las milicias.	*to deny*

desnudarse	ø	Al llegar a casa, se desnudó y se bañó.	*to undress*
despachar	ø [business]	Esta oficina no despacha los viernes.	*to receive*
	a uno	Ahora mismo le despacho.	*to attend to*
despedir	a uno	Fuimos al tren a despedir a Juan.	*to say goodby to*
	a uno de alg	Le despidieron del trabajo.	*to dismiss*
	alg	El motor despide gas tóxico.	*to release*
despedirse	de uno	Se despidió de su madre y salió.	*to take one's leave*
despertarse	ø	Todos los días me despierto a las ocho.	*to wake up*
despojar	uno de alg	Lo despojaron de todas sus posesiones.	*to strip of*
desprender	alg	El viento desprendió su casa de la costa.	*to tear apart*
desprenderse	ø	Se desprendió una roca y cayó en la vía.	*to fall off*
	de alg	El alcalde se desprendió de su autoridad.	*to give off*
destinar	(a) uno a alg	Al oficial lo destinaron a la Capital.	*to appoint*
	alg a uno	Este es el trabajo que me han destinado.	*to assigne*
destrozar	alg/uno	El granizo destrozó las cosechas.	*to ruin*
destruir	alg	El terremoto destruyó la ciudad.	*to destroy*
desvelar	a uno	Una taza de café basta para desvelarme.	*to keep awake*
	alg	Desveló el secreto de su familia.	*to unveil*
desvelarse	por alg	Se desvela por la educación de sus hijos.	*to care*
desviar	alg	Desviaron el cauce del río hacia el valle.	*to divert*
desviarse	de alg	Me desvié de la autopista para ver el pueblo donde nació mi abuela.	*to divert*
detener	(a) uno/alg	La policía detuvo a tres manifestantes.	*to detain*
		Los bomberos lograron detener el fuego.	*to stop*
detenerse	a inf	Se detuvo a hablar con los vecinos.	*to stop*
determinar	alg	No determinaron las causas del crimen.	*to determine*
	[date]	Determinamos la fecha del examen.	*to fix*
determinarse	a inf	No se determina a abandonar el puesto.	*to decide to*
devolver	alg (a uno)	Presté mi diccionario a Pepe pero no me lo ha devuelto.	*to return*
dibujar	(a) uno/alg	Los niños dibujaron a sus familias.	*to draw*
	a uno	Ella dibuja a su jefe como un dictador.	*to depict*

dictar	*alg*	La alcaldesa dictó la carta al secretario.	*to dictate*
		Ella dictó una conferencia magistral.	*to give*
	exp	*Lo dicta el sentido común./It is what common sense suggests.*	
diferenciar	*a uno de uno*	Lo que diferencia a Tim de Noé es el valor.	*to be differentiated*
diferenciarse	*por alg*	Nos diferenciamos por la altura.	*to differentiate*
	en que	Luisa y María se diferencian en que una tiene dinero y la otra no lo tiene.	*to be differentiated*
digerir	*alg*	Hay que digerir la comida antes de entrar en la alberca.	*to digest*
dirigir	*alg a uno*	El periodista dirigió la pregunta al ministro.	*to address*
	(a) uno/alg	Ella es la profesora que dirigió mi tesis.	*to direct*
	alg	Goizueta dirige una gran empresa.	*to manage*
		Dirigió la Orquesta durante 20 años.	*to conduct*
dirigirse	*a uno*	Me dirijo a Vd. para que me escuche.	*to address*
	a [place]	Al llegar al lago, se dirigió a la cabaña.	*to go towards*
disculpar	*alg*	Disculpe la molestia.	*to excuse*
	a uno por alg	Le pido me disculpe por el olvido.	*to pardon*
	que sub	Disculpe que no le haya llamado.	*to forgive*
	exp	*¡Disculpa! ¡Disculpe usted!*	*I'm sorry.*
discutir	*(de) alg*	Pasaron la tarde discutiendo de política.	*to discuss*
	con uno	Le gusta discutir con su papá.	*to discuss*
	exp	*¡No discutas!*	*Don't argue.*
disentir	*de uno/alg*	Ella disiente de la opinión general.	*to disagree*
disfrazarse	*de alg*	En el carnaval me disfracé de Zorro.	*to disguise*
disfrutar	*de alg*	Los novios disfrutaron mucho del viaje.	*to enjoy*
	con alg	Siempre disfruto con un buen libro.	*to enjoy*
disgustar [like **gustar**]	*a uno*	Me disgusta su conducta.	*to upset*
	a uno que sub	Me disgusta que mis hijos hayan dejado la casa en esta condición.	*to upset*
disolver	*alg*	Hay que disolver la pastilla en el agua.	*to melt*
	(a) uno	La policía disolvió a los manifestantes.	*to break up*
disparar	*alg*	Dispararon cuatro tiros al Presidente, pero salió ileso del atentado.	*to fire*
dispensar	*(a) uno/alg*	Le dispensaron una acogida excepcional.	*to give out*
		Dispense al camarero por su error.	*to excuse*
	exp	*¡Dispense usted!*	*I beg you pardon!*

disponer	*alg*	Dispuso las cosas sobre la mesa.	*to arrange*
	de uno/alg	Disponemos de 4 buenos jugadores.	*to have*
	que sub	La alcaldesa dispuso que se comenzara la investigación.	*to order*
disponerse	*a inf*	Me disponía a salir cuando sonó el teléfono.	*to get ready*
distinguir	*entre alg*	No distingue entre un buen vino y un vino ordinario.	*to distinguish*
	(a) uno con alg		
		Lo distinguieron con una medalla.	*to honor*
	exp	*saber distinguir / to have a critical sense*	
distinguirse	*por alg*	Alfonso se distingue por su educación, inteligencia y modestia.	*to stand out*
distraer	*(a) uno*	Luis y María saben distraer a los niños.	*to amuse*
distraerse	*ø*	Se distrajo mirando las vitrinas.	*to entertain o.s*
	exp	*estar distraído/a*	*to be absent-minded*
disuadir	*a uno de alg*	A pesar de los consejos, no pudimos disuadirle de su intención de atravesar el desierto a pié.	*to dissuade*
divertirse	*ø*	¿Te divertiste en la fiesta?	*to have fun*
divorciarse	*ø*	Tras dos años de casados, se divorciaron.	*to get a divorce*
doblar	*ø*	El número de turistas ha doblado.	*to double*
	alg	¡Doblen la hoja en dos!	*to fold*
	[movie]	Doblaron la película.	*to dub*
	a [place]	Al llegar al cruce, ¡doblen a la derecha!	*to turn*
doler	*a uno*	Con tanta TV, me duele la cabeza.	*to hurt*
		Le duele la actitud de su padre.	*to grieve*
	a uno que sub	Le duele que lo hayan tratado mal.	*to be upset*
	exp	*estar dolido*	*to be upset*
dolerse	*de que sub*	Se duele de que nadie le llame por teléfono.	*to complain*
dormir	*ø*	Ayer dormí solamente cinco horas.	*to sleep*
	exp	*dormir como un tronco*	*to sleep like a log*
dormirse	*ø*	Estaba tan cansado que me dormí durante el concierto.	*to fall sleep*
dudar	*de uno*	Ella duda de Isabel.	*to doubt, mistrust*
	en/entre inf	Dudo entre salir o quedarme a leer.	*to hesitate*
	(de) que sub	Dudo que tenga tiempo para ir a bailar.	*to doubt*

e

economizar	*alg*	Con la nueva impresora economizamos tiempo y dinero.	*to save*
echar	*alg*	Echó su vieja máquina a la basura.	*to throw*
		¡Échame un poco de leche en la taza!	*to add*
		¡No te olvides de echar la carta!	*to post*
	(a) uno	A Luis lo echaron del internado.	*to dismiss*
	a inf	Al ver al policía, echó a correr.	*to begin*
	exp	*echar abajo algo*	*to pull down*
		echar de menos	*to miss*
		echar la culpa	*to blame*
		echar un vistazo	*to glance at*
echarse	*en alg*	Al llegar a casa, se echó en el sofá.	*to lie down*
	a inf	Se echó a dormir un rato.	*to lie to*
	exp	*echarse a perder*	*to get ruined*
edificar	*alg*	Van a edificar viviendas en el centro de la ciudad.	*to build*
egresar	*de* [place]	Elena egresó de la UDLA el año 96.	*to graduate from*
ejercer	*alg*	Ejerce mucha influencia sobre su hijo.	*to exert*
	de alg	Ejerció de médico rural dos años.	*to practice as*
elegir	*(a) uno/alg*	He elegido la corbata a rayas.	*to choose*
	(a) uno de	Lo eligieron de Presidente.	*to elect*
	exp	*a elegir*	*with a choice of*
elevar	*(a) uno a alg*	Lo elevaron a Director General.	*to promote*
elevarse	*ø*	En medio de la plaza se eleva una estatua.	*to rise up*
	a [height]	El volcán se eleva a 3000 metros.	*to rise up*
eliminar	*(a) uno*	Eliminaron al candidato a Presidente.	*to eliminate*
embalar	*alg*	Hay que embalar la mercancía.	*to pack*
embalarse	*ø*	Se embaló en su discurso y no paró.	*to rush off*
embarazar	*(a) uno*	Embarazó a su novia por no usar medios anticonceptivos.	*to make pregnant*
embarcar	*alg*	Vamos a embarcar la mercancía.	*to load*
embarcarse	*en* [boat]	Se embarcó en el San Juan rumbo a Cuba.	*to board*
	en alg	Se embarcó en un mal negocio.	*to embark on*
	para [place]	Me embarqué para los mares del sur.	*to sail for*
embestir	*a/contra*	El toro embistió contra el picador.	*to charge*

362

emborracharse ∅		Como no tenía costumbre de beber cerveza, se emborrachó con dos vasos.	*to get drunk*
emigrar	*a* [place]	Muchos jóvenes emigraron al Norte.	*to emigrate*
emitir	∅	Radio Latina emite desde Dallas.	*to broadcast*
empapar	*alg*	¡Empapa el algodón en alcohol!	*to soak*
	(a) uno	La lluvia nos empapó hasta los huesos.	*to soak in*
empaparse *de alg*		Se empapó de filosofía oriental.	*to become imbued*
empatar	*a* [number]	Los equipos empataron a tres goles.	*to tie*
empeñar	*alg a uno*	Le empeñaron el carro deportivo.	*to pawn*
empeñarse	*en inf*	Se empeñó en terminar el trabajo a pesar de que estaba muy cansado.	*to persist*
	en que sub	Se empeñaron en que tocara la guitarra.	*to be determined*
empezar	∅	El festival empezó a las seis de la tarde.	*to start*
	a inf	Al llegar a la playa, empezó a llover.	*to start*
	por alg	Empecé por un plato de camarones.	*to begin by*
empujar	∅	¡No empujes!	*to push*
	(a) uno/alg	Nos empujó para entrar en la cola.	*to push*
		¡Empuja la puerta!	*to push*
enamorarse *de uno*		Antonio se enamoró de Carmen.	*to fall in love with*
encabezar	*alg*	Carlos encabeza la lista de los finalistas.	*to come first*
		Chávez encabezó el movimiento chicano.	*to lead*
encantar [like **gustar**]	*a uno*	Le encantan las fresas.	*to delight*
	a uno que sub	Me encantaría que fuéramos a Andalucía de luna de miel.	*to delight*
encargar	*alg a uno*	Me encargaron varios libros de México.	*to request*
encargarse	*de alg/inf*	Yo me encargo de avisarle que llegaron sus libros.	*to take care of*
encender	*alg*	Encendieron las luces para ver mejor.	*to tun on*
encerrar	*(a) uno/alg*	Encerramos los medicamentos en el armario para que no toquen los niños.	*to lock*
		El libro encierra una gran sabiduría.	*to contain*
encerrarse	*en* [place]	Se encerró en su casa sin salir dos días.	*to lock oneself*
encoger	∅	Metí mi nuevo suéter en la máquina de lavar y encogió.	*to shrink*

encontrar	*alg*	Encontré la foto que había perdido.	*to find*
encontrarse	*con uno*	Me encontré con Juan en el Mercado.	*to run into*
	en alg [place]	La biblioteca se encuentra en el Zócalo.	*to be located*
	exp	*encontrarse bien/mal*	*to feel good/bad*
enderezar	*alg*	Enderezaron el poste de la luz porque estaba torcido.	*to straighten*
endulzar	*alg*	Las historias de mi abuelo endulzaron mi infancia.	*to sweeten*
enfadarse	*con uno*	Se enfadó con su mamá y salió de casa.	*to get angry*
enfermarse	*de alg*	Me enfermé del estómago y fui al doctor.	*to fall ill*
enfrentarse	*con alg*	Hay que enfrentarse con la situación.	*to face up to*
engañar	*a uno*	El vendedor nos dijo que el carro funcionaba bien; pero nos engañó.	*to deceive*
		Engañó a su marido con un bombero.	*to be unfaithful*
	exp	*Las apariencias engañan. / Appearances are deceptive.*	
engañarse	*exp*	*¡No te engañes! / Do not fool yourself.*	
enojarse	*de/por alg*	Se enoja por cualquier cosa.	*to get angry at*
	contra uno	Se enojó contra su director.	*to get angry at*
	exp	*¡No te enojes!*	*Don't be angry!*
enredar	*alg*	Vino y enredó todos los papeles.	*to make a mess*
enredarse	*en alg*	Se le enredó el anzuelo en la red.	*to get entangled*
	[tongue]	En pleno discurso, se le enredó la lengua.	*to become entangled*
enrollar	*alg*	El gato desenrolló el ovillo que yo había enrollado con tanto cuidado.	*to roll*
enseñar	*alg a uno*	Me enseñó su colección de estampillas.	*to show*
	a uno a inf	Mi hermana la mayor me enseñó a leer.	*to teach*
ensuciar	*alg*	Por favor, ¡no ensucien los baños!	*to dirty*
entender	*alg*	No entendí bien la explicación.	*to understand*
	de alg	No entiendo de mecánica.	*to know about*
entenderse	*adv*	Luis y María se entienden muy bien.	*to get along*
	con uno	Usted debe entenderse con el Director.	*to deal with*
enterarse	*de alg*	Acabo de enterarme del accidente.	*to find out about*
enterrar	*a uno/alg*	Ayer enterraron al papá de Alfredo.	*to bury*
entrar	*en* [place]	Entró en la casa por la puerta del patio.	*to enter*
	en alg	Me entró algo en el ojo.	*to get into*
	ø	¡Abre la puerta y entra!	*to go in*

entregar	*alg a uno/alg*	Le entregaron el piano en mal estado.	*to deliver*
		Debes entregar los libros a la biblioteca.	*to give back*
entregarse	*a uno*	Los terroristas se entregaron a la policía.	*to surrender*
	a alg	Ella se entregó a la vida religiosa.	*to devote oneself*
entretener	*alg*	Para conservar el carro en buenas condiciones hay que entretenerlo con regularidad.	*to maintain*
	(a) uno	¡Entretén a nuestros amigos mientras preparo el café!	*to entertain*
	ger	Lo siento, pero me entretuve mirando unos libros en la librería.	*to delay*
entretenerse	*ø*	El niño se entretiene solo.	*to amuse oneself*
enviar	*alg a uno*	Enviamos un paquete a Juan.	*to send*
	a inf	Me enviaron a acompañar al Senador.	*to send sb to*
envolver	*alg*	¿Le envuelvo la caja de chocolate?	*to wrap up*
	(a) uno en alg	Lo envolvieron en un asunto delicado.	*to get involved*
equivocarse	*en alg*	Se equivocó en los ejercicios.	*to be mistaken*
	de alg	Llegó tarde porque se equivocó de ruta.	*to take the wrong way*
errar	*ø*	El concursante erró dos veces.	*to make a mistake*
	por [place]	El vagabundo erró por las calles.	*to wander*
escalar	*alg*	El equipo escaló el pico más alto.	*to climb*
escaparse	*de* [place]	Dos ladrones se escaparon de la cárcel.	*to escape*
	ø	El gas se está escapando.	*to leak out*
escasear	*ø*	En esta época, escasean los turistas.	*to be scarce*
escoger	*(a) uno/alg*	Escogió la mejor colonia de la ciudad para construir una casa.	*to choose*
	entre uno/alg	Debes escoger entre los tres candidatos.	*to choose*
esconder	*(a) uno/alg*	El pirata escondió el tesoro en la isla.	*to hide*
esconderse	*ø*	En este juego uno cuenta hasta veinte y los otros niños se esconden.	*to hide*
	de uno	El ladrón se escondió de la policía.	*to hide*
escribir	*(alg) a uno*	Voy a escribir a mis amigos de Canadá.	*to write*
	exp	*escribir a máquina; a mano / type, write in longhand*	
		¿Cómo se escribe "..."? / How is "..." spelled?	

365

escuchar	*(a) uno/alg*	Me gusta escuchar la música clásica.	*to listen to*
escupir	*a uno*	Se pelearon y le escupió a la cara.	*to spit at*
escurrir	*alg*	Hay que escurrir el aceite de las papas.	*to drain*
	[cloth]	Puse a escurrir las toallas.	*to wring out*
escurrirse	*de/entre*	Se me escurrió el pez de las manos.	*to slip*
esforzar	*alg*	Tuve que esforzar la vista para leer.	*to strain*
esforzarse	*en/por inf*	Se esforzó por terminar a tiempo.	*to try hard*
espantar	*(a)* [animal]	El ruido espantó a los pájaros.	*to scare away*
	a uno	Las películas de terror me espantan.	*to scare*
espantarse	*ø*	Se espanta facilmente.	*to get scared*
	con alg	Se espantan con el menor ruido.	*to get frightened*
esparcir	*alg*	El viento esparció los papeles.	*to spread*
	(a) uno	La policía esparció a los manifestantes.	*to scatter*
	exp	*esparcir el ánimo*	*to relax*
esparcirse	*por* [place]	Mis papeles se esparcieron por el piso.	*to spread*
		La lengua española se esparció por todo el mundo.	*to disseminate*
esperar	*(a) uno/alg*	Espero una carta de Brasil.	*to wait for*
	inf	No esperaba tener esta nota.	*to expect*
	en alg	Espero en su poder de decisión.	*to trust in*
	que sub	Espero que el accidente no sea grave.	*to hope*
	a que sub	Esperábamos a que llegara la carta.	*to wait for*
esquivar	*alg*	No pudo esquivar un perro que estaba cruzando la calle y lo atropelló.	*to avoid*
	exp	*esquivar las preguntas.*	*to elude*
estar	*adj*	El televisor está roto.	*to be*
	de alg	José está de maestro.	*to act as*
	ger	Estoy mirando la televisión.	*to be Ving*
	en [place]	Estamos en casa toda la tarde.	*to be*
	en que ind	El problema está en que no hay agua.	*to lie in*
	a [time]	Estamos a doce de diciembre.	*the date is*
	a [time] *de*	Estamos a una hora de la salida.	*to be from*
	para inf	Está para graduarse este semestre.	*to be about to*
	por uno/alg	Está por los derechos del trabajador.	*to be in favor of*
	por inf	Estaba por salir cuando llegó Roberto.	*to be about*
estimar	*alg*	Estimaron sus bienes en varios millones.	*to estimate*
	(a) uno	Estima mucho al nuevo maestro.	*to have a high regard*
	que ind	Estimo que no llegaremos a tiempo.	*to think that*

estirar	*alg*	Estiré una cuerda para secar la ropa.	*to stretch*
		Es bueno estirar las piernas en el avión.	*to stretch*
estirarse	*ø*	El gato se despertó y se estiró.	*to stretch*
estrechar	*a uno*	Estrechó a su hijo entre sus brazos.	*to hug*
estrecharse	*exp*	Se estrecharon la mano.	*to shake hands*
estrellarse	*contra alg*	El carro se estrelló contra un árbol.	*to crash into*
estrenar	*alg*	Hoy estrené mis nuevos zapatos.	*to wear for the first time*
estropear	*alg*	Alguien estropeó mi bicicleta.	*to damage*
estudiar	*alg*	Gabriel estudia medicina en Madrid.	*to study*
	para alg	Gabriel estudia para médico.	*to study to become*
evacuar	*(a) uno/alg*	Evacuaron del campo a los refugiados.	*to evacuate*
	exp	*evacuar de vientre* / *have a bowel movement*	
evitar	*alg*	Hemos evitado un gran desastre.	*to avoid, prevent*
	inf	Siempre evito usar materias tóxicas para el medio ambiente.	*to avoid*
examinar	*(a) uno/alg*	Examinó los documentos con cuidado.	*to examine*
examinarse	*de alg*	Hoy me examiné de matemáticas.	*to take an exam in*
excluir	*(a) uno de alg*	Lo excluyeron de la lista de participantes.	*to exclude from*
excusar	*(a) uno por alg*	Nunca te excusaré por tu actitud.	*to excuse*
	a uno de alg	Siempre excusa a los de su oficina de toda responsabilidad.	*to exempt*
excusarse	*de inf*	Se excusó de haber llegado tarde.	*to apologize*
exigir	*alg*	Este puesto exige mucha experiencia.	*to require*
	que sub	El médico exige que guardes cama.	*to demand*
existir	*ø*	Esa palabra no existe en el diccionario.	*to exist*
experimentar	*alg*	El laboratorio ha experimentado un nuevo producto.	*to test*
		El enfermo experimentó una mejoría.	*to show*
explicar	*ø*	Este profesor explica muy bien.	*to explain*
	alg a uno	El investigador va a explicarnos su método de trabajo.	*to explain*
	a uno quest	¡Explícame cómo se llega a la plaza!	*to explain*

explicarse	*alg*	Ahora me explico su actitud.	*to understand*
	quest	No logro explicarme cómo ocurrió el accidente.	*to understand*
	exp	*No me lo explico. / I can't understand it.*	
explorar	*alg*	Antes de lanzar el producto, hemos explorado el mercado latino.	*to explore*
explotar	*a uno*	El público protesta porque hay fábricas que explotan a los niños.	*to exploit*
	ø	Una bomba explotó en el metro.	*to explode*
exponer	*alg*	El ingeniero agrónomo expuso el plan para hacer frente a la sequía.	*to explain*
		El joven pintor expone hoy sus cuadros.	*to exhibit*
exponerse	*a inf*	Si sales con esta tormenta, te expones a permanecer atrapado en el monte.	*to run the risk of*
exportar	*alg*	Se exportan libros a Estados Unidos.	*to export*
expresar	*alg a uno*	Permita expresarle mi profundo agradecimiento por su servicio.	*to express*
		En la carta, el cliente olvidó expresar la cantidad de libros que requería.	*to say*
expresarse	*ø*	John se expresa muy bien en español.	*to express oneself*
exprimir	*alg*	¡Exprime tres limones!	*to squeeze*
expulsar	*de* [place]	Lo expulsaron del colegio por cuestión de disciplina.	*to expel from*
extender	*alg*	Extendió un mantel en la mesa.	*to spread*
extenderse	*en* [place]	San Diego se extiende en el valle.	*to spread*
	por [place]	Sus sucursales se extienden por el país.	*to spread over*
	[time]	La conferencia se extendió dos horas.	*to last*
	sobre alg	El conferenciante se extendió sobre la relación entre Europa y América.	*to develop*
extinguir	*alg*	Los bomberos extinguieron el incendio.	*to extinguish*
extraer	*alg*	El dentista me extrajo una muela.	*to pull out*
extrañar	*(a) uno/alg*	Extraño a mi familia y mis amigos.	*to miss*
	a uno que sub	Me extraña que Julio no conteste.	*to find strange*
extraviarse	*ø*	El equipo de rescate busca el avión que se extravió en la selva.	*to get lost*

368

f

fabricar	*alg*	No fabrican más ese modelo de carro.	*to manufacture*
	exp	*fabricar en serie*	*to massproduce*
faltar	*ø*	Esta mañana, Pedro faltó.	*to be absent*
	a alg	Sansón faltó a la clase de gimnasia.	*to miss*
	a uno	Miré en mi bolsa y me falta el libro.	*to be missing*
	a uno para inf	Le falta voluntad para dejar de fumar.	*to be lacking*
		Me faltan 100 dólares para poder viajar.	*to be lacking*
	[time]	Faltan tres días para la graduación.	*there are... left*
	a uno por inf	Me falta por escribir el último capítulo.	*to still need to*
	exp	*faltar al respeto*	*to be disrespectful*
		¡Lo que faltaba!	*It's all I needed!*
		¡No faltaría más!	*Naturally!*
fallar	*ø*	Falló su pronóstico del tiempo.	*to go wrong*
	alg	En el concurso de tiro, falló todos sus disparos.	*to miss*
	a uno	¡No me falles!	*to let uno down*
	exp	*Le falló el corazón.*	*His heart failed.*
familiarizarse			
	con uno/alg	En tres días se familiarizó con la ciudad.	*to get acquainted*
fastidiar	*a uno que sub*	Me fastidia que usen mi motocicleta.	*to annoy*
	exp	*¡No me fastidies! / Stop bothering me!*	
felicitar	*a uno por alg*	Le felicitaron por su contribución.	*to congratulate*
	a uno por inf	Le felicité por haber escrito un libro.	*to congratulate*
festejar	*alg*	He festejado mi cumpleaños.	*to celebrate*
fiar	*ø*	Disculpe, pero la Casa no fía.	*to sell on credit*
fiarse	*de uno*	No se fía de su abogado.	*to trust*
fichar	*por alg*	Mendoza fichó por el Real Madrid.	*to sign up*
	exp	*Luis está fichado. / Luis has a police record.*	
figurar	*ø*	Su nombre no figura en la lista.	*to appear*
fijar	*alg*	Fijó la puerta con el destornillador.	*to fasten*
	[date/price]	Fijaron un día para reunirse.	*to fix*
fijarse	*en uno/alg*	No me fijé en la ropa que llevaba.	*to notice*
	exp	*¡Fíjate bien! / Pay close attention!*	
filtrar	*alg*	Hay que filtrar el agua antes de beber.	*to filter*
filtrarse	*por alg*	El agua se filtra por el tejado.	*to filter*

finalizar	*ø*	El partido finalizó a las ocho.	*to finish*
		El programa finalizó con baile folklórico.	*to end*
	alg	Finalizamos el programa con una lotería.	*to end*
fingir	*alg*	Él fingía una cojera delante del juez.	*to pretend*
	inf	Ella finge estar enojada pero no lo está.	*to pretend*
firmar	*alg*	La Señora Salas firmó su testamento.	*to sign*
flotar	*ø*	Una botella flota en el agua.	*to float*
fomentar	*alg*	La campaña fomentó el número de socios.	*to increase*
formar	*(a) uno/alg*	Con la tierra, formó el primer hombre.	*to make (up)*
		Esta escuela formó a la primera generación de pilotos.	*to educate*
formarse	*ø*	Se formó una cola enorme a la entrada.	*to form*
	en alg	Teresa se formó en la Enseñanza del Español como Lengua Extranjera.	*to be educated*
	exp	*formarse una opinión / to form an opinion*	
forrar	*alg*	Antes de ir a la escuela forra sus libros.	*to cover*
forrarse	*ger*	Se forró vendiendo casas en la costa.	*to make one's pile*
fortalecer	*(a) uno/alg*	La vitamina D fortalece los huesos.	*to strengthen*
forzar	*a uno inf*	Le forzaron a firmar contra su voluntad.	*to force*
	alg	El ladrón forzó la puerta del garaje.	*to force open*
fotocopiar	*alg*	Necesito fotocopiar 20 páginas.	*to photocopy*
fracasar	*ø*	El nuevo experimento fracasó.	*to fail*
fregar	*alg*	Friego el piso con agua y cepillo.	*to wash, to mop*
	a uno	¡No me friegues con esa historia!	*to annoy*
freír	*alg*	Le gusta freír el pescado y las papas.	*to fry*
frenar	*ø*	Al ver al gato, frenó bruscamente.	*to brake*
	alg	Las medidas frenaron la violencia.	*to slow down*
fumar	*ø*	Está prohibido fumar en el Campus.	*to smoke*
	alg	Fumo un paquete de cigarrillos al día.	*to smoke*
funcionar	*ø*	Esta máquina no funciona.	*to work*
	exp	*no funciona*	*out of order*
fundar	*alg*	Los españoles fundaron la ciudad de San Agustín en el siglo XVI.	*to found*
	exp	*¿En qué te fundas? / On what grounds can you maintain this?*	

fundir	*alg*	Fundieron todos los metales para hacer la campana de la Misión.	*to melt*
fundirse	*ø*	Los tres bancos se fundieron.	*to merge*

g

ganar	*alg*	Los pescadores ganaron mucho dinero.	*to earn*
	(a) uno	Ganamos al equipo de Santa Fé.	*to beat*
	exp	*ganar a la lotería / to win the lottery*	
		ganar el pan / to earn one's daily bread	
garantizar	*alg*	Les garantizamos satisfacción completa.	*to guarantee*
gastar	*alg*	Hoy gasté mucho dinero en la tienda.	*to spend*
	exp	*¿Qué número/talla gastas? (Spain) /What size do you wear?*	
girar	*a* [direction]	Al llegar a la esquina, gira a la derecha.	*to turn*
	exp	*gira alrededor de...* [number]	*to be about...*
gobernar	*ø*	El nuevo presidente del gobierno dijo que gobernará con mano dura.	*to govern*
gozar	*ger*	La gozo jugando al dominó.	*to enjoy*
	de alg	Gozo de un buen plato de mariscos.	*to enjoy*
	exp	*gozar de buena salud*	*be in good health*
grabar	*alg*	Ayer grabé el programa de música.	*to record*
		Grabó su nombre en la pulsera.	*to engrave*
gritar	*a uno*	Gritó a los niños para que se pararan.	*to shout*
guardar	*(a) uno/alg*	Se quedó en casa guardando los niños.	*to watch*
		Guardó la pluma en su bolsillo.	*to keep*
	exp	*guardar cama*	*to stay in bed*
guardarse	*de uno/alg*	¡Guárdate del sol!	*to avoid*
	de inf	¡Guárdate de beber agua del grifo porque no es buena.	*be careful not to*
guiar	*a uno*	Guió a los turistas por la ciudad.	*to guide*
guiarse	*por alg*	Me guié por el plano para llegar.	*to be guided by*
	exp	*guiarse por las apariencias / to trust appearances*	
guiñar	*a uno*	Al pasar a su lado, le guiñó el ojo.	*to wink at*
guisar	*ø*	Puedo guisar para toda la familia.	*to cook*
gustar	*a uno alg*	A Eva le gustan las comedias.	*to like*
	a uno inf	Me gusta salir a pasear por la mañana.	*to like to*
	a uno que sub	Me gusta que me traten bien.	*to like*
	exp	*¿Gusta/s?*	*Would you like?*

h

haber	*uno/alg*	Hay un florero en la mesa.	*there is/are*
	que inf	Hay que leer el libro.	*it is necessary to*
	participio	He tomado café.	*I/you... have V*
hablar	*con uno*	Hoy hablé con mi tía de Monterrey.	*to speak with*
	contra uno	El testigo habló contra él.	*to speak against*
	de uno/alg	El conferenciante habló del Arte.	*to speak about*
	exp	*hablar alto/en voz alta*	*to speak loudly*
		hablar bajo/en voz baja	*to speak in a low voice*
hacer	*alg*	Yo siempre hago mi tarea.	*to do*
	a uno inf	Nos hizo trabajar el sábado.	*to make*
	exp	*hace... que* [see 110 - 111]	*for, ago*
hacerse	*exp*	*hacerse a la idea* / to become accustomed to	
halagar [like gustar]	*a uno que sub*	Me halaga que hayan pensado en mí.	*to flatter*
hallar	*(a) uno/alg*	Hallé unas monedas antiguas en el baul.	*to find*
hallarse	*en* [place]	El castillo se halla en el bosque.	*to be located*
	exp	*hallarse fuera*	*to be away*
hartarse	*de alg*	En la fiesta, me harté de pasteles.	*to stuff oneself*
	de uno	La criada se hartó de su señora y la dejó.	*to get tired of*
	de inf	Me harté de esperarle y me fui.	*to get tired of*
helar	*ø*	Está helando en el norte del país.	*to freeze*
heredar	*alg (de uno)*	Heredó una gran fortuna de su abuela.	*to inherit*
herir	*a uno*	Me hieren sus palabras.	*to offend*
herirse	*ø*	Jugando con el martillo, se hirió en la mano.	*to hurt oneself*
hervir	*alg*	¡Hierve los huevos en una cazuela!	*to boil*
	exp	*hervir a fuego lento*	*to simmer*
hincar	*alg*	Hincó el parasol en la playa.	*to stick in*
	exp	*hincarse de rodillas*	*to kneel*
honrar	*a uno*	¡Honra a tus padres!	*to honor*
	a uno con alg	Nos honra con su asistencia.	*to honor with*
huir	*de/a* [place]	Un preso huyó de la cárcel.	*to escape*

hundir	*alg*	Hundió la cabeza en el agua.	*to submerge*
hundirse	*en* [place]	El barco se hundió en el Golfo de México.	*to sink*
	ø	La economía del país se hundió.	*to collapse*

I

ignorar	*alg*	Ignoro los detalles del asunto.	*not to know*
	(a) uno	El grupo lo ignora completamente.	*to ignore*
	que sub	Ignoraba que tuviera seis hijos.	*to be unaware*
igualarse	*con uno*	Quería igualarse con el campeón.	*to be equal to*
imaginarse	*alg*	¿Te imaginas la vida en la Edad Media?	*to visualize*
	que ind	Me imagino que nadie vendrá hoy.	*to suppose*
	que sub	No puedo imaginarme que sea así.	*to imagine*
impedir	*alg*	La policía impide la entrada al edicio.	*to forbid*
	inf	El museo impide tomar fotos.	*to forbid*
	que sub	El clima impide que continuemos escalando la montaña.	*to prevent*
implorar	*a uno (para) que sub*		
		Imploró al Presidente para que no ejecutaran a su hijo.	*to implore*
imponer	*alg a uno*	Le impusieron una multa muy grande.	*to impose*
imponerse	*a uno*	Gómez se impuso al resto del equipo.	*to dominate*
importar	*inf*	Me importa saber quién lo hizo.	*it is important to*
	quest	No me importa quién lo hizo.	
	que sub	Me importa mucho que lo hagas tú.	*it is important that*
	exp	¿Le importa si... ?	*Do you mind if...?*
		¡No importa!	*Never mind!*
incendiar	*alg*	Los soldados incendiaron el pueblo.	*to set fire to*
incendiarse	*ø*	Se incendió la biblioteca municipal.	*to catch fire*
inclinarse	*ante alg/uno*	Me inclino ante la labor que hicieron.	*to bow*
	a inf	Me inclino a dudar de su sinceridad.	*to be inclined*
	por uno	Yo me inclino por el nuevo candidato.	*to be in favour*
incluir	*a uno/alg*	El museo incluye a todos los pintores.	*to include*
indicar	*alg a uno*	Me indicaron esta dirección.	*to indicate*
inducir	*a uno a inf*	La falta de escuelas para los niños le indujo a hacer una campaña política.	*to induce*

373

infectarse	*ø*	La herida se me infectó.	*to become infected*
inferir	*alg*	¿Cómo pudo inferir tal conclusión?	*to deduce*
influir	*en/sobre alg*	La sequía va a influir en el costo de la leche.	*to affect*
informar	*que ind*	El Ministerio de Cultura informó que se celebrará el año del cuento infantil.	*to announce*
informarse	*sobre alg*	No logré informarme sobre la situación.	*to gather information*
ingresar	*a/en alg*	Vargas Llosa ingresó en la Academia de la Lengua Española.	*to be admitted*
	alg [money]	Ingresó 300 dólares en su cuenta.	*to deposit*
inquietar	*a uno*	Me inquieta la situación del enfermo.	*to worry*
	a uno que sub	Me inquieta que no hayan vuelto.	*to worry*
inscribir	*(a) uno/alg*	He inscrito mi nombre en la lista.	*to write down*
inscribirse	*en alg*	Me inscribí en el club de tenis.	*to register*
	dentro de alg	La nueva ley se incribe dentro del programa humanitario del gobierno.	*to lie within the scope*
insistir	*en inf*	Insiste en salir a pesar del tiempo.	*to insist on*
	en que sub	Insistió en que llevara el paraguas.	*to insist that*
instruir	*(a) uno en alg*	A Ramón lo instruyeron en la Aviación.	*to instruct*
	exp	*instruir el caso / to conduct the investigation*	
instruirse	*ø*	Teresa es una persona que se instruye.	*to educate oneself*
intentar	*inf*	Intenté abrir la puerta pero no pude.	*to try*
interesar	*a uno*	Me interesó mucho la conferencia.	*to interest*
	a uno inf	Me interesa saber lo que pasó.	*to be interested in*
interesarse	*en uno/alg*	Se interesa en la arqueolgía.	*to be interested in*
	por/en inf	El periodista se interesa por conocer los detalles del crimen.	*to be interested in*
interrogar	*(a) uno*	El juez interrogó tres testigos.	*to question*
intervenir	*en alg*	El alcalde intervino en el debate.	*to take part*
	en favor de	Nadie intervino en su favor.	*to intercede on one's behalf*
intoxicar	*(a) uno*	El escape de gas intoxicó cuatro niños.	*to poison*
introducir	*(a) uno*	El jefe introdujo al nuevo empleado.	*to introduce*
	alg	El presidente introdujo las reformas.	*to bring in*

introducirse *en* [place]		El ladrón se introdujo en el sótano.	*to get into*
inundar	*alg*	Las lluvias inundaron los campos.	*to flood*
invertir	*alg*	Nos toca invertir los horarios.	*to reverse*
	alg [time]	¿Cuánto tiempo has invertido en esto?	*to spend*
	alg [money]	Invertí todos mis ahorros en la casa.	*to invest*
investir	*(a) uno con alg*	La Universidad investió al Señor Gómez con el título de Doctor.	*to confer title*
invitar	*a uno a alg*	Invité a todos mis colegas a la boda.	*to invite*
	a uno a inf	El concejal invitó al público a votar.	*to invite*
	a uno a que sub	Te invito a que participes en la reunión.	*to invite*
ir	*a* [place]	Todos los días voy a la universidad.	*to go*
	a inf	Mañana voy a salir de excursión.	*to be going to*
	para alg	Manolo va para arquitecto.	*to be going to become*
	para inf	Vamos para ver la exposición.	*to go to*
	por uno	Voy por ti a las ocho de la tarde.	*to go for*
	tras uno/alg	Iban tras el dinero de la tía Rosa.	*to go after*
	exp	*ir a pié*	*to walk*
		ir en bicicleta/carro/tren... / *to go by...*	
		¡Qué te vaya bien! / *Goodbye!*	
		¿Me va bien el sombrero...? / *Does the hat... suit me?*	
irse	*de* [place]	La bibliotecaria se va de su trabajo.	*to leave*
	a [place]	Se fue a Perú.	*to go*
	a inf	Se fue a terminar su tarea.	*to go away*
	exp	*irse a pique*	*to sink*
izar	*alg*	Al alzarse el viento, los marineros izaron las velas.	*to haul up*

j

jalar	*alg*	¡Jala la puerta y entra!	*to pull*
jubilarse	*ø*	Tras 20 años se servicio en el Ejército, el papá de Luis se ha jubilado.	*to retire*
jugar	*ø*	Los niños no pararon de jugar.	*to play*
	a alg	A mí me gusta mucho jugar al tenis.	*to play*
jugarse	*exp*	*jugarse el todo por el todo*	*to stake one's all*
		jugarse la vida	*to risk one's life*
		¿Qué te juegas a qué ...? / *What do you want to bet?*	

375

juntar	*alg*	Juntaron mucho dinero para el viaje.	*to collect*
juntarse	*en* [place]	Nos juntamos en el Zócalo a las ocho.	*to meet*
	con uno	Él se junta con muchachos de su edad.	*to associate with*
jurar	*alg*	Juró fidelidad a la bandera de su país.	*to swear*
	sobre uno/alg	El testigo juró sobre la Biblia.	*to swear*
	por alg	Juro por el nombre de mi madre que es verdad.	*to swear*
	contra uno/alg	Estaba tan furioso que juró contra todos.	*to swear, curse at*
	inf	Juró no volver a hacerlo.	*to swear*
	exp	*jurar en falso / to commit perjury*	
		jurar decir la verdad / to swear to tell the truth	
juzgar	*ø*	La función del tribunal es de juzgar.	*to judge*
	(a) uno	Lo detuvieron, lo juzgaron, y lo condenaron a cien años de cárcel.	*to judge*
	por alg	No juzgues por la apariencia.	*to judge by*
	exp	*juzgar necesario*	*to consider*

1

labrar	[wood]	El artesano labró mi nombre en la pieza.	*to carve*
	[land]	Labraron el campo para plantar algodón.	*to farm*
ladrar	*ø*	Ese perro ladra pero no muerde.	*to bark*
lamentar	*alg*	Lamentamos la pérdida de Octavio Paz.	*to be sorry*
	que sub	Lamento que no haya podido venir.	*to regret*
lanzar	*alg*	Lanzó el balón a Julia.	*to throw*
		Ford acaba de lanzar su nuevo modelo.	*to launch*
lanzarse	*tras uno*	La policía se lanzó tras el agresor.	*to rush*
	contra uno/alg	Lanzaron tomates contra el Ministerio.	*to throw*
	exp	*lanzarse en paracaidas*	*to parachut*
lastimarse	*alg*	Me lastimé el dedo con un martillo.	*to injure*
lavar	*alg*	Lava los platos con mucho jabón.	*to wash*
leer	*ø*	Aprendió a leer a los cuatro años.	*to read*
	alg	En esta clase leemos mucha poesía.	*to read*
	que ind	Leí que hubo un terremoto en Lima.	*to read that*
levantar	*alg*	¡Levanten la mano los que están a favor!	*to raise*
levantarse	*ø*	Me levanto a las siete todos los días.	*to get up*
liberar	*(a) uno*	Un comando liberó a los rehenes.	*to release*

liberarse	*de uno/alg*	La isla se liberó de la tiranía.	*to free oneself*
licenciar	*(a) uno*	La empresa licenció mil empleados.	*to dismiss*
licenciarse	*en alg*	Alfredo se licenció en Contabilidad.	*to graduate*
limitar	*alg*	Esta ley limita la libertad de expresión.	*to restrict*
	con alg	La casa limita con un hospital.	*to be adjacent*
limitarse	*a inf*	Me limito a resumir lo que dijo Pepe.	*to limit oneself*
	a alg	Se limita a un vaso de vino por día.	*to limit oneself*
limpiar	*alg*	Cada mañana limpia su patio con agua.	*to clean*
	exp	*limpiar en seco*	*to dry-clean*
lograr	*alg*	Los obreros lograron un aumento.	*to obtain*
	inf	No logra concentrarse en su trabajo.	*to succeed in*
luchar	*contra uno/alg*		
		Luchó contra el comercio de drogas.	*to fight*
	por alg/inf	Luchó por los derechos de los braceros.	*to struggle*
	para inf	Lucha para salvar el medio ambiente.	*to struggle*

11

llamar	*a uno*	¡Llama a Alfredo!	*to call*
	a uno [noun]	Le llamaron Alfredo Ruiz Vargas.	*to call*
	a uno alg	Le llamaron "Pepito rompetodo"	*to call*
	exp	*estar llamado a + inf*	*to be destined to*
		llamar las cosas por su nombre / to call a spade a spade	
llamarse	*exp* [noun]	*Me llamo Alfredo.*	*my name is*
llegar	*a* [place]	La secretaria llega a casa muy cansada.	*to arrive*
	a inf	Pablo llegó a ser un famoso arquitecto.	*to succeed*
llenar	*alg de alg*	Llenó la casa de plantas tropicales.	*to fill with*
llenarse	*de alg*	Me llené de pasteles de chocolate.	*to stuff*
llevar	*a uno*	Llevé a María al aeropuerto.	*to drive uno*
	exp	*llevar a cabo*	*to carry out*
llevarse	*a cabo*	La fiesta se llevó a cabo en el salón Rex.	*to take place*
	exp	*llevarse bien/mal*	*to get on well/badly*
llorar	*ø*	Al oir la noticia, lloró desesperadamente.	*to cry*
	por uno/alg	No deja de llorar por lo ocurrido.	*to cry over*
llover	*ø*	Ayer llovió mucho durante la noche.	*to rain*

377

m

maldecir	*(a) uno*	Dios maldijo a Caín por su crimen.	*to curse*
	de uno/alg	Maldice de todos sus vecinos.	*to speak ill of*
	alg	Al perder todo su dinero, maldijo su mala suerte.	*to curse*
mandar	*alg a uno*	Nos mandaron un fax de Colombia.	*to send*
	a uno inf	Su mamá le mandó limpiar su alcoba.	*to ask uno to*
	a uno por uno/alg		
		La maestra mandó a Julián por su mamá.	*to send for*
	a uno que sub		
		Le mandó que fuera a la tienda.	*to command*
	exp	*mandar de paseo / to send sb packing*	
		¿Mande?	*Pardon?*
		mandar recuerdos	*to send regards*
manejar	*ø*	¿Quieres manejar?	*to drive*
manejarse	*(adv) en alg*	Se maneja bien en los negocios.	*to manage*
manifestar	*ø*	Las madres manifiestan en la plaza.	*to demonstrate*
	alg	Todos manifestaron el apoyo al Rey.	*to show*
	en favor/contra uno/alg		
		Manifestaron contra la violencia.	*to demonstrate*
manifestarse *ø*		La justicia terminó por manifestarse.	*to show oneself*
mantener	*(a) uno/alg*	Varias columnas mantienen el edificio.	*to support*
		Queremos mantener las tradiciones.	*to keep*
		Yo mantengo mi palabra.	*to maintain*
	(a) uno/alg adj	¡Mantén tu ciudad limpia !	*to keep*
mantenerse	*con/de alg*	Se mantienen con papas y arroz.	*to sustain oneself*
	exp	*mantenerse en forma*	*to keep fit*
maquillar	*(a) uno*	Él maquilla a todo el equipo de TV.	*to make up*
	alg	Maquillaron el carro para venderlo.	*to disguise*
maravillar	*a uno*	Me maravillan las ciudades coloniales.	*to fill with wonder*
[like **gustar**]			
maravillarse *de alg*		Alicia se maravillaba de lo que veía.	*to wonder*
marcar	*(a) uno/alg*	Varios sucesos marcaron su vida.	*to leave a mark*
	alg	Marcamos todos los árboles de la finca.	*to mark*
		Marqué las expresiones interesantes.	*to write*
		Las agujas marcan las tres de la tarde.	*to show*
		¿Qué número has marcado?	*to dial*
	exp	*Marcaron dos goles/puntos.*	*to score*
marcharse	*de* [place]	El peluquero se marchó del barrio.	*to leave*
	a inf	Se marchó a trabajar a la capital.	*to go to*

378

masticar	*alg*	Se prohíbe masticar goma de mascar.	*to chew*
matar	*(a) uno*	El incendio mató muchos animales.	*to kill*
	exp	*matar dos pájaros de un tiro / to kill two birds with one stone*	
matarse	*en alg*	Se mató en un accidente de aviación.	*to kill oneself*
	por inf	Se mata por ser el primero en clase.	*to struggle to*
medir	*alg*	Medimos el dormitorio para comprar una alfombra.	*to measure*
	[measure]	La alfombra mide 10 metros cuadrados.	*to measure*
	alg	No se puede medir las consecuencias del abuso de las drogas.	*to evaluate*
	adv	*¡Mide bien lo que vas a responder!*	*Think twice.*
medirse	*con uno*	Él no puede medirse con su adversario.	*to measure up*
mejorar	ø	Mejoró el transporte público.	*to improve*
mejorarse	ø	¡Ojalá que te mejores pronto!	*to become better*
mencionar	*(a) uno/alg*	En el artículo no mencionan a Fuentes.	*to mention*
mentir	*a uno*	Mintió a su mamá, pero ne le sirvió.	*to lie to*
merecer	*alg*	Ella recibió el premio pues lo merecía.	*to deserve*
	inf	La noticia merece ser anunciada.	*to deserve*
	que sub	Merece que le castigue por su conducta.	*to deserve*
	exp	*Se lo tiene merecido. / It serves him right.*	
merendar	*alg*	Le gusta merendar pan con chocolate.	*to have an afternoon snack*
meter	*alg en* [place]	Metió sus cosas en la cartera.	*to put*
	(a) uno en	Lo metieron en una escuela privada.	*to place*
	exp	*meter la pata / to put one's foot in it*	
meterse	*en* [place]	Pulgarcito se metió en lo más profundo del bosque.	*to go into*
	a inf	Me metí a averiguar lo que pasó.	*to start*
	de alg	Se metió de investigador.	*to take a job as*
	con uno	¡No te metas con la Carmen!	*to provoke*
mezclar	*alg*	¡Mezclen todos los ingredientes!	*to mix*
	en alg	Yo no me mezclo en esos asuntos.	*to get involved*
	con uno	No se mezcla con esa pandilla.	*to mingle with*
mirar	*alg*	Miró todos los escaparates de la ciudad.	*to look at*
	(a) uno	Miró a Pedro y comprendió que éste había mentido.	*to look at*
mojar	*(a) uno/alg*	Todos los días moja el patio de su casa.	*to wet*

379

mojarse	ø	Llovió tanto que me mojé.	*to get oneself wet*
		¡No te mojes en ese asunto!	*to kept out of*
moler	*alg*	Recordaba a su abuela moliendo café.	*to grind*
	a uno	Esta caminata me ha molido.	*to exhaust*
	exp	*moler a palos*	*to beat uno up*
molestar	*a uno que sub*	Me molesta que hagan tanto ruido.	*to annoy*
molestarse	*con uno/alg*	Se molestó con la secretaria.	*to get annoyed*
	en inf	¡No te molestes en responderle!	*to bother*
montar	ø	Montó hasta lo alto de la cuesta.	*to go up*
	exp	*montar a caballo/en bicileta*	*to ride*
		tanto monta...	*it's all the same*
morder	ø	Mi perro ladra pero no muerde.	*to bite*
	alg	El perro mordió todos mis juguetes.	*to bite*
	exp	*está que muerde*	*to be furious*
morir	ø	Mi mamá murió hace cuatro años.	*to die*
	exp	*morir de frío/ de calor*	*to die of cold/heat*
		morir de hambre/de sed	*to die of hunger/thirst*
		morir de vergüenza/de pena	*to die of shame/ sorrow*
		morir del corazón	*of a heart-attack*
morirse	*por inf*	Carlos se muere por salir con Conchita.	*to be dying for*
	exp	*Es para morirse de risa.*	*It's hilarious.*
mostrar	*alg a uno*	Mostramos las fotos a nuestros amigos.	*to show*
	que ind	Los resultados muestran que no estudió.	*to show that*
mostrarse	*adj*	Se mostró descontento de la mercancía.	*to appear*
mover	*alg*	El piano es tan pesado que no logré moverlo.	*to move*
mudar	*(a) uno a* [job]	Mudaron al inspector Vargas a otra estación de policía.	*to move*
	exp	*mudar de color*	*to change color*
mudarse	*de* [clothes]	Me voy a mudar de camisa.	*to change*
	a [place]	El año 91 nos mudamos a Boca Ratón.	*to move*
multiplicar	ø	Ha multiplicado el número de accidentes.	*to increase*
	alg [numbers]	¡Multiplica 17 por 25!	*to multiply*
murmurar	ø	Murmuró unas palabras a mi oído.	*to murmur*
	de uno	Se pasa el día murmurando de su jefe.	*to grumble*

n

nacer	[date]	Julio nació el 6 de octubre de 1985.	*to be born*
	en [place]	Diego Rivera nació en Guanajuato.	*to be born in*
	para alg/inf	Picasso nació para pintor.	*to be born to be*
nadar	**ø**	Como no sabía nadar, casi se ahogó.	*to swim*
	exp	*nadar en la riqueza* / *to be rolling in money*	
		nadar como un pez / *to swim like a fish*	
necesitar	**(a) uno/alg**	Para hacer la tarea, necesitamos un buen diccionario bilingüe.	*to need*
	inf	Necesito terminar este trabajo hoy.	*to need*
	que sub	Necesito que me mandes dinero.	*to need*
negar	**alg**	El acusado negó su culpabilidad.	*to deny*
	inf	Niega estar al corriente del asunto.	*to deny*
	que sub	Sofía niega que haya salido por la noche.	*to deny that*
negarse	**a inf**	Se niega a contar la vida de sus hijos.	*to refuse to*
nevar	**ø**	Es raro que nieve en este pueblo.	*to snow*
nombrar	**(a) uno**	El acusado no nombró a sus cómplices.	*to name*
	(a) uno alg	Lo nombraron Luis María en honor al abuelo paterno.	*to name*
		Lo nombraron presidente del Club.	*to appoint*
		Nombró solamente a dos escritores.	*to mention*
notar	**alg**	Yo noto todas mis citas en la agenda.	*to note down*
		El maestro notó severamente el test.	*to grade*
	exp	*se nota que*	*one notes that*

o

obedecer	**a uno**	Los estudiantes obedecen al maestro.	*to obey*
obligar	**a uno a inf**	Le obligaron a renunciar al puesto.	*to force sb*
	a uno a que sub	Le obligaron a que se vacunara antes de viajar.	*to force*
observar	**(a) uno/alg**	El sociólogo observa la sociedad.	*to examine*
		La gente observa buenas costumbres.	*to keep*
obtener	**alg**	Obtuvo el permiso tras pasar el examen.	*to get*
ocupar	[place]	El ejército ocupó el noreste del país.	*to occupy*
	[time]	La TV ocupa gran parte de su tiempo.	*to take up*
ocuparse	**de inf**	Yo me ocupo de regar las plantas.	*to take care of*
	exp	*¡Ocúpate de lo tuyo!* / *Mind your own business!*	

ocurrir	*ø*	Ocurrió un accidente en la autopista 20.	*to take place*
ocurrirse	*a uno*	Se le ocurren unas cosas increíbles.	*to occur to sb*
	a uno inf	Se me ocurrió visitar a mi suegra.	*to occur to sb*
odiar	*(a) uno/alg*	Limpia su casa porque odia la suciedad.	*to hate*
	inf	Odio ver la basura tirada en la calle.	*to hate*
	que sub	Odia que sus niños le ensucien la casa.	*to hate*
ofrecer	*alg a uno*	Quisiera ofrecerle un buen regalo.	*to give*
	por alg	¿Cuánto ofreces por mi coche?	*to offer*
ofrecerse	*(a) inf*	Un vecino se ofreció repararle el carro.	*to offer*
	exp	¿Se te/le ofrece algo? / *Do you want anything?*	
oír	*alg*	Esta mañana, no oí el despertador.	*to hear*
	inf	Al despertarme, oí cantar al gallo.	*to hear*
	que ind	Oyó que alguien llamaba a la puerta.	*to hear*
oler	*a alg*	Toda la casa huele a chocolate.	*to smell*
olerse	*alg*	Los narcotraficantes se olieron el peligro.	*to sense*
olvidar	*(a) uno/alg*	No olvidaré nunca mi pueblo natal.	*to forget*
	(de) inf	Olvidaron de cerrar las ventanas.	*to forget to*
operar	*a uno de alg*	Le operaron del estómago/corazón...	*to operate on*
	alg	Este obrero no sabe operar la máquina.	*to operate*
oponerse	*a alg*	Los padres de José se oponen a la boda.	*to oppose*
	a inf	Me opongo a permanecer callado.	*to refuse*
	a que sub	Mi mamá se opone a que haga el viaje.	*to oppose to*
optar	*por alg/inf*	Optó por viajar en avión.	*to choose*
	entre uno/alg	Tuvo que optar entre trabajo o familia.	*to choose between*
ordenar	*alg*	¿Cuándo vas a ordenar tu dormitorio?	*to arrange*
	a uno inf	El comandante ordena a la compañía prepararse para el desfile.	*to order*
	a uno que sub	Te ordeno que hagas el trabajo hoy.	*to order unoy to*
	exp	*ordenarse sacerdote*	*to take holy orders*
organizar	*alg*	El comité organizó el Cinco de Mayo.	*to organize*
organizarse	*ø*	Tengo trabajo y no logro organizarme.	*to get oneself organized*
orientar	*(a) uno/alg hacia*		
		Hay que orientar la antena hacia el sur.	*to turn*
		Lo orientaron hacia la medicina.	*to orient toward*
orientarse	*ø*	Con un buen mapa puedes orientarte.	*to find one's bearings*
osar	*inf*	No osa dirigirme la palabra.	*to dare to*

p			
padecer	*de alg*	Mi papá padece del corazón.	*to suffer from*
pagar	*alg por*	Pagué 20 dólares por la raqueta.	*to pay for*
	alg	Terminamos de pagar las deudas.	*to pay*
	exp	*pagar por adelantado*	*to pay in advance*
		pagar al contado	*to pay cash*
parar	*alg*	Paró su coche enfrente del hotel.	*to stop*
	de inf	El vecino paró de tocar el tambor.	*to stop*
	a inf	Vamos a parar a tomar un refresco.	*to stop to*
	en alg	¿En qué paró el proyecto del parque?	*to end up as*
pararse	*ø*	Al llegar a la esquina, ¡párate!	*to stop*
		¡Párate! [in Mexico]	*to stand up*
	a inf	Me paré a hablar con mi amiga.	*to stop*
parecer	*inf*	La alfombra parece estar mojada.	*to seem*
parecerse	*a uno*	Luis se parece a su tío Ramón.	*to resemble*
partir	*a/para/hacia*	Partieron para la playa en la camioneta.	*to leave*
	alg en	¡Parte el pastel en 10 porciones!	*to split*
	exp	*a partir de* [time]	*from*
partirse	*ø*	Con el golpe se ha partido el jarrón.	*to crack*
pasar	*ø*	¿Ha pasado el autobús?	*to come*
		¿Qué ha pasado aquí?	*to happen*
	alg	¡Pásame la sal, por favor!	*to pass*
	por alg	Pasaré por San Diego de camino a L.A.	*to go through*
	por uno	Con el uniforme se hizo pasar por médico.	*to be taken for*
	a inf	Pasaré a charlar un rato con ustedes.	*to drop in*
	[time]	Pasé el fin de semana en la cama.	*to spend*
	exp	*pasar la aspiradora*	*to vacuum*
		pasar los exámenes	*to take*
		pasarlo bien	*to have a good time*
pasarse	*por* [body]	Se pasó la mano por la frente.	*to pass*
	de adj	Se pasó de listo.	*to be too*
	exp	*Se me pasó.* / *it slipped my mind.*	
		No se le pasa nada. / *nothing escapes her/him.*	
pasearse	*ø*	Todas las tardes, la gente sale y se pasea.	*to take a walk*
	por [place]	Se pasearon por el centro de la ciudad.	*to go for a walk*
pecar	*ø*	Incriminaba a los que habían pecado.	*to sin*
	de adj	Peca de imprudente.	*to be too adj*
	por alg	Peca por imprudencia.	*to be too adj*

383

pedir	*alg*	Pide 1000 dólares por su colección.	*to ask for*
	a uno que sub	Me pidió que organizara el viaje.	*to ask that*
	exp	*a pedir de boca*	*perfectly*
pegar	*alg*	He pegado el cartel en el salón.	*to glue*
	a uno/alg	Está prohibido pegar a los niños.	*to hit*
	a uno en [body]	Una piedra le pegó en la cabeza.	*to hit*
	exp	*no pegar ojo / not to sleep a wink all night*	
pegarse	*a uno*	Felipe se me pegó durante todo el viaje.	*to stick to*
	exp	*pegársela a alguien*	*to deceive*
peinarse	*ø*	Isabel, se pasa una hora peinándose.	*to comb*
penetrar	*en alg/uno*	El ladrón penetró en el banco por el techo.	*to enter*
		La bala penetró en su pecho.	*to enter*
		Penetró en lo más profundo de la vida.	*to understand fully*
pensar	*ø*	El mejor sistema educativo es el que enseña a pensar.	*to think*
	alg de uno/alg	¿Qué piensas del nuevo director?	*to have an opinion*
	en uno	Paso el día pensando en mi hijo.	*to think about*
	que ind	Yo pienso que no deben inquietarse.	*to think that*
	[negative] *que sub*		
		No pienso que sea una buena idea.	*not to think, doubt*
	inf	Pensaron salir de la isla en un barco.	*to plan*
percatarse	*de alg*	No se percataron de la salida del tren.	*to notice*
percibir	*alg*	Por su trabajo, percibió una fuerte suma.	*to be paid*
		Percibo muy bien la intención de Luis.	*to perceive*
perder	*(a) uno/alg*	Perdió a su padre cuando tenía 5 años.	*to lose sb*
		Te presto mi llave, pero no la pierdas.	*to lose*
		Perdió el tiempo buscando un carro.	*to waste*
perderse	*ø*	Caminó por el bosque y se perdió.	*to get lost*
		Tras el granizo se perdió la cosecha.	*to be ruined*
	exp	¡No te lo pierdas!	*Don't miss it!*
perdonar	*ø*	Solamente Dios puede perdonar.	*to pardon*
	alg a uno	Perdonó a su hijo lo que le había hecho.	*to forgive*
	exp	*perdonar la vida*	*to spare sb's life*
		Esta... no perdona.	*to be fatal*
perjudicar	*alg*	El incidente va a perjudicar las relaciones entre los dos países.	*to harm*
	a uno	La nueva ley nos perjudica.	*to harm*
	que sub	Perjudica que haya ocurrido tal cosa.	*to damage*

384

permitir	*alg*	El reglamento permite el uso de botas.	*to allow*
	a uno inf	Esta medicina me permitió continuar.	*to permit to*
	que sub	El profesor no permite que lleguemos	*to allow*
		tarde a su clase.	
	exp	¿Me permite?	*May I?*
permitirse	*alg*	No me permito tal lenguaje con mi madre.	*to dare to*
	inf	No se permite tirar basura.	*to be permitted*
perseguir	*(a) uno/alg*	La policía los persiguió en la carretera.	*to chase*
persistir	*en alg*	Debemos persistir en el estudio.	*to persist*
	en inf	Persiste en creer que ganaremos.	*to persist in*
pertenecer	*a uno*	¿A quién pertenece esta llave?	*to belong*
	a uno inf	Al Presidente de la Asociación	*to be uno's job*
		le pertenece entregar los premios.	
pervertir	*(a) uno*	Algunos acusan a la televisión de	*to pervert*
		pervertir a la juventud.	
pesar	*alg*	Pesó las naranjas y las puso en la bolsa.	*to weigh sth*
	[weight]	Yo peso 10 kilos más que tú.	*to weigh*
	exp	¡Te pesará!	*You'll be sorry.*
pescar	*ø*	Pasó el fin de semana pescando.	*to go fishing*
	alg	Hoy tuve suerte, pesqué seis truchas.	*to catch*
	exp	*pescarse un marido/una mujer...*	*to get*
picar	*ø*	No me gusta esta comida porque pica.	*to be hot*
		A estas horas del día los peces no pican.	*to bite*
	(a) uno	Me picó un mosquito y se me infló	*to bite*
		la nariz.	
picarse	*ø*	Fernando se pica siempre que se le	*to take offence*
		hace una broma.	
picotear	*alg*	Picoteamos unas tapas antes de cenar.	*to nibble sth*
pillar	*a uno* [body]	La puerta del taxi le pilló el pié.	*to catch*
	exp	*Le pilló la policía.*	*to catch*
		¡Te pillé!	*I got you.*
pintar	*alg*	¿Quién pintó "Guernica"?	*to paint*
	(a) uno/alg	Esquivel pintó a la perfección la	*to depict*
		sensibilidad femenina.	
	exp	*No pinta nada./¿Qué pinta aquí?*	*He has no place.*
pintarse	*alg*	Se pintó los labios de rojo vivo.	*to make-up*
pisar	*ø*	¡Cuidado, que me estás pisando!	*to step on*
	exp	*No se deja pisar por nadie./*	*He doesn't let anybody walk all*
			over him/her

385

plantar	*alg*	Planté varias legumbres en mi jardín.	*to plant*
	exp	*Plantar en la calle.*	*to get fired*
plantarse	*a/en* [place]	Se plantó a la entrada y nadie pudo entrar.	*to stand firm*
platicar	*sobre alg*	Platicamos sobre la película.	*to talk about*
	con uno	Me gusta platicar con la familia Navarro.	*to talk with*
poder	*inf*	Podemos pararnos a comer ahora.	*to be able , can*
	que sub	Puede que esta tarde llueva.	*it is possible*
	[negative] *con uno/alg*		
		No puedo con este animal.	*to be exhauted with*
poner	*alg*	Pusieron una escultura de Tumarkin en el centro de la plaza.	*to put*
	a uno a inf	Puso a sus estudiantes a pintar.	*to set sb to V*
ponerse	*alg*	Hoy me puse mi traje azul.	*to put on*
	a inf	Al llegar a casa, me puse a cocinar.	*to begin to*
	adj	Se puso furiosa cuando supo lo sucedido.	*to become*
	exp	*ponerse rojo*	*to blush*
		ponerse la carne de gallina	*to get goosebumps*
posar	*alg*	Posó todas sus cosas en la mesa.	*to lay*
	ø	La modelo posó para las revistas.	*to pose for*
posarse	*ø*	El avión se posó sin dificultad.	*to land*
poseer	*alg*	Los López poseen una casa en la playa.	*to have*
		El guía posee un buen conocimiento de la arquitectura colonial.	*to have knowledge*
practicar	*ø*	Para ser buen pianista, es necesario practicar varias horas por día.	*to practice*
	alg	Siempre que puedo, practico el español.	*to practice*
precipitar	*alg*	La nevada precipitó nuestra salida.	*to hasten*
	(a) uno	Precipitó a su víctima por el acantilado.	*to throw down*
precipitarse	*a inf*	Los clientes se precipitaron a comprar antes de la subida de precios.	*to rush*
	a [place]	El público se precipitó a la salida.	*to rush*
preferir	*alg*	¿Prefieres pan tostado o pan blanco?	*to prefer*
	inf	¿Prefieres ir a Florida o a California?	*to prefer*
	que sub	Prefiero que vayamos a Florida.	*to prefer*
preguntar	*alg a uno*	¿Qué te preguntaron en el examen?	*to ask*
	por uno	Teresa preguntó por ti.	*to ask about*
	quest	Me preguntó si había leído este libro.	*to ask if*
		Me preguntaron dónde había vivido.	*to ask*
preguntarse	*quest*	Me pregunto si ha recibido el mensaje.	*to wonder*

386

prender	*(a) uno*	La policía prendió al ladrón sin disparar.	*to capture*
	alg	En cuanto llega a casa, prende la TV.	*to switch on*
	exp	*prender fuego*	*to catch fire*
preocupar	*a uno*	Me preocupa el futuro de mis hijos.	*to worry*
preocuparse	*por uno/alg*	Se preocupa mucho por su hijo.	*to worry*
	de que sub	Se preocupa de que todo esté bien.	*to care*
	exp	*No te preocupes.*	*Don't worry.*
preparar	*(a) uno/alg*	Preparo mis cosas para comenzar el nuevo año escolar.	*to prepare*
presentar	*(a) uno/alg a uno*		
		Te presento a mi amigo Alfonso.	*to introduce*
presentarse	*a uno/alg*	Debes presentarte al director.	*to report*
		Teresa no se presentó al examen.	*to take*
	adv	El fin de semana se presenta bien.	*to appear*
presentir	*que ind*	Presentía que la guerra era inevitable.	*to have a premonition*
prestar	*alg a uno*	¿Podrías prestarme tu cámara?	*to lend*
		Tu cámara me prestó un gran servicio.	*to render*
	exp	*prestar atención*	*to pay attention*
prestarse	*para alg*	Esta moto no se presta para el terreno.	*to be for*
	para inf	La tarde se presta para salir.	*to be for*
pretender	*inf*	Pretende convencerme para que pase el verano con ellos.	*to try to*
prevenir	*alg*	No se ha podido prevenir el accidente.	*to avoid*
	(a) uno	Yo solamente te prevengo.	*to warn*
	exp	*Es mejor prevenir que lamentar. / Prevent is better than regret.*	
privar	*a uno de alg*	El doctor le priva de comer chocolate.	*to forbid*
privarse	*de alg*	Se priva de vino y de jamón.	*to deprive oneself*
	exp	*No se priva de nada. / He (she) has everything he (she) wants.*	
probar	*alg*	¡Prueba esta carne! Está estupenda.	*to try*
	que ind	El resultado de los exámenes prueba que el niño no estudió.	*to prove that*
	exp	*No cuesta nada probar. / There's no harm in trying.*	
probarse	*alg*	Me voy a probar estos zapatos.	*to try on*
proceder	*de alg*	Procede de una familia de Monterrey.	*to come from*
procurar	*inf*	Procuró hacerlo lo mejor que pudo.	*to try to*
	que sub	Procura que nadie se entere.	*to try to*

producir	*alg*	La empresa produce 80% del sector.	*to produce*
	alg a uno	La visita a la empresa me produjo una buena impresión.	*to give*
producirse	*ø*	En los últimos años se han producido grandes cambios en el país.	*to come about*
proferir	*alg*	El invitado al debate no paró de proferir insultos y maldiciones.	*to hurl, utter*
prohibir	*(a uno) inf*	Te prohibo usar la moto sin casco.	*to forbid*
	que sub	El museo prohibe que se tomen fotos.	*to forbid*
	exp	*prohibido fumar/llevar arma...*	*no smoking...*
prometer	*alg a uno*	Mi mamá me prometió un pastel de manzana.	*to promise*
	a uno inf	Te prometo escribirte a mi llegada.	*to promise*
promover	*alg*	IBM está haciendo una campaña de TV para promover el último modelo.	*to promote*
	a uno	A Daniel, le promovieron en su trabajo.	*to promote*
proteger	*(a) uno de alg*		
		Esta crema nos protege del sol.	*to protect*
	alg de alg	La pintura protege el piso de la lluvia.	*to protect*
protestar	*contra uno/alg*		
		Los padres protestaron contra la situación de las escuelas públicas.	*to protest*
proveer	*alg a uno*	La lechería provee leche a todo el valle.	*to supply*
proveerse	*de alg*	Debemos proveernos de víveres con vistas al huracán.	*to provide oneself*
provenir	*de alg*	Su familia proviene de Nuevo León.	*to come from*
provocar	*alg*	El terremoto provocó el pánico.	*to cause*
	a uno	¿Te provoca un pastel de manzana? [LA]	*I/you...would like*
		Fue Luis quien provocó a Martín.	*to provoke*

q

quebrar	*ø*	La fábrica de papel quebró.	*to go out of business*
	alg	Quebró la mesa con el peso.	*to break*
quedar	*a uno*	¿Cuánto dinero te queda?	*to remain*
	con uno en/por inf		
		Quedé con Juan en ir al cine.	*to agree to*
	en que ind	Quedó en que me llamaría.	*to agree that*

388

quedarse	***con uno***	Me quedé con la familia tres semanas.	*to stay*
	con alg	Se quedó con mi libro.	*to keep*
	a inf	Nos quedamos a tomar café con Julián.	*to remain*
	exp	*quedarse boquiabierto/a*	*to be left gaping*
quejarse	***a uno***	No le gustó el servicio y se quejó a la dirección del hotel.	*to complain*
	de alg	Me quejé del sevicio.	*to complain*
	de que sub	Se queja de que le hayan recibido mal.	*to complain*
quemar	***alg***	El sol quema las plantas.	*to burn*
quemarse	***con alg***	Se quemó con la plancha.	*to burn oneself*
querer	***(a) uno/alg***	Quiere mucho a sus hermanos.	*to love*
	inf	Queremos jugar al tenis con ustedes.	*to want to*
	que sub	Quiero que vayamos juntos a la charla.	*to want*
quitar	***alg***	Yo quito la piel del durazno para comerlo.	*to remove*
	alg a uno	Si no te portas bien, te quitaré tus juguetes.	*to take from*
	uno a uno	Tras el divorcio, le quitaron su hijo.	*to take away from*
quitarse	***alg***	Llegó a la playa y se quitó los zapatos.	*to take off*

r

rajarse	***ø***	Con el calor se rajan la carreteras.	*to crack*
	exp	¡No te rajes!	*Don't quit!*
raptar	***a uno***	Hoy, raptaron al hijo del Embajador.	*to kidnap*
rascar	***alg***	Hay que rascar con lija antes de pintar.	*to scrape*
rascarse	[body]	Tiene la manía de rascarse la cabeza.	*to scratch*
rayar	***alg***	Alguien rayó mi nuevo carro.	*to scratch*
	con alg	El Paso raya con la frontera de México.	*to border on*
	en [age]	Maximiliano raya en los sesenta.	*to be nearly*
reaccionar	***adv***	No sé como va a reaccionar cuando se entere de la noticia.	*to react*
		Reaccionó muy bien.	*to react*
	adv a alg	Reaccionó muy mal a la vacuna.	*to have a reaction*
realizar	***alg***	Por fin logró realizar su sueño.	*to fulfil*
		Es un proyecto muy difícil; pero estoy dispuesto a realizarlo.	*to carry out*
		No realiza la consecuencia de sus acciones.	*to realize*

rebajar	*alg*	En esta tienda no rebajan el precio.	*to reduce*
	(a) uno	Es tan soberbio que siempre rebaja a los otros.	*to belittle*
rebajarse	*ø*	Me niego a rebajarme ante la autoridad.	*to bow*
rebelarse	*contra*	El ejército se rebeló contra el gobierno.	*to revolt*
recibir	*ø*	La familia Fuentes recibe mucho.	*to entertain*
		El médico recibe de 8 a 5.	*to receive*
	alg	Recibimos dos paquetes de libros.	*to receive*
	exp	*recibir con los brazos abiertos* / to welcome with open arms	
reclamar	*alg*	Si no estas satisfecho de la compra, reclama el dinero que has pagado.	*to claim*
reclinar	*alg*	Reclinó la cabeza sobre su novio.	*to lean*
recobrar	*alg*	Está en jucio para recobrar su Hacienda.	*to recover*
recoger	*(a) uno/alg*	En esta ciudad recogen la basura dos veces por semana.	*to pick up*
recomendar	*alg a uno*	¿Puedes recomendarnos un buen restaurante en el Centro Histórico?	*to recommend*
	inf	Me recomendó ir a la enfermería.	*to advise to*
	a uno que sub	Les recomiendo que visiten Taxco.	*to recommend*
reconocer	*(a) uno/alg*	Reconocí a Felipe en cuanto lo vi.	*to recognize*
	inf	Reconozco haber cometido un error.	*to admit*
recordar	*quest*	No recuerdo dónde puse mi mochila.	*to remember*
	a uno (a) uno/alg		
		Ella me recuerda a mi madre.	*to remind*
	que ind	Recuerda que debemos llegar a las ocho.	*to remember*
recorrer	*alg*	El tren recorre los pueblos de la costa.	*to go through*
		Hoy hemos recorrido 300 kilómetros.	*to cover*
rechazar	*alg a uno*	Le rechazaron su primer manuscrito.	*to reject*
		Ofrecí flores a Lola pero me las rechazó.	*to reject*
reducir	*alg*	Hemos reducido el consumo de tabaco.	*to diminish*
		Necesito reducir el tamaño de la copia.	*to reduce*
	(a) uno/alg a alg		
		Aquella administración redujo el país a la miseria.	*to bring down to*
referir	*alg*	El escritor refiere lo que le sucedió en su viaje a la India.	*to tell*
referirse	*a uno/alg*	¿A quién te refieres?	*to refer to*
	a lo que ind	Me refiero a lo que dijo el director.	*to refer to what*
	exp	*en (por) lo que se refiere a...*	*as for...*

390

reflejar	*en alg*	La luna refleja en la superficie del lago.	*to reflect on*
	alg	Sus palabras reflejan buena voluntad.	*to show*
reflejarse	*en alg*	La vida del artista se refleja en su obra.	*to be reflected*
reforzar	*alg*	Hay que reforzar los lazos con China.	*to reinforce*
refrescar	*ø*	Por la noche, la temperatura refresca.	*to cool down*
	alg	Hay que refrescar el vino blanco.	*to cool*
	exp	*refrescar la memoria*	*to refresh*
refugiarse	*en* [place]	Los alpinistas se refugiaron en la cueva.	*to take refuge*
regalar	*alg a uno*	Se acostumbra regalar una camiseta a los visitantes de la universidad.	*to give a present*
regalarse	*con alg*	Me regalé con un plato de ostras.	*to treat oneself*
regañar	*a uno*	La maestra le regañó por llegar tarde.	*to reprimand*
regar	*alg*	¡No olvides regar las plantas!	*to water*
regatear	*ø*	En este mercado hay que regatear.	*to bargain*
regir	*a uno/alg*	La nueva ley rige a todas las escuelas.	*to apply*
regirse	*por alg*	Nos regimos por la ley del estado.	*to follow*
registrar	*alg*	Voy a registrar las maletas.	*to register*
		El aduanero registra las maletas de todos los pasajeros.	*to search*
registrarse	*ø*	Si quieres participar en el concurso, debes registrarte.	*to register*
regocijar	*(a) uno*	La llegada del circo regocijó a todos.	*to fill with joy*
regresar	*a* [place/time]	Regresaremos a las diez de la noche.	*to come back*
	a inf	Va a regresar a cenar con nosotros.	*to return to*
rehusar	*alg*	Rehusó el Premio Nobel de Literatura.	*to refuse*
	inf	Rehusa comprar cosas de piel de animal.	*to refuse to*
reinar	*ø*	Carlos IV reinó en la época de Goya.	*to reign*
reír	*exp*	*hacer reír / to make uno laugh*	
		Es mejor reír que llorar. / It is better to laugh than to cry.	
		El que ríe el último ríe mejor / He who laughs last laughs best.	
reírse	*ø*	Ricardo es tan cómico que no paramos de reírnos cuando estamos con él.	*to laugh*
	de uno/alg	Todos se reían de sus ideas.	*to laugh at*

391

relacionar	*alg*	No consigue relacionar dos ideas.	*to connect*
relacionarse	*con uno*	Se relaciona con los más ricos del pueblo.	*to be connected with*
	exp	*en lo que se relaciona a/con algo*	*with regard to*
relajar	*(a) uno/alg*	El ruido del mar me relaja.	*to relax*
		No consigo relajar los músculos.	*to relax*
relajarse	*ø*	Va al monte para relajarse.	*to relax*
relevar	*(a) uno de alg*	Lo relevaron de su cargo de Ministro.	*to replace*
rematar	*(a) uno*	Remató al reo con un tiro de gracia.	*to finish off*
	alg	Remató su tesis con una buena conclusión.	*to finish off*
	[sport]	El delantero remató de cabeza.	*to head a goal*
	exp	*para rematar*	*to crown it all*
remediar	*ø*	Ahora es demasiado tarde para remediar.	*to remedy*
	exp	*No se remedia llorando.* / *You won't do any good by crying.*	
remitir	*alg*	Remití el paquete a mis padres.	*to send*
remitirse	*a uno/alg*	Me remito a lo expuesto por el abogado.	*to refer*
remontar	*alg*	Logramos remontar todos los obstáculos.	*to surmount*
remontarse	*a* [time]	Esto se remonta a la época de la Colonia.	*to go back to*
remover	*alg*	Remueve los papeles que están en el piso.	*to remove*
		Alguien removió todos mis papeles.	*to turn over*
rendir	[business]	La exportación de cerveza rinde bien.	*to pay*
	exp	*rendir honores*	*to pay tribute*
rendirse	[army]	Las tropas francesas se rindieron.	*to surrender*
	exp	*No me rindo.*	*I don't give up.*
renegar	*de* [religion]	Renegó de sus creencias religiosas.	*to apostatize*
	de uno	Si es así, reniego de su amistad.	*to break with*
renovar	*alg*	Rubén renovó su restaurante.	*to remodel*
renunciar	*a alg*	Tuvo que renunciar al viaje a Chile.	*to give up*
reñir	*ø*	Él y su esposa se pasan el día riñendo.	*to quarrel*
	a uno por alg	Su mamá le riñó por haber roto el florero de porcelana.	*to reprimand*
	por alg	Los dos hermanos riñeron por una cuestión de herencia.	*to quarrel*

reparar	*alg*	El carpintero reparó la mesa.	*to repair*
	en alg	El detective reparó en una mancha que había en el piso.	*to notice*
repartir	*alg entre/a*	Benito Juárez repartió la tierra entre los campesinos.	*to distribute*
		Gana dinero repartiendo periódicos.	*to deliver*
	[cards]	¿A quién le toca repartir?	*to deal*
repasar	*alg*	Esta semana vamos a repasar la lección.	*to review*
	[clothe]	Repasé la camisa y el pantalón.	*to iron*
repetir	*ø*	¿Puedes repetir, por favor?	*to repeat*
		La cebolla y el ajo repiten.	*to come back*
	alg a uno	Se lo repetí pero no hizo caso.	*to say again*
	alg	Vamos a volver a repetir esta escena.	*to repeat*
repetirse	*ø*	La Historia se repite.	*to repeat itself*
	exp	¡Qué no se repita! / I hope this won't happen again.	
representar	*(a) uno/alg*	Lola va a representar la universidad.	*to represent*
	alg [age]	No representa su edad.	*to look*
	[show]	La Compañía va a representar "Evita."	*to perform*
reproducir	*alg*	Tengo que llevar a reproducir las fotos.	*to reproduce*
reproducirse	*ø*	Se le volvió a reproducir la úlcera.	*to recur*
		Los conejos se reproducen en gran número.	*to reproduce*
repugnar [like **gustar**]	*a uno*	Me repugnan los caracoles.	*to disgust*
		Me repugna ver la miseria en el país.	*to revolt*
	exp	ser repugnante	*to be disgusting*
resbalar	*ø*	Como el piso estaba mojado, resbalé.	*to slip up*
rescatar	*(a) uno/alg*	Lograron rescatar a 20 pasajeros.	*to rescue*
	alg	El ejército rescató la isla que estaba ocupada por el enemigo.	*to recover*
resentir	*alg*	Hoy resiento el esfuerzo de la carrera.	*to feel the effects*
resentirse	*ø*	El cansancio se resiente al día siguiente.	*to be felt*
reservar	*alg*	Reservamos una mesa para diez.	*to reserve*
reservarse	*ø*	El campeón se reserva para la final.	*to keep up one's strength*
resignarse	*ø*	A pesar de todo, no me resigno.	*to resign oneself*
	a inf	No me resigno a creer que haya muerto.	*to resign oneself*
resistir	*ø*	El neumático que compré no va a resistir mucho.	*to last*
	a uno/alg	El barco resistió al agua y al viento.	*to resist*

resistirse	*a inf*	Me resisto a abandonar la búsqueda de los alpinistas.	*to refuse to*
resolver	*alg*	No podemos resolver el problema.	*to solve*
	inf	Resolvieron dejar el carro y caminar.	*to resolve*
respirar	*alg*	Salimos al monte a respirar aire puro.	*to breathe*
	exp	*trabajar sin respirar / to work without a break*	
		¡Uf, respiro! / That's a relief!	
responder	*ø*	Llamé a su casa pero no responde.	*to answer*
	a uno	¡No me respondas!	*to answer back*
	a alg	No supe responder a su pregunta.	*to answer*
	de uno/alg	Yo no respondo de lo que ellos decidan.	*to be responsible for*
	por uno	¿Quién responde por Vd.?	*to vouch for*
restar	*a uno*	Me restan cuatro días para ir a México.	*to remain*
	inf	Sólo resta saber quién robó la pulsera.	*to remain*
resultar	*adj*	Dos muertos resultaron heridos en el accidente de carretera.	*to turn out*
		La excursión resultó estupenda.	*to turn out*
	de alg	¿Qué resultó de aquella idea?	*to result from*
	en alg	La acción del ejército resultó en protesta.	*to result in*
	como ind	La crema no resultó como yo esperaba.	*to come out*
	que ind	Resulta que ya tenía una novia formal.	*It turned out that*
	exp	*Me resulta simpático/a.*	*I like him/her.*
resumir	*alg*	Tiene que resumir el artículo.	*to summarize*
retirar	*alg*	Retiró todas las espinas del pescado.	*to remove*
		Voy a retirar 200 dólares de mi cuenta.	*to withdraw*
retirarse	*ø*	El señor López se retiró este año.	*to retire*
	de alg	El caballo 3 se retiró de la competición.	*to withdraw*
	a inf	Luis se retiró a trabajar en su pueblo.	*to go off to*
retorcerse	*[body]*	Me caí y me retorcí la muñeca.	*to twist*
retraerse	*de alg*	Aunque tenga hambre, me retraigo de la comida de los vendedores ambulantes.	*to stay away*
retroceder	*alg*	La cantante retrocedió tres puestos en la escala de éxitos.	*to move back*
reunir	*(a) uno/alg*	El director reune a los profesores cada fin de año.	*to assemble*
		Este producto reune las condiciones.	*to meet*
reunirse	*ø*	La comisión se reune en la escuela.	*to get together*
	con uno	Me reuno con mis compañeros a las seis.	*to meet*
	para inf	Nos reuniremos para organizarlo todo.	*to get together to*

reventar	*alg*	Se me reventó un neumático.	*to have a flat tire*
revolver	*alg*	¡Pon los ingredientes y revuélvelos!	*to mix*
rezar	*ø*	Está prohibido rezar en las escuelas públicas.	*to pray*
	alg [prayer]	Rezaron una oración por el alma del difunto.	*to pray*
	exp	*El anuncio del periódico reza así:...*	*to read*
robar	*alg a uno*	A Susana le robaron el carro.	*to steal from*
rogar	*a uno que sub*	Rogó a la Virgen que cuidara de su hijo que salía al Norte.	*to ask that*
	exp	*hacerse de rogar / to like to be asked twice*	
romper	*alg*	El camarero rompió todos los platos.	*to break*
	a inf	Al ver el suceso, el dueño rompió a gritar.	*to burst out*
	con uno	Lupita rompió con su amigo.	*to break up with*
roncar	*ø*	Se pasó la noche roncando.	*to snore*
rozar	*alg*	Una bala le rozó la cabeza.	*to touch lightly*
	en alg	Sus palabras rozan en racismo.	*to border on*
rozarse	*con alg*	Me rocé el brazo con un clavo.	*to touch lightly*
	con uno	Ella no se roza con un obrero.	*to mix with*

S

saber	*alg*	Isabel García sabe español y francés.	*to know*
	inf	Sé jugar al tenis.	*to know how to*
	adv de alg	Carlos sabe mucho de ajedrez.	*to know about*
	[algo/nada]	No sé nada de Luis.	*to have news about*
	que ind	Yo sé que Bárbara no vendrá.	*to know*
	exp	*No se sabe.*	*Nobody knows.*
saber	*a alg*	Este postre sabe a miel.	*to taste like*
saborear	*alg*	Pude saborear los vinos de Jerez.	*to savour*
sacar	*alg*	Sacó la bicicleta del garaje.	*to get out*
		El dentista me sacó una muela.	*to extract*
	a inf	Sacó a su novia a cenar al "Club Vasco"	*to take out*
sacudir	*alg*	El terremotó sacudió la ciudad.	*to shake*
		Después de comer, ¡sacude el mantel!	*to brush off*

395

salir	∅	Vamos a salir a hacer unas compras.	*to leave for*
	de [place]	Salimos de Miami a las 8 de la tarde.	*to leave*
	adj	Te salió la sopa estupenda.	*to turn out*
	adv	Isabel salió bien/mal en el examen.	*to pass/fail*
	con uno	Josefina sale con Ramón.	*to date*
	a inf	Voy a salir a comprar el periódico.	*to go out to*
salpicar	*a uno*	Estaba esperando el bus, cuando un carro pasó y me salpicó.	*to splash*
saltar	∅	Al ver el fuego, todos saltaron por las ventanas del edificio.	*to jump*
	alg	Siempre salta palabras cuando lee.	*to skip*
	exp	*saltar a los ojos / to be patently obvious*	
saludar	*a uno*	Voy a saludar a la nueva secretaria.	*to greet*
	[negative]	Ese nunca me saluda.	*to acknowledge*
salvar	*(a) uno/alg*	Los médicos salvaron la vida de la niña.	*to save*
salvarse	*de alg*	Cuatro prisioneros se salvaron de la pena de muerte.	*to escape from*
	de inf	El soldado se salvó de ir a la guerra.	*to escape from*
	exp	*¡Sálvese quien pueda!*	*Run for your life!*
sangrar	∅	Cuando llegó la ambulancia, su herida sangraba mucho.	*to bleed*
	de/por [body]	Sangraba de la cabeza.	*to bleed from*
saquear	*a uno/alg*	Los bandidos saquearon el pueblo.	*to loot*
satisfacer	*alg*	No pudo satisfacer las condiciones.	*to meet*
	a uno	El resultado del partido me satisface.	*to please*
satisfacerse	*con alg*	Me satisfago con una nota mediana.	*to be satisfied with*
	con inf	Se satisface con ver pasar a la gente.	*to be satisfied to*
secar	*alg*	Sequé la ropa en la terraza.	*to dry*
secarse	[body]	Tengo que secarme el cabello.	*to dry*
seducir	*(a) uno*	En su papel de Don Juan siempre seducía a varias mujeres.	*to seduce*
		Nos sedujo con su sonrisa.	*to charm*
		No me seduce la idea de viajar en esta época del año.	*to like*
segar	*alg*	¡Hay que segar el pasto!	*to mow*
		Salieron los segadores a segar el trigo.	*to harvest*
seguir	∅	¡Sigue/Siga!	*to go on*
	a uno/alg	En la semifinal, Paredes sigue a Chang.	*to follow*
		¡Vaya adelante! y yo le sigo.	*to follow*

	adj	Ella sigue contenta en su trabajo.	*to be still adj*
	ger	Aún, sigue lloviendo.	*to be still Ving*
	en alg	Sigue en problemas con su novio.	*to be still in*
	sin inf	Seguimos sin tener noticias de Juan.	*to be still without*
	exp	*¡Que siga Vd. bien!*	*I hope you keep well.*
sembrar	*alg*	¿Cuándo vamos a sembrar el algodón?	*to sow*
	alg de alg	El candidato al cargo de alcalde, sembró la calle de papeletas.	*to spread*
sentarse	*ø*	¡Siéntense, por favor!	*to sit down*
	a inf	Nos sentamos a jugar a las cartas.	*to sit down to*
sentir	*alg*	Me sacaron una muela, pero no sentí nada.	*to feel*
	a uno adv	Una buena sopa me sienta bien.	*to do sb good*
	que sub	Siento que esté enfermo.	*to regret*
	exp	*Lo siento.*	*I'm sorry.*
sentirse	*adj*	Me siento enfermo.	*to feel*
	[bien/mal]	Me sentó bien la comida.	*to take it well*
	[bien/mal] *que sub*		
		Le sentó mal que lo dijeras.	*to take it badly*
separar	*(a) uno/alg*	Empezaron a pegarse y hubo que separalos.	*to separate*
		El divorcio, separó a las dos hermanas.	*to separate*
	(a) uno/alg de uno/alg		
		Separaron los hombres de las mujeres.	*to separate from*
separarse	*ø*	Los estados del sur querían separarse.	*to secede*
		Llegaron juntos a Atlanta y allí se separaron.	*to part*
	de uno	Se separó del grupo y tomó el autobús.	*to leave*
ser	*adj*	Ivana es peruana.	*to be*
	alg	José es maestro.	*to be*
	[time]	Son las doce de la tarde.	*It is*
	de [place]	Elena Cabeza es de Nuevo México.	*to be from*
	para uno	Este regalo es para la Señorita Rosa.	*to be for*
	para inf	Esta lámpara es para matar moscas.	*to be for*
servir	*alg a uno*	Nos sirvieron un buen plato de salmón.	*to serve*
	de alg	Este carro sirve de transporte escolar.	*to be used for*
	de alg [role]	Sirvió de cocinero en el ejército.	*to serve as*
	para inf	Este contenedor sirve para transportar gas.	*to be used for*
significar	[word]	¿Qué significa "noria"?	*to mean*
silbar	*ø*	El minero va por la calle silbando.	*to whistle*

simpatizar	*a uno*	Yo no le simpatizo.	*to like*
	con uno	Yo no simpatizo con ese tipo.	*to get on well*
situarse	*en* [time]	La acción se sitúa en la época de Cortés.	*to take place*
sobrar	*alg*	Sobró mucha comida en la fiesta.	*to be left*
sobreponerse *a alg*		Luis se sobrepuso a la crisis familiar.	*to overcome*
sobresalir	*ø*	Las ramas del árbol sobresalen a la calle.	*to stick out*
	en alg	Mi hijo sobresale en matemáticas.	*to be outstanding*
soler	*inf*	Por la mañana, suele ir a la cafetería.	*to be in the habit of*
		Cuando era pequeño, solía pasar las vacaciones en California.	*I/you... used to*
solicitar	*(a) uno/alg*	Carmen solicitó el puesto de ingeniero.	*to apply for*
	(a uno) que sub	Le solicitamos que nos escuchen.	*to request*
	exp	*El puesto está muy solicitado. / to be in great demand*	
soltar	*(a) uno/alg*	El Instituto Oceanográfico soltó las jóvenes ballenas en la playa.	*to let go of*
someter	*(a) uno/alg a alg*		
		Sometió a su familia a una dieta estricta.	*to subject sb to*
		Sometí mi ensayo al concurso.	*to present*
sonar	*ø*	El telefonó sonó varias veces.	*to ring*
	exp	*El nombre me suena / he name sounds familiar.*	
		Sonarse las narices / to blow one's nose	
sonreír	*a uno*	Siempre que Juanito pasa por la calle me sonríe.	*to smile at*
soñar	*ø*	Pasé la noche soñando.	*to dream*
	con uno/alg	Por la noche, soñaba con bisontes.	*to dream of*
	que ind	Soñé que hablaba japonés en la TV.	*to dream that*
soplar	*alg*	La niña sopló las velas del pastel.	*to blow off*
	alg a uno	En el examen, José le sopló la respuesta.	*to whisper*
soplarse	*alg* [drink]	Pepe Botella se soplaba diez botellas de vino por día.	*to knock back*
soportar	*(a) uno/alg*	La verdad, yo no soporto a este tipo.	*to stand*
sorprender	*ger*	Le sorprendí copiando en el exámen.	*to catch*
	a uno que sub	Me sorprende que no haya llegado.	*it is surprising*
sortear	*alg*	Sortearon dos billetes de avión en la fiesta.	*to raffle*

sospechar	*que ind*	Sospechaba que su esposo no le era fiel.	*to suspect*
sostener	*alg*	Dos columnas sostienen el balcón.	*to hold up*
		No es posible sostener tal tesis.	*to defend*
sostenerse	*de alg*	Se sostenía de una pequeña pensión.	*to support oneself*
subir	*ø*	¿Puedes subir?	*to go up*
	a [place]	Subí al desván para buscar una foto.	*to go up*
	alg	¡Suba la maleta a mi habitación!	*to take up*
suceder	*ø*	Sucedieron varios acontecimientos de gran importancia en el país.	*to happen*
	a uno	El vicepresidente le sucede en el cargo.	*to succeed*
	con uno/alg	¿Qué sucedió con aquel plan?	*to happen*
	exp	¿Qué sucede?	*What's going on?*
sudar	*ø*	No paré de sudar en todo el partido.	*to sweat*
sufrir	*de alg*	Mi mamá sufre de los riñones.	*to suffer from*
	alg	El senador sufrió un ataque cardíaco.	*to have*
sugerir	*a uno que sub*	Si quieres un carro disponible, te sugiero que hagas la reserva.	*to suggest that*
sujetar	*ø*	¡Sujeta aquí! mientras busco el martillo.	*to hold*
	(a) uno/alg	El tenista sujeta su pelo con una cinta.	*to hold in place*
sumar	*alg* [quantity]	En total, suma 120 dólares.	*to add up to*
sumarse	*a uno/alg*	Lupe se sumó al grupo de investigación.	*to join*
superar	*(a) uno/alg*	Superó el record de natación.	*to surpass*
		Mi empresa supera a todas en calidad.	*to be superior to*
suplicar	*a uno que sub*	Te suplico que dejes de hacer ruido.	*to implore*
suponer	*que ind*	Ella supone que todo está listo.	*to assume*
		Supongo que no estás contenta.	*to assume*
	exp	*Supongamos que* + ind	*suppose that*
surgir	*ø*	Este año han surgido varios problemas.	*to arise*
	de [place]	De repente, el lobo surgió del bosque.	*to emerge from*
suscribirse	*a alg*	Me suscribí a la revista "Contenido"	*to subscribe*
suspender	*de* [place]	Los jamones suspenden del techo.	*to suspend*
	a uno	Le suspendieron en tres asignaturas	*to fail*
suspenderse	*alg*	Debido al tiempo se supendió el carnaval.	*to be suspended*
suspirar	*por alg*	Suspira por tener una casa en Morelia.	*to long to*

sustituir	*(a) uno*	Van a sustituir al portero del equipo.	*to replace*
	alg por alg	Sustituí el neumático por uno nuevo.	*to replace*
sustraer	*alg de alg*	Debo sustraer 7 dólares de la cuenta.	*to substract*
		En su país, le sustraen los impuestos de la paga mensual.	*to deduct*
sustraerse	*a alg*	No podía sustraerse al deseo de confesar lo que había pasado.	*to get out of*
susurrar	*alg*	Me susurró un secreto al oído.	*to whisper*

t

tapar	*alg*	Tapé la mesa con un mantel de plástico.	*to cover*
tardar	*ø*	Llamamos un taxi pero tardó mucho.	*to take a long time*
	[time] **en inf**	Tardamos dos horas en llegar a casa.	*to take*
telefonear	*a uno*	Se pasa el día telefoneando a sus amigos.	*to phone*
temblar	*ø*	Hacía tanto frío que estaba temblando.	*to shiver*
	exp	*temblar de frío / to shiver with cold*	
		temblar de miedo / to tremble with fright	
temer	*a uno/alg*	En esta época, temo a los huracanes.	*to be afraid of*
	inf	Con este tiempo, temo viajar en avión.	*to fear to*
	que ind	Temo que ha salido sin avisarnos.	*to be afraid*
	que sub	Sus padres temen que sea grave.	*to be afraid*
	exp	¡No temas!	*Don't be afraid!*
tender	*(a) uno*	Tendieron al herido en la camilla.	*to lay down*
	alg	¡Tienda el brazo!	*to stretch*
	a inf	Esta madera tiende a curbarse.	*to tend to*
tener	*alg*	Tiene un Cadillac de los años 60.	*to have*
	que inf	Tengo que tomar el avión a las seis.	*to have to*
	por adj	Me tiene por idiota, pero un día verá.	*to consider to be*
	exp	*tener hambre*	*to be hungry*
		tener miedo que + sub	*to be afraid*
		tener razón	*to be right*
		tener sed	*to be thirsty*
		tener sueño	*to be sleepy*
		tener vergüenza	*to be ashamed*
		tener en cuenta	*to take into account*
		tener presente	*to bear in mind*
tenerse	*por adj*	Se tiene por un aristócrata.	*to consider oneself*
tentar	*alg*	Tentó la mesa en la oscuridad.	*to feel*
	[idea]	Me tienta la idea.	*to tempt*
	inf	Tenté tomar la sopa pero no pude.	*to try to*

400

teñirse	*alg* [hair]	Se tiñó el cabello de verde.	*to dye*
terminar	*alg*	Me voy porque he terminado mi trabajo.	*to complete*
	de inf	Acabo de terminar de escribir a José.	*to finish doing*
	adv	La historia de Pinocho termina bien.	*to end*
	en alg	Su amistad terminó en matrimonio.	*to end in*
	ger	Terminó yéndose sin despedirse.	*to finish by*
	por inf	Terminó por confesar su crimen.	*to finally V*
tildar	*a uno de adj*	Tildó a su novio de mentiroso.	*to brand*
timar	*a uno*	Le timaron con el precio del carro.	*to swindle*
tirar	*alg a uno*	¡Tírame la pelota!	*to throw*
	alg	Tiró todos los viejos muebles.	*to throw away*
		Tiró dos disparos al aire.	*to shoot*
	de alg	¡Tira fuerte de la cuerda!	*to pull*
	a uno	Mi esposa Josefa tira a su madre	*to take after*
tirarse	*a/de/en alg*	Los vaqueros se tiraron del tren.	*to jump from*
	a inf	Me tiré a descansar un rato.	*to abandon oneself*
tocar	*(a) uno/alg*	¡No me toques con la mano sucia!	*to touch*
	a uno inf	A nosotros nos toca invitarles esta vez.	*it's sb's turn to*
	[instrument]	Toca muy bien la guitarra y el piano.	*to play*
	alg a uno	Le tocó 200 dólares a la lotería.	*to get*
	exp	¿A quién le toca?	*Whose turn is it?*
		¡Toca madera!	*Touch wood!*
		por lo que a mí me toca / as far as I am concerned	
tolerar	*alg*	El gobernador no tolera la crítica.	*to tolerate*
	que sub	No tolero que me hables de esa forma.	*to allow*
tomar	*alg*	Tomó la maleta y subió al tren.	*to take*
		Tomé camarones y cerveza.	*to have*
		Al llegar a la esquina, tomó a la derecha.	*to turn*
	por uno	Al entrar en casa, me tomó por un ladrón.	*to take for*
	exp	tomar el sol / to sunbathe	
		¿Por quién se toma? / Who does think he/she is?	
topar	*con alg*	El carro derrapó y topó con un árbol.	*to run into*
toparse	*con uno/alg*	Me topé con Rosa y Elena en el Teatro.	*to run into*
torcer	*alg*	El viento tuerce los árboles de la playa.	*to bend*
		El periodista torció el sentido de las palabras de la Ministra de Educación.	*to distort*
	ø	El taxi torció a la derecha.	*to turn*
torcerse	*alg* [body]	No puedo jugar hoy porque me torcí el tobillo.	*to twist*
toser	*ø*	En toda la noche, no he parado de toser.	*to cough*

401

trabajar	**ø**	Trabaja por la noche en una panadería.	*to work*
	de alg	Trabaja de cocinero en el Hotel Ritz.	*to work as*
traducir	**alg**	Yo traduje el primer capítulo del libro.	*to translate*
	(del)... al...	Hay que traducir del francés al inglés.	*to translate into*
traer	**alg a uno/alg**	Se me olvidó traer los discos a la fiesta.	*to bring*
tragarse	**alg**	Me tragué una espina del pescado.	*to swallow*
trasnochar	**en** [place]	Trasnochamos en un hotelito de la costa.	*to spend the night*
tratar	**(a) uno**	Al enfermo, lo trataron con penicilina.	*to treat*
	(a) uno adv	Nos trataron muy bien en Michoacán.	*to treat*
	(a) uno de adj	Trataron al cocinero de incompetente.	*to call sb adj*
	de alg	La película trata de la vida de Dalí.	*to be about*
	de inf	Traté de hablar con ella pero no estaba.	*to try to*
tratarse	**de adj**	Se trataron de idiotas y otros nombres.	*to call by*
	exp	*se trata de...*	*it's a question of*
trazar	**alg**	El ingeniero trazó en el mapa la línea de la nueva autopista.	*to design*
	alg	Antes de comenzar la campaña, debemos trazar el plan de trabajo.	*to lay down*
	alg	El conferenciante trazó en su discurso la historia de la literatura chicana.	*to describe*
triunfar	**ø**	El equipo de Albuquerque triunfó.	*to triumph*
	exp	*triunfar en la vida*	*to succeed in life*
tropezar	**con uno**	Tropecé con mi maestra en la plaza.	*to run into*
tumbar	**(a) uno/alg**	Le dió tal golpe que lo tumbó.	*to knock down*
tumbarse	**ø**	Se tumbó debajo de una palmera.	*to lie down*
turnar	**(a) uno/ alg**	Turnaron las horas de trabajo.	*to take turns*
turnarse	**para inf**	Se turnaron para guardar las cosas.	*to take turns*

u

ubicar	**(a) uno/alg**	No consigo ubicar su pueblo en el mapa.	*to locate*
	exp	*estar ubicado*	*to be located*
unir	**(a) uno/alg**	Los dos países unieron sus esfuerzos.	*to join*
unirse	**ø**	Los braceros del Sur del país, se unieron para defender sus derechos.	*to unite*
		Las compañías de teléfonos se unieron.	*to merge*
	exp	*unirse en matrimonio*	*to get married*

urgir	*a uno*	Urgió al Jefe para terminar el conflicto.	*to press*
	inf	Urge encontrar una solución ecológica.	*to urge*
usar	*alg*	Mi abuelo usa un bastón para caminar.	*to use*
usarse	*ø*	¿Cómo se usa esta computadora?	*to be used*
utilizar	*alg*	Se recomienda utilizar el cinturón de seguridad.	*to use*

V

vaciar	*alg*	Vació la caja en la mesa.	*to empty*
vacilar	*ø*	Respondió a la pregunta sin vacilar.	*to hesitate*
	con uno	¡No vaciles conmigo!	*to make fun of*
	en inf	No vaciles en llamarme.	*to hesitate*
	entre uno/alg y uno/alg		
		Vacilaba entre Juan y Luis.	*to hesitate*
	exp	A mí, no me vaciles. / *Stop messing me about.*	
vacunar	*(a) uno contra alg*		
		Vacunaron a la gente contra el tifus.	*to vaccinate*
vagar	*ø*	Los perros sin amo vagan por las calles.	*to wander*
valer	*alg*	Este mueble de cocina vale mil dólares.	*to cost*
		Este hombre vale mucho.	*to be worthy*
	a uno inf	No le valió de nada falsificar la foto.	*to serve*
	por alg	Este tipo vale por un millón.	*to be worthy of*
	exp	¡Vale!	*O.K.*
valerse	*de uno/alg*	Se vale de la influencia de su tío.	*to take advantage*
	exp	*valerse por sí mismo* / *to be able to manage*	
velar	*(a) uno/alg*	Se quedó la noche velando al enfermo.	*to stay by*
	por alg	Hay que velar por el futuro del planeta.	*to watch over*
	ø	¡No te quedes velando! pues mañana tienes que madrugar.	*to stay awake*
vencer	*(a) uno*	El equipo de Perú venció al de Quebec por 2 a 0.	*to beat*
	ø	Las escaleras vencieron debido al peso.	*to break down*
	exp	*vencer el plazo*	*to expire*
		Se vence el plazo.	*Time is up.*
vender	*alg*	Vendió la casa al primer cliente.	*to sell*
	exp	*vender al por mayor*	*to sell wholesale*
		vender al por menor	*to retail*

vengarse	*de uno*	Emma tomó la pistola y se vengó del director de la fábrica.	*to take revenge*
	por alg	Emma se vengó por la injusticia y la muerte de su padre.	*to take revenge*
venir	*ø*	Hoy Victor no vino a la universidad.	*to come*
	a inf	Mi familia de Houston vino a visitarme.	*to come to*
ver	*(a) uno/alg*	Ayer vi una buena película italiana.	*to see*
	(a) uno inf	La vi cantar en la Ópera.	*to see*
	exp	*ver claro*	*to understand*
verse	*ø*	José y su hermano se ven amenudo.	*to see each other*
	con uno	Mañana me veo con mi ex-esposa.	*to meet*
	exp	*verselas con alguien*	*to confront*
vestir	*(a) uno*	Calvin Klein viste a la gente joven.	*to make clothes for*
	alg	Viste pantalón negro con camisa roja.	*to wear*
vestirse	*ø*	La novia se está vistiendo.	*to get dressed*
	de alg	Este carnaval me visto de pirata.	*to dress up as*
	exp	*vestirse de sport*	*to dress casually*
		vestirse de [color]	*to dress in*
viajar	*ø*	Me gusta mucho viajar.	*to travel*
	en alg	Viajé a Londres en tren.	*to go in*
	por [place]	Viajé por Chile y Argentina.	*to travel through*
vigilar	*(a) uno/alg*	Se quedó vigilando a los niños.	*to watch over*
		El guarda vigila la fábrica.	*to guard*
virar	*a [direction]*	En la esquina, viré a la derecha.	*to turn*
visitar	*a uno/alg*	Voy a visitar a mis amigos de Laredo.	*to visit*
vivir	*en [place]*	Los padres de Alfonso viven en Toledo.	*to live*
	de alg	Esta escritora vive de sus libros.	*to live on/by sth*
	exp	*¡Viva alguien/algo!*	*Hurray!*
volar	*a [place]*	Mañana volamos a Australia con la TWA.	*to fly*
	en alg	El carro del ministro voló en pedazos.	*to blow up*
	ø	¡Voló mi cartera!	*to disappear*
volcar	*ø*	El carro salió de la carretera y volcó.	*to overturn*
	alg	El camión volcó la carga en el monte.	*to dump*
volver	*a [place]*	Volveremos a casa a las diez.	*to return*
	a inf	No volveré a comprar ese producto.	*to do sth again*
	alg en alg	Volvió la casa en una mansión.	*to transform*
	exp	*volver en sí / to regain consciousness*	
volverse	*ø*	¡Vuélvete!	*to turn around*
	contra uno	Se volvió contra su propio hermano.	*to turn against*
votar	*por uno*	La mayoría del estado votó por Morales.	*to vote*

404

y			
yacer	*exp*	*Aquí yace...*	*Here lies...*

z			
zambullirse	*en alg*	Le gusta zambullirse en el agua.	*to plunge*
zumbar	*(a) uno*	Se riñó con la pandilla y lo zumbaron.	*to hit*
	a uno	En el avión me zumban los oídos.	*to buzz*

	conj.	compl.		conj.	compl.
abalanzarse	298	330	acertar	305	333
abandonar	294	330	aclamar	294	333
abarcar	314	330	aclarar (se)	294	333
abarrotar (se)	294	330	acoger (se)	290	333-4
abastecer	281	330	acometer	279	334
abatir (se)	320	330	acomodar (se)	294	334
abdicar	314	330	acompañar	294	334
ablandar	294	330	aconsejar (se)	294	334
abochornar (se)	294	330	acordar (se)	319	334
abofetear	294	330	acortar	294	334
abogar	304	330	acostar (se)	319	334
abolir	320	330	acostumbrar (se)	294	334
abominar	294	330	acribillar	294	335
abonar (se)	294	331	actuar	294	335
abordar	294	331	acudir	320	335
aborrecer	281	331	acumular	294	335
abortar	294	331	acusar (se)	294	335
abotonar	294	331	achacar	314	335
abrasar (se)	294	331	adaptar (se)	294	335
abrazar (se)	298	331	adelantar (se)	294	335
abreviar	294	331	adelgazar	298	335
abrigar (se)	304	331	adentrarse	294	335
abrir (se)	320	331	aderezar	298	335
abrochar (se)	294	331	adherir (se)	309	335
abrumar	294	331	adivinar	294	335
absolver	300	331	adjudicar (se)	314	336
absorber	279	332	administrar (se)	294	336
abstenerse	321	332	admirar	294	336
abstraerse	323	332	admitir	320	336
abundar	294	332	adoptar	294	336
aburrir (se)	320	332	adormecer (se)	281	336
abusar	294	332	adornar	294	336
acabar (se)	294	332	adquirir	309	336
acaecer	281	332	adueñarse	294	336
acalorarse	294	332	advertir	309	336
acallar	294	332	afanarse	294	336
acaparar	294	332	afectar	294	336
acariciar	294	332	afeitarse	294	336
acarrear	294	333	aferrarse	294	336
acatarrarse	294	333	aficionarse	294	337
acceder	279	333	afiliarse	294	337
acelerar	294	333	afirmar	294	337
acentuar	289	333	agarrar (se)	294	337
aceptar	294	333	agitar	294	337
acercar (se)	314	333	agradar	294	337

	conj.	compl.		conj.	compl.
aumentar	294	343	cambiar (se)	294	346-7
autorizar	298	343	caminar	294	347
avanzar	298	343	cansarse	294	347
aventurarse	294	343	cantar	294	347
avergonzarse	273	343	captar	294	347
averiguar	294	343	carecer	281	347
avisar	294	344	cargar (se)	304	347
ayudar	294	344	casar (se)	294	347
			castigar	304	347
bailar	294	344	causar	294	347
bajar (se)	294	344	cazar	298	347
bañarse	294	344	ceder	279	347
barrer	279	344	cegar (se)	301	347
basarse	294	344	cejar	294	347
bastar (se)	294	344	celebrar	294	348
batallar	294	344	cenar	294	348
batir (se)	320	344	cepillarse	294	348
beber	279	344	cerrar (se)	305	348
bendecir	285	344	cesar	294	348
beneficiarse	294	344	clasificarse	314	348
besar (se)	294	345	cobrar	294	348
bloquear	294	345	cocer	276	348
bordear	294	345	cocinar	294	348
borrar (se)	294	345	coger	290	348
bostezar	298	345	cohibirse	320	348
botar	294	345	coincidir	320	348
brillar	294	345	cojear	294	348
brincar	314	345	colar (se)	319	348
brindar (se)	294	345	colgar	277	348
bromear	294	345	colmar	294	349
broncearse	294	345	colocar (se)	314	349
brotar	294	345	columpiarse	294	349
bucear	294	345	combatir	320	349
bullir	320	345	combinar (se)	294	349
burlar (se)	294	345-6	comentar	294	349
buscar	314	346	comenzar	278	349
			comer (se)	279	349
caber	275	346	comerciar	294	349
caer (se)	323	346	cometer	279	349
calarse	294	346	compadecerse	281	349
calcular	294	346	compaginar	294	349
calentar (se)	305	346	comparar	294	349
calificar	314	346	compartir	320	349
calzar	294	346	compensar	294	350
callar (se)	294	346	competir	312	350

	conj.	compl.		conj.	compl.
complacer (se)	281	350	convencer (se)	282	354
componer (se)	308	350	convenir	325	354
comportarse	294	350	converger	290	354
comprar	294	350	conversar	294	354
comprender	279	350	convertir (se)	309	354
comprimir	320	350	convidar	294	354
comprobar	319	350	convocar	314	354
comprometer (se)	279	350	corregir (se)	283	354
comunicar (se)	314	350	correr	279	354
concebir	283	351	corresponder	279	355
conceder	279	351	cortar	294	355
concentrar (se)	294	351	costar	319	355
concernir	317	351	crecer	281	355
concertar (se)	305	351	creer (se)	299	355
conciliar (se)	294	351	criticar	314	355
concluir	280	351	cruzar (se)	298	355
concurrir	320	351	cubrir	320	355
condenar	294	351	cuidar (se)	294	355
conducir (se)	322	351	culpar	294	355
conectar (se)	294	351-2	cultivar	294	355
confesar	305	352	cumplir	320	355
confiar	294	352	curar (se)	294	355
conformarse	294	352			
confundir (se)	320	352	charlar	294	356
conmover (se)	300	352	chiflar	294	356
conocer [109]	281	352	chismear	294	356
conquistar	294	352	chocar	314	356
consagrar (se)	294	352	chupar (se)	294	356
conseguir	316	352			
consentir	317	352	dar (se)	284	356
conservar (se)	294	353	deber	279	356
consistir	320	353	decidir (se)	320	356
consolar (se)	319	353	decir	285	357
constar	294	353	decretar	294	357
constituir	280	353	dedicar (se)	294	357
construir	280	353	defender (se)	306	357
consultar	294	353	dejar (se)	294	357
consumir	320	353	demostrar	319	357
contar	319	353	denunciar	294	357
contener (se)	321	353	depender	279	357
contentar (se)	294	353	derivar	294	357
contestar	294	353	derramar	294	357
continuar	289	354	derribar	294	357
contraer	323	354	derrotar	294	357
contribuir	280	354	desafiar	294	357

	conj.	compl.		conj.	compl.
desahogarse	304	358	distinguir (se)	287	361
desalojar	294	358	distraer (se)	323	361
descalzarse	298	358	disuadir	320	361
descansar	294	358	divertirse	309	361
descender	306	358	divorciarse	294	361
descomponerse	308	358	doblar	294	361
descubrir	320	358	doler (se)	300	361
descuidar (se)	294	358	dormir (se)	288	361
desear	294	358	dudar	294	361
desempeñar	294	358			
desgajar	294	358	economizar	298	362
desgarrar	294	358	echar (se)	294	362
deshacer (se)	295	358	edificar	314	362
desistir	320	358	egresar	294	362
deslizar (se)	298	358	ejercer	282	362
desmentir	317	358	elegir	283	362
desnudarse	314	359	elevar (se)	294	362
despachar	294	359	eliminar	294	362
despedir (se)	312	359	embalar (se)	294	362
despertarse	305	359	embarazar	298	362
despojar	294	359	embarcar (se)	314	362
desprender (se)	279	359	embestir	312	362
destinar	294	359	emborracharse	294	363
destrozar	298	359	emigrar	294	363
destruir	280	359	emitir	320	363
desvelar (se)	294	359	empapar (se)	294	363
desviar (se)	289	359	empatar	294	363
detener (se)	321	359	empeñar (se)	294	363
determinar (se)	294	359	empezar	278	363
devolver	300	359	empujar	294	363
dibujar	294	359	enamorarse	294	363
dictar	294	360	encabezar	298	363
diferenciar (se)	294	360	encantar	294	363
digerir	309	360	encargar (se)	304	363
dirigir (se)	286	360	encender	306	363
disculpar	294	360	encerrar (se)	305	363
discutir	320	360	encoger	290	363
disentir	317	360	encontrar (se)	319	364
disfrazarse	298	360	enderezar	298	364
disfrutar	294	360	endulzar	298	364
disgustar	294	360	enfadarse	294	364
disolver	300	360	enfermarse	294	264
disparar	294	360	enfrentarse	294	364
dispensar	294	360	engañar (se)	294	364
disponer (se)	308	361	enojarse	294	364

421

	conj.	compl.		conj.	compl.
enredar (se)	294	364	explorar	294	368
enrollar	294	364	explotar	294	368
enseñar	294	364	exponer (se)	308	368
ensuciar	294	364	exportar	294	368
entender (se)	306	364	expresar (se)	294	368
enterarse	294	364	exprimir	320	368
enterrar	305	364	expulsar	294	368
entrar	294	364	extender (se)	306	368
entregar (se)	304	365	extinguir	287	368
entretener (se)	321	365	extraer	323	368
enviar	289	365	extrañar	294	368
envolver	300	365	extraviarse	289	368
equivocarse	314	365			
errar	305	365	fabricar	314	369
escalar	294	365	faltar	294	369
escaparse	294	365	fallar	294	369
escasear	294	365	familiarizarse	298	369
escoger	290	365	fastidiar	294	369
esconder (se)	279	365	felicitar	294	369
escribir	320	365	festejar	294	369
escuchar	294	366	fiar (se)	289	369
escupir	320	366	fichar	289	369
escurrir (se)	320	366	figurar	294	369
esforzar (se)	273	366	fijar (se)	294	369
espantar (se)	294	366	filtrar (se)	294	369
esparcir (se)	291	366	finalizar	298	370
esperar	294	366	fingir	283	370
esquivar	294	366	firmar	294	370
estar	292	366	flotar	294	370
estimar	294	366	fomentar	294	370
estirar (se)	294	367	formar (se)	294	370
estrechar (se)	294	367	forrar (se)	294	370
estrellarse	294	367	fortalecer	281	370
estrenar	294	367	forzar	273	370
estropear	294	367	fotocopiar	294	370
estudiar	294	367	fracasar	294	370
evacuar	294	367	fregar	301	370
evitar	294	367	freir	311	370
examinar (se)	294	367	frenar	294	370
excluir	280	367	fumar	294	370
excusar (se)	294	367	funcionar	294	370
exigir	286	367	fundar	294	370
existir	320	367	fundir (se)	320	371
experimentar	294	367			
explicar (se)	314	367-8			

	conj.	compl.		conj.	compl.
ganar	294	371	informar (se)	294	374
garantizar	298	371	ingresar	294	374
gastar	294	371	inquietar	294	374
girar	294	371	inscribir (se)	320	374
gobernar	305	371	insistir	320	374
gozar	298	371	instruir (se)	280	374
grabar	294	371	intentar	294	374
granizar	[117]		interesar (se)	294	374
gritar	294	371	interrogar	304	374
guardar (se)	294	371	intervenir	325	374
guiar (se)	289	371	intoxicar	314	374
guiñar	294	371	introducir (se)	322	374-5
guisar	294	371	inundar	294	375
gustar	[112]	371	invertir	309	375
			investir	309	375
haber [107]	293	372	invitar	294	375
hablar	294	372	ir (se)	296	375
hacer [110-111]	295	372	izar	298	375
halagar	304	372			
hallar (se)	294	372	jalar	294	375
hartarse	294	372	jubilarse	294	375
helar [117]	305	372	jugar (se)	297	375
heredar	294	372	juntar (se)	294	376
herir (se)	309	372	jurar	294	376
hervir	309	372	juzgar	304	376
hincar	314	372			
honrar	294	372	labrar	294	376
huir	280	372	ladrar	294	376
hundir (se)	320	373	lamentar	294	376
			lanzar (se)	298	376
ignorar	294	373	lastimarse	294	376
igualarse	294	373	lavar	294	376
imaginarse	294	373	leer	299	376
impedir	312	373	levantar (se)	294	376
implorar	294	373	liberar (se)	294	376-7
imponer (se)	308	373	licenciar (se)	294	377
importar	294	373	limitar (se)	294	377
incendiar (se)	294	373	limpiar	294	377
inclinarse	294	373	lograr	294	377
incluir	280	373	luchar	294	377
indicar	314	373			
inducir	322	373	llamar (se)	294	377
infectarse	294	374	llegar	304	377
inferir	317	374	llenar (se)	294	377
influir	280	374	llevar (se)	294	377

	conj.	compl.		conj.	compl.
llorar	294	377	obligar	304	381
llover [117]	300	377	observar	294	381
			obtener	321	381
maldecir	285	378	ocupar (se)	294	381
mandar	294	378	ocurrir (se)	320	382
manejar (se)	294	378	odiar	294	382
manifestar (se)	305	378	ofrecer (se)	281	382
mantener (se)	321	378	oír	302	382
maquillar	294	378	oler (se)	303	382
maravillar (se)	294	378	olvidar	294	382
marcar	314	378	operar	294	382
marcharse	294	378	oponerse	308	382
masticar	314	379	optar	294	382
matar (se)	294	379	ordenar	294	382
medir (se)	312	379	organizar (se)	298	382
mejorar (se)	294	379	orientar (se)	294	382
mencionar	294	379	osar	294	382
mentir	317	379			
merecer	281	379	padecer	281	383
merendar	305	379	pagar	304	383
meter (se)	279	379	parar (se)	294	383
mezclar	314	379	parecer (se)	281	383
mirar	294	379	partir (se)	320	383
mojar (se)	294	379-80	pasar (se)	294	383
moler	300	380	pasearse	294	383
molestar (se)	294	380	pecar	314	383
montar	294	380	pedir	312	384
morder	300	380	pegar (se)	304	384
morir (se)	288	380	peinarse	294	384
mostrar (se)	319	380	penetrar	294	384
mover	300	380	pensar	305	384
mudar (se)	294	380	percatarse	294	384
multiplicar	314	380	percibir	320	384
murmurar	294	380	perder (se)	306	384
			perdonar	294	384
nacer	281	381	perjudicar	314	384
nadar	294	381	permitir (se)	320	385
necesitar	294	381	perseguir	316	385
negar	301	381	persistir	320	385
negarse	301	381	pertenecer	281	385
nevar [117]	305	381	pervertir	317	385
nombrar	294	381	pesar	294	385
notar	294	381	pescar	314	385
			picar (se)	314	385
obedecer	281	381	picotear	294	385

	conj.	compl.		conj.	compl.
pillar	294	385	rascar (se)	314	389
pintar (se)	294	385	rayar	294	389
pisar	294	385	reaccionar	294	389
plantar (se)	294	386	realizar	298	389
platicar	314	386	rebajar (se)	294	390
poder	307	386	rebelarse	294	390
poner (se)	308	386	recibir	320	390
posar (se)	294	386	reclamar	294	390
poseer	299	386	reclinar	294	390
practicar	314	386	recobrar	294	390
precipitar (se)	294	386	recoger	290	390
preferir	309	386	recomendar	305	390
preguntar (se)	294	386	reconocer	281	390
prender	279	387	recordar	319	390
preocupar (se)	294	387	recorrer	279	390
preparar	294	387	rechazar	298	390
presentar (se)	294	387	reducir	322	390
presentir	317	387	referir (se)	309	390
prestar (se)	294	387	reflejar (se)	294	391
pretender	279	387	reforzar	273	391
prevenir	325	387	refrescar	314	391
privar (se)	294	387	refugiarse	294	391
probar (se)	319	387	regalar (se)	294	391
proceder	279	387	regañar	294	391
procurar	294	387	regar	301	391
producir (se)	322	388	regatear	294	391
proferir	317	388	regir (se)	283	391
prohibir	320	388	registrar (se)	294	391
prometer	279	388	regocijar	294	391
promover	300	388	regresar	294	391
proteger	290	388	rehusar	320	391
protestar	294	388	reinar	294	391
proveer	299	388	reír (se)	311	391
provenir	325	388	relacionar (se)	294	392
provocar	314	388	relajar (se)	294	392
			relampaguear	[117]	
quebrar	305	388	relevar	294	392
quedar (se)	294	388-9	rematar	294	392
quejarse	294	389	remediar	294	392
quemar (se)	294	389	remitir (se)	320	392
querer	310	389	remontar (se)	294	392
quitar (se)	294	389	remover	300	392
			rendir (se)	312	392
rajarse	294	389	renegar	301	392
raptar	294	389	renovar	319	392

	conj.	compl.		conj.	compl.
suspender (se)	279	399	vaciar	294	403
suspirar	294	399	vacilar	294	403
sustituir	280	400	vacunar	294	403
sustraer (se)	323	400	vagar	304	403
susurrar	294	400	valer (se)	324	403
			velar	294	403
tapar	294	400	vencer	282	403
tardar	294	400	vender	279	403
telefonear	294	400	vengarse	304	404
temblar	294	400	venir	325	404
temer	279	400	ver (se)	326	404
tender	306	400	vestir (se)	312	404
tener (se)	321	400	viajar	294	404
tentar	305	400	vigilar	294	404
teñirse	312	401	virar	294	404
terminar	294	401	visitar	294	404
tildar	294	401	vivir	320	404
timar	294	401	volar	319	404
tirar (se)	294	401	volcar	314	404
tocar	314	401	volver (se)	300	404
tolerar	294	401	votar	294	404
tomar	294	401			
topar (se)	294	401	yacer	281	405
torcer (se)	276	401			
toser	279	401	zambullirse	320	405
trabajar	294	402	zumbar	294	405
traducir	322	402			
traer	323	402			
tragarse	304	402			
trasnochar	294	402			
tratar (se)	294	402			
trazar	298	402			
triunfar	294	402			
tronar	[117]				
tropezar	278	402			
tumbar (se)	294	402			
turnar (se)	294	**402**			
ubicar	294	402			
unir (se)	320	402			
urgir	286	403			
usar (se)	294	403			
utilizar	298	403			

A

to **abandon**, abandonar
to **abdicate**, abdicar
to **abide-by**, atenerse
to **abolish**, abolir
to **abominate**, abominar
to **abound**, abundar
to **absolve**, absolver
to **absorb**, chupar, absorber
to **abstain**, abstenerse
to **abuse**, abusar
to **accelerate**, acelerar
to **accept**, aceptar, admitir
to **acclaim**, aclamar
to **accompany**, acompañar
to **accost**, abordar
to **accumulate**, acumular
to **accuse**, acusar
to **acquire**, adquirir
to **acquit**, absolver
to **act**, actuar
to **adapt**, adaptar
to **add**, agregar, añadir, sumar
to **address**, dirigir
to **administer**, administrar
to **admire**, admirar
to **admit**, admitir, reconocer, confesar, conceder
to **adopt**, adoptar
to **advance**, adelantar, avanzar
to **advise**, aconsejar, advertir
to **advocate**, abogar
to **affect**, afectar, influir
to **affirm**, afirmar, asegurar
to **agitate**, agitar
to **agree**, aceptar, acceder, acordar, concertar, coincidir, consentir, convenir
to **allow**, consentir, permitir, dejar
to **amount**, ascender, sumar
to **amuse**, distraer, entretenerse, divertirse
to **analyze**, analizar
to **announce**, anunciar
to **annoy**, fastidiar, molestar
to **answer**, contestar, responder
to **anticipate**, calcular
to **apologize**, excusarse
to **apostatize**, renegar
to **appear**, presentarse, aparecer, figurar
to **appease**, ablandar
to **applaud**, aclamar, aplaudir

to **apply**, aplicar, regir, solicitar
to **appreciate**, apreciar
to **approach**, acercarse, abordar
to **appropriate**, adjudicarse, apropiarse
to **approve**, aceptar, aprobar
to **arise**, surgir
to **arrange**, acomodar, arreglar, disponer
to **arrive**, llegar
to **ask**, pedir
to **ask**, preguntar
to **aspire**, aspirar
to **assemble**, reunir
to **assign**, adjudicar, asignar, destinar
to **assist**, asistir
to **associate**, asociarse, juntarse
to **assume**, suponer
to **astonish**, admirar, asombrar
to **attack**, acometer, atacar
to **attempt**, atentar, intentar
to **attend**, asistir, atender, concurrir, despachar
to **attract**, atraer(se)
to **authorize**, autorizar
to **avenge**, vengar
to **avoid**, esquivar, evitar, guardarse

B

to **bargain**, regatear
to **bark**, ladrar
to **base**, basar(se)
to **bathe**, bañarse
to **be**, estar
to **be**, ser
to **be able**, poder
to **be absent**, faltar
to **be accustomed to**, acostumbrar, soler
to **be adjacent**, limitar
to **be admitted**, ingresar
to **be alike**, asemejarse
to **be amazed**, asombrarse
to **be annoyed**, molestarse
to **be ashamed**, avergonzarse
to **be astonished**, asombrar(se)
to **be bored**, aburrirse
to **be born**, nacer
to **be bothered**, molestarse
to **be careful**, cuidarse
to **be composed of**, componerse, consistir
to **be content with**, conformarse
to **be convinced**, convencerse
to **be cured**, curarse

429

to be distressed, apenarse
to be enough, bastar
to be equal, igualarse
to be familiar with, conocer
to be frightened, asustarse
to be glad, alegrarse, celebrar
to be grateful, agradecer
to be hot, picar
to be inclined, inclinarse
to be included, constar
to be lacking, faltar
to be left, sobrar
to be located, hallarse
to be lodged, alojarse
to be missing, faltar
to be mistaken, equivocarse
to be pleased, agradar
to be promoted, ascender, acceder
to be satisfied, contentarse
to be scarce, escasear
to be self sufficient, bastarse
to be sorry for, alegrarse, arrepentirse
    sentir
to be stuffed, abarrotarse
to be thankful, agradecer
to be the end of, acabar
to be upset, doler
to be used, soler
to be worth, valer
to bear, soportar, aguantar
to bear the burden, acarrear
to beat, batir, ganar. vencer, pegar
to become, ponerse, volver
to become attached, apegarse
to become bored, aburrirse
to become blinded, cegarse
to become worse, agravarse
to beg, rogar, suplicar
to begin, comenzar, empezar
to behave, conducirse, comportarse
to believe, creer(se)
to belittle, rebajar
to belong, pertenecer
to bend, torcer
to benefit, beneficiar(se)
to bet, apostar
to bite, morder, picar
to blame, culpar
to bleed, sangrar
to blend, mezclar
to bless, bendecir
to blind, cegar
to block, bloquear

to block up, cegar
to blow, soplar
to blow out, reventar
to blow up, volar
to board, embarcarse
to boast, alabarse
to boil, bullir, cocer, hervir
to border, bordear
to bore, aburrir
to bother, molestar
to bounce, botar
to bow, inclinarse
to brake, frenar
to brand, tildar
to break, quebrar, romper desgarrar
to break down, descomponerse
to break up, disolver
to breathe, aspirar, respirar
to brighten, aclarar
to bring, aportar, llevar, traer
to bring closer, acercar
to bring in, entrar
to bring on, traer
to broadcast, emitir
to brush, cepillar(se)
to build, edificar
to bump, topar
to burn, abrasar, arder, quemar
to bury, enterrar
to button, abrocharse, abotonar
to buy, comprar
to buzz, zumbar

C

to calculate, calcular
to call, llamar(se), avisar
to can, poder
to cancel, cancelar, borrar
to capsize, volcar
to captivate, seducir
to capture, apresar, prender
to care, desvelarse
to caress, acariciar
to carry, llevar, cargar
to carry off, alzarse
to carve, labrar
to cash, cobrar
to catch, pillar, coger, agarrar,
    alcanzar, cazar
to catch a cold, acatarrarse
to catch fire, incendiarse
to cause, causar, producir, provocar

to **celebrate**, celebrar, festejar
to **challenge**, desafiar
to **change**, cambiar(se), convertirse, mudarse
to **charge**, cargar, cobrar, embestir
to **charm**, encantar
to **chase**, perseguir
to **chat**, charlar, platicar
to **check**, comprobar
to **cheer**, alegrarse
to **cherish**, acariciar
to **chew**, masticar
to **choke**, atorarse
to **choose**, elegir, decidirse, escoger, optar
to **claim**, reclamar
to **clarify**, aclarar
to **clean**, limpiar
to **climb**, escalar
to **cling to**, abrazarse
to **close**, cerrar
to **close oneself**, cerrarse
to **collapse**, derrumbarse
to **collect**, cobrar, juntar
to **collide**, chocar
to **color**, teñir
to **comb**, peinar(se)
to **combine**, combinar
to **come**, acudir, llegar, venir
to **come closer**, acercarse
to **come from**, proceder, provenir
to **come to terms**, arreglarse
to **comfort**, consolar
to **command**, mandar
to **comment**, comentar
to **communicate**, comunicar, conectarse
to **compare**, comparar
to **compel**, obligar
to **compensate**, compensar
to **compete**, competir
to **complain**, dolerse, quejarse
to **complete**, terminar, acabar
to **compose**, componer
to **comprehend**, comprender
to **concede**, conceder
to **conceive**, concebir
to **concentrate**, concentrar(se)
to **concern**, concernir
to **conclude**, concluir
to **concur**, concurrir
to **condemn**, condenar
to **condense**, contraer
to **conduct**, dirigir

to **confer title**, investir
to **confess**, confesar, acusarse
to **confide in**, fiarse, abrirse
to **confirm**, comprobar
to **confuse**, confundir
to **congeal**, helar
to **congratulate**, felicitar
to **connect**, conecta, relacionar(se)
to **conquer**, conquistar
to **consider**, juzgar
to **consist of**, constar
to **conspire**, concertarse
to **constitute**, constituir
to **construct**, construir
to **consult**, aconsejarse
to **consume**, consumir
to **contain**, abarcar, contener, encerrar
to **content oneself**, conformarse, consolarse
to **continue**, continuar, seguir
to **contract**, contraer
to **contribute**, contribuir
to **converge**, converger
to **convert**, convertirse
to **convince**, convencer
to **cook**, cocer, cocinar, guisar
to **cool down**, refrescar
to **correct**, corregir
to **correspond**, corresponder
to **cost**, costar, valer
to **cough**, toser
to **counsel**, aconsejar
to **count**, contar
to **cover**, cubrir, forrar, tapar
to **crack**, partirse, rajarse
to **crah into**, chocar, estrellarse
to **criticize**, criticar
to **cross**, atravesar, cruzar
to **crowd**, amontonarse
to **cry**, llorar
to **cultivate**, cultivar
to **cure**, curar
to **curse**, maldecir
to **cut down**, abatir
to **cut off**, tajar
to **cut**, cortar

D

to **damage**, estropear
to **dance**, bailar
to **dare**, osar
to **dare to do**, atreverse

431

to date, salir
to deal cards, repartir
to deceive, engañar
to decide, acordar, decidir, terminarse
to decorate, adornar
to decree, decretar
to dedicate, dedicar
to deduce, inferir
to deduct, sustraer
to defeat, derrotar, vencer
to defend, defender
to degenerate, derivar
to delete, borrar
to delight, encantar
to deliver, entregar, repartir
to demand, exigir
to demonstrate, manifestar
to deny, desmentir, negar
to depend, depender
to depict, dibujar
to deposit, ingresar
to deprive, privar(se)
to derive, derivar
to descend, descender
to desert, abandonar
to deserve, merecer
to design, trazar
to desire, desear
to desist from, desistir
to destroy, acabar, destruir
to detain, detener
to determine, determinar
to detest, aborrecer
to develop, extenderse
to devote, consagrar, darse
to devote oneself, aplicarse, consagrarse
  dedicarse, entregarse
to dictate, dictar
to die, morir(se)
to differentiate, diferenciar(se)
to digest, digerir
to diminish, reducir
to direct, dirigir
to dirty, ensuciar
to disagree, disentir
to disappear, volar
to discuss, consultar, discutir
to disguise, disfrazarse
to disgust, repugnar
to dismiss, cesar, despedir, echar
  licenciar
to disseminate, esparcirse
to dissuade, disuadir

to distinguish, distinguir
to distort, torcer
to distribute, repartir
to divert, desviar(se), derivar
to dive, zambullirse
to do, hacer
to do business, comerciar
to dock, atracar
to dominate, imponerse
to double, doblar
to doubt, dudar
to drag, arrastrar
to drain, escurrir
to draw, dibujar, trazar
to dream, soñar
to dress, vestir, aderezar
to drink, beber, tomar
to drink to, brindar
to drink up, apurar
to drive, conducir, manejar
to drown, ahogarse
to dry, secar
to dub, doblar
to dump, volcar
to dye, teñirse

E

to earn, ganar
to eat, comer
to educate, formar(se)
to eject, desalojar
to elect, elegir
to elevate, alzar
to eliminate, eliminar
to elude, esquivar
to embark on, embarcarse
to embarrass, abochornar
to embellish, hadornar
to embrace, abrazarse
to emigrate, emigrar
to empty, vaciar
to enclose, acompañar
to encourage, alentar, animar
to encumber, afectar
to end, acabarse, concluir, finalizar,
  terminar
to end up by, acabar
to endure, aguantar, soportar
to engrave, grabar
to enjoy, disfrutar, gozar
to enter, entrar
to entertain, entretener

to entertain oneself, distraerse
to entrust, confiar
to erase, borrar(se)
to escape, escaparse, huir
to esteem, apreciar, estimar
to evacuate, evacuar
to examine, examinar, observar
to exchange, cambiar
to exclude, excluir
to excuse, disculpar, dispensar
　　excusar
to exempt, excusar
to exert, ejercer
to exhibit, exponer
to exist, existir
to expect, atenerse, esperar
to expel, expulsar
to expire, vencer
to explain, explicar, exponer
to explode, explotar
to exploit, explotar
to explore, explorar
to export, exportar
to express, expresar(se), opinar
to extinguish, apagar, extinguir
to extract, arrancar, sacar

F

to face up to, enfrentarse
to fail, abortar, fracasar
to fall, bajar, caer(se)
to fall ill, enfermarse
to fall in love, enamorarse
to fall off, desprenderse
to fall asleep, dormirse
to farm, labrar
to fasten, abrochar, amarrar, atarse
　　fijar
to fear, temer
to feed, alimentar
to feel inhibited, cohibirse
to feel, resentir(se), sentir(se),
　　tentar
to feel like, antojarse
to fight, batallar, batirse, combatir,
　　luchar
to fill, lenar(se)
to fill up, colmar
to fill with joy, regocijar
to filter, colar, filtrar(se)
to find, acertar, dar, encontar, hallar
to find out, averiguar

to find it hard to, costar
to find out, enterarse
to finish, acabar, concluir, finalizar
　　terminar
to finish off, rematar
to fire, botar, disparar
to fit with, compaginar
to fix, arreglar, fijar
to flatter, halagar
to float, flotar
to flood, inundar
to flunk, suspender
to fly, volar
to fold, doblar
to follow, regirse, seguir
to forbid, impedir, prohibir
to force, forzar, obligar
to forget, olvidar, dejarse
to forgive, disculpar
to form, constituir
to found, fundar
to free oneself, liberarse
to freeze, helar
to fry, freír
to fulfil, cumplir, realizar

G

to gather, amontonar
to gather information, informarse
to get, obtener, cobrar
to get acquainted, familiarizarse
to get a divorce, divorciarse
to get adjusted, ajustarse
to get along, compaginar, entenderse
to get angry, acalorarse, calentarse,
　　enojarse, enfadarse
to get by, arreglarse
to get close, acercarse
to get down, descender
to get dressed, vestirse
to get drunk, emborracharse
to get embarrassed about, abochornarse
to get engaged, comprometerse
to get excited about, apasionar
to get entangled, enredarse
to get fond of, aficionarse
to get into, adentrarse, entrar
to get involved, comprometerse
to get lost, extraviarse
to get out, sacar
to get ready, disponerse
to get rid of, deshacerse

to get soaked, calarse
to get scared, espantarse
to get tired, cansarse
to get tired of, hartarse
to get tongue tied, atorarse
to get up, levantarse
to get used, acostumbrarse, aficionarse
to get worked up, acalorarse
to give, dar, regalar
to give back, entregar
to give off, desprenderse
to give out, dispensar
to give up the post, abandonar
to give (talk), dictar
to give up, ceder, renunciar
to glue, pegar
to go, ir, acudir
to go ahead, adelantarse
to go after, andar
to go around, alternar
to go away from, alejarse
to go deeply into, ahondar
to go down, bajar, descender
to go fishing, pescar
to go numb, adormecerse
to go out, salir
to go through, recorrer
to go towards, dirigirse
to go up, ascender, montar, subir
to go to bed, acostarse
to go wrong, fallar
to gossip, chismear
to govern, gobernar
to grade, calificar, notar
to graduate, egresar, licenciarse
to grant, acordar
to grant permission, autorizar
to grapple, aferrarse
to grasp, agarrar, captar
to greet, saludar
to grieve, doler
to grind, moler
to grow, crecer
to guarantee, garantizar
to guard, vigilar
to guess, adivinar
to guess correctly, acertar
to guide, conducir, guiar(se)

H

to hang, colgar, suspender
to happen, acaecer, pasar, suceder

to harbor, acoger
to harmonize, conciliar
to harm, perjudicar
to harvest, segar
to hasten, precipitar
to hasten to, apresurarse
to hate, odiar
to haul up, izar
to have, tener
to have, haber
to have, disponer
to have, tomar
to have a birthday, cumplir años
to have a high regard, estimar
to have a premonition, presentir
to have a snack, merendar
to have an abortion, abortar
to have bad intention, abrigar
to have fun, divertirse
to have lunch, almorzar
to have recourse to, ampararse, acogerse
to have supper, cenar
to have to, deber
to hear, oír
to help, amparar, ayudar
to hesitate, vacilar
to hide, esconder(se)
to hit, acertar, pegar, zumbar
to hold, agarrarse, coger, contener, sujetar
to hold up, atracar, sostener
to honor, distinguir, honrar
to hope, esperar
to hug, abrazar, adopt, embrace, estrechar
to hunt, cazar
to hurl, proferir
to hurl upon, abalanzarse
to hurry, apresurar(se), apurarse
to hurt, doler
to hurt oneself, herirse

I

to ignore, ignorar
to imagin, imaginarse
to implicate, comprometer
to implore, implorar, suplicar
to impose, imponer
to improve, mejorar(se)
to include, comprender, incluir
to increase, aumentar, fomentar

to indicate, indicar
to induce, inducir
to inform, informar
to inherit, heredar
to injure, lastimar(se)
to insist, insistir
to instruct, instruir(se)
to insure, asegurar
to interest, interesar(se)
to interrupt, atajar
to introduce, introducir(se), presentar
to invest, invertir
to invite, convidar, invitar
to iron, repasar

J

to join, adherir(se), afiliarse, apuntarse,
   sumarse, unir
to joke, bromear
to judge, juzgar
to jump, brincar, saltar
to jump into, arrojarse

K

to keep, guardar
to keep, quedarse
to keep awake, desvelar
to keep on, cejar
to keep warm, abrigar
to keep well, conservarse
to kid, bromear
to kidnap, raptar
to kill, matar, cargarse
to kiss, besar(se)
to kneel, hincar
to knock down, derribar, tumbar
to know, conocer
to know, saber

L

to lack, carecer
to land, aterrizar, posarse
to last, extenderse
to laugh, reír(se)
to launch, lanzar
to lay, posar
to lay down, tender
to lay the blame, achacar
to lead, conducir, encabezar
to leak out, escaparse

to lean, apoyar(se), reclinar
to lean on, descansar
to learn, aprender
to leave, irse
to leave, marcharse, partir, salir
to leave, arrojar
to leave aside, abstraerse
to lend, prestar
to lend itself, brindarse
to let, dejar
to let go, soltar
to let oneself be, dejarse
to license, autorizar
to lie, mentir
to lie down, echarse, tumbarse
to lie in, consistir
to lie in the grave, yacer
to like, gustar, caer bien, simpatizar
to limp, cojear
to listen, escuchar
to live, vivir
to live on, alimentarse
to load, cargar, embarcar
to locate, ubicar
to lock oneself, encerrarse
to look, mirar
to look for, buscar
to look out of, asomarse
to look up, consultar
to loot, saquear
to lose, perder
to lose weight, adelgazar
to love, amar, querer
to lower oneself, bajarse

M

to maintain, entretener, mantener
to make, hacer, causar, cometer, formar
to make a commitment, comprometerse
to make a mess, enredar
to make a mistake, errar
to make fun of, burlarse
to make pregnant, embarazar
to make up, maquillar, pintarse
to make sleepy, adormecer
to make sure, asegurarse
to manage, acertar, arreglarse,
   administrarse, alcanzar, componerse
   conseguir, defenderse, dirigir,
   manejarse
to manufacture, fabricar
to mark, marcar

435

to marry, casar(se)
to match, casar, combinar
to mean, significar
to measure, medir(se)
to meet, conocer, concurrir, juntarse, reunir(se)
to melt, disolver, fundir
to mention, mencionar
to merge, fundirse
to mingle, confundir, mezclar
to miss, extrañar,
to mix, mezclar, batir, revolver
to monopolize, acaparar
to move, mover, mudarse
to move back, retroceder
to move forward, avanzar
to move from, apartarse
to moved, conmoverse
to move out, desalojar
to mow, segar
to multiply, multiplicar
to murmur, murmurar

N

to name, nombrar
to need, necesitar
to neglect, descuidar
to nibble, picotear
to nod, asentir
to notice, advertir, apercibirse, fijarse, percatarse, reparar
to notify, avisar

O

to obey, obedecer
to obstruct, bloquear
to obtain, conseguir, lograr
to occupy, desempeñar, ocupar
to offend, herir
to offer, brindar, ofrecer(se)
to open, abrir
to operate, operar
to oppose, fight, oponerse
to order, disponer, ordenar
to organize, organizar(se)
to orient, orientar(se)
to originate in, arrancar
to over come, sobreponerse
to over crowd, abarrotar
to overfill, abarrotar
to over turn, volcar

to over whelm, abrumar
to owe, deber

P

to pack, embalar
to paint, pintar
to pardon, disculpar, perdonar
to park, aparcar
to part, apartarse, separarse
to pass, adelantar, aprobar, pasar(se) cruzarse
to pass through, atravesar
to pawn, empeñar
to pay, pagar, abonar
to pay attention, atender
to pay tribute, rendir
to penetrate, penetrar
to perceive, percibir
to perform, actuar, representar
to persist, empeñarse, persistir
to pervert, pervertir
to pester with questions, acribillar
to phone, telefonear
to photocopy, fotocopiar
to pick up, recoger
to pile up, amontonarse
to pinch, apretar
to place, colocar
to place, meter(se)
to place oneself, colocarse
to plant, plantar
to play, jugar(se)
to play, tocar
to plead, abogar
to please, complacer, contentar, satisfacer
to plunge, zambullirse
to point out, apuntar
to poison, intoxicar
to possess, poseer
to post, apostarse
to postpone, aplazar
to practice, ejercer, practicar
to praise, alabar
to pray, rezar
to prefer, preferir
to prepare, preparar
to preserve, conservar
to press hard, atacar
to pretend, fingir
to prevent, impedir
to produce, producir

436

to **promise**, prometer
to **promise to be**, anunciarse
to **promote**, ascender, avanzar, elevar, promover
to **protect**, proteger
to **protest**, protestar
to **prove**, probar
to **provoke**, meterse, provocar
to **pull**, jalar, tirar
to **pull down**, echar
to **pull out**, extraer
to **punish**, castigar
to **pursue**, seguir
to **push along**, correr
to **push**, empujar
to **pull**, jalar
to **put**, meter, poner
to **put to bed**, acostar
to **put an end**, acabar, atajar
to **put make up**, componerse

Q

to **quarrel**, reñir
to **question**, interrogar

R

to **raffle**, sortear
to **rain**, llover
to **raise**, levantar
to **rank**, clasificarse
to **reach**, alcanzar
to **react**, reaccionar
to **read**, leer
to **realize**, darse cuenta, realizar
to **rease**, aumentar
to **receive**, acoger, despachar, recibir
to **reciprocate with**, corresponder
to **recognize**, conocer, reconocer
to **recommend**, aconsejar, recomendar
to **record**, grabar
to **recover**, curarse, recobrar, rescatar
to **recur**, reproducirse
to **educe**, rebajar, reducir
to **refer**, referirse, remitirse
to **reflect**, reflejar
to **reform**, corregirse
to **refresh**, refrescar
to **refuse**, negarse, rehusar, resistirse
to **register**, inscribirse, registrar(se)
to **regret**, arrepentirse, lamentar, sentir
to **reign**, reinar

to **reinforce**, reforzar
to **reject**, rechazar
to **relax**, relajar(se)
to **release**, despedir, liberar
to **relieve stress**, desahogarse
to **rely on**, confiar
to **rely upon**, contar
to **remain**, quedar(se), restar
to **remedy**, remediar
to **remember**, acordarse, recordar
to **remind**, recordar
to **remodel**, renovar
to **remove**, quitar, remover, retirar
to **rent**, alquilar, arrendar
to **repair**, reparar
to **repeat**, repetir
to **replace**, relevar, sustituir
to **report**, denunciar
to **represent**, representar
to **reprimand**, regañar, reñir
to **reproduce**, reproducir(se)
to **request**, solicitar, encargar
to **require**, exigir
to **rescue**, rescatar
to **resemble**, parecerse
to **reserve**, reservar
to **resign**, resignar
to **resign oneself**, resignarse
to **resist**, resistir
to **resolve**, resolver
to **rest**, descansar
to **restrain**, aguantarse, contenerse
to **restrict**, limitar(se)
to **result**, resultar
to **retire**, jubilarse, retirarse
to **return**, devolver, regresar, volver
to **revenge**, vengarse
to **reverse**, invertir
to **review**, repasar
to **revolt**, alzarse, rebelarse
to **riddle with bullets**, acribillar
to **ring**, sonar
to **rise up**, elevarse
to **risk**, arriesgarse
to **risk to**, aventurarse
to **rival**, competir
to **roll**, enrollar
to **ruin**, deshacer, destrozar
to **run**, correr
to **run out of**, acabarse
to **run into**, encontrarse, topar(se)
to **run the risk**, exponerse
to **rush**, precipitarse

437

to rush at, abalanzarse
to rush off, embalarse
to rush toward, abalanzarse

S

to sail for, embarcarse
to satisfy, satisfacer
to save, ahorrar, economizar
to save, salvar(se)
to savour, saborear
to say, decir
to say goodby to, despedir
to say nothing, callar
to scare, asustar
to scatter, esparcir
to score, marcar
to scrape, rascar
to scratch, rascarse, rayar
to scuba dive, bucear
to seduce, seducir
to seem, parecer
to see, ver
to seize, apresar
to sell, vender
to send, enviar, mandar, remitir
to sense, olerse
to sentence, condenar
to separate, separar
to serve, servir
to set fire, incendiar
to shake, agitar, conmover, sacudir
to share, compartir
to shave, afeitarse
to shine, brillar
to shiver, temblar
to shock, chocar
to shoot, tirar
to shorten, abreviar, acortar
to shot down, abatir
to shout, gritar
to show, demostrar, enseñar, marcar,
    mostrar(se)
to shrink, encoger
to shut up, callarse
to sigh, suspirar
to sign, firmar
to sign up, fichar
to silence, acallar
to simmer, hervir
to sing, cantar
to sin, pecar
to sit down, sentarse

to skip, saltar
to skirt around, bordear
to slap, abofetear
to sleep, dormir
to sleep with, acostarse
to slide, deslizar
to slip, deslizarse, escurrirse
to slip in, colarse
to slip up, resbalar
to smell, oler
to smile, sonreír
to smoke, fumar
to sneak in, colarse
to snore, roncar
to snow, nevar
to soak, empapar
to solicit, solicitar
to solve, resolver
to sow, sembrar
to speak, hablar
to speak to, comunicarse
to speed up, acelerar
to spend, gastar, invertir
to spill, derramar
to spit, escupir
to splash, salpicar
to spread, esparcir(se), extender(se),
    sembrar
to sprout, brotar
to squeeze, comprimir, exprimir
to stand out, distinguirse
to start, comenzar, arrancar, empezar
to stay, quedarse
to stay awake, velar
to stay away, retraerse
to steal, robar
to step, pisar
to stick, adherir, hincar
to stick out, sobresalir
to stigmatize, tildar
to still have, continuar
to stop, parar(se), cesar, detener(se),
    dejar
to straighten, enderezar
to strain, esforzar
to strengthen, fortalecer
to stress, acentuar
to stretch, estirar(se), tender
to stretch scare, espantar
to strike, dar
to strip of, despojar
to strive, afanarse
to struggle, batallar, luchar

438

to study, estudiar
to stuff oneself, atracarse, hartarse
to stumble, tropezar
to subject, someter
to submerge, hundir(se)
to subscribe, abonarse, suscribirse
to substitute, sustituir
to substract, sustraer
to succeed, lograr, suceder
to suck, chupar
to suffer, padecer, sufrir
to suggest, sugerir
to summarize, resumir
to summon, convocar
to sun bathe, broncearse
to supply, abastecer, proveer
to support, alimentar, apoyar, mantener, sostener
to suppose, imaginarse, suponer
to surmount, remontar
to surpass, superar
to surprise, sorprender
to surrender, entregarse, rendirse
to suspect, sospechar
to suspend, suspender
to sustain, mantenerse
to swallow, tragarse
to swear, jurar
to sweat, sudar
to sweep, barrer, arrastrar
to sweeten, endulzar
to swim, nadar
to swindle, timar
to swing, columpiarse
to switch off, apagar
to switch on, prender
to swoop on, abatirse

T

to take, tomar
to take advantage, abusar, aprovechar(se)
to take a walk, pasearse
to take an exam, examinarse
to take away, apartar
to take care of, cuidar, encargarse
to take it in turns, combinarse
to take long, tardar
to take notes, apuntar
to take off (shoes), descalzarse
to take offence, picarse
to take one's leave, despedirse

to take out, sacar
to take part, intervenir
to take place, llevarse, ocurrir(se)
to take pleasure in, complacerse
to take possession, adueñarse, apoderarse
to take refuge, refugiarse, acogerse
to take shelter, abrigarse
to take turns, alternarse, turnar(se)
to talk, conversar, platicar
to taste like, saber
to teach, enseñar
to tear apart, desprender
to tear off, desgajar
to tell, contar, referir
to tempt, tentar
to tend to, tender
to test, experimentar
to thank, agradecer
to think, creer, pensar
to threaten, amenazar
to throw, arrojar, botar, echar, lanzar, tirar
to tie, atar
to tie, empatar
to tighten, ajustarse, apretar
to discover, descubrir
to fit, caber
to tolerate, tolerar
to prove that, demostrar
to touch, tocar
to touch lightly, rozar
to transfer, ceder
to transform, volver
to translate, traducir
to transport, acarrear
to travel, viajar
to treat, tratar
to trick, burlar
to triumph, triunfar
to trust, confiar, fiarse
to trust in, esperar
to try, intentar, pretender, probar(se), procurar
to try hard, esforzarse
to tune, ajustar
to tune in, captar
to turn, torcer, virar, convertir, doblar, girar
to turn around, volverse
to turn on, encender
to turn out, salir, resultar
to twist, retorcerse, torcerse

U

to undergo, acusar
to understand, comprender
to understand, entender, explicarse
to undertake, acometer
to undo, deshacer
to undress, desnudarse
to unite, unir(se)
to unveil, desvelar
to upset, disgustar
to urge, urgir
to use, usar, utilizar

V

to vaccinate, vacunar
to vacillate, vacilar
to value, apreciar
to verify, comprobar
to visit, visitar
to visualize, imaginarse
to vote, votar

W

to wait, aguardar
to wait for, esperar
to wake up, despertarse
to walk, andar, caminar
to wander, errar, vagar
to want, querer, antojarse
to warm, calentar
to warm up, calentarse
to warn, advertir, avisar, prevenir
to wash, lavar, fregar
to waste, perder
to watch, guardar, velar
to watch over, vigilar
to water, regar
to wave, agitar
to wear, vestir(se), calzar
to wear for the first time, estrenar
to weigh, pesar
to wet, mojar(se)
to whisper, soplar, susurrar
to whistle, chiflar, silbar
to winckle, arrugarse
to win, ganar, conquistar
to wink, guiñar
to wish, desear
to withdraw, retirar
to wonder, maravillarse, preguntarse

to work, trabajar, funcionar
to worry, apurarse, inquietar(se),
  preocupar(se)
to wrap up, envolver
to wring out, escurrir
to write, escribir
to write down, inscribir

Y

to yawn, bostezar
to yield, ceder, dar